THE OAKWOOD PRESS

TORTILLARDS OF ARTOIS

The
Metre Gauge Railways and Tramways of the Western Pas-de-Calais

by
Martin & Joan Farebrother

THE OAKWOOD PRESS

© Oakwood Press & Martin & Joan Farebrother 2008

British Library Cataloguing in Publication Data
A Record for this book is available from the British Library
ISBN 978 0 85361 679 5

Typeset by Oakwood Graphics.
Repro by PKmediaworks, Cranborne, Dorset.
Printed by Cambrian Printers, Aberystwyth, Ceredigion.

A train heading towards Berck waits at Hucqueliers station on the Aire-Berck line, postcard postmarked 1924. The locomotive is ARB (Aire-Berck) No. 45, a 21 tonne Corpet 0-6-2 tank locomotive delivered in 1892. *Authors' Collection*

Front cover, top: A train coming from the Calais direction at the halt at Andres on the Anvin-Calais line. No date but the dress indicates before 1914. The locomotive is an AC (Anvin-Calais) 18.5 tonne SACM 0-6-2 tank with the original water tanks, probably No. 6 *Lumbres* built in 1881. *Édition J. Cerf; Authors' Collection*
Front cover, bottom: Arrival of a train at Berck-Plage, western terminus of the Aire-Berck line. There is no date but the original station buildings date it before 1909. The locomotive is Aire-Berck No. 42, a 21 tonne Corpet 0-6-2 tank locomotive delivered in 1892. *Authors' Collection*
Rear cover, top: The station at Licques on the Boulogne-Bonningues line. A Blanc-Misseron 0-6-0 *bicabine* tank locomotive is heading a passenger train in the direction of Boulogne. This station is now a private house and the lavatory block in the foreground has been demolished. *Collection André Artur*
Rear cover, bottom: The station at Merlimont-Plage on the Berck-Plage-Paris-Plage line, with a train headed towards Berck-Plage. The tank locomotive, hauling the train backwards, is the 0-6-0 Decauville put into service in 1910. Undated. *Authors' Collection*

Published by The Oakwood Press (Usk), P.O. Box 13, Usk, Mon., NP15 1YS.
E-mail: sales@oakwoodpress.co.uk
Website: www.oakwoodpress.co.uk

Contents

A passenger train at Berck-Ville station on the Aire-Berck line in 1954. The diesel locomotive is 0-6-0 No. 651, built at Ateliers CF Dordogne in 1947.

J. Bazin; Collection Bernard Guéret, formerly BVA

Acknowledgements

We wish to thank the following, without whose help this book could not have been produced.

Our friend Derek Jordan, Joan's father Allan Woodhead, and Martin's mother Stella Farebrother, for their help in exploring the lines and other remains; and Allan Woodhead for the line drawings at the head of each chapter and for some of the station diagrams.

Philip Pacey, author of *Railways of the Baie de Somme* (Oakwood Press, 2000), for help with the history of rolling stock now at CFBS (*see 'Abbreviations' on following page*), and Geoffrey Nickson for hosting a visit to this rolling stock at the CFBS workshops at St-Valery.

The Pas-de-Calais archives at Arras, and the National Archives at Kew. The Imperial War Museum (IWM) Photograph Archive for their assistance and for permission to reproduce photographs from the archive. The IWM map archive at Duxford, for help with finding other information on World War I.

The Royal Engineers Museum and Library, Brompton Barracks, Gillingham, Kent for help, and access to War Diaries of the Royal Engineers Railway Companies.

Henri Dupuis, and other staff at the *Musée de Tramways à Vapeurs et des chemins de fer Secondaires français* (MTVS) at Valmondois.

The SNCF Society Archivist Francis Carline, Librarian Roger Ongley, and members André Artur, Bram van der Velden, Bob Vice, and Jean Willig.

Claude Wagner, Christian Levasseur (Montreuil), Gabriel Richard (Bimont), Mme Jeannine Couvreur (Montcavrel), Mme Paulette Hénon and Claude Hénon (Audenfort), Phillipe Valcq (Montreuil), and Daniel Piton (*Amis du Musée de Berck*).

Rémy Marquis, who worked on the Anvin-Calais line, member of *Les Amis du PP* (Friends of the *Chemin de fer de Pont-de-la-Deule à Pont-à-Marcq*), and Guy Desbiens, President of the same.

Karl-Heinz Buchholz (Bombardier, Kassel) and the Henschel Museum, Kassel, Germany.

D.C. Davies, of the *Musée du Mur de l'Atlantique (Batterie Todt)* at Audinghen, and Daniel Leunens (Bazinghen), for information on railways in the Cap Gris Nez area in World War II, and on other railway plans in that area.

M. Bernard Guéret, for permission to reproduce pictures from the 1950s series of photographs formerly held by the Bureau Vaudois d'Addresses (BVA), Lausanne.

To many other friends, especially those who have continued to encourage us in spite of being frequently bored by hearing all about it.

Last but by no means least, Jane Kennedy and Ian Kennedy of the Oakwood Press, for encouraging us to persist with this book, and for their help and advice.

Abbreviations

French titles for people:

M.	*Monsieur* (Mr)
Mme.	*Madame* (Mrs)
MM.	*Messieurs* (Messrs)

Metre gauge lines in this book (abbreviations mainly used for tables and figures):

AC	Anvin-Calais
ARB	Aire-(Rimeux-)Berck
BB	Boulogne-Bonningues
CEN	*Compagnie des Chemins de Fer Économiques du Nord*
BPPP	Berck-Plage-Paris-Plage
TEPP	Tramway from Étaples to Paris-Plage
TEB	*Tramways Électriques de Boulogne-sur-Mer*
VFIL (CGL)	*Compagnie Générale des Voies Ferrées d'Intérêt Local*

Other abbreviations:

ACNF	*Ateliers de Construction du Nord de la France (de Blanc Misseron)*
BEF	British Expeditionary Force (WWI)
BV	*Bâtiment des Voyageurs* (passenger building)
CdN	*Compagnie du Nord*
CF	*Chemin de Fer*
CFBS	*Chemin de Fer de la Baie de Somme*
HM	*Halle aux Marchandises* (goods building)
IWM	Imperial War Museum, London
MTVS	*Musée de Tramways à Vapeurs et des chemins de fer Secondaires français* (Valmondois)
MVA	*Marine Verpflegungsamt* (Naval Supply and Maintenance organization) (German, WWII)
OFK	*Oberfeldkommandantur* (Senior field headquarters) (German, WWII)
PN	*passage à niveau* (level crossing)
RAF	Royal Air Force
RE	Royal Engineers
RFC	Royal Flying Corps (WWI, became RAF)
ROD	Railway Operating Division (British Army, WWI)
SACM	*Société Alsacienne de Constructions Mécaniques*
SE	*Société Générale des Chemins de Fer Économiques*
SLM	*Schweizerische Locomotive u Maschinenfabrik*, Winterthür, Switzerland
SNCF	*Société Nationale des Chemins de Fer Français*
STO	*Service du Travail Obligatoire* (Forced labour service) (WWII)
WWI	World War I
WWII	World War II

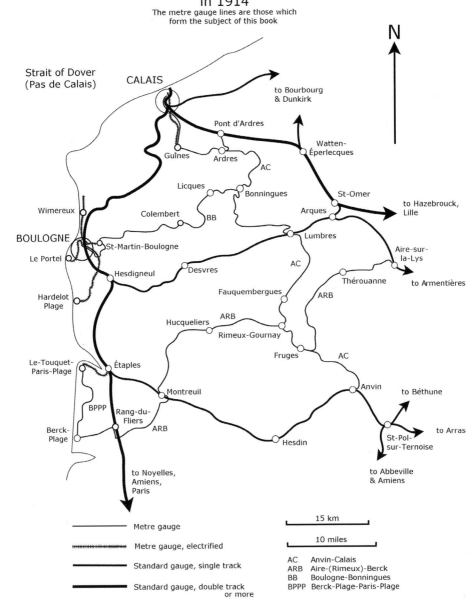

Standard gauge & metre gauge lines in the western Pas-de-Calais in 1914

The metre gauge lines are those which form the subject of this book

N

Strait of Dover (Pas de Calais)

CALAIS

to Bourbourg & Dunkirk

Pont d'Ardres

Watten-Éperlecques

Guînes

Ardres

AC

Licques

Bonningues

St-Omer

to Hazebrouck, Lille

Wimereux

Colembert

BB

Arques

Lumbres

BOULOGNE

St-Martin-Boulogne

Aire-sur-la-Lys

Le Portel

AC

to Armentières

Hesdigneul

Desvres

Thérouanne

Hardelot Plage

Fauquembergues

ARB

Hucqueliers

ARB

Rimeux-Gournay

Le-Touquet-Paris-Plage

Fruges

AC

Étaples

Anvin

to Béthune

Montreuil

BPPP

Rang-du-Fliers

to Arras

Berck-Plage

ARB

St-Pol-sur-Ternoise

Hesdin

to Noyelles, Amiens, Paris

to Abbeville & Amiens

15 km

10 miles

——————— Metre gauge

+++++++++++ Metre gauge, electrified

——————— Standard gauge, single track

━━━━━━━ Standard gauge, double track or more

AC Anvin-Calais
ARB Aire-(Rimeux)-Berck
BB Boulogne-Bonningues
BPPP Berck-Plage-Paris-Plage

Introduction

In the issue of 29th September, 1896, *The Queen*, a London magazine, carried an article about Berck. The writer, having left Paris on a Sunday morning, arrived at 'that queer little junction with a long name, Rang-du-Fliers-Verton, with tickets for Berck-sur-Mer'. He took the train to Berck, and then hired a cart to take him north through the forest to visit the developing resort of Paris-Plage.

In his book *The End of the Line* (Cleaver-Hume Press, 1955), Bryan Morgan describes his journey on the Anvin-Calais-Aire-Berck lines. This journey must have been between September 1952 and February 1955, because the lines from Fruges to Anvin and to Aire had already closed when he travelled. He lamented that, as all over France, 'what had been a valuable cross-country service has been truncated or snapped so that now it serves only very local needs'. Nonetheless he travelled from Calais, in a 'battered, lightly-built but upholstered little vehicle' from 'Calais Town's remotest bay' across 'a good deal of scruffy Artois'. After changing at Lumbres, he reached Rimeux. From here he travelled on the Aire-Berck line at least as far as Rang-du-Fliers.

These two descriptions almost span the lifetime of the principal lines described in this book. The metre gauge network of the western Pas-de-Calais began with the opening of the first part of the Anvin-Calais line in 1881, and ended with the closure of the rump of the Anvin-Calais and Aire-Berck lines in 1955. At its most extensive in the early 1920s there were 302 km (188 miles) of metre gauge railways and urban and inter-urban tramways in the area covered by this book. The two principal lines, Anvin-Calais and Aire-Berck, were 95 km (59 miles) and 97 km (60 miles) long respectively, with shared running for 9 km (5½ miles).

In 1990, we bought a cottage near Montreuil-sur-Mer in the Pas-de-Calais, and began to discover in the surrounding countryside tantalising remnants of an extensive narrow gauge railway network. Beginning with village houses that had begun life as stations, our interest grew, and six years ago we began to visit the lines and stations and to collect information more systematically. We also looked for a book we could read to guide us. We found that no comprehensive description of these lines exists in English. The lines are, of course, listed and briefly described in *Minor Railways of France* (W.J.K. Davies, Plateway Press, 2000). There is also coverage in French in *Les Petits Trains de Jadis (Nord)* (Éditions Cabri, 1995), and there are some other articles in French about some of these lines. So two years ago we decided to complete our researches and write such a book ourselves. There were a very few narrow gauge lines which were not metre gauge in our area. They were all of 60 cm gauge, and we have mentioned these briefly for the sake of completeness.

There is no good collective term covering all the metre gauge lines in the area we have described. From 1919, the two major lines, Anvin-Calais and Aire-Berck, were managed by the *Compagnie Générale des Voies Ferrées d'Intérêt Local* (VFIL), but this company managed many other lines. They also later took over the rump of the other major line, Boulogne-Bonningues, from 1936. During and after World War II this grouping of lines is referred to in some documents as the *réseau cotier* (coastal network), but this has not been a sufficiently regular appellation for us to use it. In the end we have simply fallen back on Anvin-Calais-Aire-Berck for the two principal lines working together, latterly under VFIL.

The Pas-de-Calais is a major tourist destination for the British, but few know of the presence of these reminders of the age of steam, some in major tourist spots. For instance, many walk the walls of Montreuil every year, but few know about the old railway route below. We have done our best to make this book as accurate as possible. We are responsible for any errors, and would be pleased to hear about

The beach at Berck-Plage in high season. No date but probably before World War I.
Authors' Collection

Diesel railcar ARB No. 5, built by VFIL at Lumbres in 1933 or 1934, pointing in the arrival direction in the Anvin-Calais line terminus bay platform at Calais-Ville in 1953. The carriage is of the 1886-built third class only type purchased for the Calais to Guînes section of the line.
J. Bazin; Collection Bernard Guéret, formerly BVA

them. All translations from French are our own, and are indicated in the text with single inverted commas. We have followed the British convention for the configuration of wheels on locomotives. Readers new to railways in France should, however, be aware that the French convention is only to count the wheels on one side of the locomotive and not to use hyphens, so that a locomotive that is to us a 2-6-0 is to the French a 130.

We have had great fun, and we have learned a lot, in writing this book. We hope that readers will derive as much enjoyment from it.

Tortillard

The name *tortillard* (noun, masculine) (or occasionally *tortilleur* or *tortillart*) has been widely applied to narrow gauge steam railways and trains in France. The derivation is probably from the verb *tortiller*, to twist or twirl. The word has been used since the early 20th century, with examples of this on old photographs and postcards of many lines from that period. It probably began as a comment on the twisting or tortuous nature of many narrow gauge lines. The word has also been widely used as an adjective for the *hêtre tortillard* (twisted beech tree; *Fagus sylvatica* L. var. *tortuosa* Pépin), which occurs in France, especially in the forest of Verzy near Rheims. The earliest we have found of this usage is 1891, when a letter and photographs of the *hêtre tortillard de Dain* appeared in the Paris periodical *La Nature*, and this usage probably preceded that for trains. These trains have also from time to time attracted the title *le tacot*, *tacot* being an informal term for an old-fashioned and defective vehicle, or 'old banger'.

Times and timetables

In summary timetables all times have been given in the 24 hour clock. All these tables are abstracted from the originals; the originals often contain too much information, and we spent too much time during the research for this book peering at copies of timetables which were difficult to read to wish to inflict this on readers. All of the original timetables are in the 24 hour clock, except for some in the 19th century which are in the 12 hour clock, with the trains marked *matin* (morning) or *soir* (evening) over the departure from the station of origin. In the text we have given all times in the 24 hour clock.

Units of measurement

Here are a few notes for those unfamiliar with metric units:

Length and distance
1 metre = 100 centimetres (cm) = 1,000 millimetres (mm) = 3.28 feet = 3 feet 3⅜ inches
1 kilometre (km) = 1,000 metres = 0.62 miles = approx. ⅝ mile
1 mile = 1.609 kilometres

In this book distances are in metres or kilometres, except for those very few instances where the originals are in Imperial units, as for instance in British Army

documents from World War I. For some other important distances in the text we
have added the distance in miles in brackets to the nearest ¼ mile. Heights are in
metres but again important heights are also given in feet to the nearest foot.

Weight
1 kilogram (kg) = 1,000 grams (gm) = 2.2046 pounds (lb.)
1 tonne (metric ton) = 1,000 kilograms = 2,204.6 pounds
1 ton (Imperial ton) = 2,240 pounds

Money and Prices

It is always difficult to compare prices and value for money over long periods of
time. We have, however, given some fares and prices in the text, so we will try to put
these into context. Using the Retail Price Index, £1 sterling in 1881, the year of
opening of the first part of the Anvin-Calais line, would now be worth about £69.
The French franc in 1860 would now be worth £1.34 in current values, and rather
more, about £1.60, in 1900. In 1880 a large loaf of bread and one litre of red wine each
cost about 45 centimes (68 pence at current values). The French franc was devalued
during World War I, and again rather sharply after World War II. By 1959 £1 was
worth about 1,000 francs, and in 1960 France brought in the New Franc, worth 100
of the old francs, but this was after the time of the railways in this book. It is an
indication of the devaluation of the franc that the first class fare when the Anvin-
Calais line opened was 8 centimes per km. By 1950 it was 4 francs 52 centimes. We
have reported in Chapter Two that the original SACM steam locomotives of the
Anvin-Calais line cost 32,375 francs each in 1880, which would be the equivalent of
about £50,000 today. However in this area comparisons are more difficult. Buying a
motive power unit for equivalent work would cost a lot more in real terms today,
but it would be a much more sophisticated machine.

Layout of book

In this book we have described a number of metre gauge lines, which are spread
geographically, and whose stories are spread over time. In the first part of the book,
after an introduction to the area in Chapter One, we have described each of the three
principal lines, with lesser geographically associated lines, up to the beginning of
World War I. After that we have followed the stories chronologically. At the end we
have given information on things that can be seen now, and some walks on parts of
the old lines.

In this area it is not possible to make a complete separation between railways,
inter-urban tramways, and urban tramways. Both Calais and Boulogne had an
urban electric tramway network, but including longer lines which were really inter-
urban. In Calais one of these lines, that from Calais to Guînes, competed with the
steam railway from Anvin to Calais. In Boulogne the electric tramways took over
one line, that from Boulogne to Le Portel, which had been conceived as part of the
inland steam railway. We have therefore included the urban tramways of these two
ports in this book.

Goods traffic

For those not familiar with French practice, here is an explanation of the terms *grande vitesse* and *petite vitesse*, which you will meet in this book.

As the name implies goods sent *grande vitesse* travelled faster but paid more. They travelled on passenger or mixed trains, under the eye of the *chef du train*, the man in charge of the train who also fulfilled the functions of conductor and guard. Baggage, dogs, small parcels, money and valuables, and freight packages of a manageable size travelled in this category. For accounting purposes passenger receipts were also classed under *grande vitesse*.

Goods going *petite vitesse* would be all others, but principally those goods which were heavy or loose or went as whole wagon loads. They would go in wagons in mixed or goods trains. The price lists for *petite vitesse* have a very long list of such goods, more than 60 items, including coal, coke, wheat, marble, oil, and of course sugar beet. For charging purposes these were put into four categories. Cattle and other large animals also went *petite vitesse*.

Glossary of railway and related words in French

Note: some of these words have other meanings outside the context of railways. adj = adjective, nf = noun, feminine; nm = noun, masculine; pl = plural

abri	nm	shelter
accotement	nm	verge
aiguille	nf	points
appareil	nm	device, probably points
arrêt	nm	stop (lower grade than halt)
autorail	nm	railcar
baladeuse	nf	open passenger trailer
bascule	nf	weighbridge
bâtiment	nm	building
bâton-pilote	nm	single line working token
bestiaux	nmpl	livestock
betterave (à sucre, sucrière)	nf	beet (sugar beet)
(pont) biais	adj	oblique, angled (bridge)
boulon	nm	bolt
buse	nf	pipe, duct, conduit
(chef) cantonnier	nm	(chief) platelayer (permanent way maintenance man)
chauffeur	nm	(of steam locomotive) fireman; (of railcar) driver
cheminot	nm	railway worker
colis (postaux)	nmpl	small parcels (parcel post)
déclassement	nm	declassification
département	nm	department
desserte (ferroviare)	nf	(rail) service

éclisse	nf	joint plate (rails)
entretoise	nf	brace, strut, stay
essieu(x)	nm	axle(s)
fourgon	nm	baggage van intended for a passenger train
galet	nm	flint, silica, pebble
garage (de machines)	nm	siding (engine shed)
gare	nf	station
gestion	nf	management
glace	nf	window
guérite	nf	booth
halage (chemin de halage)	nm	towing (towpath)
houille	nf	coal
impériale	nf	upper deck
à l' impériale	adj	double-decker (bus, train, tram)
lampisterie	nf	lamp store
locotracteur	nm	diesel locomotive
machine (à vapeur)	nf	(steam) locomotive
magasinage	nm	warehousing
marchandise(s)	nf	(in plural) goods
mécanicien	nm	engine driver
messagerie	nf	freight forwarding
Micheline	nf	railcar (colloquial)
navette	nf	shuttle
nœud (de voie ferrée)	nm	junction (railway)
octroi	nm	tax office
oyat	nm	Picardy name for a grass which stabilises sand dunes
passage à niveau (PN)	nm	level crossing
passerelle	nf	footbridge
pétard	nm	explosive fog signal
plaque tournante	nf	turntable
poutre	nf	beam (wooden) girder (metal)
raccordement	nm	chord, loop line, connection line
raffinerie	nf	refinery (oil or sugar)
ramassage	nm	trains of odd vehicles/ miscellaneous traffic
rame	nf	rake/ group of vehicles or wagons
remaniement	nm	modification
remblai	nm	embankment
remorque	nf	trailer
sucrerie	nf	sugar factory or refinery
tablier (métallique)	nm	(metal) platform (of bridges)
talus	nm	bank
tampon (de wagon)	nm	buffer
terrassement	nm	excavation
tirefond	nm	large screw for fixing rail to sleeper
triage (gare de triage)	nm	sorting sidings/marshalling yard
tranchée	nf	(railway)cutting; (military) trench
traverse	nf	sleeper
vasista	nm	fanlight
voie (de garage)	nf	track (siding)
voirie	nf	(rail) network
voyageur (-euse)	nm(f)	passenger
wattman	nm	tram driver

Chapter One

Introducing the Pas-de-Calais

The *département* of Pas-de-Calais, through which our railways pass, was only created in December 1789, on the eve of the French Revolution. Although it was given this very localised name, the French equivalent of the Strait of Dover, the *département* is a bulky one, stretching south-east well beyond Arras. With its eastern neighbour Nord, these *départements* form the Region Nord-Pas-de-Calais. The population of Pas-de-Calais has risen from 692,000 in 1851 to a present figure of 1.4 million. This rise is due in the most part to the growth of its two famous ports, Boulogne and Calais. These are the nearest ports to England and have, for many centuries, been British travellers' first taste of mainland Europe.

Boulogne was founded by a Celtic tribe, *les Belges*, who called it Bononia. After Julius Caesar conquered Gaul it became, with Bavay and Amiens, a major Roman town. It was always an important centre for fishing and now tops the French league table for fishing ports. In addition it is now the biggest European centre for fish processing – the smell around the port proves it! Prior to railway transport, horses pulled carts of fish to Paris. The journey alone would have taken approximately 24 hours and Paris was the farthest it could be taken and remain edible. Today's catch comes off the boats at midnight and is on the train by 11 am, having been sorted, weighed, auctioned, filleted, and chilled.

Calais is much younger than Boulogne; it obtained its charter in 1181. It has for centuries shared Boulogne's eminence as a passenger port but in the 20th century it began to creep ahead. This was largely due to its better developed railway networks. The high-speed train (TGV) connects Calais with an increasing range of destinations in Europe and the Channel Tunnel is very close. In addition, Calais has enormous marshalling yards for the Channel Tunnel and the earliest motorways in the north of France went through Calais. This is now France's busiest port and is the second busiest in the world for passenger traffic.

The Pas-de-Calais' other claim to fame is its 19th century seaside resorts. With the increasing prosperity brought by the Industrial Revolution and better, faster, safer transport, our area became an attractive holiday destination. Many small resorts sprang up, usually close to the ports, adjacent to the wonderful beaches. The concept of 'beach holidays' had begun to take hold. Berck-Plage and Paris-Plage are the two that became the most popular.

Part of the reason for Berck-Plage's success, however, lies elsewhere. It became a celebrated health resort, a 19th century spa. Instead of 'taking the waters', at Berck-Plage one 'took' fresh air by walking on its amazing beach. Even its air was said to have therapeutic properties. This idea probably arose out of Berck's reputation as a centre for the treatment of scrofula, a form of tuberculosis. Earlier in the 19th century, two local widows, Mme Duhamel and Mme Brillard, the latter evocatively called '*Marianne Toute Seule*' (Marianne All Alone), had begun to take in sick children, at first from local towns, ultimately from Paris. The children were suffering from scrofula. In 1861, a little wooden

Patients with tuberculosis receiving the fresh sea air treatment at the Sanatorium Vincent at Berck-Plage. Postcard postmarked 1920.   *Authors' Collection*

The beach at Le-Touquet-Paris-Plage in high season. No date but the dress and especially the cloche hats suggest 1920s.   *Authors' Collection*

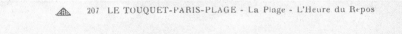

hospital was built here. The benefits of fresh sea air, better food and the opportunity to play on the beach had dramatic effects and the two widows became famous.

Later in the century further hospitals were built, notably one funded by the Rothschild family. In 1869, the Empress Eugenie paid her second visit to Berck. She was concerned for the health of her son Louis, the Prince Imperial, and presumably had heard of Berck's reputation as a health resort. She arrived by special train at Rang-du-Fliers-Verton at 13.30 and took a carriage to the town, where she opened a hospital, *L'Hôpital Napoleon*, named after her husband. She was back in Rang-du-Fliers by 16.30, having had luncheon at the hospital, provided by Queen Victoria's Parisian bakers. Two streets in Berck commemorate her visits, Rue de l'Impératrice and Rue du Prince Impérial. Some of these hospitals still stand.

Paris-Plage, however, only became prominent at the start of the 20th century. Up until the 1830s, the villagers of Le Touquet, a hamlet slightly inland in the *commune* of Cucq, used to live by raising Jerusalem artichokes, rye and potatoes. From 1855, a *notaire* (solicitor), Alphonse Daloz, planted a forest in the large area of dunes by the sea. By the end of the century, it had been turned into a seaside resort by an Englishman, John Whitley. An English syndicate developed the golf course. It has been claimed that it was renamed Le-Touquet-Paris-Plage by the editor of the Paris newspaper, *le Figaro*, in 1912: however, it was called Paris-Plage from the 1890s. Its posters called it *'L'Arcachon du Nord'*, after the famous resort area south of Bordeaux and *'le jardin de la Manche'*. By the 1930s it was established as one of the most elegant and expensive resorts in Europe. By now the rich and famous mostly arrived at the newly-opened airport. It is worth visiting the Hotel Westminster to look at the signed photographs of celebrities, such as Greta Garbo and the Duke of Windsor. These decorate the wall of the main corridor. Today the resort is celebrated for its sporting events.

History of the Pas-de-Calais

Historically the area was owned and controlled by the Counts of Artois, Boulogne, Picardy, and Flanders. This book is focusing on what used to be Artois and the area around Boulogne, the Boulonnais. By the time of the revolution, Artois included the Boulonnais and Calais and was almost the same as the present Pas-de-Calais. The Nord *département* roughly corresponds to that part of Flanders now in France, the rest of Flanders now being part of Belgium. Our area faced the melting pot that finally became Belgium and Holland, and this fact ensured that its ownership was always crucial to France, and was often contested. In addition, the flat coastal area offered invading armies access to the riches of Western Europe.

This changing ownership over the centuries has given the Pas-de-Calais a remarkable diversity. This can be seen in the glories of its Flemish architecture, marvellously combining northern discipline with Spanish exuberance, seen perhaps at its best in the squares of Arras. But everyday life displays the same curious mix. It is fascinating to watch the place names gradually change from Flemish to French as you travel south and west across the Region. The Pas-de-Calais can be seen as a melting-pot where powerful cultures met, fought and gradually combined.

The first change of ownership we can identify is the conquest by Belgian Celts about 300 BC. They held it until Julius Caesar arrived in 57 BC. From the Romans via the Franks we come ultimately to Charlemagne, the greatest of the Frankish kings, who ruled an empire that at its peak, in the middle of the 9th century, took in parts of Spain, Italy and Germany.

The town hall and the Place des Héros at Arras in 2007.   *Authors*

The Rodin sculpture *The Burghers of Calais*, sited in front of the town hall, and close to Calais-Ville station.
Galerie de l'Hôtel de Ville, Calais; Authors' Collection

Over the subsequent centuries the kingdom of France shrank, with the nobility increasing their local power. The first notable move to expand the kingdom of France into our area was in 1223, when Artois was added on the accession of Louis VIII. He made his second son, Robert, Count of Artois. In 1314, Phillip IV annexed Flanders. Although he had three sons, they had no male issue and the crown passed to a nephew, Phillip VI of Valois. Edward I of England contested this succession, claiming the French crown for his daughter-in-law, Isabella, only daughter of Phillip IV. Various other contentious issues about land ownership added fuel to this fire and ultimately, in the middle of the 14th century, this led to the Hundred Years War.

Our area saw much fighting, as the Duke of Burgundy, seeing his chance with the dismemberment of France, joined the English. The first major battle was Crécy, fought in 1346. Crécy is now in the Somme *département* a few miles south of the River Authie, the border with the Pas-de-Calais. Edward III oversaw his archers' victory and a viewing tower on the site marks the position of the windmill that he used as an observation post. After their victory, the English marched via St-Josse, Étaples and Wissant to Calais, which they besieged until it capitulated after eight months. The story of the burghers of Calais is well known. Edward was intent on executing them until his wife, Phillipa, intervened. Rodin's famous statue of 1895 stands near Calais town hall. The statue near the Palace of Westminster, in London, is a copy.

In 1369, Flanders was lost to the French crown when Phillip the Bold, Duke of Burgundy, married Margaret of Flanders. Henry V now appears on the scene, landing at Harfleur, in Normandy, in 1415. He then marched north to meet the French at Agincourt (now called Azincourt), near Fruges, in the Pas-de-Calais. The battlefield has an excellent visitor's centre. In 1420, because her husband Charles VI was insane, the French queen, Isabeau of Bavaria, signed the treaty of Troyes, giving Henry V the French crown on Charles' death. Nothing came of this as Henry died near Paris in 1422. His body, being taken to the coast, was blessed at the church of Notre-Dame in Montreuil. French writers at the time suggested this was done to obtain forgiveness for his sins against France! It took Joan of Arc to restore the French position and bring Charles VII to his coronation in Rheims in 1429.

Further shifts of power led, in 1435, to the treaty of Arras, whereby Picardy and the Boulonnais were ceded to Burgundy. The war continued until 1453 when the English left France. The only territory they had to show for 100 years of fighting was the area around Calais, protected by the forts of Guînes and Hammes on the frontier with Burgundy. This was a marshy area of 20 square miles, called The Pale. The garrison strength was 2,000 men-at-arms and archers. It is noteworthy that they were the only professional army that England had at the time. It seems likely that the only reason Calais remained in English hands was the continuing enmity between France and Burgundy. Calais was extremely important to England at this time. This importance lay in commerce not military strategy. The merchants of the Calais Wool Staple held a monopoly of most of the wool produced in England. It was to Calais that the Flemish weavers had to come to buy. Flanders had by now become the main weaving centre of Europe. This had not always been the case. In the 12th century, Artois had been foremost in cloth production, when merchants from Arras and Hesdin traded their cloth at fairs in Champagne. They brought back oils and spices. The Artois cloth was then sold by the Italian traders in Genoa and travelled as far as Turkey and the Middle East. The 13th and 14th centuries saw a decline. This was due in part to severe outbreaks of the 'Black Death'. In 1349, the population of Arras was halved by the plague. The Arras weavers survived by concentrating on up-market items such as wall-hangings. In *Hamlet*, Polonius is stabbed whilst hiding behind an 'arras'.

The entrance to the citadel at Calais. Postcard postmarked 1905. *Authors' Collection*

In 1456, a legendary figure, Richard Neville, Earl of Warwick, became Captain of Calais. Later, in the Wars of the Roses, he became known as 'Warwick the Kingmaker' because of his ruthless use of family power. Calais, however, was where he found his feet. He was 28 years old. He found the fortifications in Calais in a bad way. The troops were mutinous, not having been paid for some time, and the walls had begun to crumble. At once he began to put things to rights and realising that Calais' strength lay in her mastery of the Channel, he taught himself seamanship and set about creating a marine fighting force. By 1458, he was able to take on 28 Spanish galleons. After six hours, having two ships sunk and six captured, the Spanish retired.

In 1461, France acquired a king to be reckoned with, Louis XI. As Dauphin, at odds with his father, Charles VII, he had gone to Flanders, where Duke Philip had welcomed him as a thorn in Charles' side. As king, through a mixture of statecraft, cunning and determination, he managed to bring his feuding nobility under control and unite France. Ultimately the 'Spider King' increased French territory. In the north he added Picardy to the French crown but Artois and the Boulonnais remained out of reach.

The Dukes of Burgundy at this time, held Flanders, Artois and the Boulonnais, and the Burgundian court was the most luxurious and ostentatious in Europe. Their favourite summer residence was at Hesdin in the Pas-de-Calais. Here, they took over the gardens of the Counts of Artois. These had been famous since the Middle-Ages with their joke fountains and drenchings for the unwary. There were to be only four Dukes of Burgundy. By the death of Charles the Bold at Nancy in 1477, Burgundian power in France was on the wane. In that year, Mary, his heiress, needing strong military support, had married Maximilian of Austria. Thus, the Hapsburgs enter our story. After the death of Mary in 1482, Maximilian ruled the remaining Burgundian possessions. Thus for a while our area became Austrian. Their son, Phillip 'the Handsome', married the heiress to Spain in 1496 and that was how our *départements* came under Spanish rule in the 16th century.

Our area continues to be a battle-ground. Only the leaders change. On Phillip's death in 1506, his son Charles inherited a vast range of territory. French documents refer to him as *Charles Quint* which in older French means 'fifth of that name', so called because he was the fifth Austrian Archduke of that name. In Spain he was crowned as Charles I. His French opponent was now François I and he was determined to push the Hapsburgs out of Artois. Across the Channel too we have a new king, Henry VIII. In June 1520, a meeting was arranged between Henry and François. François lodged in the castle at Ardres and Henry at Guînes, which was still in English hands. Presentation was everything and each king wanted to have the most expensive and gorgeous accoutrements. Henry had a large pavilion built of glass. François had a luxurious tent of gold brocade. This meeting later became known as 'The Field of the Cloth of Gold' (*Camp du Drap d'Or*). The field itself is between Guînes and Ardres, just south of the line of the later Anvin-Calais railway, but there is nothing there to see now. Nothing was achieved at the meeting. Henry left in a huff after the wind damaged his pavilion and he was unhorsed in a joust.

As a result, Henry acquired a new ally, Charles Quint. The old partnership of England and Burgundy was to be revived. By 1544, relations between England and France had deteriorated to such an extent that Henry was planning to invade. Although unwell, he intended to lead this himself. Landing at Calais in June of that year, he rode into French territory with a huge lance and a heavy musket across his saddle. He besieged Boulogne and although he had to be winched onto his horse, he led the attacks. Boulogne fell on 14th September and the English army moved on to besiege Montreuil. Since the 11th century this had been a French royal town and therefore was a prize for Henry and Charles. Along with Thérouanne, Montreuil had been under attack by the Spaniards since 1537, with much damage being done to the medieval fortifications. Henry took Montreuil and was keen to march on Paris but Charles had other ideas and the two parted. Since it was now September and the campaigning season nearly over, Henry went home. The Dauphin, who was leading the French army and on his way to retake Boulogne in 1544, destroyed much of Berck. Prior to this the town had a population of 1,800, living in 300 dwellings. After the attack only 200 people were left, and 20 dwellings.

England finally lost her only remaining French territory, Calais, in 1558, after a siege of only eight days. Everyone knows that Mary Tudor's last words are purported to have been that they would find 'Calais' engraved on her heart. The next 50 years saw a shift from wars against foreigners to civil wars fed by religious hate. Peace came with Henri

MONTREUIL-sur-MER — Promenade des Remparts

Flahaut, Débit de Tabacs, Grande Rue

Part of the walls at Montreuil-sur-Mer, built by Jen Errard and later altered by Vauban. Postcard written in 1911.   *Authors' Collection*

IV's Edict of Nantes of 1598, which gave respite to the Protestant Huguenots. In 1659, Louis XIV secured a lasting peace with Spain and France finally gained Artois and the Boulonnais. The years 1661-2 saw a revolt break out in the Boulonnais. This was a reaction to Louis' excessive tax demands. The revolt was harshly suppressed, its leaders executed in front of Boulogne cathedral and 400 sent to serve for ever in the galleys. In order to protect his northern borders against the Spaniards and to promote his own expansionist intent, Louis employed his brilliant military architect Sebastien le Prestre de Vauban to build an amazing string of forts. He built two lines along what was then the Spanish-Hapsburg border and is now the Belgian border. There were 15 in one line and 13 in the other, and many of these are still standing, notably Lille, Maubeuge and Gravelines. These are all worth a visit. The fort at Aire-sur-la Lys has unfortunately gone. The fort at Montreuil was created by an earlier master, Jean Errard, but Vauban made alterations. In 1689, James II fled England and landed at Ambleteuse, north of Boulogne. Until his death in 1701, he lived in France under the protection of Louis, his cousin.

With its incorporation into France, our area steps back from the forefront of history. After his great-grandfather's long reign, Louis XV came to the throne and another long reign ensued. At the end of the 18th century the French Revolution left its mark, particularly in its destruction of religious houses and churches. Boulogne Cathedral was demolished. This had been a place of pilgrimage since the year 636, when worshippers at a shrine, where the cathedral now stands, saw a vision of the Virgin. At the same moment a statue arrived on the shore in an unmanned boat. The result was an annual pilgrimage, so celebrated that 14 kings of France and five kings of England performed it over the centuries.

Napoleon Bonaparte came to Boulogne in June 1803. There, he gathered a large army and a fleet to carry them on an invasion of Britain. He hoped to slip past the superior British Navy under cover of mist but the weather remained clear. A complicated plan to lure Nelson to the West Indies failed and he was back in time to win at Trafalgar. Some historians think it unlikely that Napoleon, a superb military strategist, would have believed an invasion was feasible and maintain that the 'invasion' was a pretext for collecting a huge army, ready to strike anywhere in Europe. In any event, trouble from the Austrians, in 1805, caused him to withdraw his enormous army from Boulogne to meet them on the Rhine. To commemorate the 'invasion', Napoleon began, in 1804, the *Colonne de la Grande Armée*. It was completed by Louis-Phillipe many years later and remains a notable landmark on the N1 road to the north. Although a bridge or tunnel crossing of the Channel had been a dream for centuries, and there had been projects since 1750, Napoleon was the first to set the dream in motion. An engineer called Matthieu actually began work that was not abandoned until 1870.

The opening years of the 19th century saw industrial developments in our area. In 1816, expertise was imported from Nottingham to begin lace manufacture in Calais. At its peak, Calais lace-making employed 2,000 workers, many of them working at home. In the 1830s, a Lyonnaise manufacturer invented the Jacquard loom, named after him, and production really took off. The church of St-Pierre in Calais has his statue. In 1988, Calais still had 500 lace looms, and Calais lace is still exported to many countries.

Of the other industries that developed in the area the one of most interest here is sugar production. It was in the Pas-de-Calais, near Arras, in 1810, that the first sugar was produced from sugar-beet. The inventor of the industrial process, Benjamin Delessert, was well rewarded by Napoleon, because of the shortage of West Indian sugar cane during the British blockade. As we will describe later the sugar refineries used narrow-gauge lines extensively. Nord-Pas-de-Calais is still a major producer of French sugar, providing one-fifth of the total.

225 *BOULOGNE-SUR-MER. — La Colonne de la Grande-Armée. — LL.*

The *Colonne de la Grande Armée* at Boulogne.   *Authors' Collection*

In August, 1840, pursuing his claim to the French throne as Napoleon Bonaparte's nephew, Louis Napoleon made a rash attempt to invade France. Having lashed a dishevelled vulture to the mast to represent the Imperial eagle, he landed with 56 men on the coast near Boulogne. Since the men had been recruited to join a pleasure cruise that had been well supplied with drink, they were not sober. It was quite a performance ferrying them ashore, and they were then informed that they were invading infantry and told to march on Boulogne. On arriving in the upper town, Louis issued proclamations of his return but the citizens just watched from their windows as at a travelling circus.

He then made for the *Colonne de la Grande Armée*. He planted his flag there and was captured trying to regain his boat. He was imprisoned in the gloomy fortress of Ham, south-east of Amiens. This fortress stood from the 10th century but was destroyed in 1917 by the retreating German army. With the help of a girl, and dressed as a workman, Louis Napoleon escaped to London in 1846. In 1848, a republic was declared and Louis Napoleon was elected to Parliament. Ultimately he became President, and later ruled as Emperor Napoleon III, of France's Second Empire. He was always popular in our area, and in the plebiscite of 1870 he obtained 92 per cent of the vote.

Since then, northern France has been invaded three times by a German army. The first was in 1870, in the Franco-Prussian War. Napoleon III was defeated at Sedan and went into exile in England. The Prussian army occupied Paris but withdrew in 1871, when France ceded Alsace and part of Lorraine. In World War I (1914-1918), the area in this book was never occupied, but in World War II the whole area came under German military rule from spring 1940 to autumn 1944. In the summer of 1940, a large German force was assembled in the Pas-de-Calais, particularly around Boulogne, for the invasion of Britain, echoing that of Napoleon, but with probably more serious intent. The invasion plans were abandoned in autumn 1940 after the failure of the Luftwaffe to obtain air supremacy. From 1942 the stance of the German forces became defensive with the building of coastal fortifications, the 'Atlantic Wall'. Finally from 1943 the area was used for the construction of sites for the launching of the 'V' weapons against England. More details of World War I and World War II are given in Chapters Five and Seven because of the involvement of our railways in these conflicts.

This has been a gallop through more than a thousand years of events in the Pas-de-Calais. The last decade has seen the area return to the front pages again. The long-awaited Channel Tunnel was completed in May 1994. At the same time poverty and lack of opportunity for betterment has led people from poorer countries to seek a better life in the West. The majority of these immigrants speak English as their second language and therefore to work in Britain is their dream. To this end, therefore, they have found ways of heading towards England. As always the Channel is a barrier that must be crossed and the Channel Tunnel and the Car Ferries must seem tantalising. Some found illegal ways of crossing, in lorry containers or under trains in the Tunnel, but many were stranded in the Pas-de-Calais. The notorious camp at Sangatte, near Calais, was the French Government's answer to the problem. It has now been closed but the Pas-de-Calais remains the frontline in this new economic war.

Geology and Geography

Looking back around two million years, during the time geologists call the Secondary Period, our area was covered by sea and remained so for many thousands of years. Gradually the chalk ridges formed, the sea retreated and land appeared. Overall the land is very similar to large parts of southern England, being mostly chalk; indeed the whole is sometimes called the Wealden-Artois formation. However, the effects of the people on the land over centuries have made it very different.

Artois and Picardy form the division between two extensive basins, the Paris basin, which now in part forms the Ile de France, and the Anglo-Belgian basin, stretching away to the north. In the Ile de France this results in an extensive chalk plain which extends up into the Pas de Calais, forming the fertile agricultural area around Arras. From the Middle Ages this area was a major wheat producer for the more populous weaving areas of Flanders. In Artois, however, we find a plateau of chalk running in a north-west to south-east direction. This plateau ends in an escarpment before falling to the Flanders plain. Because of the contrast with these plains, we feel safe in calling this escarpment 'dramatic' although it never rises more than 100 metres. The escarpment's drama has been put to good use at Vimy Ridge and Notre-Dame de Lorette with their memorials to World War I. The battle for Vimy Ridge continued through much of the war. The ridge was critical because it overlooked the German held positions around Lens. The memorial records the loss of life by the Canadian troops who took the ridge in 1917. The escarpment of Notre-Dame de Lorette now carries the imposing memorial to the French dead of World War I.

In the north-east corner of the Pas-de-Calais are the cliffs of the *Caps*. Cap Blanc-Nez ('white nose'), just west of Calais, is chalk as the name suggests. It rises 145 metres (475 feet) above the sea. Cap Gris-Nez ('grey nose'), further along the coast towards Boulogne, is less spectacular. From both one can see the English coast on a clear day.

Overall the watershed runs through the western Pas-de-Calais from north-west at Cap Blanc-Nez to south-east. South and west of this the main rivers run north-west to the English Channel, from the Liane at Boulogne to the Authie just south of Berck. The Authie is for most of its course the boundary between *départements* of Pas-de-Calais and Somme, and therefore historically the division between Artois and Picardy. To the north and east of the watershed, the main rivers run north or east to the North Sea.

In the south of Artois, in the area named after the river Ternoise, a large tributary of the river Canche, we find hills that, although they are well watered, appear bare and inhospitable, with wind and water erosion revealing their chalk substance in places. For non-geologists amongst us, local building materials can give a quick answer to the question, 'what sort of soil do we get around here?' In the area of the Ternoise, we find brick replacing the *torchis* of further north. *Torchis* is the northern French equivalent of our 'wattle and daub' and this needs clayey soil. Hard chalk blocks are also used as a building material. The hills to the north-west are more fertile with their chalk overlaid by clay. This clay carries the flints that you can also find used in many local buildings. This area supports the dense greenery of Hesdin Forest and the damp hedged fields, the *bocage*, that surround the forest.

The area around Boulogne, the Boulonnais, is a curious feature. A guide to the Pas de Calais, produced by the local authorities, describes it as a *boutonnière*, a button-hole. It is a basin enclosed in the chalk shell. This basin extends under the Channel. As a result, we find, in the Boulonnais, very different countryside from that in the surrounding areas. The clay soils are very fertile and have encouraged the rearing of the famous dappled grey, extremely strong Boulonnais horses. These horses crop up again in this book, pulling trams at Berck-Plage. The fertile soils also support numerous forests, notably those of Boulogne and Desvres.

Along the coast from Calais to the east, the land is low-lying and relatively recently relinquished by the sea. Inland there is marshy land, both near the coast (the *marais* of Guînes) and around St-Omer, where the water appears trapped in low-lying ground inland of the narrow passage of the river Aa through the line of hills at Watten. From south of Boulogne all the way to the Somme estuary, there are spectacular sand dunes, and in places, as at Rang-du-Fliers, there is also *marais* between the dunes and the inland hills.

Development of railways in Pas-de-Calais

The first section of the first metre gauge railway in the area of this book, part of the Anvin-Calais line, opened in 1881, and was one of the earliest such lines in France. By that time the standard gauge network in the western Pas-de-Calais was already fully developed. The *Loi Migneret* of 1865 codified the definitions of lines of *Intérêt Général* and those of *Intérêt Local*. The former were those of sufficient length, importance, or strategic worth to be at least partially a charge on the State. The latter were the responsibility of the *département* concerned. In 1879-1880 the Freyciney Plan further encouraged the development of lines of *Intérêt Local*, and within this category also defined tramways, which were lines built at least 70 per cent in roads, or on the verges of roads. For a full discussion of these decisions and their effects we recommend Chapter One of *Minor Railways of France* (W.J.K. Davies, Plateway Press, 2000).

Lines of *Intérêt Général* were administered by the Ministry of Public Works in Paris, whereas those of *Intérêt Local* were administered by the *département* concerned. This was a responsibility of the *Préfet*, the chief administrator, of the *département*, with the Chief Engineer of *Ponts et Chaussées* (bridges and highways) and his local Engineers reporting to him. Local Engineers were based in the chief towns. References to the 'Chief Engineer' and the 'Engineer' in this book refer to these departmental employees, not to employees of the operating companies. Although the right to build and operate the railways was conceded to companies, the State and the *départements* kept a very tight grip on them. They had to give permission for all changes, however minor, to the *Cahier des Charges*, the original very detailed agreement about building and operating each line. It is fortunate for us that this was so, since most of the paperwork survives in the departmental archives even when, as in this case, most of the companies' archives have disappeared.

Plans for railways of *Intérêt Local* would be brought forward by a businessman or company, usually with local encouragement. After suitable public enquiries, the

The north side of Calais-Ville station, postcard postmarked 1905. The distinctive footbridge on the right allowed pedestrians to cross from one side of the station to the other without going to the road bridge beyond the left end of the station. *Édition Le Raincy; Authors' Collection*

The second Gare Maritime at Calais, opened in 1889. *Authors' Collection*

proposed line would be declared of *utilité publique* ('in the public interest'), and the concession to build and operate the line would be granted for a fixed number of years to the businessman or company. At about this stage a businessman who had not already formed a *Compagnie* or *Société Anonyme* (limited company) for this purpose would usually do so. At the end of the life of the line it could be closed by local agreement but the decree of *déclassement* (declassification) had to come from the office of the President of the Republic, and would be published in the official journal of the Republic.

It was in general the case that standard gauge lines were of *Intérêt Général*, and those of metre and other narrow gauges were of *Intérêt Local*, but there were exceptions both ways. In the area described in this book there was only one exception. The industrial line from La Lacque, on the St-Omer to Berguette line just east of Aire, to Estrée-Blanche, was of standard gauge but of *Intérêt Local*.

Development of standard gauge railways in the Pas-de-Calais

The *Compagnie du Nord* was formed in 1845 and was eventually responsible for all lines of *Intérêt Général* in the area covered by this book. The first lines north from Paris were to Lille and Valenciennes, opened in 1846. The line to Lille ran via Amiens, the principal town of the Somme *département*, and Arras, principal town of the Pas-de-Calais. A branch of this from Lille to Calais via Hazebrouck and St-Omer opened in 1848. The first, provisional, terminal station at Calais, opened in 1848, was at Calais-St-Pierre, probably in the marshalling yard area close to the first terminal of the Anvin-Calais metre gauge railway (*see Chapter Two*). The line extended to the first permanent station of Calais-Ville, situated where it still stands, between old Calais and St-Pierre, in 1849. This station was rebuilt in 1888-1889, with passenger buildings on both sides of the station, and a striking footbridge linking the two sides. This was the station to which the Anvin-Calais metre gauge line was extended in 1900.

There was a line to the port at Calais from 1860. The first passenger station in the port area, Calais-Maritime, was established in 1882, but a much grander station was opened in 1889 with extensions to the port. It is claimed that at the end of the 19th century, the steam ferries, provided three times daily by the *Compagnie du Nord* and the London, Chatham & Dover Railway Company, enabled a journey time from Paris to London of seven hours.

A double track main line to Boulogne left the Lille line at Amiens. From November 1847, trains ran from Paris via Amiens to Neufchatel, 12 km south of Boulogne, and the line was open all the way to Boulogne in 1848. A major feature of this line was the 300 metre-long, 15-arch, bridge of brick and stone across the river Canche at Étaples. From 1891 to 1955 the metre gauge Aire-Berck line crossed this coast main line at Verton just south of Rang-du-Fliers, where there was a shared station (*see Chapter Three*). From 1900 to 1940 the metre gauge tramway from Étaples to Paris-Plage began at Étaples station (*see Chapter Three*).

The imposing central station at Boulogne, Boulogne-Ville, or sometimes Boulogne-gare-Centrale, was not built until the 1850s, and until then passengers had to make do with the goods terminal. Boulogne-Ville was on the left bank (west) of the river Liane and close to the port, in the neighbourhood of Capécure. The station building had red and yellow bricks with a stone base and pointed with red, yellow and white mortar, and it is pity this cannot be seen on the contemporary black and white photographs. There were polygonal towers flanking the main entrance, and smaller matching gate-towers. This building was destroyed in World War II, and by the 1960s a new Boulogne-Ville had been built on the through line on the other side

A goods train on the Compagnie du Nord main line from Abbeville to Boulogne crossing the bridge over the river Canche at Étaples. No date but the locomotive design indicates before World War I.   *Éditions Stévenard/Authors' Collection*

The central station of the Compagnie du Nord at Boulogne (Boulogne-Ville). No date but the dress indicates before World War I. The standard gauge line bottom left is one of two through lines to the Gare Maritime.   *Authors' Collection*

A cross-channel paddle steamer leaving Boulogne Harbour for Folkestone. *Authors' Collection*

The Gare Maritime at Boulogne following the arrival of a boat. Postcard postmarked 1927.
Authors' Collection

Montreuil-sur-Mer (P.-de-C.) — La Gare

Fontaine-Segrez, lib.-édit.

The Compagnie du Nord standard gauge station at Montreuil-sur-Mer. The Aire-Berck metre gauge lines are to the left beyond the island platform. Postcard postmarked 1912.

Authors' Collection

The Compagnie du Nord standard gauge station at Aire-sur-la-Lys. The Aire-Berck metre gauge line is crossing the foreground behind the nearest lamp post, into the terminus of this line, off picture to the right. This arrangement nearly led to an accident in 1903. Postcard written in 1909.

L. Paresys, Aire; Authors' Collection

Vue de la Gare d'AIRE-sur-la-LYS

L. Paresys, Aire-sur-la-Lys

of the river Liane. From 1902 to 1935 the metre gauge line from Boulogne to Bonningues began outside Boulogne-Ville station (*see Chapter Four*).

The remaining part of the coastal main line, from Boulogne to Calais, was not opened until 1867, after long discussion about the route. The same year the boat trains to Calais from Paris began to use this route rather than go via Arras and Hazebrouck. Boulogne-Ville was a terminus and originally through trains had to reverse. On leaving Boulogne-Ville towards Calais there was a curved viaduct 362 metres long, built of stone with 18 arches, over the river Liane. This bridge ended about where the entrance to the new Boulogne-Ville station is now. Later, in 1887, a chord on a new metal bridge across the Liane was built and fast through trains then missed Boulogne-Ville and stopped at Boulogne-Tintelleries. This is situated in the gardens of the same name where the line emerges from a tunnel under the corner of the old town, The line to Calais leaves the coast at Wimereux, and follows a rather winding inland route through the hills towards Calais. At the Calais end the line joins those from St-Omer, and from Dunkirk (opened 1876), at Calais-Fontinettes.

Boulogne has been an important entry point to France for centuries and so naturally, from the earliest days of the railways, ferries wanted to discharge their passengers onto trains. In 1875, lines were extended along the Quai Chanzy from Boulogne-Ville station. The first *Gare Maritime* at Boulogne burned down, but a new and better one was built in 1877. The route via Boulogne and Folkestone became the shortest way from Paris to London. Boulogne also became a port of call for transatlantic steamers.

The cross-country line from St-Omer to Boulogne opened in 1874. It was double track as far as Arques, shared with the line to Berguette and Armentières. From there it went west via Lumbres and Desvres to join the Amiens to Boulogne main line at Hesdigneul, south-west of Boulogne. From Arques to Hesdigneul it was single track. The gradients were steep and at its summit near Lottinghem, going over the watershed between the Aa and the Liane valleys, it reached almost 200 metres (650 feet), the highest point of any railway in the Pas-de-Calais. From 1882 to 1955 this line was crossed at Lumbres by the metre gauge Anvin-Calais line, which also had its main depot and workshops at Lumbres (*see Chapter Two*). The passenger service from Arques to Desvres closed in 1959 and from Desvres to Boulogne in 1968. The line is still used for goods services from Arques to Lumbres and from Desvres to Hesdigneul, and a summer weekend tourist railway operates from Arques to Lumbres.

The other cross-country line, from Arras to Étaples, opened from Arras to St-Pol-sur-Ternoise and from Étaples to Montreuil in 1875. The central section from Montreuil to St-Pol did not open until 1878. The line has always been single track except during World War I when it was doubled by French and British railway engineers. The station at Anvin, on this line between Hesdin and St-Pol, was, from 1882 to 1952, the southern terminus of the metre gauge Anvin-Calais line (*see Chapter Two*). From 1893 to 1955 the metre gauge Aire-Berck line crossed this line at Montreuil (*see Chapter Three*).

The line from St-Omer to Armentières opened between Arques and Berguette in 1878. The line was single track from Arques where it left the line to Boulogne. Between St-Omer and Berguette it served Aire-sur-la-Lys. From 1893 to 1952 this was the eastern terminus of the metre gauge Aire-Berck line (*see Chapter Three*). Passenger services between St-Omer and Berguette ceased in October 1954, and the track has been lifted for most of the section from Arques to just east of Aire.

So by the end of the 1870s the framework of standard gauge railways in the western Pas-de-Calais was established. The scene was set for the addition of the metre gauge network of lines of *Intérêt Local*, beginning with the first part of the Anvin-Calais line, from Calais-St-Pierre to Guînes, in 1881.

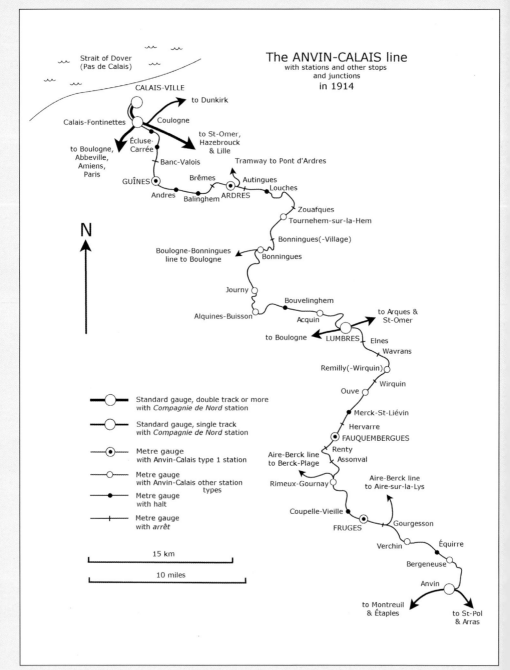

The ANVIN-CALAIS line
with stations and other stops
and junctions
in 1914

Strait of Dover
(Pas de Calais)

CALAIS-VILLE

to Dunkirk

Calais-Fontinettes

Coulogne

Écluse-
Carrée

to St-Omer,
Hazebrouck
& Lille

to Boulogne,
Abbeville,
Amiens,
Paris

Banc-Valois

Tramway to Pont d'Ardres

GUÎNES

Brêmes

Autingues

Andres

Balinghem

ARDRES

Louches

Zouafques
Tournehem-sur-la-Hem

Bonningues(-Village)

Boulogne-Bonningues
line to Boulogne

Bonningues

N

Journy

Bouvelinghem

Alquines-Buisson

Acquin

to Arques &
St-Omer

to Boulogne

LUMBRES

Elnes

Wavrans

Remilly(-Wirquin)

Wirquin

Ouve

Merck-St-Liévin

Hervarre

FAUQUEMBERGUES

Aire-Berck line
to Berck-Plage

Renty

Assonval

Rimeux-Gournay

Aire-Berck line
to Aire-sur-la-Lys

Coupelle-Vieille

Gourgesson

FRUGES

Verchin

Équirre

Bergeneuse

Anvin

to Montreuil
& Étaples

to St-Pol
& Arras

Standard gauge, double track or more
with *Compagnie de Nord* station

Standard gauge, single track
with *Compagnie de Nord* station

Metre gauge
with Anvin-Calais type 1 station

Metre gauge
with Anvin-Calais other station
types

Metre gauge
with halt

Metre gauge
with *arrêt*

15 km

10 miles

Chapter Two

The Line from Anvin to Calais up to 1914
and related and competing lines and tramways

Anvin to Calais

Permission to build this metre gauge *ligne d'Intérêt Local* (line of local importance) was given to M. Émile Level, who had been an Engineer in the *Compagnie des Chemins de Fer du Nord*, in 1874. It was one of the earliest lines of local interest constructed under the Freyciney plan of 1880, and the first in the Pas de Calais. M. Level set up the *Compagnie du Chemin de Fer d'Anvin à Calais* to build and operate the line. It was always known as 'Anvin à Calais' (Anvin to Calais, abbreviated as AC), even though Calais is a major city and port and Anvin is a small rural town, hardly more than a village. It is likely that this order, being alphabetical, satisfied the passion of the French, then as now, for tidiness and bureaucratic convention.

Building and opening the line

Construction was started at both ends simultaneously. The line was opened from its first station in Calais, Calais-St-Pierre, to Guînes, a distance of 9 km (5½ miles) on 1st October, 1881. Anvin to Fruges was opened 1st January, 1882; Fruges to Lumbres on 1st April; Guînes to Ardres on 1st July; and the final section from Lumbres to Ardres on 10th August, 1882. The total length was then 94 km (58½ miles). Finally, in or just before 1900, the station at Calais-St-Pierre was closed and the line opened a further kilometre to the main standard gauge terminus at Calais-Ville. This was part of a programme of changes to railways between Calais-Fontinettes and Calais-Ville agreed in 1895 to 'ameliorate local services and welcome the Anvin to Calais line at Calais Ville'. The final full length of the line was 95 km (59 miles). The cost of building the line was reported to be 77,000 francs per kilometre, about a quarter to a third the cost of a single track standard gauge line.

The line was visited on 3rd December, 1882, by several Deputies and Senators from the French National Assembly, and by many engineers and industrialists. Most of the visitors left Paris at 07.40 and arrived at Calais-St-Pierre at 13.00. They then travelled the whole length of the line. They inspected Guînes as an example of a main station and Tournehem as an example of a village one. Arriving at Lumbres after 3 hours and 30 minutes, the visitors 'assisted in the trans-shipment of a wagon of coal, toured the workshops, and then saw a siding on the open track serving a paper factory'. At Fauquembergues, reached after 4 hours and 10 minutes, a train was on display made up of various stock including phosphate wagons. The visitors arrived at Anvin after 5 hours and 24 minutes, which would have been well after 6 pm. No doubt this long day was well lubricated with French hospitality. Probably this amount of interest in the line was due to the fact that Anvin-Calais was one of the earliest local railways in France.

<o>
31

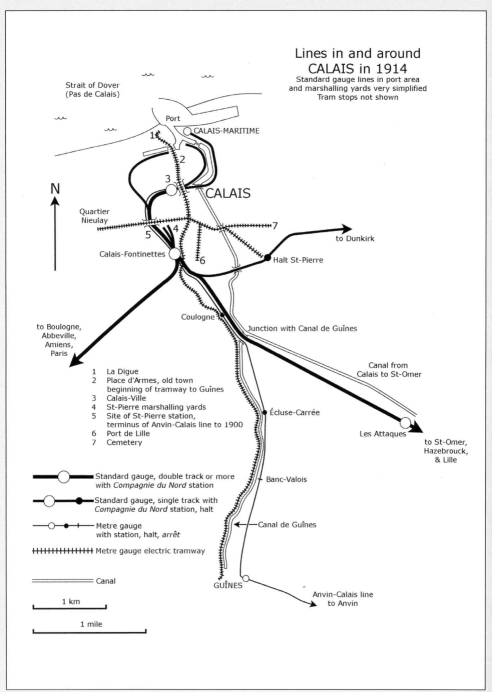

Lines in and around
CALAIS in 1914
Standard gauge lines in port area
and marshalling yards very simplified
Tram stops not shown

Strait of Dover
(Pas de Calais)

Port

CALAIS-MARITIME

1

2

3

CALAIS

N

Quartier
Nieulay

7

5   4

Calais-Fontinettes

6

Halt St-Pierre

to Dunkirk

Coulogne

Junction with Canal de Guînes

to Boulogne,
Abbeville,
Amiens,
Paris

Canal from
Calais to St-Omer

1   La Digue
2   Place d'Armes, old town
    beginning of tramway to Guînes
3   Calais-Ville
4   St-Pierre marshalling yards
5   Site of St-Pierre station,
    terminus of Anvin-Calais line to 1900
6   Port de Lille
7   Cemetery

Écluse-Carrée

Les Attaques

to St-Omer,
Hazebrouck,
& Lille

Standard gauge, double track or more
with *Compagnie du Nord* station

Banc-Valois

Standard gauge, single track with
Compagnie du Nord station, halt

Metre gauge
with station, halt, *arrêt*

Canal de Guînes

Metre gauge electric tramway

Canal

1 km

GUÎNES

Anvin-Calais line
to Anvin

1 mile

Description of the line

The line ran in general north-north-east from Anvin to Calais, but wound about considerably. This can easily be demonstrated by comparing its actual length of 95 km (59 miles) with the distance of 62 km (38.5 miles) 'as the crow flies'. The tortuous nature of the line was partly determined by the need to serve the local communities, surely the *raison d'être* for the line. There were, however, also economic reasons. By following the contours, earthworks were minimised and costs kept down. As well as connecting rural communities, the line visited the chief towns of five of the cantons it passed through: Guînes, Ardres, Lumbres, Fauquembergues and Fruges. Apart from these towns and the run from Calais through its suburbs towards Guînes, the line ran through the country. This countryside is quite hilly, especially the central area from Bonningues to Fruges, with areas of chalk downs interspersed with woods and river valleys. Most of the line between Lumbres and Guînes ran through what is now the *Parc Naturel Régional des Caps et Marais d'Opale*. This designation recognises the particular beauty of this landscape.

Since the line was known as the Anvin to Calais, we will start our journey at Anvin. Here the line shared the standard gauge station of the *Companie du Nord*, whose line ran from Étaples to St-Pol-sur-Ternoise and Arras. Anvin station stands 60 metres (197 ft) above sea level and is in the valley of the river Ternoise, which flows west to join the river Canche which in turn enters the English Channel between Étaples and Le Touquet. The line left Anvin station eastwards with the standard gauge line before turning north, crossing the Ternoise and following a tributary. Towards Fruges the line crossed the plateau between the Ternoise and the river Lys. The highest point reached on this part of the line was 131 metres (430 ft) between Équirre and Verchin. The latter lies in the upper valley of the Lys which eventually reaches Belgium, where, as the river Leie, it joins the river Schelde flowing through Gent and Antwerp to the North Sea. Our railway has thus crossed the watershed between the English Channel and the North Sea.

From Verchin, the line ran north-west along the valley of the Lys, then along the valley of the river Traxène, a tributary of the Lys, to Fruges. Continuing north-west beyond Fruges, the line left the Traxène beyond Coupelle-Vieille and climbed in a series of curves up onto the plateau between the Lys and the valley of the river Aa, reaching the top at Rimeux-Gournay station. The line then headed north, descending into the Aa valley down another series of curves on the hillside, to reach the valley bottom just before Fauquembergues. At this point the line had descended to 78 metres (256 ft) in about 6 kilometres. From Fauquembergues the line continued north along the valley of the Aa to Lumbres. Here it shared the station with the standard gauge line running from Hesdigneuil on the main Boulogne-Paris line in the west, to Arques and St-Omer on the Calais-Lille line in the east. Part of this line from Arques to Lumbres survives as a tourist railway (*see Chapter Eight*).

The Anvin-Calais line now swung north again to climb over a ridge to Acquin. It then climbed again westward for six kilometres along the side of a wooded valley to the summit of the whole line at Le Buisson, where the halt known as Alquines-Buisson was in a shallow cutting at the top of the hill at 177 metres (580 ft) - and they say that this part of France is flat and boring! From here the line turned north again, curving along a spectacular west-facing chalk down for seven kilometres to Bonningues-lès-Ardres, where the station was a little above the main village, which lies in the valley of the river Hem. The line wound down into the valley before crossing the Hem. Beyond Tournehem-sur-la-Hem the line climbed a little again, to 50 metres (164 ft) as it curved to the north-west, rounded the end of the range of forested hills which run west from here to Marquise, and descended gradually to Ardres. From Ardres it ran west across flatter farmland, descending gradually again to Guînes.

A train alongside the river Traxène west of Fruges, heading towards Coupelle-Vieille. Date unknown. The locomotive is a Corpet 0-6-2 tank locomotive of Aire-Berck, probably ARB No. 44 delivered in 1892.   *Authors' Collection*

The type 1 station at Fauquembergues. Date unknown.   *Authors' Collection*

The Compagnie du Nord station at Lumbres on the standard gauge line from Boulogne to St-Omer. No date, but the dress indicates before World War I. The Anvin-Calais metre gauge lines are in the foreground with passengers waiting for a train. *Authors' Collection*

The halt at Alquines-Buisson, the highest point on the Anvin-Calais line, in 2006. The old halt building is unique, and has a modern extension to the right. The line ran in front. *Authors*

The Rue de la Gare (station approach) at Ardres with the station (AC type 1) at the end. Postcard written in 1903. *Authors' Collection*

The same view in 2006; the station has gone and the road is now the Rue Léon Delaches, Adjoint 1841-1921. *Authors*

Between Guînes and Calais the line took on a different aspect, crossing the *marais* (marshland) northwards by or close to the Guînes canal, only 1.5 metres (5 ft) above sea level. Just east of the junction of the Guînes canal with the Calais to St-Omer canal the line joined the main Calais-St-Omer-Lille line, which it followed, staying on its west side, to Calais. At the station of Calais-Fontinettes our line crossed the main line from Calais to Boulogne and Paris at its junction with the St-Omer line. When first opened, the terminus at the station called Calais-St-Pierre was on the west side of the standard gauge marshalling yards outside the main Calais station, Calais-Ville. This was the station abandoned in 1900 when the line continued with the main line to Calais-Ville.

Engineering

The railway was constructed with its own formation, and no sections ran alongside roads. The metre gauge single track was laid using Vignole rails weighing 20 kg per metre, initially of iron but later replaced with similar steel rails. Later papers indicate that the sleepers were of oak. According to a report of 1883, the maximum gradient was 1.5 per cent (15 mm per metre) and the maximum curvature on the main running track was of radius 130 metres (426 ft). However, at the meeting held on completion between the company and local officials, the company admitted that the gradient of 1.5 per cent, the maximum allowed in the agreements, had been exceeded for 2.6 km on the way up to the top at Alquines-Buisson, where it was 1.6 per cent. This was probably on the side towards Journy. The Journy area also had the deepest cutting, at 8.14 metres, and the highest embankment, at 9.53 metres. Curves down to 100 metres radius were allowed in the agreements. In general, the company had only used curves down to 130 metres radius, but found it necessary to employ the tighter curves in Fruges town centre, and near the exit from Lumbres station in the Calais direction, where the line curved away from the standard gauge line. At all times, at least 50 metres of straight track was provided between curves of different directions, and at least 50 metres of level track between down and up gradients.

Stations were fenced but the main running track was not enclosed. The general construction aimed to minimize earthworks and building works; there were some cuttings and embankments, but very few bridges and no tunnels. Unavoidably, there was a lot of terracing on the hillside sections. On the section between Calais and the point where it left the standard gauge line south of Pont-de-Coulogne, the line shared the bridges and level crossings of the standard gauge line.

Level crossings (*passages à niveau*, abbreviated as PN) were classified into four categories. First, those which were public and had barriers; second, those which were public with no barriers; third, those for private use (often on farm land); and fourth, those only for pedestrians. In the first category the barriers were of rolling type, pulled across the road. The railway could therefore be closed off from the road but not vice versa. Barriers were closed 10 minutes before a train was due, and reopened immediately the train had passed. The barriers were left open at night. From 1912 it was agreed that trains could use seven first category crossings at night. A light would be shown 10 minutes before the arrival of the train. At second category crossings there were warning signs, indicating that users must be sure that no train was coming before crossing. At the third, private, category, proprietors could provide barriers across the road or track if they wished, and be responsible for opening them for use when required.

At the opening of the line there were 161 level crossings, of which only 16 were gated; these were over more major roads in larger towns and villages. In the second

24 — Fruges (P.-de-C.) - Passage à niveau - Rue de Saint-Omer

The level crossing at Fruges on the Anvin-Calais line, in the Rue de St-Omer, looking towards the town centre. One of the rolling barriers is pulled across the road. The shelter on the left has a square lead roof similar to those of the lavatory blocks on this line. Postcard written in 1915.

Éditions Paul Boulanger, Fruges; Authors' Collection

The station at Calais-Fontinettes. A standard gauge train coming from Calais-Ville on the line to Boulogne is crossing the Anvin-Calais line. The two standard gauge tracks to the right of the Anvin-Calais line are those to St-Omer and Hazebrouck, and that on the far right is to Gravelines and Dunkirk. Postcard postmarked 1906.   *Authors' Collection*

The bridge over the road at Bouvelinghem, August 2006. The halt is to the right.   *Authors*

The bridge of *tablier métallique* (metal platform) type over the River Ternoise at Anvin, July 2007. The end of the Anvin-Calais line at Anvin is round the curve to the right.   *Authors*

The bridge of *tablier métallique* type over the River Aa between Fauquembergues and
Hervarre, November 2006.   *Authors*

category there were 111, in the third 31, and in the fourth only three. In respect of the
unprotected nature of most of the crossings, it was reported in 1883 that no accidents
had resulted from these arrangements and that 'the inhabitants find it convenient to
cross the line when they please, rather than waiting in front of a closed barrier for a
train which is not yet in view'. That this was safely possible reflects the very slow
line speeds. Later, level crossings were to become a significant source of accidents.

When the Anvin-Calais line crossed standard gauge lines, it was done on the level.
This occurred west of Lumbres station, crossing the single track Boulogne-St-Omer
line, and at Calais-Fontinettes, crossing the double track Calais-Ville-Paris line. It is
likely that this was considered safe only two kilometres from Calais-Ville station, with
lower speeds. Later and further south both the Aire-Berck metre gauge line at Verton
(*see Chapter Three*), and the Somme metre gauge network at Noyelles, had bridges over
the main Calais-Paris line, where standard gauge line speeds, especially for non-
stopping trains, would have been much greater. After the move from St-Pierre to
Calais-Ville about 1900 there were more crossings of standard gauge lines, but only
sidings and secondary lines, as our line became entangled in this major transport web.

Bridges were of two types. One type appeared as a brick arch but was in fact, in most
and probably all cases, a concrete structure. The other type was of *tablier métallique*
(metal platform) type. These consisted of steel girders laid across the opening between
vertical brick-faced concrete abutments. On top of the main girders, smaller ones were
placed across, then a sheet steel platform which carried the track. These were the ones
which were normally built over rivers, and any ditches too large for just a pipe culvert.
In general road bridges were of brick arch type, but there were exceptions.

Apart from the shared bridge with the standard gauge between Calais-Ville and
Calais- Fontinettes, which goes under the beginning of the N1, the main road to Paris,
there were seven road bridges, five of them taking the railway over the road and two
under. Starting from the Anvin end, the first is over the Vieux Chemin, a minor road,

at Bergueneuse. This is a brick arch and survives. The second was over a minor road west of Verchin station, which has been demolished. The third was between Rimeux-Gournay and Assonval, on the descent into the Aa valley at Renty. This was shown as a bridge on maps only 20 years ago, but has now been demolished. The fourth and fifth both crossed what is now the D208. Both were on the section climbing along the hillside from Acquin up to Alquines-Buisson. One was at Acquin. This was the exception for a bridge over a road, being of *tablier métallique* type. Only the vertical side abutments, of concrete faced in brick, now remain. The other was at Bouvelinghem halt, which is a brick arch and which survives. Turning now to bridges where the road crossed the railway, the first was a small bridge under a minor road, the Rue du Moulin, 500 metres south-east of the halt at Louches. This has completely disappeared in new housing. The other bridge was at the D224 at Ardres, between the junction with the line to Pont d'Ardres and Ardres station. This has completely gone and the cuttings both sides are filled in. These two bridges taking the line under roads both had three metre openings and were of *tablier métallique* type. All of the road bridges were probably determined by the lie of the land and the gradients rather than by a desire to avoid a level crossing.

There were many river bridges, over the Ternoise, the Traxène, the Aa, the Bléquin, and the Hem, and more over smaller streams, canals and ditches. Bridges over water were almost always of *tablier métallique* type. Exceptions were a bridge of two brick arches over the main stream of the Aa, 250 metres south of Fauquembergues station, and a bridge of one arch over the Bléquin 400 metres from Lumbres station in the Calais direction. Bridges in the Aa valley needed repairing after floods on 24th January, 1891, and 30th and 31st October, 1894. The shared bridge over the beginning of the Guînes canal, just before the parting from the standard gauge line to St-Omer, carried the two standard gauge lines and the single metre gauge line. It had two central steel openings 5 metres (17 ft) wide for the canal, and two masonry arches at the sides for the footpaths each with 2 metre (6 ft) openings.

Stations

The stations on the line, and other stops, are listed in *Table One*. Where stations were shared with the standard gauge (*Compagnie du Nord*) the Anvin-Calais line made use of their buildings and facilities; this was the case at Calais-Ville (from 1900), Calais-Fontinettes, Lumbres, and Anvin. There were inter-gauge goods transhipment facilities at Calais, Lumbres, and Anvin.

Stops were classified as a *gare* (station), *halte* (halt) or *arrêt* (stop). Chief towns of cantons which did not have standard gauge stations had larger stations than the others, known to the company as type 1; these were at Guînes, Ardres, Fauquembergues, and Fruges. Because these large stations were in town centres where land is at a premium, all have disappeared except that at Guînes. The passenger part of the station (*bâtiment des voyageurs*) was of two storeys with an attic floor lit only by large windows in the end walls. It was originally of brick with brick ornamentation over the windows, at the corners and under the roof. The same ornamentation can be seen on the smaller stations too. There were three doors or windows front and back on each storey. Unlike the smaller stations, Guînes and other type 1 stations carried their name on the side walls as well as on the track side. On the far side there was a single-storey goods building (*halle aux marchandises*) with platforms, road and track side. This road area was called the *cour aux marchandises* (goods yard). There was also a station forecourt for passenger access (*cour des voyageurs*).

Table One
Anvin-Calais line, stations and other stops

Name	Type	Distance km	Altitude m	(ft)
Anvin	Shared	0	60	(197)
Bergeneuse	Station type 2	3.0	83	
Équirre	Halt type 18 (1)	4.8	106	
(Highest point between Équirre and Verchin)			131	(430)
Verchin	Station type 2	9.3	105	
Gourgesson	Arrêt (2) (3) (4) (5)	12.6	95	
Fruges	Station type 1	15.0	96	(315)
Coupelle-Vieille	Halt type 18 (1)	17.1	106	
Rimeux-Gournay	Station type 2 (5)	21.3	162	(531)
Assonval	Arrêt (2) (3)	23.4	137	
Renty	Arrêt (2) (3)	25.8	103	
Fauquembergues	Station type 1	28.6	76	(249)
Hervarre	Arrêt (2) (3)	30.6	70	
Merck-St-Liévin	Halt type 18 (1)	31.7	66	
Ouve	Halt type 18 (6)	34.6	57	
Wirquin	Arrêt (2) (7)	36.6		
Remilly (-Wirquin)	Station type 2 (8)	37.9	53	
Wavrans	Arrêt (2) (9)	40.7	49	
Elnes	Arrêt (2) (3)	45		
Lumbres	Shared	43.4	47	(154)
Acquin	Station type 2	49.7	83	
Bouvelinghem	Halt type 18 (1)	53.1	132	
Alquines-Buisson	Special type (10)	55.9	177	(580)
Journy	Halt type 18 (11)	58.1	143	
Bonningues	Station type 2 (12)	63.2	68	(223)
Bonningues	Arrêt (2) (3)	65.2	42	
Tournehem-sur-la-Hem	Station type 2	67.5	40	
Zouafques	Arrêt (2) (13)	68.5	48	(157)
Louches	Halt type 18 (1)	72.8	17	
Autingues	Arrêt (2)	74.9	16	
Ardres	Station type 1	76.4	12	(39)
Brêmes	Arrêt (2) (3)	77.6	5	
Balinghem	Halt type 18 (1)	79.5	9	
Andres	Halt type 18 (1)	81.6	13	
Guînes	Station type 1	84.1	7	(23)
Banc-Valois	Arrêt (2) (14)	86.6	2	
(L')Écluse-Carrée	Halt type 18 (1)	88.3	2	(6)
Coulogne	Halt (2)	90.9	3	
Calais-Fontinettes	Shared (15)	92.9	3	
Calais-St-Pierre	to 1900, special	94.0	3	
Calais-Ville	Shared (CdN), from 1900	95.0	5	(16)

Unless indicated otherwise, all stations and other stops in service from the opening of the line.
All distances are from Anvin.
Heights in feet given only for the line ends, high points, and other important stations.
Shared stations are those shared with the standard gauge (*Compagnie du Nord*) and using their facilities and passenger buildings.

(1) Halts and *arrêts* in service for passengers, baggage and dogs (May 1909).
(2) Halts and *arrêts* in service for passengers without baggage and without dogs (May 1909).
(3) In use in 1909, not in 1892.
(4) Probably in use from opening of Aire-Berck line in 1893.
(5) Junction with Aire-Berck line from 1893.
(6) Halt type building but classed as station.
(7) Known as Garage Avot up to some time between 1889 and 1892.
(8) Remilly-Wirquin up to some time between 1889 and 1892, then just Remilly.
(9) Classed as halt in 1892, *arrêt* by 1909.
(10) Not listed up to some time between 1885 and 1889. Known as Haut-Buisson in 1889, halt in 1892, classed as station by 1909.
(11) Halt type building, halt in 1898, classed as station by 1909.
(12) Junction with Boulogne line from 1900.
(13) In use in 1892, not in 1889.
(14) Classed as halt in 1889, *arrêt* by 1892. Called Banc Aug. Boulanger from 1945.
(15) Classed by Anvin-Calais line as halt in 1892, station by 1909.

Smaller towns had stations of a standard type, known by the company as type 2. These stations were also of two storeys with an attic floor. The most obvious difference, apart from size, is a very recognisable round window to the attic; and there are only two doors or windows front and back on each storey. These also had a building for goods, with platforms for loading on the road side and on the rail side, and one for passengers. The exception was at Journy, later classified as a station but given a halt type building, with a goods building across the road, on the other side of the level crossing. It is interesting to note that the architecture of the stations gives clues to the way the lines were planned. The station at Rimeux-Gournay, which later gained prominence as a junction with the Aire-Berck line, was only a type 2 building. Likewise, the station at Bonningues which later became the junction with the Boulogne line, was also only a type 2. Clearly when these stations were built no one had an inkling that such developments would take place, in 10 years at Rimeux-Gournay and 18 years at Bonningues.

Stations of both types also had lavatories (*cabinets d'aisance*) which were installed in small square brick buildings with charming lead roofs. Good examples can still be seen at Bonningues, Remilly, Rimeux-Gournay, Verchin (where the station building has been replaced by a modern bungalow but the *cabinet d'aisance* and the goods building remain) and at Bergueneuse. The stations also held a lamp store (*lampisterie*).

Halts were of single-storey appearance front and back, but also had attics with large end windows. They were also of brick with brick embellishments, and all remaining examples except Journy have a single-storey extension at the back (away from the track) with a sloping roof. Their appearance suggests that these were later additions and early photographs of halts prove that this was the case. It must have been felt that the halts had inadequate accommodation and identical rear extensions were added. The Engineer's list of station buildings in 1895 states that all halts had lavatories, and had done since the opening of the line, but there does not seem to have been a separate building at halts. The exception was at Coulogne, where old photographs show that there was an atypical halt building or shelter, with a typical lavatory block.

The Anvin-Calais type 1 station at Fruges, with the Calais direction to the left. A train with a bogie carriage is in the station. Postcard postmarked 1905.   *Authors' Collection*

The Anvin-Calais type 1 station at Guînes, January 2007, with the former track side to the left.
Authors

The Anvin-Calais type 2 station at Verchin. Postcard postmarked 1914. The photograph was taken between the removal of the second (loop) running line, before 1892, and its re-instatement by the British Army in 1918. There remain only the goods loop to the left and single running line going off picture to the right.   *Paul Boulanger, Fruges; Collection Jean Willig*

The station at Journy in August 2006. This had a halt type building but was classified as a full station on the timetables by 1909. It is the only halt type building which does not now have a back extension. The site is halfway up a hill.   *Authors*

The Anvin-Calais type 2 station at Tournehem. Postcard postmarked 1906.
J. Gates; Tirmarche, Tournehem; Authors' Collection

TOURNEHEM (P.-de-C.). - La Gare

The former Anvin-Calais type 2 station at Rimeux-Gournay in September 2007. The square
lavatory block is to the left.   *Authors*

The halt at Bouvelinghen in August 2006, which is typical of halts on this line. The back
extensions are probably post-World War I.   *Authors*

COULOGNE — La Gare

The halt at Coulogne (Pont de Coulogne) on the standard gauge main line from Calais to St-Omer and on the Anvin-Calais line (*left*). An Anvin-Calais train hauled by an SACM 0-6-2 is waiting to leave in the Anvin direction and the rolling crossing gates (*near right*) are closed ready for this.
Authors' Collection

The arrival of a train at Guînes. Note how far the passengers have to walk to reach the station building, with the line nearest being goods. Postcard postmarked 1907. *Authors' Collection*

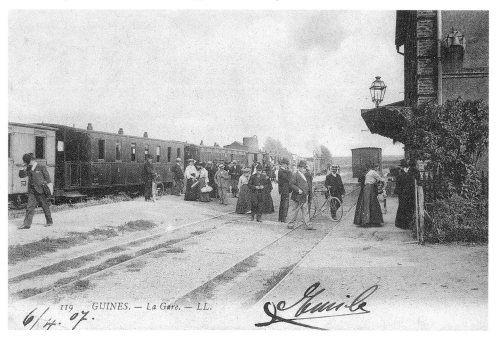

119 GUINES. — La Gare. — LL.

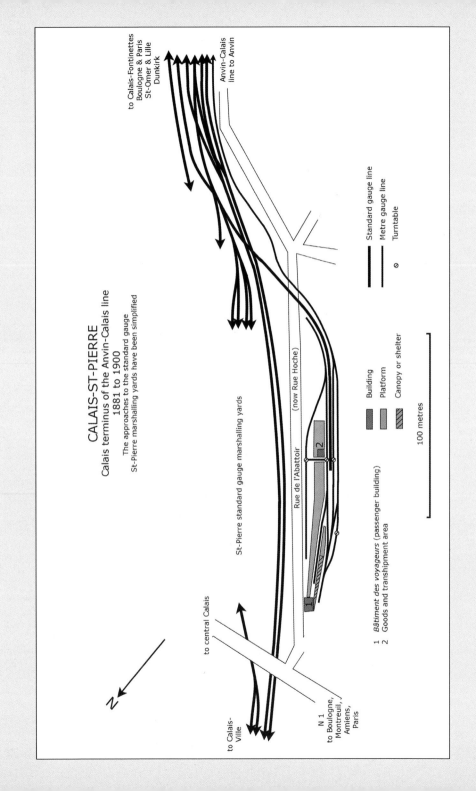

CALAIS-ST-PIERRE
Calais terminus of the Anvin-Calais line
1881 to 1900
The approaches to the standard gauge
St-Pierre marshalling yards have been simplified

to Calais-Fontinettes
Boulogne & Paris
St-Omer & Lille
Dunkirk

Anvin-Calais
line to Anvin

St-Pierre standard gauge marshalling yards

Rue de l'Abattoir

(now Rue Hoche)

to central Calais

N 1
to Boulogne,
Montreuil,
Amiens,
Paris

to Calais-
Ville

N

1   Bâtiment des voyageurs (passenger building)
2   Goods and transhipment area

Building

Platform

Canopy or shelter

Standard gauge line

Metre gauge line

ø   Turntable

100 metres

There were non-standard buildings at the halt at Alquines-Buisson, where the track layout and platforms were in a wide cutting, at the summit of the line. A shelter and a house for the station and crossing keeper were provided. The *arrêts* were just places where the train would stop, probably on demand, and they probably only had shelters. There were plans in 1905 for a small shelter at Banc-Valois, which was probably built. At Bonningues, where the line crossed the GC 217 (now D217), there was a crossing keeper's cottage, resembling a halt building but facing the road not the line. In 1906 a ticket window was added to the corner of this building. The platform in front of the cottage continued across the road for about 50 metres, towards Tournehem. In 1906 an *arrêt* was also recommended at Berthem (Zutquerque), between Zouafques and Louches. The *commune* offered to provide the funding. This was already an industrial stop for mixed or goods trains to pick up or drop off wagons at the sand quarry. However, it seems the company did not want to provide a stop here, and the *département* commented that they could not be made to do so. It never appeared in the passenger timetable.

Layouts at stations

From 1881 to about 1900 the station at Calais was at Calais-St-Pierre. Between Calais-Fontinettes and Calais-Ville the main standard gauge marshalling yards were on the east side of the Rue de l'Abattoir. The metre gauge station was on the west side of the road. A standard gauge siding also crossed the road to transhipment sidings in the metre gauge station. From about 1900 the line used newly built platforms at Calais-Ville station with a siding into the goods area and transhipment facilities.

For stations not sharing with the standard gauge, the most complex was at Fruges, because of the depot. Here there were two island platforms, as well as extensive goods facilities, the depot, and a larger paint workshop. It is notable that because of the layouts, passengers wishing to board a train had to cross the lines. This was because the passenger platforms were not immediately adjacent to the passenger building. The only other type 1 stations were at Fauquembergues, where the layout was similar to a type 2 station; at Ardres which in 1902 became the start of the tramway to Pont d'Ardres; and at Guînes where there were additional facilities because of the local services into Calais.

Type 2 stations had a single island platform, initially with one line on each side. There was a third line alongside the goods area, and one or more sidings. However by 1892, as indicated by the Engineer's report of that date, one of the running lines by the platforms had been removed at five out of the seven type 2 stations (Bergueneuse, Verchin, Remilly, Acquin and Bonningues). Probably with the infrequency of trains, the passing facilities were not needed at all these stations. The second running line at Bonningues had been re-instated when this became the junction with the Boulogne line in 1900. The second running line was re-instated at the other stations by the British Army in 1918 (*see Chapter Five*).

At Bonningues there were, by 1909, five through lines including that past the goods building. It was proposed to provide, in addition, a siding with a 5 metre manual turntable and a shed for one locomotive, so that the first train to Calais in the morning could start from Bonningues, and the last return there, rather than finishing at Tournehem. This was supported by the Calais Chamber of Commerce, to be paid for over 15 years by a small surcharge on tickets and other charges to and from Bonningues. We are not sure when these works were completed, but by 1913 the 07.01 from Tournehem to Calais had become the 07.00 from Bonningues, and the 19.20 from Calais finished at Bonningues at 21.01.

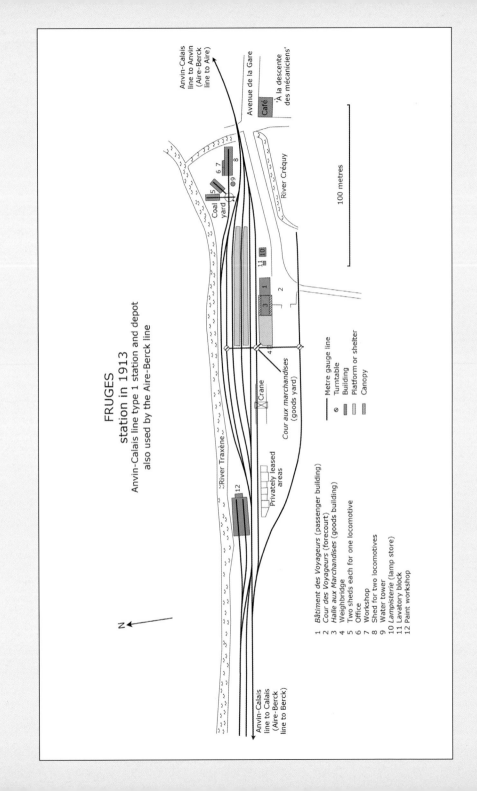

FRUGES
station in 1913
Anvin-Calais line type 1 station and depot
also used by the Aire-Berck line

Anvin-Calais
line to Anvin
(Aire-Berck
line to Aire)

Avenue de la Gare

Café   'À la descente
       des mécaniciens'

Coal
yard

River Créquy

100 metres

River Créquy

River Traxène

Crane

Cour aux marchandises
(goods yard)

Privately leased
areas

N

Anvin-Calais
line to Calais
(Aire-Berck
line to Berck)

——— Metre gauge line
⊘   Turntable
▨   Building
▨   Platform or shelter
▨   Canopy

1   Bâtiment des Voyageurs (passenger building)
2   Cour des Voyageurs (forecourt)
3   Halle aux Marchandises (goods building)
4   Weighbridge
5   Two sheds each for one locomotive
6   Office
7   Workshop
8   Shed for two locomotives
9   Water tower
10 Lampisterie (lamp store)
11 Lavatory block
12 Paint workshop

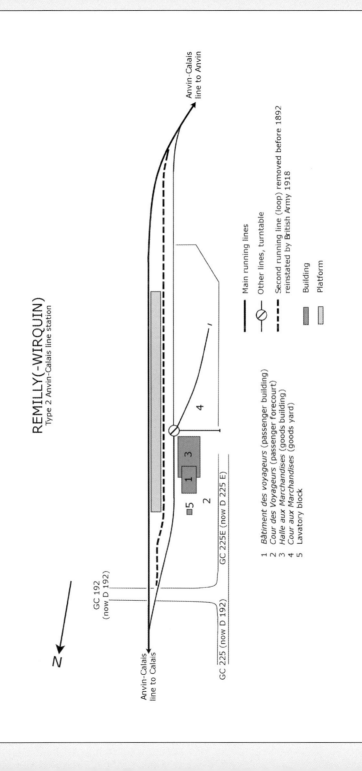

REMILLY(-WIRQUIN)
Type 2 Anvin-Calais line station

Anvin-Calais
line to Anvin

Anvin-Calais
line to Calais

GC 192
(now D 192)

GC 225 (now D 192)

GC 225E (now D 225 E)

N

Main running lines

Other lines, turntable

Second running line (loop) removed before 1892
reinstated by British Army 1918

Building

Platform

1 *Bâtiment des voyageurs* (passenger building)
2 *Cour des Voyageurs* (passenger forecourt)
3 *Halle aux Marchandises* (goods building)
4 *Cour aux Marchandises* (goods yard)
5 Lavatory block

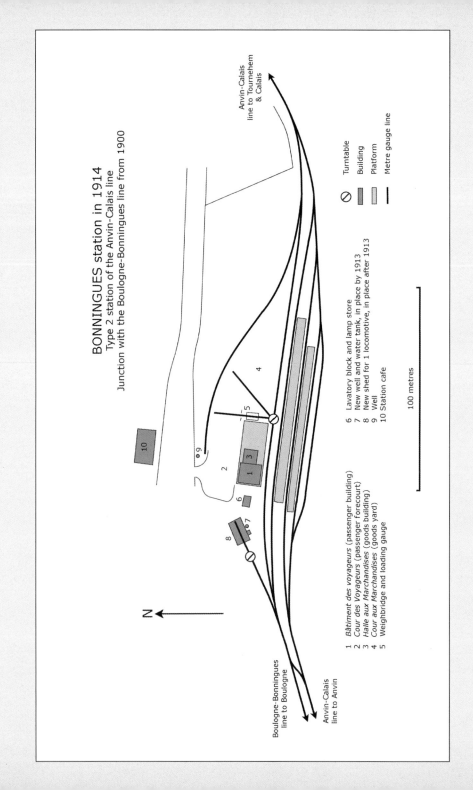

BONNINGUES station in 1914
Type 2 station of the Anvin-Calais line
Junction with the Boulogne-Bonningues line from 1900

N

Boulogne-Bonningues
line to Boulogne

Anvin-Calais
line to Anvin

Anvin-Calais
line to Tournehem
& Calais

1 Bâtiment des voyageurs (passenger building)
2 Cour des Voyageurs (passenger forecourt)
3 Halle aux Marchandises (goods building)
4 Cour aux Marchandises (goods yard)
5 Weighbridge and loading gauge

6 Lavatory block and lamp store
7 New well and water tank, in place by 1913
8 New shed for 1 locomotive, in place after 1913
9 Well
10 Station cafe

⊘ Turntable
▮ Building
▮ Platform
— Metre gauge line

100 metres

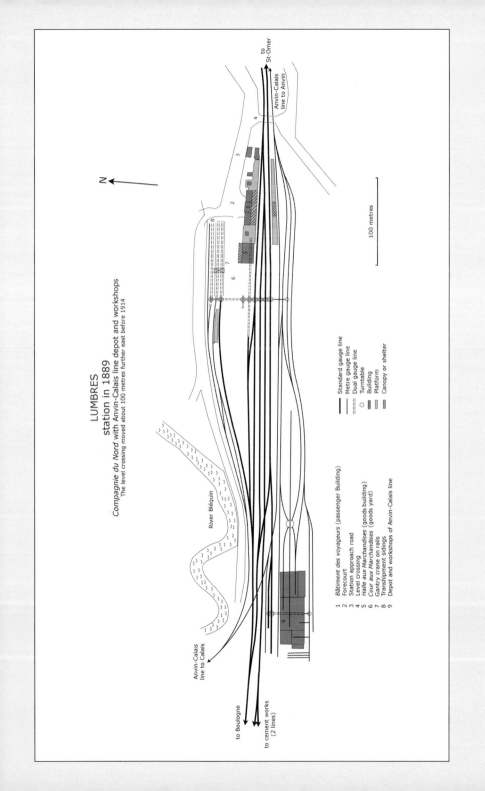

LUMBRES
station in 1889
Compagnie du Nord with Anvin-Calais line depot and workshops
The level crossing moved about 100 metres further east before 1914

N

to
St-Omer

Anvin-Calais
line to Anvin

4

3

2

8

5

7

6

9

River Bléquin

Anvin-Calais
line to Calais

to Boulogne

to cement works
(2 lines)

100 metres

—————— Standard gauge line
- - - - - - Metre gauge line
═══════ Dual gauge line
○ Turntable
▬ Building
▨ Platform
▨ Canopy or shelter

1 *Bâtiment des voyageurs* (passenger Building)
2 Forecourt
3 Station approach road
4 Level crossing
5 *Halle aux Marchandises* (goods building)
6 *Cour aux Marchandises* (goods yard)
7 Gantry crane on rails
8 Transhipment sidings
9 Depot and workshops of Anvin-Calais line

The Aa valley, with the former paper factory at Vedringhem, in 2006. This was where the dual gauge from Lumbres was extended to after World War II. The river and the old path of the railway run in the dead ground in the foreground where the treetops can be seen.   *Authors*

Manual turntable on loop line by the River Aa at Wavrans, with the bridge for the siding at right angles going across river to the former paper mill, owned by the Dambricourt family, July 2006.
Authors

At a halt there would be a platform with a passing loop. Again, at both type 2 stations and at halts, the platforms were not adjacent to the passenger building. At an *arrêt* there might have been a small platform and passenger access would have been from the road. Since these *arrêts* were almost all positioned by level crossings, they often had a crossing keeper's cottage.

Depots and workshops

The main workshops for the Anvin-Calais line were established at Lumbres. Up to World War I these only undertook maintenance, but from the 1930s they also built diesel railcars and locomotives (*see Chapter Six*). There were also workshops and a depot at Fruges, but since this part of the line was shared with the Aire-Berck line from 1893 (*see Chapter Three*), it is likely that these facilities were shared. Later there were also some workshop facilities at Bonningues.

Industrial links

As was usually the case with railways in the 19th and early 20th centuries, many factories and other industries along the route had sidings from the line, and some of these had their own locomotives within the works area. From the 18th century the valleys of the Aa and its tributaries had many paper factories. In 1900 there were eight such factories drawing water from the river and all these were on or close to the Anvin-Calais line between Fauquembergues and Lumbres. Many were owned by various branches of the Avot family. The other big name in the valley was Dambricourt, but most of their factories were further down the valley between Lumbres and St-Omer on the standard gauge line. We do not have a complete list of factories which had sidings and made use of the railway, but it is likely that most, if not all, did so. We know that a paper mill with a siding, probably that at Elnes, was visited by the delegation led by Deputies and Senators in December 1882. Businesses recorded as paying money to the Anvin-Calais company in 1897 for the use of sidings linked to the line were (listed in order along the line starting from Anvin):

Place	Business and nature of business	Income 1897 (francs)
Coupelle Vieille	Debuire (nature unknown)	62.55
Wirquin	Avot - paper mill	1269.55
Coteaux de l'Aa	Unknown	263.15
Val d'Elnes	Paper and cardboard mill, Emile Avot	1100.30
Zutkerque	*Sablières* (sand pit)	2129.30
Louches	*Sucrerie* (sugar factory) Say - siding	2638.30
Balinghem	*Sucrerie* Say - siding	1644.40
Andres	*Sucrerie* Say - siding	1377.45

From 1899 there was also a siding to the Vedringhem paper mill. The sidings for the Say sugar factory do not indicate a factory at that site, only that there was a siding there for the loading of sugar beet. The major local sugar factory, owned by Say, was at Pont d'Ardres (*see Ardres-Pont d'Ardres tramway later in this chapter*).

In 1912 MM. Emile Avot et fils, proprietors of the paper and cardboard factory at Elnes, put forward plans for a standard gauge line from Lumbres to their factory. A branch line and sidings of metre gauge already existed for the factory. The standard gauge line was approved and built in 4-rail dual gauge with the Anvin-Calais line by

Anvin-Calais 0-6-2 SACM
18.5 tonne steam locomotives Nos. 1 to 8
as originally supplied between 1880 and 1882
Collection Jean Willig

the end of 1913. The dual gauge on the through line extended for a distance of 520 metres from the east end of Lumbres station, and the bridge over the river Aa in this section was strengthened. MM. Avot reached agreement with M. Level, for the Anvin-Calais company, that the factory would pay 5,000 francs per year for the use of this part of the metre gauge line. The Anvin-Calais company would take no part in the movement of standard gauge wagons between the factory and Lumbres station. How the practical aspects, such as safety and signalling, would work, is not described.

A siding across the river Aa to the paper mill at Wavrans, owned by the Dambricourt family, was installed at an unknown date, with a loop off the through line and a turntable on this giving access to the siding. A similar loop line and turntable leading to a siding at right angles to the line was installed at a tannery at Fruges in 1913. The large cement factory and associated quarry at Lumbres, just west of the site of the former VFIL works and depot, was always served by the standard gauge line at Lumbres. There were many smaller businesses beside the line which almost certainly made use of the line, and many probably sprang up because the line was there. Examples are, a small quarry between Journy and Bonningues (*see walk 2 in Chapter Eight*), and a marl pit at Zouafques, just east of Tournehem. At some locations where there were private sidings, mixed trains would stop to pick up or drop off wagons, but partial loads could not be handled. These were shown on the detailed timetable produced for staff, but not on the public timetables. The only one of these on the Anvin-Calais line in 1913 was at *La Sablière* (sand pit) at Berthem, between Zouafques and Louches.

Rolling Stock

Locomotives

Technical details of steam locomotives acquired by the Anvin-Calais line up to 1914 are shown in *Table Two*. A full motive power list for all the lines in this book is given in *Appendix One*.

At the beginning the Anvin-Calais line bought eight 0-6-2 tank locomotives from the *Société Alsacienne de Contructions Mécaniques* (SACM) in Belfort. These were given the numbers 1 to 8. Nos. 1 to 3 were delivered in 1880, Nos. 4 to 6 in 1881, and Nos. 7 & 8 in 1882. They cost 32,375 francs each. Permission was given in August 1881 to put No. 3 *Guînes*, No. 4 *Calais* and No. 5 *Ardres* into service between Calais and Guînes, in time for the opening of that section in October. In January 1882 permission was given to put No. 1 *Fruges*, No. 2 *Fauquembergues*, and No. 6 *Lumbres* into service, and these were initially for the section between Anvin and Fruges which opened in January 1882. Permission was given on 4th July, 1882 to put No. 7 *Heuchin* into service. At the same time permission to put No. 8 *Saint Pierre* into service was refused because there was some problem with the buffers. Clearly the necessary work was done and No. 8 was put into service in May 1883. It is interesting that the locomotives were mostly named for a town on the part of the line where they first served.

A Batignolles 0-6-0 tank locomotive built in 1878 had been used as a construction locomotive. In September 1882 this was authorized for use for passenger and goods traffic on the line. It was given No. 8 and named *Anvin*. It appears from the details to have been very underpowered for this work. Perhaps this was just to bridge the gap until permission was given to put the permanent No. 8 into service in May 1883. It was sold to the Allier line in 1886. However, at the time of the opening of the final section from Lumbres to Guînes in August 1882 the company only had seven locomotives in service, Nos. 1 to 7.

Anvin-Calais 2-6-0 Nord-Belge

(Ateliers de St-Martin) 24 tonne steam locomotive No. 20
as originally supplied in 1906

This locomotive was first used on the Aire-Berck line
These lines later acquired seven further similar locomotives
manufactured in 1909 (Nos. 22 to 25) and 1924 (Nos. 120, 121 and 126)

Collection Jean Willig

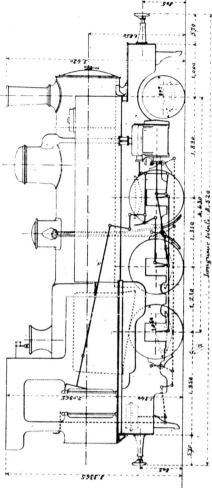

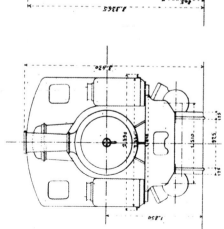

Two Pinguely 0-6-0 tank locomotives were purchased in 1900, and given the numbers and names 9 *Tournehem* and 10 *Rimeux*. No. 10 was later transferred to the Aire-Berck line as their No. 46. It is not known when or why this occurred; the decision appears odd because, by 1900, stock on the two lines was being run interchangeably. Perhaps it was an accounting stratagem. Later No. 9 was used on the line from Ardres to Pont d'Ardres.

In 1906 the Anvin-Calais company purchased and was authorized to put into use a 24 tonne locomotive manufactured in 1906 at the *Ateliers du Chemin de Fer du Nord de St-Martin* (Belgium), which was given the number 20. The initial authorization was for use on the Aire-Berck line between Rimeux-Gournay and Berck, but later it must have been given permission for general use on the Anvin-Calais-Aire-Berck network. In 1910 the line put into use another identical locomotive, which had been No. 1 on the Guise-Hirson line. From January 1910 there was permission to use this locomotive on the whole network. The Anvin-Calais company purchased this locomotive in 1912, giving it the number 22. The characteristics of these two locomotives were identical to the three further such locomotives acquired from the Guise-Hirson line after World War I and numbered 23 to 25, and to another three manufactured by the same works in 1924 and numbered 120, 121 and 126.

Table Two
Technical details of Anvin-Calais locomotives up to 1914

Manufacturer	Batignolles	SACM	Pinguely	ANB
Year(s) of manufacture	1878	1880-1882	1900	1906 & 1910
Type	0-6-0T	0-6-2T	0-6-0T	2-6-0T
Works No(s)	975			
Company No(s)	8 (temp)	1 to 8	9 & 10	20 & 22
Year(s) put in service	1882 *	1881-1883	1900 †	1906 & 1910
No. put in service	1	8	2	2
Length (m)		7.99		8.52
Height (m)		3.62		3.42
Width (m)		2.54		2.59
Weight empty (tonnes)	10	18.5	18	24
Weight loaded (tonnes)	13	23.8	23	31
Wheelbase (m)		3.97		4.43
Driving wheelbase (m)		2.07		2.54
Dia. of driving wheels (m)	0.80	0.90	0.90	1.06
Boiler capacity (m³)	0.98	2.899	1.950	3.500
Boiler pressure (kg/cm²)	8.5	8.5	12.5	14
Heating surface (m²)	25.4	60	43.8	65.51
Water capacity (L)		3,000		3,200
Coal capacity (kg)		1,100		1,200
Dia. of valves (mm)	53	104	55	100
Dia. of pistons (m)	0.26	0.35	0.30	0.36
Piston travel (m)	0.38	0.46	0.45	0.46
Load pulled (tonnes)				
At 15 kph level		690		
At 40 kph level		250		
At 15 kph at 2% gradient		80		
At 40 kph at 2% gradient		38		

Batignolles	Société de construction des Batignolles
SACM	Société Alsacienne de Constructions Mécanique, Belfort
Pinguely	Pinguely, Lyon
ANB	Chemin de Fer du Nord, Ateliers de St-Martin (Nord-Belge)

* For passenger work, previously construction locomotive.
† No. 10 transferred to Aire-Berck line as No. 46 in 1900.

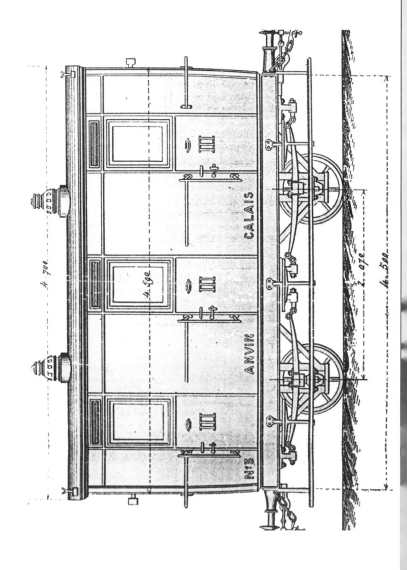

Anvin-Calais carriage No. 3
one of 20 of 3rd class only with 24 seats
purchased for the opening of the line in 1881
Collection Jean Willig

Passenger carriages

Thirty-two 2-axle carriages with side doors were purchased in 1881 for the opening of the line. Seven of these were mixed first and second class (22 seats), five were mixed first , second and third class (19 seats), and 20 were third class only (24 seats). These cost from 3,650 to 5,725 francs according to the class mix. One 'special' coach of 56 places, a bogie coach, was available for full opening of the line in August 1882. This coach cost 8,000 francs and had end doors and platforms in the American style, and was probably one of the earliest examples of these. Such coaches were later commonplace in France. In June 1882 the departmental Engineer reported that this coach was 0.56 metres shorter than it should have been. Nonetheless he considered it to have advantages. Permission was given to put it into service, initially for a trial of two months. It was forbidden to ride on the platforms while the train was in motion. In 1886 three further bogie coaches, third class only, with end platforms and access, were purchased for the Guînes-Calais services. These had rather widely spaced windows and must have been dark inside.

By 1893 the line also had at least one, and possibly up to three, additional bogie coaches. These were mixed first (16 seats) and second (20 seats) class, with space for baggage (including dog kennels) and for post. They also had end platforms, one end being for access to the first class compartment, but there were side doors for the second class compartment (in the middle) and for the baggage spaces. Four further bogie coaches were purchased from Blanc-Misseron in 1912, two first, second, and third class, and two second and third class only. As the mix of classes suggests, these had multiple compartments with side doors, and no end platforms. The line also had four flat wagons which could be converted for passenger use in the summer. There were initially eight and eventually 10 baggage vans.

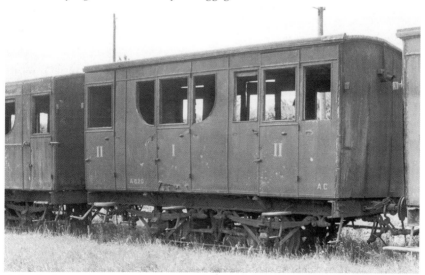

A 2-axle first and second class carriage (numbered AB 20, but also labelled 'AC') at Acquin, probably for scrapping, in 1955. Although it has an AB number, the Aire-Berck line never purchased any 2-axle carriages, and this was probably one of the original 1st and 2nd, or 1st, 2nd and 3rd, class carriages of the Anvin-Calais line.

M. Rifault; Collection Bernard Guéret, formerly BVA

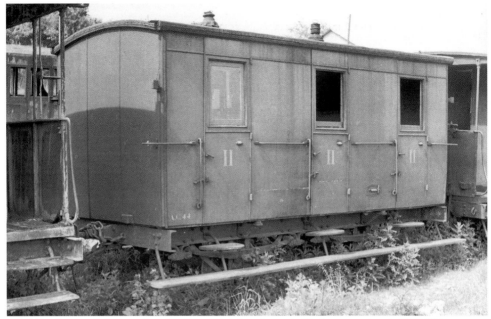

A 2-axle second class carriage (AC No. 44) at Acquin, probably for scrapping, in 1955. This was one of the 3rd class only carriages purchased for the Anvin-Calais line in 1881, changed to second class with the abolition of third class by VFIL in 1930.

M. Rifault; Collection Bernard Guéret, formerly BVA

A second class bogie carriage with end doors and platforms at Acquin, probably for scrapping, in 1955. The carriage is of the 1886 3rd class only type purchased for the Calais to Guînes section of the line, changed to second class with the abolition of third class by VFIL in 1930.

M. Rifault; Collection Bernard Guéret, formerly BVA

Goods rolling stock

By the time of full opening in August 1882, the line had 60 covered wagons, 40 open wagons with sides, 42 flat wagons (including those convertible for passenger use), and 30 ballast wagons. At that time wagons cost from 1,123 to 2,350 francs.

Operations

The regulations for operating the line were very complex. In the early 20th century the pocket handbook for employees, common to all the lines in the Level empire in Pas-de-Calais, Nord and Aisne, but with local additions, ran to nearly 100 pages. Steam trains were operated with crews of three. The *conducteur/chef de train* was in charge of the train and the rest of the crew, of movements and operations, overall safety, hand braking of coaches and wagons, and the care of passengers and baggage. The *mécanicien* (driver) was responsible for driving the locomotive and seeing to running maintenance, assisted by the *chauffeur* (fireman). The departure of a train was signalled by the station master blowing a whistle, followed by the *conducteur* blowing a small trumpet, which indicated to the *mécanicien* that he agreed that the train was ready to leave.

Disc signals, turned by hand, were installed to protect the main stations and junctions, but the remainder of the line was run using brass tokens, called *bâtons-*

36 — Fruges (P.-de-C.) - L'Avenue de la Gare

Paul Boulanger, imp.-édit., à Fruges

L'Avenue de la Gare at Fruges, looking away from the station towards the town. Note the *estaminet* to the right with A LA DESCENTE DES MECANICIENS ('where the engine drivers alight') on the top of the signboard over the entrance. Fruges was a major railway depot, and we assume that this was where the drivers took their refreshment. This is supported by the man on the pavement wearing a typical driver's cap. Date unknown, possibly 1918.   *Éditions Paul Boulanger; Authors' Collection pilotes*. These were slabs of brass with different shapes for each section. They were handed over to the driver, in the presence of the conductor, by the station master at the beginning of each section and handed back to the station master at the end. They were unusual for France, where there was usually a paper permission system for local lines. The regulations for the line make it clear that the normal section, for each of which there was unique token, would be between two consecutive stations, where trains would have to stop, and might cross. As already noted, the second through running line had been removed at five of the type 2 stations by 1892. Presumably the lightness of traffic meant that trains never had to cross at these stations. We do not have details of the sections for the tokens on the Anvin-Calais line but it must be presumed that the sections became longer with this change. The system required that all junctions should be section ends. This must have been the case at Gourgesson junction after the opening of the Aire-Berck line in 1893. Rimeux-Gournay junction was probably already a section end, as the second running line at this station had been retained. From 1900 Bonningues, one of the stations which lost the second through line before 1892, became the junction with the line to Boulogne and must have been a section end. An additional section was put in with the opening of the line from Ardres to Pont d'Ardres in 1902, from Ardres station to the junction. In 1918, when the British Army reinstated the second running line at all remaining type 2 stations, the sections must have been shortened to include these so that traffic could increase.

There were some circumstances in which trains could proceed without the token. Station masters could give trains written authority to proceed if they had consulted by telegraph with the station master at the other end of the section. One reason for this might be that more than one train was going in the same direction, in which case the second or last train would be given the token.

The summary timetable starting from 18th November, 1889 is shown in *Table Three* and that starting 1st May, 1913 in *Table Four*. Before World War I, two trains per day ran the whole length of the line in each direction, taking at least five hours and usually more than six, depending on the waiting times at main stations with connections. This represents an average speed of, at most, 11½ mph. In 1913 the second train of the day from Calais to Anvin took 8½ hours, thanks to a waiting time of 2¾ hours at Fruges, during which time there were (after 1893) connections to Berck and to Aire. Even in 1889, when there were no connections at Fruges, this train took almost eight hours.

Table Three
Anvin to Calais
Summary Timetable from 18th November, 1889

		(1)	(2)						
Anvin			07.10				10.05		15.55	20.17
Fruges	arr.		07.55				10.50		16.40	21.02
	dep.	06.01				08.03	10.57		16.48	
Rimeux-Gournay		06.10				08.24	11.18		17.02	
Lumbres	arr.	07.18				09.33	12.33		18.26	
	dep.					10.19	12.45		18.42	
Bonningues						11.26	13.47		19.37	
Tournehem				07.34		11.43	13.59		19.48	
Ardres				07.50		12.15	14.26	18.28	20.12	
Guînes		06.25		08.17	10.45	12.44	14.52	18.46	20.37	
Calais-St-Pierre		06.50		08.43	11.10	13.15	15.20	19.08	21.03	

Station		(2)		(1)								
Calais-St-Pierre					07.50	10.15	11.30	15.25	17.45		19.26	21.50
Guînes					08.15	10.40	11.55	15.50	18.06		19.51	22.15
Ardres					08.39		12.19	16.21	18.25		20.12	
Tournehem					09.02		12.46	16.52			20.43	
Bonningues					09.13		13.07	17.10				
Lumbres	arr.				10.05		14.15	18.25				
	dep.			07.28	10.18		14.30	18.50				
Rimeux-Gournay				08.23	11.18		15.47	20.04				
Fruges	arr.			08.41	11.37		16.10	20.25				
	dep.	05.30	08.30	08.42	11.40					18.39		
Anvin		06.09	09.15	09.21	12.25					19.29		

(1) Saturdays only (market day in Fruges).   (2) Mondays and Thursdays only.

Note: The original on which this timetable is based is in the 12 hour clock with times headed *'matin'* or *'soir'*

Table Four
Anvin to Calais
Summary Timetable from 1st May, 1913

Station		(1)			(2)						
Anvin							10.12	12.48		15.51	21.15
Fruges	arr.						10.52	13.25		16.31	21.58
	dep.					08.32	11.44			16.50	
Rimeux-Gournay						08.53	12.05			17.10	
Lumbres	arr.					10.05	13.24			18.28	
	dep.					10.35	13.55			18.56	
Bonningues				07.00		11.24	14.51			19.46	
Tournehem				07.12		11.36	15.05			20.01	
Ardres				07.39	09.23	12.02	15.32		18.03	20.25	
Guînes		04.55	05.58	08.07	09.42	12.26	16.00		18.28	20.50	
Calais-Ville		05.23	06.27	08.35	10.06	12.52	16.28		18.55	21.16	

Station		(1)(3)	(2)									
Calais-Ville		05.28	06.30		07.30		10.55	15.30		17.05	19.20	21.30
Guînes		05.51	06.52		08.09		11.30	16.08		17.35	19.58	22.00
Ardres			07.10		08.33		12.03	16.37		17.55	20.26	
Tournehem					09.00		12.28	17.05			20.51	
Bonningues					09.11		12.39	17.20			21.01	
Lumbres	arr.				10.04		13.29	18.18				
	dep.				10.34		14.10	18.58				
Rimeux-Gournay					11.28		15.36	20.12				
Fruges	arr.				11.43		15.53	20.28				
	dep.			08.10	11.49	14.15			18.40			
Anvin				08.55	12.25	14.50			19.25			

(1) 1st April to 30th September except Sundays and Feast Days, as well as the Mondays and Tuesdays of the feasts at Calais-St-Pierre and Guînes.
(2) Tuesdays only (market day in Ardres). Train non-stop between Ardres and Guînes, and Guînes and Calais-Fontinettes.
(3) Train non-stop between Calais-Fontinettes and Guînes

In the Anvin to Calais direction there were two more trains from Anvin to Fruges, one from Fruges to Calais, one from Tournehem or later Bonningues to Calais, and one from Ardres to Calais. There was also one, and by 1909 there were two, in the early morning from Guînes to Calais. In 1913 one of these was at 04.55 on working days and the other at 05.58 every day. In all, this meant that there were at least three trains per day at every station. Anvin to Fruges and Tournehem or Bonningues to

SACM 0-6-2 tank locomotive AC No. 7 *Heuchin* entering Guînes with a train from Calais. Date unknown. *Authors' Collection*

2/24
SACM 0-6-2 tank locomotive AC No. 1 *Fruges* entering Guînes with a train from Calais. The water tanks of the locomotive have been enlarged since delivery. Postcard postmarked 1909. *Authors' Collection*

GUINES — La Gare

Calais had four, Ardres to Calais had five, and Guînes to Calais had five and later six. The service to Calais that had, in 1909, started in the mornings from Tournehem at 07.01 became the 07.00 from Bonningues when the extra facilities there were ready, sometime between 1909 and 1913. At the same time, the evening service to Tournehem was extended to Bonningues. A note on the 1909 timetable states that, for the morning service, the locomotive ran tender first from Tournehem to Ardres. This would be because there was no turntable at Tournehem.

In the other direction, the same pattern operated in reverse, but with the short distance trains going back when needed, e.g. Calais to Guînes at the end of the working day. Guînes was regarded as being on the edge of the suburbs of Calais. This is reflected by Guînes to Calais having the most frequent service on the line, but the railway was also in competition on this section with the Calais to Guînes Tramway (*see later in this chapter*). In addition to the passenger services, which were mixed passenger and goods, there were scheduled wholly goods trains, although these had the option not to run if there was no business. In 1913 there was one each way between Lumbres and Anvin, two between Lumbres and Guînes, and one between Lumbres and Ardres. There were certainly more on a less regularly scheduled basis, especially in the sugar beet season.

In 1914 fares for the whole route were from 5 francs 30 centimes, third class to 9 francs 70 centimes, first class. In general, halts were open for passengers, baggage and dogs, but *arrêts* were only open for passengers without baggage or dogs. This was because dogs as well as baggage were carried in the baggage van or area, with special kennels being provided; and presumably the extra time to open the baggage van was not allowed at *arrêts*.

The 1894 *Baedeker Guide to Northern France* offered three itineraries from Calais to Amiens. The first, on the main line via Boulogne and Abbeville, was 107¼ miles and took 2½ to 5 hours: fares were from 8 francs 30 centimes, to 18 francs 90 centimes. The second followed the standard gauge route to the east, via St-Omer, Hazebrouck, Béthune, Lens and Arras. This was 121½ miles and took 5½ to 7½ hours: fares were 9 francs 25 centimes to 20 francs 95 centimes. The third route took the metre gauge train from Calais to Anvin, then changing, onto the standard gauge from Anvin to Amiens via St-Pol, Frévent and Doullens. This was 115 miles and took 11½ hours: fares were 10 francs 25 centimes to 19 francs 90 centimes for the whole journey. The guide comments that 'there are no through trains or through tickets on this route as the narrow gauge line from Calais to Anvin does not belong to the *Compagnie du Nord'*. Now not only the Anvin-Calais line but also the standard gauge line from St-Pol to Amiens via Doullens have long gone.

The full opening of the Aire-Berck line in 1893 provided the opportunity for passengers to connect with trains on the Anvin-Calais line at Fruges and at Rimeux-Gournay. In mid-morning it was possible to make all the connections in both directions on both lines at Fruges, except for the connection from the direction of Calais-Ville on the Anvin-Calais line and going in the direction of Berck-Plage on the Aire-Berck line; however, this connection could be made at Rimeux-Gournay. In the late afternoon all connections in all directions could be made at Fruges. In both the mornings and the afternoons the price was paid in some long stops at Fruges. Some of the changes could also be made at Rimeux-Gournay.

With all these lines there were always endless disputes, usually initiated by the communities concerned, about the pattern of connections, both with other metre gauge lines and with the standard gauge *Compagnie du Nord* lines. It was never possible, with the small number of services on all these lines, to please everybody, and compromises had to be made. However, we should not forget the major impact these railways had, especially on village life, where prior to the railways horses provided the fastest transport. To give a random example, in 1913, a person could leave Assonval, an obscure hamlet about 4 km from Fauquembergues, at 11.22, and arrive at Anvin at 12.25. Changing to the standard gauge and leaving Anvin at 12.42, via St-Pol and Arras, they could be in Paris by 17.10 in good time for dinner! Prior to the railways this would have taken days!

The numbers of passengers using the interchange stations on the Anvin-Calais line are shown in the *Table Five* for 1897 and 1911. This information is based on the annual reports of the Anvin-Calais company for 1898 and 1912. The numbers using the opportunities to change between lines for these years are also shown (figures in brackets). For the possible changes with the Aire- Berck line, at Fruges and at Rimeux-Gournay, the numbers changing in this way were not very large. Of course changes would mainly be made for intermediate stations. Passengers for the ends of the lines, for example going from Calais to Rang-du-Fliers or Aire, would use the standard gauge network. However, it is interesting that a lot more people changed at Rimeux-Gournay than at Fruges, and that this was more marked in 1911 than in 1897. This is surprising since the change at Fruges would be more comfortable if there was a wait, with nearby cafés and other facilities. Some of the figures seem improbable; for instance the fact that arrivals at Calais-Ville on the metre gauge line exceed departures many times over. This is consistent in the two years. There remains a suspicion that it may have been more important to collect the statistics than that they were checked to be right.

Table Five
Passenger arrivals and departures, and numbers changing,
at interchange stations on Anvin-Calais (AC) line

Station	Line changing to or from	1897 AC arrivals (to other)	AC departures (from other)	1911 AC arrivals (to other)	AC departures (from other)
Anvin	Étaples	13,117	13,064	14,671	14,631
	to Arras (1)	(3,079)	(1,580)	(4,509)	(3,703)
Fruges	Aire to Berck	20,304	19,307	25,009	21,752
		(80)	(48)	(80)	(80)
Rimeux-Gournay	Aire to Berck	2,242	5,081	3,611	7,056
		(316)	(189)	(716)	(531)
Lumbres	Boulogne	19,077	16,902	28,486	19,535
	to St-Omer (1)	(4,375)	(3,302)	(6,616)	(3,186)
Bonningues	Boulogne to Bonningues (2)	3,350	2,969	6,109	8,510
Ardres	Tramway Ardres to Pont d'Ardres (3)	30,410	26,012	33,436	31,273
Calais-Fontinettes	Calais to Boulogne, Dunkirk & St-Omer (1)	71,673 (3,414)	65,994 (382)	48,182 (2,086)	31,174 (402)
Calais-St-Pierre (4)		150,174	23,491		
Calais-Ville (5)	Calais to Boulogne, Dunkirk & St-Omer (1)(6)			372,272	31,765

Arrivals and departures do not include passengers changing

(1) *Compagnie du Nord* standard gauge
(2) Boulogne-Bonningues open from 1900. No figures for numbers changing even in 1911
(3) Ardres-Pont d'Ardres open from 1902. No figures for numbers changing even in 1911
(4) Until 1900. No direct interchange with *Compagnie du Nord* standard gauge
(5) From 1900
(6) No figures for numbers changing in 1911

The Boulogne-Bonningues line was not open in 1897 but in 1911 it had been fully open for nine years, and the pattern of connections is discussed in *Chapter Four*. It is therefore perhaps surprising that no figures are presented in the Anvin-Calais line annual report for changes to and from the Boulogne line at Bonningues. There can be little doubt however, that the relatively large increase in the number of passengers arriving at and leaving Bonningues on the Anvin-Calais line between 1897 and 1911 is attributable to the connection. Perhaps there was no through ticketing. Through ticketing was more likely between the Anvin-Calais and Aire-Berck lines, and between both and the *Compagnie du Nord* standard gauge lines, because of the close associations between these companies.

Some activity and financial figures for the line for the years 1897 and 1911 are shown in the *Table Six*. We do not have these figures for this line for any years after 1911. There was a substantial increase in passenger traffic and an even bigger increase in goods over these years. The increase in number of trains is smaller and clearly load per train has increased. Profits have increased from just under 30 per cent of takings in 1897 to nearly 50 per cent in 1911. It would appear that in the years just before World War I this was a healthy business.

Table Six
Some activity figures and financial results for the Anvin-Calais line

Activity		*1897*	*1911*
Distance run	(train km)	274,830	302,973
Passengers			
First class		766	1,643
Second class		11,316	10,373
Third class		479,856	708,997
Total		491,938	721,013
Grande Vitesse			
Registered baggage	(No. of items registered)	18,793	25,735
Dogs carried		1,920	2,324
Parcels carried	(No. of items)	23,396	30,596
Freight forwarding	(No. of registrations)	19,192	29,160
	(weight, tonnes)	679	1,372
Petite Vitesse			
Goods	(tonnes)	37,213	141,280
Coal and coke	(tonnes)	11,419	19,210
Livestock	(complete wagons)	12,017	17,310
plus	(heads)	1,025	1,695
Financial			
Total receipts	(francs)	359,816	572,792
Total expenses	(francs)	257,391	295,761
Receipts	(per train km, francs)	1.309	1.890
Expenses	(per train km, francs)	0.935	0.968
Profit	(per train km, francs)	0.374	0.922
Coefficient of exploitation	(= expenses/receipts, per cent)	71	51

Accidents

There are numerous reports of accidents on the Anvin-Calais line. There seem to be numerous ways of collating these incidents. Some records merely list numbers of events. For example, for this line: 1881 - 3, 1882 - 29, 1883 - 12.

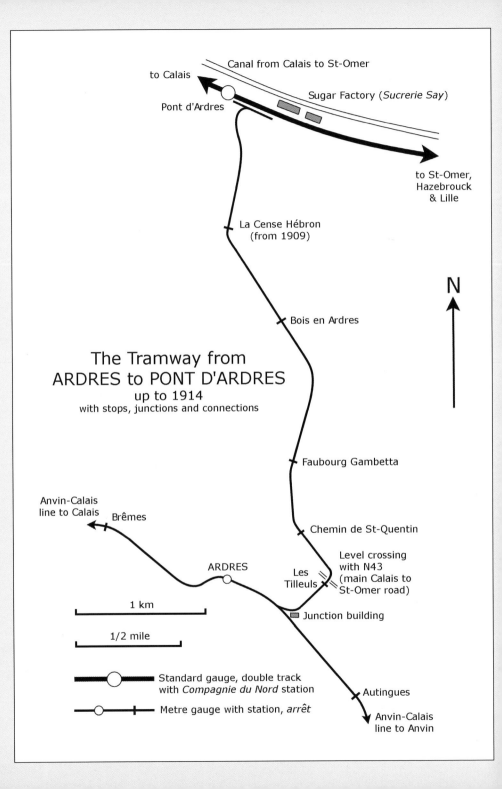

Canal from Calais to St-Omer

to Calais

Pont d'Ardres

Sugar Factory (*Sucrerie Say*)

to St-Omer,
Hazebrouck
& Lille

La Cense Hébron
(from 1909)

N

Bois en Ardres

The Tramway from
ARDRES to PONT D'ARDRES
up to 1914
with stops, junctions and connections

Faubourg Gambetta

Anvin-Calais
line to Calais   Brêmes

Chemin de St-Quentin

Level crossing
with N43
(main Calais to
St-Omer road)

ARDRES

Les
Tilleuls

Junction building

1 km

1/2 mile

Autingues

Anvin-Calais
line to Anvin

Standard gauge, double track
with *Compagnie du Nord* station

Metre gauge with station, *arrêt*

It is tempting to see the high number of accidents in 1882 as 'teething troubles' following the full opening of the line in that year. Flesh can be put on these bones, however, by looking at the mass of extremely detailed reports in the archives. These were clearly required by the French bureaucratic machine for all incidents, however minor. Some, however, were far from minor, as our first example will show.

This occurred on 6th April, 1894. A father had been to the *ducasse* (local annual fair) at Guînes with his four year old son. They caught the train at 16.00, climbing onto the coach platform. Since he was carrying a parcel in his right hand, in order to open the carriage door, he let go of his son's hand. The train started at 16.02 and it was noted with some pride that the train was, *'comme d'habitude'*, on time. The child fell between the coaches and was killed. It seems that this was a special train for the *ducasse* and was therefore unusually long at 17 coaches. The driver remained unaware of the problem, probably because of the length of the train, and it therefore took time for the train to stop. A major preoccupation of the inquiry seems to have been that there was an irregularity with the father's ticket, but they magnanimously decided not to proceed *'en égard à son malheur'* (in respect of his misfortune)!

A few years later, on the 16th November, 1889, a railway worker was killed on level crossing No. 97 near Lumbres. The train had left Lumbres bound for Calais at 18.46. The accident report shows there had been previous concerns about the safety of this level crossing. It was located near where the Boulogne-St-Omer line crossed the narrow gauge line and was only a class 2 crossing with no lights or gates.

Another type of accident which featured regularly at that time was one involving horse-drawn vehicles. In some of these the horses were frightened by the train and carts were overturned. An example occurred on 28th April, 1886, in the early evening at the level crossing at Brêmes. Two horses were killed and the train derailed. The carrier had sued the railway company for damages. Their reply had been that the train had sounded its hooter and that the wagon had no lights. The inquiry quoted a judgment of 1882 that had stated that the railway had no liability for damage to livestock and proceeded to turn the claim down. This was probably the place where the line crossed what is now the D231, the main road from Ardres to Guînes. This crossing caused further problems in the 1930s after the introduction of diesel railcars (*see Chapter Six*).

The events described above involve loss of life and major damage, however, in the long list of accidents many can only be described as insignificant. Two examples will suffice. On the 7th May, 1883 a railway employee was slightly injured falling off a plate-layers trolley. The inquiry decided it was his own fault. Later that same year on 12th December, a worker was squashed *legérèment* (lightly) by a wagon. Once again it was his own fault.

Tramway from Ardres to Pont D'Ardres

Before 1899 MM. Darras and Company had requested the concession to build and operate a line from Ardres to Pont d'Ardres. In 1899 petitions were organized from the *communes* around Ardres and Guînes. These were nicely printed in books for each commune, and were signed by many workers. The petitioners said that they often worked at the *Sucrerie* at Pont d'Ardres. The working day there was from 07.00 to 19.00 and with travelling this meant leaving home at 05.30 and not returning until 20.30. This would have been seasonal work in the sugar beet processing season in the autumn and early winter. The *Préfet* of the *Département* was asked to grant the concession, on condition that trains were provided between Pont d'Ardres and Guînes, each way around 07.00 and 19.00 so that both day and night shift workers could come and go, on

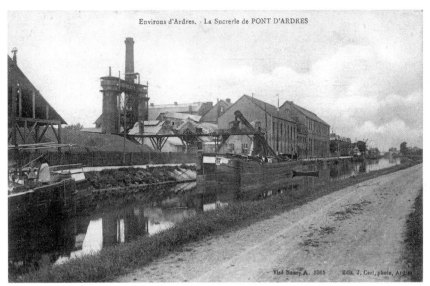

The sugar factory (*sucrerie*) at Pont d'Ardres, undated.

J. Ceri photo, Ardres; Authors' Collection

and off shift. Another similarly presented set of petitions came from the *communes* along the Anvin-Calais line from Ardres to Lumbres, and down the route of the Boulogne line, from Bonningues as far as Conteville. This petition acknowledged that M. Delori, Director of the *Sucrerie* at Pont d'Ardres, had requested the link from Ardres to Pont d'Ardres. The petition said that such a link was essential for the development of the sugar beet business in the area, and noted that the present need to take beet and pulp to Calais and tranship it was harmful to the quality of the product. It is no surprise to find that all of these petitions were submitted to *M. le Préfet* in Arras with a covering letter on the notepaper of the *Sucrerie*. It is therefore perhaps also not surprising to learn that the company owning the refinery (Say) put up 99 per cent of the finance to build the line. This ensured a near monopoly for the factory over the sugar beet growers of the region.

At an early stage three possible routes were discussed: the first ran eastwards via the hamlet called Les Pélerins, the second ran westwards along the Canal d'Ardres, and the third one mostly along the main road. The third option was selected. There were many minor variations made to the selected route at the Ardres end, before the final route was settled.

Permission to build this metre gauge line was given to MM Darras and Company, and the line was declared of *utilité publique* in June 1901. The line was opened in 1902. In 1905 the company became the *Société des Tramways à vapeur d'Ardres à Pont-d'Ardres*. However this was a trifle academic, since in October 1902 the Anvin-Calais company was authorized to operate the line.

Description of the line and Engineering

The line began at Ardres where it shared the station and facilities of the Anvin-Calais line. Leaving that line at a junction 483 metres east of the station, the line ran north, crossing the main Ardres to St-Omer road (the N43) at Les Tilleuls. It then turned west until it met the Ardres to Calais road (also the N43), which it followed along its eastern side to Pont d'Ardres. The total length of the line was just over 6 kilometres (3¾ miles).

The building at the junction of the Anvin-Calais line and the tramway from Ardres to Pont d'Ardres, east of the station at Ardres. August 2007. The extension to the right is probably modern.   *Authors*

The line had its own path from the junction with the Anvin-Calais line east of Ardres station to where it joined the N43 north of Ardres, but it then ran alongside this road, on the east side, to Pont d'Ardres, hence its designation as a tramway. It was built with Vignole steel rails at 20 kg per metre. In general the other characteristics were as for the Anvin-Calais line. The station at Ardres was 13 metres (43 ft) above sea-level and that at Pont d'Ardres 3 metres (10 ft) . There were 10 level crossings on public roads, and a few more for private access. None had gates. One over the N43 at Les Tilleuls, and two over GC roads, were 6 metres wide, the rest, over local roads, were 4 metres wide. Most of these were at the junctions of these roads with the N43 where the line was following the east verge of the road.

Stations

The line shared the Anvin-Calais line station at Ardres, where there was already a station of the larger type (type 1). Ardres station was modified in 1902 for the opening of the line to Pont d'Ardres, but we do not have detailed plans. A siding provided stabling facilities for rolling stock of the line to Pont d'Ardres. At Pont d'Ardres the line probably used the facilities of the existing *Compagnie du Nord* station, on the line from Calais to St-Omer. The line curved in alongside the standard gauge line east of the buildings of Pont d'Ardres station, and there was a spur back to the passenger building. Ahead, the line continued alongside the standard gauge for a short way. Then there must have been a crossing on the level into the *sucrerie*, but we have no plans of this. There was a halt or *arrêt* at Les Tilleuls where the line crossed the Ardres to St-Omer road (now the N43) just east of Ardres. There were also four other halts or *arrêts*. These are listed in *Table Seven*. In addition the train stopped at the junction where the tramway left the Anvin-Calais line. This time is recorded on the detailed timetables prepared by the Anvin-Calais company, for the staff, but not on the public timetables. The train also had to stop here because this was the division between the two sections of the line, and the driver needed a *bâton-pilote* (token) for the new section. There is a building here, presumably for the man who controlled the points and the *bâtons-pilotes*.

None of the intermediate stops would allow the entraining or alighting of dogs, or would handle baggage. There were by 1914, and probably a lot earlier, *abris* (shelters) at Les Tilleuls, Chemin de St-Quentin, and Bois-en-Ardres. In 1909 a new *arrêt* was opened at La Cense Hébron, in what had been quite a long gap between Bois-en-Ardres and Pont d'Ardres. You will not find La Cense Hébron on modern maps, but the *arrêt* was where the D227 leaves the N43. There is now a large roundabout here, at the entrance to the *Champion* supermarket. The large farm complex across the road is still called La Cense Hébron. In 1912 the facilities at Ardres station were extended to accommodate three locomotives rather than two. An additional siding, with another shed, new water and coal facilities, and a dormitory with two beds were also added at this time.

Table Seven
Tramway from Ardres to Pont d'Ardres, stations and other stops

Name	Type	Distance		Altitude	
		km		m	(ft)
Ardres	AC Type 1	0		13	(43)
Junction from Anvin-Calais line		0.5		17	(55)
Les Tilluels	Arrêt * †	1.0		15	
Chemin de St-Quentin	Arrêt *	1.6		11	
Faubourg Gambetta	Arrêt *	2.2		5	
Bois-en-Ardres	Arrêt *	3.6		10	
La Cense Hébron	Arrêt * #	4.4		5	
Pont d'Ardres	CdN (shared)	6.1		3	(10)

Unless indicated otherwise, all stations and other stops in service from the opening of the line
All distances are from Ardres station
Heights in feet given only for the line ends and the highest point
Shared stations are those shared with the standard gauge (*Compagnie du Nord*) and using their facilities and passenger buildings

*   Not available for alighting or entraining of baggage or dogs
†   Stop available for goods of *Petite Vitesse* in complete wagons
#   From 1909

Industrial links

The sugar refinery at Pont d'Ardres was founded in the 1870s, shortly after the change from farm based to industrial processing of sugar production from sugar beet. The refinery had an adjacent *raperie* where the sugar beet was delivered and shredded, and the juice extracted ready for the refining process. The factory became, by 1900, the largest in Europe.

The refinery was built between the main line from Calais to St-Omer and the canal from Calais to St-Omer. Apart from the railways, the sugar beet was delivered by wagon or by canal. There was also a *raperie* at Brêmes-lès-Ardres from which the juice was pumped along a pipe to the refinery, but this was slow and maintenance costs were high. After the opening of the Anvin-Calais line in 1882, sugar beet could be brought from a large area to the south, but had to be transferred onto horse-drawn wagons at Ardres or transhipped onto the standard gauge at Calais. The building of the Tramway from Ardres to Pont d'Ardres enabled the direct delivery to the refinery, on the metre gauge network, of sugar beet from the Anvin-Calais, Aire-Berck, and Boulogne-Bonningues lines.

The sugar refinery had its own motive power from an early stage, and its own standard gauge sidings. From the opening of the Ardres-Pont d'Ardres line in 1902, there must have been metre gauge sidings also, connected to the line by a crossing on the level of the standard gauge main lines. In 1903 the refinery company (Say) obtained permission to use their metre gauge steam locomotive, their No. 3, on the Ardres-Pont d'Ardres line provided that it did not leave the boundaries of Pont d'Ardres station. We do not have the details of this original private metre gauge locomotive. At the same time, they obtained similar permissions for their standard gauge locomotives Nos. 2, 2bis, and 4, to use the *Compagnie du Nord* track within the same limits. The refinery later obtained the Ardres-Pont d'Ardres locomotive No. 3 (SLM Winterthür) of 1889, and later still, the replacement No. 3 (Henschel) of 1912 (*see Rolling Stock below*).

At Les Tilleuls there was, from the opening of the line, a large area beside the track for dumping sugar beet, waiting to be taken down the factory at Pont d'Ardres by train. From 1911 the Say company provided a weighbridge and office at Les Tilleuls for the reception of the beet.

Rolling Stock

Locomotives

Technical details of steam locomotives acquired by the Ardres-Pont d'Ardres line up to 1914 are shown in *Table Eight*. A full motive power list for all the lines in this book is given in *Appendix One*.

Table Eight
Technical details of Ardres-Pont d'Ardres locomotives up to 1914

Manufacturer	Corpet-Louvet	SLM	Henschel
Year(s) of manufacture	1900 & 1882	1889	1912
Type	0-6-0T	0-6-0T	0-6-0T
Works No(s)			11393
Company No(s)	1 & 2	3*	3
Year(s) put in service	1902	1905	1912
No. put in service	2	1	1
Weight empty (tonnes)	10	13	18.4
Weight loaded (tonnes)	13	16	24
Dia. of driving wheels (m)		0.74	
Boiler capacity (m³)		0.830	
Boiler pressure (kg/cm²)	10 & 9	14	12
Heating surface (m²)		25	
Dia. of valves (mm)		48	
Dia. of pistons (m)		0.24	
Piston travel (m)		0.35	

Corpet-Louvet	Ateliers de Mme. Veuve L Corpet et M. L Louvet
SLM	Schweizerische Locomotive u Maschinenfabrik, Winterthür, Switzerland
Henschel	Henschel, Kassel, Germany

* Probably transferred to sugar factory at Pont d'Ardres by 1912.

Two 0-6-0 Corpet-Louvet tank locomotives were purchased for the opening of the line in 1902, and numbered 1 and 2. These were light locomotives, 10 tonnes unloaded. No. 2 had been manufactured in 1882 and No. 1 before 1900, so presumably they were second-hand, but we do not know where they were used before. No. 2 initially failed a braking test but was later put into service after attention.

In October 1905 a Winterthür (Switzerland) 0-6-0 tank locomotive, weighing 13 tonnes empty, was approved for use with passenger trains between Ardres and Pont d'Ardres, and given the number 3. The locomotive was constructed in 1889, and had previously been used by the tramways of Geneva. The trials were conducted on the same line, and the locomotive reached a maximum speed of 20 kph, with average 18 kph forward and backward. It was able to stop in 20 metres from 20 kph.

An 0-6-0 Henschel tank locomotive (also numbered 3) was purchased in 1912. While awaiting this, an 0-6-2 Corpet tank was borrowed from the Milly-Formerie line in the Oise *département*, another line originally owned and operated by M. Lambert of the Aire-Berck line. Special permission had to be obtained to purchase a foreign locomotive at that time. In the summer of that year the Anvin-Calais company had made the case that the forthcoming sugar beet season was forecast to be unusually heavy, and that none of the French manufacturers could deliver a suitable locomotive by 1st October; Henschel, however, could. Permission was obtained on behalf of the Anvin-Calais company for the Henschel to be used on the Anvin-Calais, Aire-Berck and Ardres-Pont d'Ardres lines. We do not know why it was given the same number as the SLM Winterthür locomotive purchased in 1905. We do know that the latter was transferred to the *Sucrerie* at Pont d'Ardres at some time, and this may have been before the Henschel was acquired in 1912. The fact that the locomotive depot at Ardres was not extended to take three locomotives until 1912 suggests that the SLM Winterthür locomotive moved soon after it arrived. The Henschel was also later transferred as a private engine to the *Sucrerie* at Pont d'Ardres; we do not know when, but it was still there in 1956, after the Tramway had closed.

Other rolling stock

At opening the line had two 2-axle passenger carriages, mixed first and second class. These had six first class seats and 20 second class, and were identical with those used on some other lines. In addition, there was one bogie carriage, all second class, with 56 places. This was similar to those used by the *Société Générale des Chemins de fer Économiques*, who ran, among other lines, the Somme networks. There were also two covered and 22 high-sided open wagons.

Operations

As already noted, from October 1902 the Anvin-Calais company was authorized to operate the line, and it is likely that in practice they did so from the opening in September 1902. They were given permission to do so in accordance with the 1881 regulations for the Anvin-Calais line, but modified in certain respects because this was a tramway.

In 1902 the service opened with six passenger trains each way per day. The first train from Ardres ran at 06.10 every day, and the first train back from Pont d'Ardres left at 07.00 from 1st October to 30th June, but at 08.04 the rest of the year. The last train arrived back at Ardres at 20.24. The trains were stabled at Ardres overnight. The journey over the whole line took 25 minutes.

By May 1913 there were still six trains per day, and the pattern was very similar. One of the morning trains ran half an hour earlier on Wednesdays, Saturdays and the eve of Feast Days than on other days. The first train from Ardres was at 06.13 every day, but it left Pont d'Ardres to return at 06.55 from 1st October to 30th June except Thursdays, and 08.04 on Thursdays and every day the rest of the year. The fares in 1914 for the whole journey were 50 centimes first class and 40 centimes second class. There was no third class accommodation.

Tramways of Calais, including the Tramway to Guînes

The Anvin-Calais line was in competition for passengers between Guînes and Calais with the line to Guînes of the Calais tramway network until 1939 (*see map page 32*). We are not sure when the first horse-drawn tram line to Guînes opened, but it would have been at the latest within a few years of the opening of this section of the Anvin-Calais line in 1881, and may have been open before it.

Building and opening

The first Calais tramways were conceded to Mr Cecil Johnson, an Englishman, on 29th October, 1877. He formed the Calais Tramways Company Limited, based in London. There may have been some misgivings about this in France, since in February 1880 the company passed a resolution that the following should be added to the Articles of Association: 'provided always that the sale of the Concession or the amalgamation of the company with another company shall not take place without the sanction of the French Government'. The concession was transferred to the company in 1881.

In 1878 the possibility of steam traction was raised, but in the end the original proposal for horses was adopted. Between 1879 and 1885, 14.5 km (9 miles) of standard gauge horse-drawn road tramway were built. Lines ran from the Place d'Armes in the centre of the old town to the Pont St-Pierre and the Halles St-Pierre in the east part of St-Pierre, to the first terminus of the Anvin-Calais line in the west part of St-Pierre, and to Les Fontinettes station in the south part of St-Pierre and on to Guînes.

The concession was bought back from the Calais Tramways Company in December 1907 for 750,000 francs. The concession passed to the *Société Anonyme des Tramways de Calais et Extensions* and the network was rebuilt and extended with metre gauge track and overhead electrification, with 20 km (12½ miles) of lines. By the end of 1908 Lines A, C, D and E had all been opened as electric tramways. They covered an area extending from the sea front north of the old town, to the Quartier Nieulay in the west, to the halte de St-Pierre and the cemetery in the east, and to the Porte de Lille on the south edge of St-Pierre. Line B, from the Place d'Armes to Guînes, had been electrified as far as Les Fontinettes station. The rest of the line to Guînes was still using horse trams in 1909, but was probably open as an electric tramway by 1910.

63 — CALAIS — Carrefour des grands Boulevards Jacquard, Gambetta, Lafayette, Pasteur
Station de Voitures de la Place du Théâtre

A standard gauge horse-drawn double-deck tram at the central cross roads in Calais-St-Pierre. This could be on the Guînes route. Postcard postmarked 1905.

Plaques Jougla/Authors' Collection

A metre gauge electric tram in the Boulevard Jacquard, Calais. Postcard postmarked 1916. This could be on the Guînes route.

Authors' Collection

193 CALAIS. — Le Boulevard Jacquard. — LL.

Description of the line to Guînes

The original horse-drawn standard gauge line and the replacement electrified metre gauge line followed the same route. Initially the horse-drawn tramway began just inside the old town in the Rue Royale but it was soon extended to the Place d'Armes. At that time the fortifications of the old town were still in place and the line passed through these from the Rue Royale, the beginning of the main road to Paris, the N1. It entered the St-Pierre district by crossing first the canal and then the standard gauge railway. It had Calais-Ville station to the west and later the new town hall, completed in 1924, to the east. The line followed the Boulevard Jacquard and then the Rue des Fontinettes to Calais-Fontinettes station, where it crossed the Calais-St-Omer and the Anvin-Calais lines with the road at a level crossing. It then followed the main road to Guînes through Pont du Leu and Pont de Cologne, and down the west side of the canal to Guînes, along what is now the D127, into the town. The line ended in the main square at Guînes. Next to this, in the Rue Mascaut, there is still a *Café Le Terminus*. The length of the line, including the shared parts in Calais, was 11.5 km (7 miles). After electrification the line was double track from near the Place d'Armes to what is now the Place d'Alsace, most of which track was shared with other lines. Beyond this it was single track with passing loops at Les Fontinettes station and at Pont de Coulogne.

Operations

At its opening, the horse tram made five journeys each way per day. The timetable for October 1885 showed that the first tram started from Guînes at 05.45 and returned from Calais at 08.00; the last from Guînes at 17.30 returning from Calais at 19.00. All times were half an hour later on Sundays and feast days. The pattern of service must mean that the tram, and the horses, were based at Guînes.

By 1896 the summer timetable lists eight departures in each direction, the first from the Place d'Armes at 06.30, and the last return from Guînes leaving at 20.30. The journey time for the whole route was 1 hour 15 minutes. This compares with 25 minutes for the Anvin-Calais line, but this only went to the station at St-Pierre prior to 1900, and ultimately to the main station. The tram, however, took you into the centre of the old town. The tram fare was 60 centimes for the whole length, with workers tickets at 25 centimes on the first two departures from Guînes in the morning and the last three from Calais in the evening. This timetable required two trams and pairs of horses, one based at Calais and one at Guînes.

In 1905, 109,353 passengers were carried on the Calais-Guînes tramway, and 1,242,928 on the rest of the tram network. In 1909 the electric network, including the service from the Place d'Armes to Les Fontinettes station, carried 4,269,868 passengers. The service to Guînes, which was still horse-drawn, carried 96,401. At that time there were 13 horses, 12 trailers (presumably horse-drawn trams), and 27 electric trams. In 1909 the horses covered 103,054 km at an average speed of 8.5 kph, and the electric trams 942,360 km at 10.5 kph.

We do not know the timetable or the journey time for the tramway to Guînes following electrification, but it is probable that the journey time was comparable to that for the section between Calais and Guînes on the Anvin-Calais line. We do know that in 1899, 43 per cent of all passengers carried on the Anvin-Calais line left from Guînes, with 251,091 departures. In 1911, which is almost certainly after the

Edit. Duporge, Calais

The station at Calais-Fontinettes. The standard gauge Boulogne line is on the extreme left, and on the right from the nearest, the Anvin-Calais line (metre gauge), the St-Omer to Hazebrouck lines (2) and the Dunkirk line (1), both standard gauge. The Calais to Guînes tramway crosses the level crossing into the foreground. Date unknown but must be before 1910 because the tramway is standard gauge and not electrified. The *Bureau d'octroi* (local tax office) is in the foreground.   *Authors' Collection*

An electric tram at the terminus of the Calais-Guînes line in the main square at Guînes. Postcard written in 1915.   *Authors' Collection*

1. - GUINES. - La Grand'Place, l'Hôtel de Ville

La Grand'Place actuelle est établie sur l'emplacement de la cour principale de l'ancien château des Comtes de Guînes. Elle est traversée par un souterrain qui va, croit-on, jusqu'aux anciens remparts

Guînes, Imp. E. Cache

tramway had been electrified, the figures were 53 per cent and 421,923 departures. Most of these passengers were going to Calais, and this suggests that the Anvin-Calais line was competing well with the tramway. Later evidence from the sale of worker's tickets confirms this.

Lines proposed but never built

Tournehem to St-Omer and St-Momelin and Tournehem to Audruicq

In June 1910 the General Council of the Pas-de-Calais approved proposals for a third network of lines of *Intérêt Local* as far as giving approval to Officers of the *département* to be allowed access to private property to make studies for these lines. The lines concerned included two beginning at Tournehem on the Anvin-Calais line. The first would link Tournehem to St-Omer, with a branch to the terminus of the lines from Bergues and Herzeele at St-Momelin. The second would link to the Calais to St-Omer main line at Audruicq (then spelt Audruick in these documents).

The line from Tournehem to Audruicq had already been discussed in 1900, when it was linked to a proposed line on from Audruicq to Bourbourg in the Nord *département*. This was in turn linked to a further proposal for another line from Bourbourg to Bollezeele, where it would have joined at Drincham the line which was eventually built (1914) from Bergues to Bollezeele. This line joined at Bollezeele the line from Herzeele to St-Momelin (opened 1912).

The 1910 discussions led to the production in December 1910 of maps showing proposed routes. The lines would leave the Anvin-Calais line at Zouafques, and divide just north-east of the junction of the N43 and the GC217 (now the D217). The line to St-Omer would follow a moderately winding route via Nordausques, Bayenghen-lès-Éperlecques, Éperlecques, Houlle, Moulle, Tilques, Salperwick, and St-Martin-du-Laert, and end at the *Compagnie du Nord* station at St-Omer. The extension of the line from St-Momelin would meet the proposed line at St-Momelin. The line to Audruicq would be via Polincove and end at the *Compagnie du Nord* station at Audruicq. The line to St-Omer would have been 18.5 km (11½ miles) long, with the branch to St-Momelin 3.5 km (2¼ miles). The line to Audruicq would have been 8.5 km (5¼ miles) long.

In March 1914 M. Level, as Director of the Anvin-Calais line, wrote to the Chief Engineer of the *département* concerning discussion which had taken place between his company and the *Société des Chemins de Fer Économiques*, who operated the Herzeele to St-Momelin line. It had been agreed that the main line was that from Tournehem to St-Omer and that the line from Salperwick to St-Momelin was a branch of this. In his view therefore, his company should have the sole right to operate trains between Salperwick and St-Omer, and if the other company insisted on operating over this section, and not terminating at Salperwick, additional dues would be payable to his company as the operators of the line. 'Additional' here is presumably meaning more than those already payable for the use of the St-Momelin to Salperwick branch.

In the event World War I intervened and the line was never built so the argument became academic. The line which was built for the British Army from Tournehem to St-Momelin in 1918 followed a different route and was lifted after the war (*see Chapter Five*).

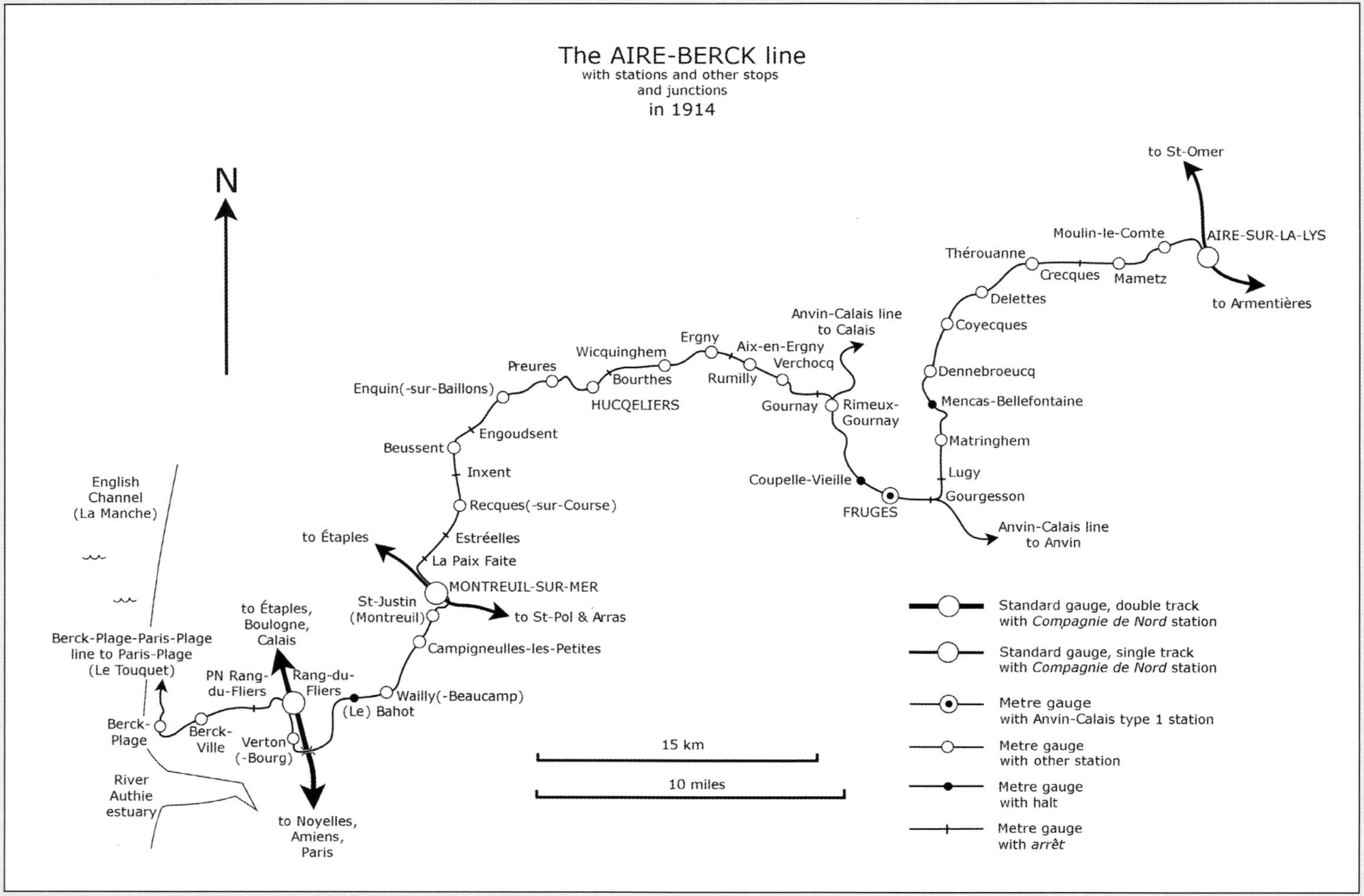

The AIRE-BERCK line
with stations and other stops
and junctions
in 1914

Legend:

○ Standard gauge, double track with *Compagnie de Nord* station

○ Standard gauge, single track with *Compagnie de Nord* station

◉ Metre gauge with Anvin-Calais type 1 station

○ Metre gauge with other station

● Metre gauge with halt

| Metre gauge with *arrêt*

15 km

10 miles

Stations and places (following the line):

AIRE-SUR-LA-LYS
to Armentières
to St-Omer
Moulin-le-Comte
Mametz
Grecques
Thérouanne
Delettes
Coyecques
Dennebroeucq
Mencas-Bellefontaine
Matringhem
Lugy
Gourgesson
Anvin-Calais line to Anvin
FRUGES
Coupelle-Vieille
Rimeux-Gournay
Gournay
Verchocq
Aix-en-Ergny
Ergny
Anvin-Calais line to Calais
Rumilly
Wicquinghem
Bourthes
HUCQELIERS
Peures
Enquin(-sur-Baillons)
Engoudsent
Inxent
Beussent
Recques(-sur-Course)
Estréelles
La Paix Faite
MONTREUIL-SUR-MER
to St-Pol & Arras
Campigneulles-les-Petites
to Étaples
St-Justin (Montreuil)
Wailly(-Beaucamp)
(Le) Bahot
Rang-du-Filiers
to Étaples, Boulogne, Calais
PN Rang-du-Filiers
Verton (-Bourg)
Berck-Ville
to Noyelles, Amiens, Paris
Berck-Plage
Berck-Plage-Paris-Plage line to Paris-Plage (Le Touquet)
English Channel (La Manche)
River Authie estuary

N

Chapter Three

The Line from Aire to Berck up to 1914
and related and competing lines and tramways

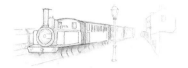

As early as November 1847 trains ran from Paris to Neufchatel, near Boulogne. They stopped at a station close to a pair of villages in the western Pas-de-Calais, Rang-du-Fliers and Verton. This station, then sporting both names, was to become much more important with the increasing popularity of Berck-Plage, 7 km away, which a little later in the century developed into a fashionable seaside and health resort.

In 1871, Berck council applied for authority to build a metre gauge line from Berck centre to Montreuil, the historic local capital. This application was turned down, only to be reauthorized, in 1882, by M. Boudenoot, a local deputy. There was also a proposal, in Berck in 1882, to build a standard gauge branch line from Rang-du-Fliers to Berck. By 1886 a tramway from Verton to Berck had been conceded to a M. Macquet, but he could not find the resources to build it. At the same time, lines proposed from Aire to Fruges, and from Renty, on the existing Anvin-Calais line, to Hucqueliers, had been conceded to another entrepreneur, M. Alfred Lambert. The *département* supported his proposal to link the whole thing together. The proposed metre gauge railway had by now increased dramatically. It was finally planned to run a single narrow gauge line from Berck to Rimeux-Gournay on the Anvin-Calais line, rather than Renty. At Rimeux-Gournay the line would join the existing Anvin-Calais line to Fruges. Here the two would separate again and the new line would head for Aire-sur-la-Lys. Agreement to the line sharing between Fruges and Rimeux-Gournay was reached with the Anvin-Calais company in April 1887.

On 8th April, 1887 local papers announced a public enquiry into the proposed line. The plans were to be on show at the council offices at St-Omer and Montreuil for a month. It seems nobody even came to see the plans and certainly no one made any comments. Therefore, in December of that year, an agreement was reached between the Prefect-General and M. Lambert to build the line as described above. On 12th December, 1889 the proposed line was declared *'d'utilité publique'*. In June of the following year, La *Compagnie des Chemins de Fer d'Aire à Fruges et de Rimeux-Gournay à Berck* was formed to build and operate the line. The *Compagnie des Chemins de Fer du Nord* advanced 3,800,000 francs to build the 87 km of line. (This represents 43,800 francs per km, which is significantly less than the 77,000 francs per km stated to be the cost for the Anvin to Calais line 10 years before.) Although the inhabitants of the area had been awaiting their railway for nearly 20 years, the end was nigh. One visible sign would surely have been the appearance on their walls, in March 1890, of a notice announcing a commission of enquiry into the placing of stations and halts. We assume this enquiry would have generated more enthusiasm than the one in 1887.

The Aire-Fruges and Rimeux-Gournay-Berck line was variously abbreviated to AFRB (Aire-Fruges-Rimeux-Berck), ARB (Aire-Rimeux-Berck) or simply AB (Aire-Berck). The latter led to the line being labelled by local jokers in the 1890s as the

'*Affreusement ballote*', roughly translated as the 'scary bouncer'. In this book we have called this the Aire-Berck line, but where appropriate have used the abbreviation ARB, because this was the one used by the line on its rolling stock, and also because it is the one most commonly used in books in English.

Building and opening the line

The line was opened from Montreuil-St-Justin to Berck-Plage in July 1891, a distance of 20 km (12½ miles). The official opening was by M. Yves Guyot, Minister for Public Works and M. Ribot, Minister for Foreign Affairs and Deputy for Pas-de-Calais, on 9th July, 1891. A poster announced the opening of the line on 28th July, 1891, with the timetables between St-Justin and Berck-Plage from that date. Perhaps this was when the public began to use the line. Some other publications have stated that none of the line was open until 1893 and then only to Berck-Ville, with the extension to Berck-Plage being opened in 1899. We think this latter may be a confusion with the opening of the 60 cm tramway from Berck-Ville to Berck-Plage on 20th August, 1899; for more on this see later in this chapter. The opening to St-Justin achieved the aim of linking Berck and Rang to Montreuil, the most important local town, since St-Justin was not far from the town centre on the south side. However, it did not link in with the *Compagnie du Nord* standard gauge line from Étaples to St-Pol, which had its station at Montreuil at the bottom of the hill in the valley of the river Canche. It had already been possible to travel by train on the standard gauge from Rang to Montreuil, changing at Étaples, since 1875 when the Étaples to Arras line was opened as far as Montreuil.

The link down the hill from Montreuil-St-Justin to Montreuil standard gauge station was opened on 6th April, 1893, a further 2 km of line (1¼ miles). The line from

The station at Montreuil-St-Justin in 2001, from the road side. The goods building is on the left. The buildings on the right are modern.   *Authors*

AIRE sur-la-LYS — La Gare

A. Lequiem, imp.

The *Compagnie du Nord* station at Aire-sur-le-Lys. Date unknown but must be after 1893 because the Aire-Berck line is crossing the left foreground just in front of the fence before crossing the road into the terminus to the right. The *Octroi* (local tax office) is also on the right. *A. Lequiem; Authors' Collection*

Aire-sur-la-Lys to Fruges was opened on the 1st June, 1893 (33 km, 20½ miles, to the junction with the Anvin-Calais line at Gourgesson), and the final section from Rimeux-Gournay to Montreuil on the 30th July, 1893 (35 km, 21¾ miles). Using the stretch of the Anvin-Calais line between Rimeux-Gournay and the junction at Gourgesson east of Fruges for 9 km (5½ miles), there was now a narrow gauge line inland from Berck-Plage for 97 km (60 miles), about the same length as the Anvin-Calais line.

Description of the line

Following the title of the original company and the usual title of the line, it will be described beginning at the eastern end at Aire-sur-la-Lys, which is as the name implies on the river Lys. The line ran, in general, west-south-west from here to Berck. Like the other lines it followed a twisting course. The 'as the crow flies' distance from Aire to Berck is 64 km (39½ miles) compared with the length of the line at 97 km. Ease of engineering and the need to serve communities along the way, particularly the chief towns of the Cantons, are, we assume, the reasons for this.

The line ran through some very attractive countryside, with river valleys winding between hills, but it was not as dramatic as parts of the Anvin-Calais line. None of this line was in what is now the *Parc Naturel Régional des Caps et Marais d'Opale*. The valley of the river Course is particularly prized by British visitors, especially as a location for holiday homes, but in our opinion is no more so than those rivers of *les Sept Vallées*, an area to the east much advertised on local road signs.

The river Lys is canalised and navigable downstream to the east from Aire and is crossed by another canal, which is the Canal de Neufossé north-west of the Lys and the Canal d'Aire à la Bassée to the south-east. The metre gauge station was in the yard of the *Compagnie du Nord* standard gauge station on the line from St-Omer to Isbergues. Aire was thus already a very accessible place for passengers and goods before the arrival of this line.

The track side of the station at Moulin-le-Comte in April 2006. The goods building with loading platform is on the right and the lavatory block in the distance. The station clock can be seen between the two further doorways. *Authors*

The ungated level crossing at Ergny on the Aire-Berck line. The station is just off picture to the right. Note that the warning notice *ATTENTION AUX TRAINS* is on the far side of the track. Postcard postmarked 1911. *Collection Gabriel Richard*

The *Compagnie du Nord* station at Montreuil, taken from the ramparts. The metre gauge lines are beyond the island platform, with the line towards Aire to the left and Berck to the right. The *Octroi* (local tax office) is just across the road on the left at the top of the steps up from the station. Date unknown but comparison with other photographs makes this probably before World War I.   *Éditions Fontaine-Segret; Authors' Collection*

The swing bridge which carried the standard gauge line to St-Omer and the metre gauge line to Berck over the canalised Lys at Aire-sur-la-Lys, in November 2006; located just north of Aire station, looking towards the station.   *Authors*

Bridge over a drainage channel between Aire and Moulin-le-Comte in April 2006. *Authors*

The standard gauge station at Rang-du-Fliers, called Rang-du-Fliers-Verton. There is no train shed over the main line tracks at the time of the picture, which is undated but almost certainly before World War I. The restaurant, now the *Buvette*, is on the right. *Authors' Collection*

3. RANG du-FLIERS — La Gare

The line to Berck left the station area, crossing the Lys with the standard gauge line and then heading off to the west. Curving round to the north of Aire the line crossed the Lys again to its south bank at Moulin-le-Comte. It then followed the Lys valley upstream all the way to the junction with the Anvin-Calais line at Gourgesson, 2 km (1¼ miles) east of Fruges. This route took the line west to Thérouanne, then south-west to Dennebrœucq. It crossed the Lys again just south-west of Delettes. The line then entered a narrow winding part of the Lys valley to Matringhem and Gourgesson junction. From Thérouanne the line was running almost parallel to, and only 5 to 7 km from, the Anvin-Calais line running in the Aa valley between Remilly-Wirquin and Renty. From Gourgesson junction, the line used the track of the Anvin-Calais line to Rimeux-Gournay. For a description of this section see *Chapter Two*. Rimeux-Gournay was the highest point on the Aire-Berck line at 162 metres (531 feet).

Immediately north of Rimeux-Gournay station, the Aire-Berck line left the Anvin-Calais line and after crossing a short plateau descended north-west into the valley of the Aa at Verchocq. From here the line ran west along the valley of the Aa, upstream to Wicquinghem, then continued across a low plateau to Hucqueliers, in the valley of the river Baillons. Continuing west the line joined the valley of the river Course at Enquin-sur-Baillons (*see Walk 6 in Chapter Eight*). It then followed the Course southwards to join the river Canche at Attin. Here the line joined the standard gauge line from Étaples to Arras and followed it south-east up the Canche to the shared station at Montreuil-sur-Mer.

Leaving Montreuil station the line turned sharply across the standard gauge line and climbed south-south-west out of the valley of the Canche, through the outer ramparts of Montreuil to Montreuil-St-Justin (*see Walk 5 in Chapter Eight*). It continued in the same direction to Wailly-Beaucamp and then west, descending gradually again to cross the standard gauge main line from Paris to Calais on a bridge just south of Verton. It then followed the main line north to Rang-du-Fliers before veering west again away from the main line at Rang. From here the line ran across the *marais*, flat salt marsh with drainage ditches, through Berck-Ville and on to the terminus at Berck-Plage, 500 metres from the beach.

Engineering

The engineering was in general similar to that of the Anvin-Calais line. The railway was constructed with its own formation and no sections ran alongside roads. The metre gauge single track had Vignole rails weighing 20 kg per metre but unlike the Anvin-Calais line these were of steel from the beginning. The rails were flat-bottomed, standard length at 11 metres, with shorter ones to construct curves. On at least part of the line the sleepers were of pine treated with copper sulphate. Within 15 years these were said by the Engineer of the *département* to be causing problems but we do not know what the problems were. The maximum gradient on the line was claimed to be 1.7 per cent (17 mm per metre) and the maximum radius of curvature on the running line was 100 metres (328 feet). It was thus slightly steeper in places than the Anvin-Calais line, but by no means severe for a metre gauge line. However, gradients were steeper for short distances. At Gournay village, where the line crossed the road at the *arrêt*, the gradient was 2.4 per cent for 40 metres.

As for the Anvin-Calais line, stations were fenced but the main running track was not enclosed. The general construction aimed to minimize construction; there were some cuttings and embankments but very few bridges and no tunnels. There was one road bridge, at Wailly-Beaucamp, over a minor road east of the station, which was of *tablier métallique* type. This was an oblique bridge with a 5 metre opening, now demolished.

Table Nine
Aire-Berck line, stations and other stops

Name	Type	Distance km	Altitude m	(ft)
Aire(-sur-la-Lys)	Shared (CdN)	0	22	(72)
Moulin-le-Comte	Station	2.7	21	
Mametz	Station	6.7	47	
Crecques	*Arrêt* (2) (3)	7.9	46	
Thérouanne	Station	11.5	38	(124)
Delettes	Station	15.2	45	
Coyeques	Station	18.2	53	
Dennebrœucq	Station	22.1	74	
Mencas-Bellefontaine	Halt (2)	24.3	68	
Matringhem	Station	26.6	77	
Lugy	*Arrêt* (2)	29.1	91	
Gourgesson	*Arrêt* (2) (4)	30.7	92	
Fruges	Station AC type 1 (4)	33.1	96	(315)
Coupelle-Vieille	Halt AC type 18 (1) (4)	35.2	106	
Rimeux-Gournay	Station AC type 2 (4)	39.5	162	(531)
Gournay	*Arrêt* (2) (3)	40.7	150	
Verchocq	Station	43.9	91	
Rumilly	Station	46.3	96	
Aix-en-Ergny	*Arrêt* (2)	47.9	101	
Ergny	Station	48.6	102	
Wicquinghem	Station	51.5	114	
Bourthes	*Arrêt* (2) (3)	53.8	149	(488)
Hucqueliers	Station	55.7	145	(475)
Preures	Station	58.3	83	
Enquin(-sur-Baillons)	Station (5)	60.8	58	
Engoudsent	*Arrêt* (2) (3)	63.7	50	
Beussent	Station	65.0	31	
Inxent	*Arrêt* (2)	66.3	29	
Recques(-sur-Course)	Station	68.1	19	
Estréelles	*Arrêt* (2)	70.4	14	
La Paix Faite	*Arrêt* (2)	72.8	8	
Montreuil-sur-Mer	Shared (CdN)	74.9	8	(26)
St-Justin (Montreuil-St-Justin)	Station	76.7	35	
Campigneulles-les-Petites	Station	78.6	46	
Wailly(-Beaucamp)	Station (6)	82.7	43	
Bahot (Le Bahot)	Halt (2) (7)	85.6	47	(154)
Verton(-Bourg)	Station	89.1	9	
Rang-du-Fliers	Shared (CdN)	90.7	9	(30)
PN Rang-du-Fliers	*Arrêt* (2)	91.9	5	
Berck-Ville	Station	95.1	8	
Berck-Plage	Station (8)	96.9	7	(23)

Unless indicated otherwise, all stations and other stops in service from the opening of the line.
All distances are from Aire-sur-la-Lys, taken from the company (staff) timetable of 1st May, 1913 .
Heights in feet given only for the line ends, high points, and other important stations.
Shared stations are those shared with the standard gauge (*Compagnie du Nord*) and using their facilities and passenger buildings.

(1) Halts and *Arrêts* in service for passengers, baggage and dogs (May 1909).
(2) Halts and *Arrêts* in service for passengers without baggage and without dogs (May 1909).
(3) In 1909, not 1894.
(4) Anvin-Calais line, with running rights.
(5) Halt from 1893, still halt in 1909, station by 1913, with addition of goods building.
(6) Always Wailly in the time of the railway, now known as Wailly-Beaucamp.
(7) Variously Bahot or Le Bahot on timetables, Bahot on the building, now le Bahot on maps.
(8) Rebuilt 1909.

We do not know the total number of level crossings there were on this line, but 43 were over roads large enough for the crossing to be marked on the 1930, 1 in 200,000 (2 km per cm) Michelin map. This number includes five on the shared running section with the Anvin-Calais line between Gourgesson and Rimeux-Gournay. A few were gated, including that across the route de St-Omer at Fruges on the shared running section. At Montreuil, the Aire-Berck line shared the gated level crossing of the standard gauge line across what was then the main road from Calais to Paris, the N1. The Aire-Berck line also crossed the N1 at La Paix Faite by the Attin sugar factory just north of Montreuil, and at Wailly-Beaucamp, but we do not know what safety arrangements were made at these crossings. At Verton the line crossed the road from Verton to Wailly-Beaucamp (then the GC142, now the D 142E) alongside the double track main line. The main line had a gated crossing but the Aire-Berck line crossing was outside these gates and was un-gated. In the early 20th century, the mayor of Verton made a plea for the metre gauge line to be included within the gated area but the response was that it would be too complicated given the differences of working between the two lines.

The section from Aire to Fruges did not cross any standard gauge lines. The section from Rimeux-Gournay to Berck crossed the standard gauge line from Étaples to Arras just to the south-west of Montreuil station. This was close to the station. A footnote to the staff timetable of 20th October, 1894, states that the *mécaniciens* (engine drivers) 'will pay the greatest attention to the crossing of the lines of the *Compagnie du Nord*'.

The other standard gauge crossing, of the double track main line from Calais to Paris just south of Verton station, was by an oblique bridge with an opening of 8 metres, of lattice girder design.

There were also a number of river bridges. The swing bridge over the canalised river Lys, which gave boats access to wharves at Aire, was shared with the standard gauge line. Whether over smaller streams or main rivers, these were of *tablier métallique* type. These were described in *Chapter Two* and had brick abutments with steel girders laid across between them. There were bridges over the Lys at Moulin-le-Comte and Delettes, and two over the Traxène, one south of Lugy and one, with the Anvin to Calais line, west of Fruges. There were two bridges over the Aa, and bridges over the Baillons, the Course and the Canche. The bridges over two branches of the Canche just north of Montreuil were shared with the standard gauge line.

Stations

The stations on the line, and other stops, are listed in *Table Nine*. Where stations were shared with the standard gauge, the Aire-Berck line made use of their buildings and facilities. This happened at Aire-sur-la-Lys, on the St-Omer-Isbergues line; at Montreuil-sur-Mer, on the line from Étaples to Arras; and at Rang-du-Fliers on the main line from Paris to Calais.

The main line station at Rang-du-Fliers opened in 1847. The history of this station's name is colourful. It was initially named Montreuil, even though Montreuil is 10 km (6¼ miles) away. Montreuil was the most important town in the area, and this was at the time the nearest station. Later it was Montreuil-Verton, then Verton, and finally from the end of 1890, Rang-du-Fliers-Verton. This was just before the opening of this part of the Aire-Berck line in 1891. At that time the station had a passenger building on both sides of the double track and a train shed covering both platforms and tracks, but the train shed was later removed. Major improvements were made for the opening of the

The station at Recques-sur-Course. Postcard written in 1910.   *Collection Gabriel Richard*

The station at Thérouanne. The man with cap and the dog is probably the station master. No date but the dress suggests before World War I.   *Authors' Collection*

The station at Campigneulles-les-Petites in June 2002, with the station name, and the goods building to the left. The name had been removed in 2006.   *Authors*

The halt at Bahot (also called Le Bahot) in June 2002. The lavatory block is to the right but there is no goods building.   *Authors*

Berck-Plage — La Gare

The first station at Berck-Plage, replaced in 1909. The station master's office is to the left of the main building, with the *salle des messageries* further left with the lower roof. The right extension is an enlargement of the normal station waiting room. *Authors' Collection*

The second station at Berck-Plage, opened in 1909. The post office with aerials is to the right. Postcard postmarked 1934. *Authors' Collection*

48 BERCK-PLAGE - La Gare et la Poste

Aire-Berck line. These included moving the shelter on the platform used by the line further away from the main building, for the convenience of the Aire-Berck passengers.

In 1905 the town council of Berck requested the *Compagnie du Nord* to put multiple signs saying 'Berck' on the station and to extend the canopies on the platforms. The full train shed had by this time gone. The *Compagnie du Nord* responded that there were already multiple signs saying *Embranchement pour Berck* (junction for Berck), especially on the down platform from Paris which was adjacent to the metre gauge platform. In addition, a large sign saying 'Berck-Plage' had been painted on the wall of a building in the neighbouring garden of the district chief, and another sign saying 'Berck' had been painted on the wall of the *buvette* close to the platforms. This was surely enough information! In addition to the canopies over the main up and down platforms, a separate shelter had been built further along the down platform adjacent to the metre gauge platform. Since the traffic to Berck was not of major importance except in the good weather, this was surely sufficient. In 2002 the station was still called Rang-du-Fliers-Verton, but by 2006 it had been renamed again, to Rang-du-Fliers-Verton-Berck. The separate station at Verton (Verton-Bourg), nearly 2 km (1 mile) to the south, served only the metre gauge line even though this was beside the standard gauge line at that point.

Apart from stations shared with the standard gauge lines of the *Compagnie du Nord*, the stops from the *arrêt* at Gourgesson junction, where it joined the Anvin-Calais line, to Rimeux-Gournay junction, where it left this line, were those of the Anvin-Calais line as described in *Chapter Two*. On the Aire-Berck line proper, the passenger buildings at the stations and the halts were all originally built to the same design. the only difference between the two was that stations had a goods building, but the halts did not. The passenger buildings were of two storeys, with three openings, doors or windows, on each side on the ground floor and three windows on each side on the first. They were built of brick, with minimal corner decoration. This was echoed in the decoration under the end eaves. There were tall thin rectangular windows in the end walls at attic level but no other end windows or doors. At the stations the goods buildings were attached to one end of the passenger buildings, with overhanging roofs, and loading platforms on both the track side and the road side. There were separate lavatory blocks, of brick also, with ridged tiled roofs, at stations and halts.

There were exceptional stations at Berck-Ville and at Berck-Plage. That at Berck-Plage reflected the town's increasing importance as a seaside and health resort. It also gained importance as the station at the end of the line and the site of one of the line's depots. The goods building was separate and the passenger building was larger than the standard stations on the line, with extensions at both ends. These provided an enlarged waiting room, an office for the station master, and a *salle des messageries* (post and parcels office). By 1909 the authorities had decided that even this was not enough for the still increasing importance of the resort. The old station was demolished and a new station erected in the 'grand hotel' style. The town thought they deserved a station fit for a *grand réseau* (major main line system). This is the building which survives today as Berck Casino. Some would say that its appearance is better suited to this than to a station. At this time the town wished to enlarge its Post Office, and this clashed with the desire to enlarge the station. There was a long dispute about this between the railway and the town from 1904 to 1908. The new station was finally built without moving the Post Office, which did, however, finally move to its present location nearby in the Rue Gabriel Peri. Berck-Ville station was smaller than the original station at Berck-Plage, but did have an extension to the side at the opposite end from the goods building. This may have been a station master's office, as this was the use for the similar extension on the original station at Berck-Plage.

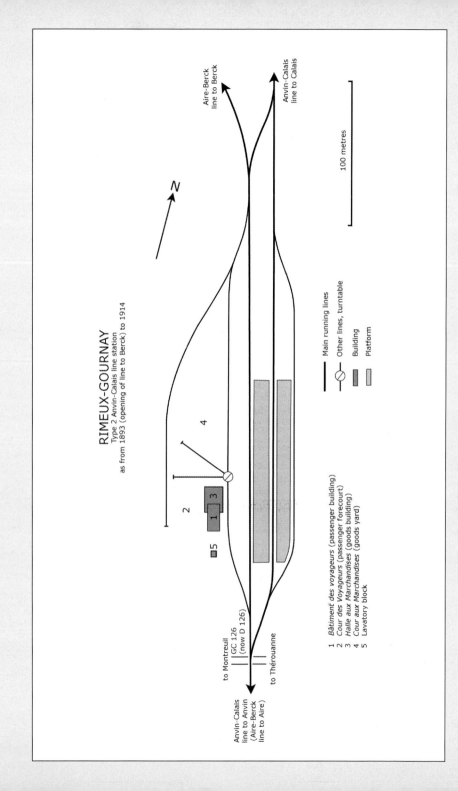

RIMEUX-GOURNAY
Type 2 Anvin-Calais line station
as from 1893 (opening of line to Berck) to 1914

N

100 metres

Aire-Berck
line to Berck

Anvin-Calais
line to Calais

to Montreuil
IGC 126
(now D 126)

to Thérouanne

Anvin-Calais
line to Anvin
(Aire-Berck
line to Aire)

1 Bâtiment des voyageurs (passenger building)
2 Cour des Voyageurs (passenger forecourt)
3 Halle aux Marchandises (goods building)
4 Cour aux Marchandises (goods yard)
5 Lavatory block

——— Main running lines
—⊘— Other lines, turntable
▨ Building
▨ Platform

The 1894 timetable shows three halts, Mencas-Bellefontaine, Enquin-sur-Baillons, and Bahot. In 1897 changes were agreed to the accommodation at halts. The waiting room and ticket office downstairs were made smaller, so that a downstairs kitchen and dining room could be provided for the *gardien*. The accommodation upstairs had only been a kitchen and two small rooms and was insufficient. Plans were put forward in 1907 for a goods building to be added at Enquin-sur-Baillons, and there was an enquiry into the proposal in 1908. In addition to adding the goods building the upgrade to the station included modifying the ground floor of the passenger building, which had not yet been done at this halt. It also involved adding a passing loop and a goods yard. Approval was given in 1909, and by 1913 Enquin had been reclassified as a station. The changes were paid for by a surcharge on fares and tariffs to and from Enquin.

Between 1894 and 1913 the four *arrêts*, at Crecques, Gournay (approved 1896), Bourthes and Engoudsent. had been added. At an *arrêt* there might be a crossing cottage or a shelter, but no shelters have survived. There was a shelter at La Paix Faite by 1908, when another was approved for the *arrêt* at PN (level crossing) Rang-du-Fliers. By 1914 there were 22 stations, two halts and 10 *arrêts*.

Track layouts at stations

A typical station on the Aire-Berck line had one loop line and an extra cross-over. The loop line ran past the goods building and the passenger building. Passengers would have to cross the loop line to reach the platform and the main running line, but in general the platform areas were much closer to the passenger buildings than of the Anvin-Calais line. Also, whereas on the Anvin-Calais line additional loops on the running line had been installed and later removed, no additional loops or running lines were ever installed at ordinary stations on the Aire-Berck line, except at Berck-Ville.

Major track works were installed at the meeting points of the Aire-Berck line with the standard gauge lines, that is at Aire-sur-la-Lys, Montreuil, and Rang-du-Fliers. Typically, there were extensive goods facilities there also. At Rang a transhipment siding had been provided from the opening of the line. A transhipment siding at Montreuil was approved in 1896, and one at Aire in 1909. Both these were approved at the Ministry of Public Works in Paris, because they involved lines of *Intérêt Général*.

At Aire the metre gauge line crossed the narrow entrance to the forecourt of the main station This arrangement led to a near accident in 1903, followed by a complaint. A reversing locomotive of the Aire-Berck line almost collided with the car of a member of the *Conseil-Général* of the *Département du Nord*. As a result it was proposed to move the metre gauge line much closer to the standard gauge passenger building, but this never happened. At Rimeux-Gournay junction the lines diverged immediately north of the station (*see diagram*). At Montreuil, the Aire-Berck line crossed a loop line to sidings on entering the station from the north-west, and then crossed the standard gauge lines again on leaving towards Berck. At Rang-du-Fliers the metre gauge line came up the west side of the double track main line from the south, and after sharing a platform with the main line diverged to the west towards Berck, behind the *buvette* (café) which is still there. Berck-Plage was a major station and the terminus. A depot and workshop were provided. From 1909 the Berck-Plage to Paris-Plage line, under different management, used the station and their line went off to the north (*see later in this chapter*). There had already been a spur line here to the Bellevue/Terminus area of Berck to aid the development of a factory and a casino. A new platform and line was provided in 1911, for the line to Paris-Plage.

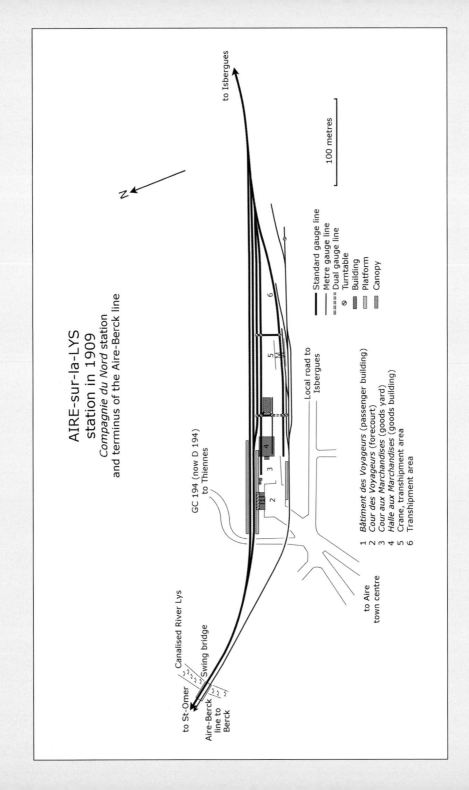

AIRE-sur-la-LYS
station in 1909
Compagnie du Nord station
and terminus of the Aire-Berck line

GC 194 (now D 194)
to Thiennes

Canalised River Lys

Swing bridge

to St-Omer

Aire-Berck
line to
Berck

to Aire
town centre

Local road to
Isbergues

to Isbergues

N

100 metres

Standard gauge line
Metre gauge line
Dual gauge line
Turntable
Building
Platform
Canopy

1 *Bâtiment des Voyageurs* (passenger building)
2 *Cour des Voyageurs* (forecourt)
3 *Cour aux Marchandises* (goods yard)
4 *Halle aux Marchandises* (goods building)
5 Crane, transhipment area
6 Transhipment area

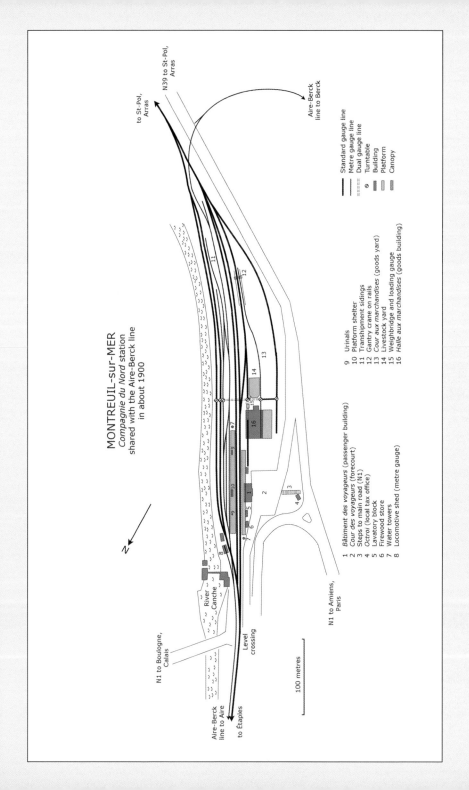

MONTREUIL-sur-MER
Compagnie du Nord station
shared with the Aire-Berck line
in about 1900

N39 to St-Pol, Arras

to St-Pol, Arras

Aire-Berck line to Berck

N1 to Boulogne, Calais

River Canche

Aire-Berck line to Aire

to Étaples

Level crossing

N1 to Amiens, Paris

100 metres

N

Standard gauge line
Metre gauge line
Dual gauge line
Turntable
Building
Platform
Canopy

1   *Bâtiment des voyageurs* (passenger building)
2   *Cour des voyageurs* (forecourt)
3   Steps to main road (N1)
4   *Octroi* (local tax office)
5   Lavatory block
6   Firewood store
7   Water towers
8   Locomotive shed (metre gauge)
9   Urinals
10 Platform shelter
11 Transhipment sidings
12 Gantry crane on rails
13 *Cour aux marchandises* (goods yard)
14 Livestock yard
15 Weighbridge and loading gauge
16 *Halle aux marchandises* (goods building)

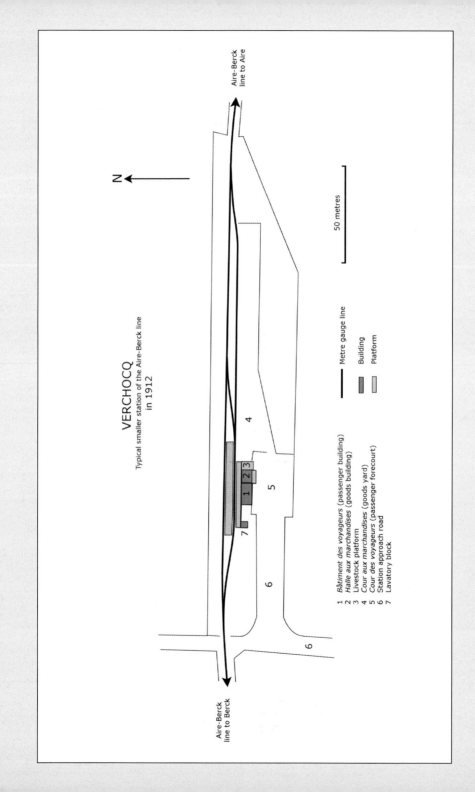

VERCHOCQ
Typical smaller station of the Aire-Berck line
in 1912

N ←

Aire-Berck
line to Aire

Aire-Berck
line to Berck

50 metres

—— Metre gauge line

■ Building

▨ Platform

1 Bâtiment des voyageurs (passenger building)
2 Halle aux marchandises (goods building)
3 Livestock platform
4 Cour aux marchandises (goods yard)
5 Cour des voyageurs (passenger forecourt)
6 Station approach road
7 Lavatory block

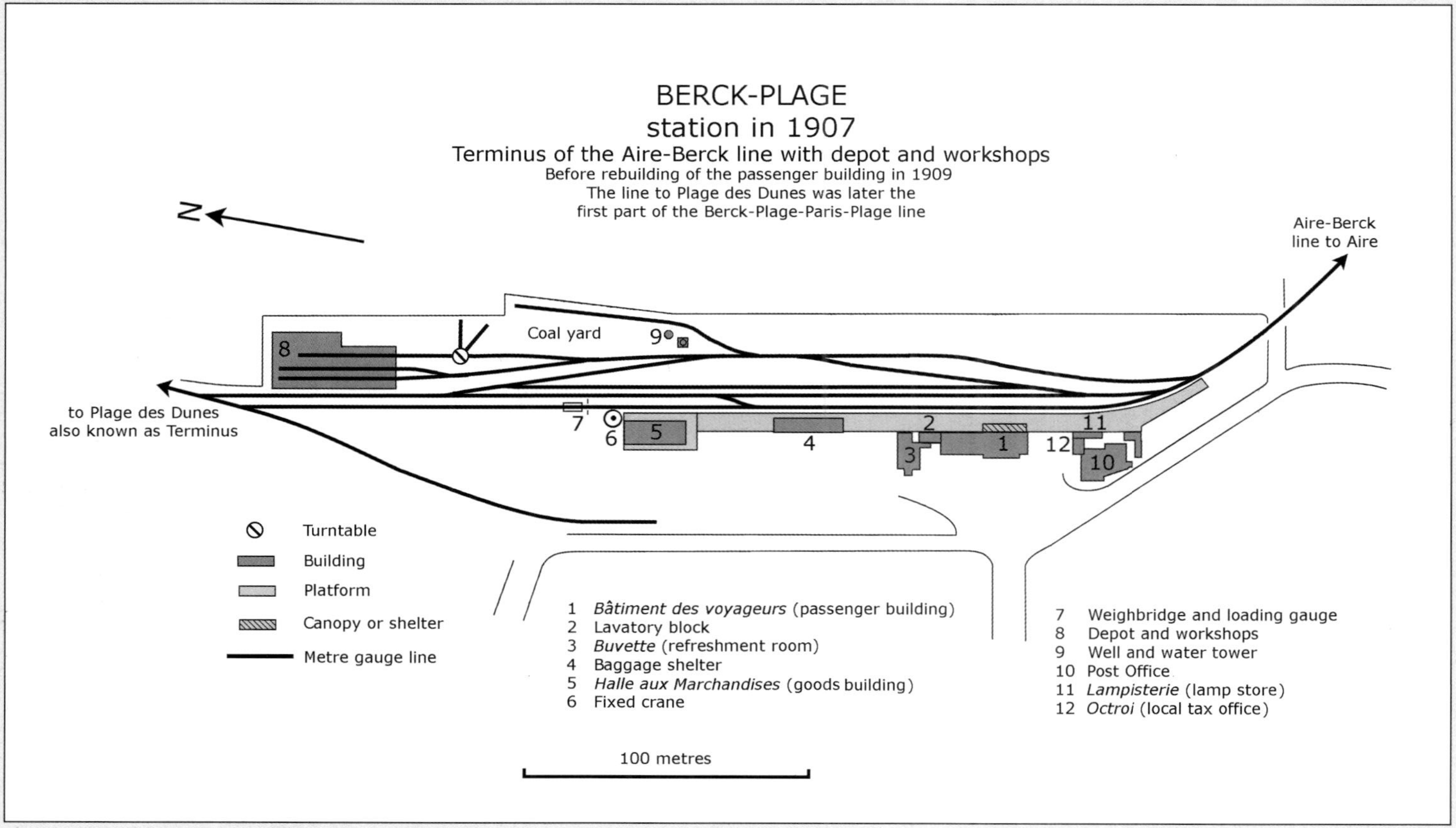

BERCK-PLAGE
station in 1907
Terminus of the Aire-Berck line with depot and workshops
Before rebuilding of the passenger building in 1909
The line to Plage des Dunes was later the
first part of the Berck-Plage-Paris-Plage line

Aire–Berck
line to Aire

Coal yard

9

N

to Plage des Dunes
also known as Terminus

Turntable
Building
Platform
Canopy or shelter
Metre gauge line

100 metres

1 *Bâtiment des voyageurs* (passenger building)
2 Lavatory block
3 *Buvette* (refreshment room)
4 Baggage shelter
5 *Halle aux Marchandises* (goods building)
6 Fixed crane

7 Weighbridge and loading gauge
8 Depot and workshops
9 Well and water tower
10 Post Office
11 *Lampisterie* (lamp store)
12 *Octroi* (local tax office)

The Compagnie du Nord station at Rang-du-Fliers-Verton, postcard postmarked 1905. The standard gauge main line is in the foreground. Behind a train hauled by an unidentifiable locomotive is arriving from Berck-Plage into the metre gauge platform, with the *buvette* to the right. On the down platform between the standard gauge and the metre gauge lines is the separate shelter provided primarily for passengers on the Aire-Berck line. Above the station name on the end of the shelter is the sign '*Embranchement pour Berck*'.   *Authors' Collection*

The sugar factory at Rang-du-Fliers. Postcard postmarked 1930.
                                        Éditions Capron-Vallois, Lille; Authors' Collection

Depots and workshops

The major depot of the Aire-Berck line was at Berck-Plage. However, the line made increasing use of the depot at Fruges especially in view of the rapid integration of stock with the Anvin-Calais line which followed the opening of the line (*see Operations*).

Industrial links

As on the Anvin-Calais line, there were many quarries, factories, and other locations along the line which used it to transport goods to and from their facilities. Some had been there before, and some, particularly quarries, started up because of the availability of rail transport close by. Some had private branch lines and agreements with the company to pay for access to the principal line. These are shown below for 1911, with the amount paid to the line, and the weight of freight (*petite vitesse*) transported. They are listed from the Aire end. A zero may just mean that there is no report. For sidings actually adjacent to stations, there is no separate report, and the totals for that station are shown in brackets. Most of these show the industrial activity, with much more leaving than arriving, but at Berck it is swamped by the other activity at this developing resort.

Place	Business and nature of business	Income (francs)	Goods (tonnes)	
			to	from
Moulin-le-Comte	Unknown	236	(1,218)	(5,416)
Vincly	Cement factory	9	0	0
Vincly	Quarry	887	0	7,410
Matringhem	Quarry	1,061	(1,082)	(10,082)
Attin	Brick works, Albert & Felix Leroy	2,091	2,718	14,814
Wailly	Quarry	86	(1,885)	(10,102)
Verton	Quarry	272	400	2,400
Rang-du-Fliers	Sugar factory, Garry company	2,847	(19,005)	(30,180)
Berck-Plage	Soubitez, sawmill & general stores	269	(39,011)	(5,909)

We are uncertain of the business of the siding at Moulin-le-Comte. This siding had originally been proposed by M. Schotsman, who was probably the proprietor of the distillery at Trézenne, near Aire. By 1911 there was a dispute about the use of this siding between M. Schotsman, the railway, and the owners of another factory. On one occasion the factory owners locked the gate to the siding so that wagons could not be delivered, and in 1914 the *Préfet* had to order them to improve the arrangements and conform with the regulations.

As noted in Chapter Two, at some locations where there were private sidings, mixed trains would stop if there were wagons to pick up or drop off. These were shown on the detailed timetable produced for staff, but not on the public timetables. On the Aire-Berck line in 1913 these were at the quarry at Vincly, between Mencas-Bellefontaine and Matringhem; at the *briqueterie* (brickworks) at Attin, close to the *arrêt* at La Paix Faite near Montreuil; and at the quarry at Verton, which was in the cutting as the line descended from Bahot to Verton-Bourg.

There was a considerable concentration of industries around Attin, near Montreuil. Apart from the Leroy brickworks, which later had a standard gauge branch from the Étaples-Arras line as well, there was a sawmill, also owned by the Leroys, and there was and still is a sugar factory. Although the sugar factory was alongside the Aire-Berck line, it made little use of it and collected most of the sugar beet from the countryside to the north-west by road. The sugar beet from the Course

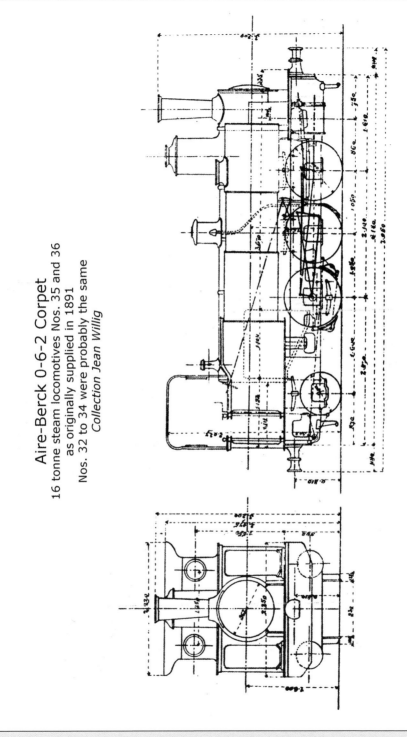

Aire-Berck 0-6-2 Corpet
16 tonne steam locomotives Nos. 35 and 36
as originally supplied in 1891
Nos. 32 to 34 were probably the same
Collection Jean Willig

valley and to the south and east of Montreuil went, mostly by train, to the factory of the Garry company at Rang-du-Fliers, or to that of the Say company at Pont d'Ardres. In 1903 a weighbridge was installed at Montreuil-St-Justin for MM. Garry and company, to weigh material for the factory at Rang-du-Fliers, and in 1907 one at Wailly for the Say factory at Pont d'Ardres. There were probably others.

Rolling stock

Locomotives

Technical details of steam locomotives acquired by the Aire-Berck line up to 1914 are shown in *Table Ten*. A full motive power list for all the lines in this book is given in *Appendix One*.

Table Ten
Technical details of Aire-Berck locomotives up to 1914

Manufacturer	Corpet	Corpet	Corpet
Year(s) of manufacture	1890	1891	1892
Type	0-6-2T	0-6-2T	0-6-2T
Company No(s)	004 (?31)	32 to 36	40 to 45
Year(s) put in service	1891	1891	1892-1893
Number put in service	1	5	6
Length (m)		7.06	7.90
Height (m)		3.20	3.46
Width (m)		2.25	2.50
Weight empty (tonnes)	16	16	21
Weight loaded (tonnes)	21	21	26.56
Wheelbase (m)		3.70	4.10
Driving wheelbase (m)		2.10	2.24
Dia. of driving wheels (m)	0.80	1.00	1.00
Boiler capacity (m³)	2.134	2.055	3.265
Boiler pressure (kg/cm²)	9	10	10
Heating surface (m²)	48	42	70.33
Water capacity (L)		2,800	3,160
Coal capacity (kg)		800	1,000
Dia. of valves (mm)	62	60	55
Dia. of pistons (m)	0.35	0.30	0.36
Piston travel (m)	0.45	0.45	0.52
Load pulled (tonnes)			
At 15 kph level		650	690
At 40 kph level		210	300
At 15 kph at 2% gradient		69	89
At 40 kph at 2% gradient		24	43

For the opening of the Aire-Berck line, six or seven 0-6-2 tank engines, weighing 16 tonnes unladen, and manufactured in 1890 or 1891 at the works of *Mme la Veuve Corpet* (the widow Corpet), were put in service in 1891 between Montreuil-St-Justin and Berck-Plage. These were numbered 004 and 31 to 36. We only have full details for Nos. 32, 33, 35, and 36, which were identical; and for No. 004, which had a slightly lower boiler pressure and smaller driving wheels. Since the line probably only had six such

Aire-Berck 0-6-2 Corpet
21 tonne steam locomotives Nos. 40 to 45
as originally supplied in 1892 and 1893
Collection Jean Willig

locomotives it is quite likely that No. 004 was renumbered 31. It is also probable that No. 34 was the same as Nos. 32, 33, 35 and 36.

It must be presumed that these were under-powered for the loads and gradients on the line since a further six Corpet 0-6-2 tank engines of 21 tonnes unladen weight were delivered in 1892 or 1893, and numbered 40 to 45. We only have full details of Nos. 40 and 41, delivered in 1892, and No. 45, delivered in 1893. These three were identical and it is almost certain that Nos. 42 to 44 were also. They had considerably larger boilers than the previously delivered 16 tonne Corpets.

In 1892 the company also applied to the *département* for permission to use engines up to 27.65 tonnes all-up weight on the section from Montreuil to Berck, whereas the metal platforms of the bridges were calculated for a maximum all-up weight of 23.80 tonnes. The company was told to produce a programme for the reinforcement of the main girders of 'openings' (bridges etc.) of three to five metres. In December 1893 the company was also given permission for the strengthening of the metal bridge at Verton, eight metres wide, for locomotives up to 27.65 tonnes. The 21 tonne locomotives Nos. 40 to 45, loaded weight 26.5 tonnes, were restricted to the section between Rang-du-Fliers and Berck-Plage until this work had been done.

In 1906 the company wanted to put into service locomotives of up to 31 tonnes, and approval was given to put this weight on the bridge at Verton. This relates to the purchase in 1906 by the Anvin-Calais company of a 24 tonne (unloaded) locomotive manufactured in 1906 at the *Ateliers du Chemin de Fer du Nord de St-Martin* (Belgium), of which the loaded weight was 31 tonnes (*see Chapter Two, Table Two, and Appendix One*). The initial authorization to put this locomotive into use in 1906 was for the Aire-Berck line between Rimeux-Gournay and Berck. The company later acquired further similar locomotives.

In 1894, the year following the full opening of the line, Corpet locomotives Nos. 31 to 33 were transferred to the *Réseau de Flandres*, followed by No. 36 in 1912. Number 34 went to the Noyon-Guiscard-Lassigny line in the *Département* of Oise, which was, like the Aire-Berck line, a business interest of M. Lambert. Presumably these lines had lesser gradients or lighter trains or both and were better suited to the lighter engines. We do not know what the early duties of the remaining 16 tonne Corpet, No. 35, were. However, we have seen a photograph of this locomotive at Calais-Fontinettes, on the Anvin-Calais line, in 1920, pulling a one-coach off-peak passenger train, perhaps only to Guînes or Ardres. This could definitely be counted as a lighter duty.

In 1900, or soon after, the 0-6-0 Pinguely tank locomotive No. 10 of the Anvin-Calais line, manufactured in 1900, was transferred to the Aire- Berck line as No. 46 (*for details see Chapter Two, Table Two*). As we have already noted in Chapter Two, this renumbering is surprising, since rolling stock had always in practice been used on both lines.

Passenger carriages and Goods rolling stock

For the opening of the line from Montreuil-St-Justin to Berck in 1891, the company purchased 10 end-platform bogie coaches. Four had six places for first class, seven places for second class, and 40 places for third class. Six had 12 places for first class and 27 places for second class only. Seats were upholstered in first and second class, and of wood in third. For the operation of the whole line they had 16 end-platform bogie coaches, which by 1911 were nine mixed first, second and third class, five mixed first and second class, and two for third class only. There were 12 baggage vans.

By 1911 the line had 34 covered wagons, 71 open wagons, 43 flat wagons, and a mobile crane.

Table Eleven
Aire to Berck
Summary Timetable from 20th October, 1894

Aire	dep.				08.55		14.12	19.45	
Fruges	arr.				10.45		15.47	21.41	
	dep.	06.00			11.00		16.05		
Rimeux-Gournay		06.22			11.22		16.26		
Montreuil	arr.	08.14			13.15		18.10		
	dep.	08.30			13.48		18.28		
Rang	arr.	09.22			14.32		19.12		
	dep.	09.40	10.40	12.56	14.37	17.43	19.28		22.57
Berck-Plage	arr.	09.55	10.57	13.11	14.54	17.59	19.48		23.13

Berck-Plage	dep.		06.50	10.06	12.08	13.50	16.05	18.47	21.37
Rang	arr.		07.06	10.22	12.26	14.09	16.26	19.00	22.00
	dep.		07.26		12.32			19.13	
Montreuil	arr.		08.13		13.20			19.58	
	dep.		08.30		13.39			20.03	
Rimeux-Gournay			10.31		15.36			21.48	
Fruges	arr.		10.46		15.51			22.03	
	dep.	06.10	11.46		17.20				
Aire	arr.	08.32	13.35		19.17				

Note: The original on which this timetable is based is in the 12 hour clock with times headed *'matin'* or *'soir'*.

Table Twelve
Aire to Berck
Summary Timetable from 1st May, 1913

Station			(1)	(2)	(3)				(4)	(5)
Aire	dep.				08.30		14.52	19.50		
Fruges	arr.				10.18		16.20	21.38		
	dep.	05.51			11.07		16.25			
Rimeux-Gournay		06.08			11.30		16.52			
Montreuil	arr.	07.54			13.23		18.30			
	dep.	08.29	10.00	11.35	14.08	17.05	18.49		19.43	19.55
Rang	arr.	09.13	10.37	12.20	14.56	17.46	19.33		20.33	20.40
	dep.	09.18	10.40	12.25	15.00	17.51	19.37 (6)		20.50	20.50
Berck-Plage	arr.	09.33	10.55	12.40	15.15	18.07	19.52 (6)		21.05	21.05

Station				(1)	(2)	(3)			(7)
Berck-Plage	dep.		06.35	08.05		12.30	15.40	17.32	18.32
Rang	arr.		06.54	08.24	09.17	12.46	15.55	17.47	18.48
	dep.		07.05	08.32	09.22	13.00	16.00	17.50	18.50
Montreuil	arr.		07.51	09.24	10.12	13.41	16.42	18.29	19.28
	dep.		08.30			14.04		18.55	
Rimeux-Gournay			10.32			16.00		20.46	
Fruges	arr.		10.48			16.15		21.01	
	dep.	05.47	11.54			17.00			
Aire	arr.	07.30	13.32			18.50			

(1) From 6th July to 30th September only.
(2) Saturdays (market day in Montreuil).
(3) Daily 28th June to 30th September, Saturdays only 1st May to 27th June.
(4) From 1st April to 30th September only, except Sundays and holidays.
(5) From 1st April to 30th September only, Sundays and holidays.
(6) 19.47 from Rang, 20.02 at Berck, from 1st October to 31st March.
(7) From 1st April to 30th September only.

Note – Up to 18 additional trains per day between Rang and Berck

Operations

Examining documents concerning the line, we find that within a few years of opening it was being run by the *Compagnie du Chemin de Fer d'Anvin à Calais*. The initial timetable from St-Justin to Berck-Plage, dated 29th July, 1891, and the timetable for the whole line of 3rd November, 1893, is headed *'Chemins de Fer d'Aire à Berck'* but the timetable of 20th October, 1894, is headed *'Chemin de Fer d'Anvin à Calais, Ligne d'Aire à Berck'*. On 27th February, 1907, the letter from the Director of *Chemins de Fer* to the *Préfecture* of Pas-de-Calais, on the subject of strengthening bridges for heavier locomotives, refers to the request of the *Compagnie d'Anvin à Calais* 'qui exploita la ligne' (who have been operating the line). Another indication of this was the early appearance on the Aire-Berck line of locomotives of the Anvin-Calais line, as evidenced in a number of photographs taken before 1909.

However the *Compagnie Anonyme des Chemins de Fer d'Aire à Fruges et de Rimeux-Gournay à Berck* continued their annual reports to shareholders, at least until 1952, with a report exclusively on the Aire-Berck line. The *Compagnie du Chemin de Fer d'Anvin à Calais* also continued to do this, with a report exclusively on the Anvin-Calais line, at least until 1912. Almost certainly this pattern continued until after the closures in 1955.

In view of all this it is not surprising that the regulations for operating the line were the same as those for the Anvin-Calais line, and for the other lines in the Level empire. Only local details differed. Please see Chapter Two for a full discussion of signalling and single line working tokens. As is true for the Anvin-Calais line, we do not know precisely the sections for each unique token, but the same considerations apply.

The initial timetable from St-Justin (Montreuil-St-Justin) provided four trains each way every day over the whole length of the line, with an additional five trains each way between Rang-du-Fliers-Verton and Berck-Plage. There was an additional late night train from Rang at 23.55, that returned from Berck at 00.23. This ran only on Saturdays and the evening before public holidays (*Fêtes*). This pattern required two trains to be circulating most of the day, but three in the early evening. The pattern also indicates that all three would be stabled at Rang-du-Fliers overnight.

The timetable from the full opening of the line in 1893 provided for two trains each way per day over the full length of the line, with additional trains starting from Fruges in the early morning to both Aire and Berck-Plage, and returning to Fruges at night. This basic pattern required three trains, two stabled at Fruges and one at Berck-Plage. There were additional trains between Rang-du-Fliers and Berck-Plage, which would require additional trains based at Berck-Plage especially in the summer season. A summary timetable from October 1894 is shown in *Table Eleven*, which would represent the winter service with fewer trains between Rang-du-Fliers and Berck-Plage.

Journey times were long, and the whole length of the line was scheduled to take from 5½ hours to just over six hours. This depended on the waiting times for connections at Rang, Montreuil and Fruges. In 1894 waiting times at Fruges were up to 1½ hours but this had improved by 1913, when the maximum wait at Fruges on Aire-Berck line services was just over an hour. Services in May 1913 are summarised in *Table Twelve*. The long journey times meant that the train which left Berck at 06.35 did not return to Berck until 19.52, assuming that it was the same train. If it was not, more than three trains would have been required. We do not know how the crews were rostered, but it is likely that they lived either at Berck or at Fruges. Basing at least two trains at Fruges, which was a main depot of the Anvin-Calais line, is another example of the close working between the two from the beginning of the Aire-Berck line.

The station at Ergny. A passenger train is waiting to leave for Berck-Plage, hauled by Corpet 0-6-2 tank locomotive ARB No. 42, delivered 1892, of 21 tonnes unladen weight. Note the loading gauge on the goods loop. Postcard postmarked 1912. *Collection Gabriel Richard*

A mixed train headed towards Berck-Plage passing the level crossing at Inxent. The *arrêt* at Inxent was just off the picture to the left on the other side of the road. The train includes a bogie carriage, a 2-axle carriage and a baggage van. The Aire-Berck line never purchased any 2-axle carriages, and this is just one of many examples of sharing rolling stock with the Anvin-Calais line. Postcard postmarked 1916. *Collection Gabriel Richard*

In addition to this service, there were by 1913 also two additional trains from Berck-Plage to Montreuil and back every day in the summer season, and one on Saturdays all year round. Saturday was, and still is, market day in Montreuil. There were also four additional trains from Berck-Plage to Rang-du-Fliers and back all year round, with more in the summer season, when there might be up to 25 trains in each direction on this section, connecting the main line from Paris with the resort. In 1906, it was agreed that, at least in the high season, an extra train from Rang to Berck-Plage would be provided to meet the 23.58 express from Paris. However, this was agreed by the *Compagnie du Nord* only on condition that the Paris express would stop for one minute and no more, and that the connection would only be available for first and second class passengers. Quite how this was controlled is not recorded. The additional trains between Berck-Plage and Montreuil and Berck-Plage and Rang-du-Fliers were based at Berck-Plage.

As on the Anvin-Calais line, there were, in addition to the passenger services, which were mostly mixed passenger and goods, scheduled goods trains. These had the option not to run if there was no business. In 1913 there were two per day each way between Fruges and Matringhem, and one between Rimeux-Gournay and Berck-Plage. There were certainly more on a less regularly scheduled basis, especially in the sugar beet season.

In May 1914 the fares for a single journey the whole length of the line were 9 francs 85 centimes first class, 7 francs 45 centimes second class and 5 francs 40 centimes third class. From 1893 the line also sold season tickets for between one month and one year at reduced rates. Reduced rates were available for groups of students and pensioners, and a wide range of special interest groups.

The full opening of the Aire-Berck line provided the opportunity for passengers to connect with trains on the Anvin-Calais line at Fruges and at Rimeux-Gournay. In mid-morning it was possible to make all the connections in both directions on both lines at Fruges, except for the connection from the direction of Calais-Ville on the Anvin-Calais line and going in the direction of Berck-Plage on the Aire-Berck line; however, this connection could be made at Rimeux-Gournay. In the late afternoon all connections in all directions could be made at Fruges. In both the mornings and the afternoons the price was paid in some long waits at Fruges. Some of the changes could also be made at Rimeux-Gournay.

The numbers of passengers using the interchange stations on the Aire-Berck line are shown in the *Table Thirteen* for 1897 and 1911. This information is based on the annual reports of the Aire-Berck company for 1898 and 1912. The numbers using the opportunities to change between lines for these years are also shown. For the possible changes with the Anvin-Calais line, at Fruges and at Rimeux-Gournay, the numbers changing in this way in this way should be the same as those in *Table Five* in Chapter Two, except that 'to other' and 'from other' are the other way round. There is agreement for Fruges for 1911, and for the others at least the numbers are of the same order of magnitude. The figures do confirm the Anvin-Calais reports that more passengers changed at Rimeux-Gournay than at Fruges. The large number of passengers changing to and from the main line at Rang-du-Fliers would almost all be on their way to or from Berck-Plage. The total number of visitors to Berck increased from 139,403 in 1900 to 244,174 in 1908. Of course changes would mainly be made for intermediate stations. Passengers for the ends of the lines, for example going from Calais to Rang-du-Fliers or Aire, would use the standard gauge network.

Some activity and financial figures for the line for the years 1897 and 1911 are shown in the *Table Fourteen*, which can be compared with *Table Six* for the Anvin-Calais line. Like the Anvin-Calais line, there was a substantial increase in passenger traffic and an even

Table Thirteen
Passenger arrivals and departures, and numbers changing, at interchange stations on Aire-Berck (ARB) line

Station	Line changing to or from	1897 ARB arr. (to other)	ARB dep. (from other)	1911 ARB arr. (to other)	ARB dep. (from other)
Aire	St-Omer to Armentière (1)	12,598 (918)	10,155 (279)	15,183 (1,774)	12,155 (739)
Fruges	Anvin to Calais	8,765 (36)	9,002 (64)	11,825 (80)	11,287 (80)
Rimeux-Gournay	Anvin to Calais	581 (181)	680 (309)	747 (169)	810 (531)
Montreuil	Étaples to Arras (1)	18,106 (3,868)	17,286 (3,960)	31,176 (7,230)	21,429 (6,987)
Rang-du-Fliers	Paris, Amiens, Boulogne, Calais (1)	31,251 (27,295)	16,680 (48,195)	58,926 (64,008)	24,996 (107,281)
Berck-Plage	Berck-Plage to Paris-Plage (2)	83,296	60,088	118,486	127,232

Arrivals and departures do not include passengers changing

(1)   *Compagnie du Nord* standard gauge.
(2)   Berck-Plage-Paris-Plage open from 1909. No figures for numbers changing in 1911.

Table Fourteen
Some activity figures and financial results for the Aire-Berck line

Activity		1897	1911
Distance run	(train km)	263,770	317,400
Passengers			
First class		5,984	
Second class		33,141	
Third class		263,433	
Total		302,558	501,208
Grande Vitesse			
Registered baggage	(No. of items registered)	23,278	42,444
Dogs carried		1,703	2,165
Parcels carried	(No. of items)	38,406	83,416
Freight forwarding	(No. of registrations)	26,296	43,216
	(weight, tonnes)	959	2,597
Petite Vitesse			
Goods	(tonnes)	54,893	143,442
Coal and coke	(tonnes)	16,490	22,833
Livestock	(in complete wagons)	6,568	12,563
plus	(heads)	563	707
Financial			
Total receipts	(francs)	323,718	570,621
Total expenses	(francs)	253,011	344,737
Receipts	(per train km, francs)	1.202	1.798
Expenses	(per train km, francs)	0.959	1.086
Profit	(per train km, francs)	0.243	0.712
Coefficient of exploitation	(= expenses/receipts, per cent)	79	60

bigger increase in goods over these years. The increase in train kilometres run is smaller and clearly load per train has increased. In general the activity is less than for the Anvin-Calais line. Receipts are about the same but expenses higher for Aire-Berck, so profitability is less. However the profits have increased from just under 21 per cent of takings in 1897 to nearly 40 per cent in 1911. It is interesting that the proportion of first and second class passengers, which we only have for 1897, is much higher than for the Anvin-Calais line. Probably this reflects more wealthy people, many no doubt from the Paris area, using the line to travel to Berck-Plage. Like the Anvin-Calais line, it would appear that in the years just before World War I this was a healthy business. This should not surprise us, since despite the separate companies and reports, it was under the same management, that of M. Émile Level and the Anvin-Calais company. Also like the Anvin-Calais line, it was a line with a large proportion of its passenger business at one end; but in the case of the Anvin-Calais line it was commuters at the Calais end, in this case it was leisure traffic between Rang-du-Fliers and Berck-Plage.

Tramway from Berck-Ville to Berck-Plage

This 60 cm horse-drawn tramway is of importance in this book firstly because it was, briefly, in competition with the Aire-Berck line from Berck-Ville to Berck-Plage. Secondly, because its opening in 1899 became confused in some quarters with the Aire-Berck line between the stations of the same names, and this is almost certainly the source of erroneous reports that the Aire-Berck line did not open from Berck-Ville to Berck-Plage until 1899.

The tramway was requested by the town council of Berck in 1897 and declared of *utilité publique* in 1899. The concession was originally granted to the town council of Berck, who passed it on to the entrepreneur M. Charles Manière in July 1899. The tram began to operate on 20th August, 1899.

The route began in the forecourt of Berck-Ville station, on the Aire-Berck line. It ran parallel with the Aire-Berck line towards Rang-du-Fliers for a short way, then turned south along what was then the quite narrow GC 119, now the much wider D 940, the main road from Étaples to Abbeville. It then turned west through Berck-Ville, along the Rue de l'Impératrice, all the way to the sea. At the sea end the line came out into the triangular open area known then and now as L'Entonnoir (literally, the funnel). The total length was 3 km (1¾ miles). There were passing loops at the town hall at Berck-Ville, at the junction of the Chemin du Calvaire Michel with the Rue de l'Impératrice (approximately where the Avenue du 8 Mai 1945 now is), and where the line came out into l'Entonnoir.

The flat-bottomed Vignole rails, of weight 12 kg/metre, were set in the roadway for the whole length of the line. They were supposed to be flush with the roadway, but one issue cropped up a few times in the town council minutes. This was the adverse effect of tram rails sitting proud of the road surface. This caused, not surprisingly, problems to other vehicles. The weight of the rails suggests that these were not suitable to be set in the roadway and this may have been the problem. The line was laid to one side of narrower roads but in the Rue de l'Impératrice they were laid down the centre, to allow parking on both sides.

The two axle tramcars were each pulled by two placid but strong Boulonnais horses, and had hard wooden seats. Closed cars had 10 seats but also standing room inside and on the end platforms. Access was through the end platforms. Open cars probably had 12 seats, with side access, and strong red and white drill curtains. These were described in one report as being like those on the Berck-Plage-Paris-Plage line, but since the latter

The station at Berck-Ville, with the goods building on the right and the lavatory block on the left. The extension to the left of the passenger building may have been a station master's office, as was the similar extension to the first station at Berck-Plage. The building on the extreme left is the depot of the horse-drawn 60 cm gauge tramway from Berck-Ville to Berck-Plage, and the line to this is crossing the forecourt in the left foreground. Postcard postmarked 1911, but the photograph must have been taken earlier (*see page 115*). *Authors' Collection*

The station at Berck-Plage. Although postmarked 1909 the picture is of the original station which was replaced in 1909. The caption says 'arrival of a train from Paris' but this is of course just from Rang-du-Fliers where there was a connection with the train from Paris.

Éditions LL; Authors' Collection

91   *BERCK-PLAGE. — Arrivée d'un train de Paris. — LL.*

did not open until 1909 if there was any copying it was the other way round. There was a depot at Berck-Ville station with two short sidings for the tramcars, and there may only have been a few tramcars. The horses were most likely kept nearby.

In 1898 it was reported that there would be 15 services per day for five months per year, 20 for three months, and 30 for four months, presumably the high season. The 'winter timetable' for April 1901 shows five services a day each way from Berck-Ville station to the sea front, with an additional 11 each way from the town hall to the sea front. The 'summer timetable' from 23rd June, 1901 has 10 and 19 each way respectively, with three extra in the evenings depending on demand. The journey time was 16 minutes from the town hall to the front and 21 minutes all the way.

By 1901 the *Compagnie du Tramway de Berck-Plage à Berck-Ville* were applying to alter the agreement for the concession so that they need only run the service in the summer season, but at the same time wanted to convert the line to electric traction. In January 1903 the Mayor of Berck expressed the discontent of the town that the line had been 'abandoned', and it seems that the *Compagnie*, still led by M. Manière, were trying to lift the line. This was in spite of the refusal of the town council and the *département* to grant permission. We do not know if the line ever ran again. In any case, in March 1905, an enquiry recommended the declassification of the line, with the depot building at Berck-Ville to be left to the town, and the track to be lifted and the roads returned to their original state. In 1906 a Departmental Engineer confirmed that this had been done, and the formal decree of *déclassement* followed in December of that year.

Given that throughout this the Aire-Berck line ran at least nine trains per day between Rang and Berck-Plage via Berck-Ville all year round, and up to 25 in the high season, and that photographs show ample horse-drawn transport meeting trains at Berck-Plage station, which was in any case only 500 metres from the beach, one wonders if the business case for the horse tramway was ever sound.

Tramway from Étaples to Paris-Plage

In 1896 the Travel Editor of *The Queen* ('The Lady's Newspaper') hired a two-wheel cart at Berck and drove north through the pine forest. He 'wanted to ascertain how far progress had been made in popularising the little bathing station of Paris-Plage and its dependence Mayville'. Paris-Plage did indeed rapidly become a very fashionable and up-market resort, which it remains to this day. In 1912 it took the name Le-Touquet-Paris-Plage, after the nearby village called Le Touquet, but today it is often just called Le Touquet.

The travel editor of *The Queen* then had to take his cart on to Étaples to catch a train to Montreuil. Étaples was and is a substantial fishing town on the estuary of the River Canche and is on the main coast line (then *Compagnie du Nord*) from Boulogne to Paris. With the resort of Paris-Plage aimed at the Paris market it was inevitable that a line should be built to serve Paris-Plage from Étaples, fulfilling the same function as did the Rang to Berck-Plage section of the Aire-Berck line for Berck-Plage.

Permission to build such a line as a tramway had been given to the entrepreneur Charles Prévost in 1894. Originally it was intended that the trams should be horse-drawn. In 1896 the line was declared to be of *utilité publique*. In 1898 the *département* agreed to the use of electric traction instead of horses. The concession was again granted to M. Prévost. The *Compagnie du Tramway d'Étaples à Paris-Plage* was founded to build and operate the line. A further public enquiry had to be held 1899, and the line in its new form was again found of *utilité publique*. The line was opened on 15th July, 1900. For this book we have used the abbreviation TEPP for this line.

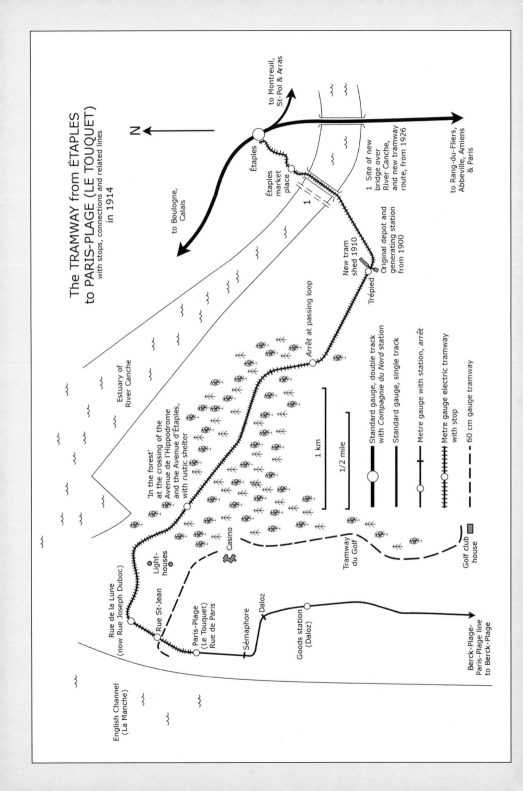

The TRAMWAY from ÉTAPLES to PARIS-PLAGE (LE TOUQUET) with stops, connections and related lines in 1914

N

to Montreuil, St-Pol & Arras

to Boulogne, Calais

Étaples

Étaples market place

1 Site of new bridge over River Canche, and new tramway route, from 1926

to Rang-du-Fliers, Abbeville, Amiens & Paris

New tram shed 1910

Original depot and generating station from 1900

Trépied

Estuary of River Canche

Arrêt at passing loop

'In the forest' at the crossing of the Avenue de l'Hippodrome and the Avenue d'Étaples, with rustic shelter

1 km

1/2 mile

Standard gauge, double track with Compagnie du Nord station

Standard gauge, single track

Metre gauge with station, arrêt

Metre gauge electric tramway

Metre gauge electric tramway with stop

60 cm gauge tramway

Golf club house

Tramway du Golf

Casino

Light-houses

Rue de la Lune (now Rue Joseph Duboc)

Rue St-Jean

Paris-Plage (Le Touquet) Rue de Paris

Sémaphore

Daloz

Goods station (Daloz)

Berck-Plage– Paris-Plage line to Berck-Plage

English Channel (La Manche)

Description of the line

The line was built as a tramway with the town and bridge sections running in roads and the middle section in the forest of Le Touquet running along the side of the road. The line was 6.4 km (4 miles) long.

The line began in the forecourt of the *Compagnie du Nord* station at Étaples. It followed the Rue de la Gare and crossed the market place to reach the river bridge. The river was crossed on the road bridge, which was then a different bridge from the present one, in a different position a little further upstream. The line then turned north-west through the forest of Le Touquet, parallel to but inland from the south shore of the estuary of the River Canche, along what was then the Avenue d'Étaples. This is now the Avenue de Picardie, but at the east end it has now been cut by the second runway of the airport. Passing the two lighthouses, it entered Paris-Plage along the Avenue L. Hubert, which then included what is now the Place Quentovic. It then turned left, that is south, along the Rue de Paris, which was parallel to and one block back from the sea front, and was then the main street. The terminus was between what is now the Rue Jean Monnet (formerly the Grand-Rue) and the Rue de la Paix.

Engineering

The line was single track and metre gauge. The maximum gradient was 36 mm per metre (3.6 per cent) and the maximum radius of curvature was 20 metres. It was therefore typical of an electric tramway. The road sections were constructed using Broca rails of 36 kg/metre set in the tarmac. Sections on the verge used Vignole rails at 18 kg/metre.

The line was electrified with overhead wire suspended from brackets mounted on wooden posts. Electricity was supplied from a steam power station at 600 volts DC. Before the tramway the bridge had been built partly of masonry piers (on the Étaples side), with an older part of wood on the south side. To strengthen it for the tramway the wooden part was rebuilt using metal. In 1909 details for the proposed crossing with the 60 cm tramway of the *Société des automobiles sur Rail de Paris-Plage* at the junction of the Rue de Paris and the Rue St. Jean were agreed, and carried out as part of the construction of the 60 cm line (*see later in this chapter*).

Stations

At the Étaples end of the line, the tramway as originally built had two sections. In one direction a single stop line and platform, accommodating three vehicles, was adjacent to the platforms of the main line. In the other was access to the goods yard and building. In 1908, or soon after, this was redesigned to provide three terminus lines by platforms, with space for up to 11 vehicles. There was eventually a brick building in the forecourt of the *Compagnie du Nord* station with the name *Gare des Tramways Étaples-Paris-Plage*, and it is most likely that this was built with the 1908 improvements.

The station at Paris-Plage in the Rue de Paris was initially a modest building of brick with a corrugated roof. Later this was replaced with a grandiose single-storey arcaded stone building surmounted by a flagpole. The name *Tramway d'Étaples à Paris-Plage* was above the centre of the arcade. We do not have an exact date for the building of this new station, but the photographic record shows that it was in use by 1907.

The Compagnie du Nord main line station at Étaples. A tram is waiting at the terminus of the tramway to Paris-Plage. The building on the right is labelled 'Gare des tramways Étaples-Paris-Plage', and there are more tramway vehicles to the right in front of this. Undated.

Éditions LL.; Authors' Collection

A tram with an enclosed passenger trailer, headed towards Paris-Plage, crossing the market place at Étaples, with a market in progress. Postcard postmarked 1906.   *Authors' Collection*

There were other stops, all *arrêts*. These were in the market place at Étaples, at the depot, at the passing loop which is now under the second runway of the airport, at the Chemin du Golf (now the Avenue du Golf), at the Avenue du Château, at the Rue de la Lune (now the Rue Joseph Duboc), and at the Rue St. Jean. The one at the Avenue du Château was probably the one often described on pictures as 'in the forest', at the corner of the Avenue de l'Hippodrome and the Avenue de Picardie (then the Avenue d'Étaples). Here, there was a wood-framed shelter with a thatched roof which can only be described as rustic. This shelter is not at the site now, but on the other side of the road there is a concrete bus shelter with fake concrete wood, clearly made in its image.

Depots and workshops

The depot and electricity generating station was at Trépied, on the then main road to Paris-Plage soon after it had turned off the road from Étaples to Berck. This is now the beginning of the Avenue des Hêtres, just off what is now the D940, although on site the road is still also called the Avenue de l'Aéroport. In addition to the generating plant there was a tram shed here with workshop facilities. In 1910 the facilities were improved, and another tram shed was built across the road. This was a long building with three lines for parking trams. There was also a shelter for passengers at the *arrêt* at the depot.

Rolling stock

The maximum allowed width of the rolling stock was 1.90 metres. Seven SACM Thomson-Houston two-axle power tramcars were delivered in 1900 and numbered one to seven. The overhead pickups were of single arm trailing pantograph type. Access was by one set of corner steps for each end platform, enabling the driver to use the other corner. By 1912 there were also nine second class passenger trailers, mostly closed but a few open (*baladeuses*), and four baggage wagons (*fourgons*). Some wagons were also available for goods traffic. Four more power tramcars, similar except for additional side windows, were delivered later when traffic increased. The company also eventually had 12 passenger trailers.

Operations

At the beginning it was agreed that the maximum length of trains would be 25 metres, although mostly the service would be provided by a single tramcar 8 metres long. The maximum speed would be 20 kph for single tramcars, 16 kph with trailers, and in any case 6 kph in the town of Étaples and on the bridge over the Canche. The minimum service would be four each way per day.

We do not have details of the summer service on opening in 1900. From October 1900 there were five trams each way per day, the first starting from Étaples at 08.20 and the last arriving back there at 18.25. The journey time was 25 minutes. Fares at the time of opening were 60 centimes, first class and 50 centimes, second class for the whole journey.

By May 1914 there were 11 services in each direction. Of these, two in each direction indicated that luggage could not be carried; presumably they did not have a baggage wagon. The first tram left Étaples at 06.10 and the last service left Paris-Plage to return at 20.05. There was an additional service each way starting at Paris-Plage at 08.10 on

A tram and trailer headed towards Paris-Plage cross the bridge over the River Canche, with the town of Étaples in the background. Note the trailing pantograph pick-up. Undated but probably before World War I.   *Authors' Collection*

The *arrêt* beside the road in the forest at Le Touquet. The rustic shelter with thatched roof can be seen on the right. A tram and trailer are headed towards Étaples. Postcard postmarked 1905.
Éditions Mme Letort 'Aux Fantaisies', Paris-Plage; Authors' Collection

19 Le Touquet — La Forêt - Le Tramway   The Touquet — The Forest - The Tramway

Edit. Mme Letort « Aux Fantaisies » Paris-Plage

·22   LE TOUQUET-PARIS-PLAGE. — Les Phares et le Tramway. — LL.

A tram with enclosed passenger trailer, headed towards Étaples, passing in front of the two lighthouses at Paris-Plage. Postcard postmarked 1915.   *Éditions LL.; Authors' Collection*

The first station in the Rue de Paris at Paris-Plage. A tram with trailer and baggage van is waiting to depart for Étaples.   *Authors' Collection*

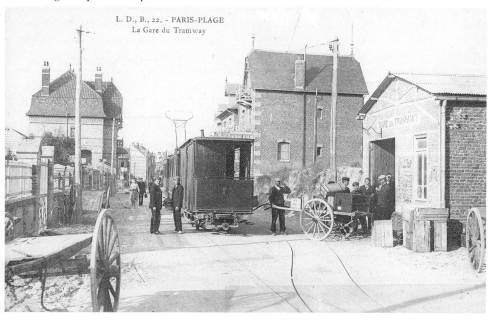

L. D., B., 22. - PARIS-PLAGE
La Gare du Tramway

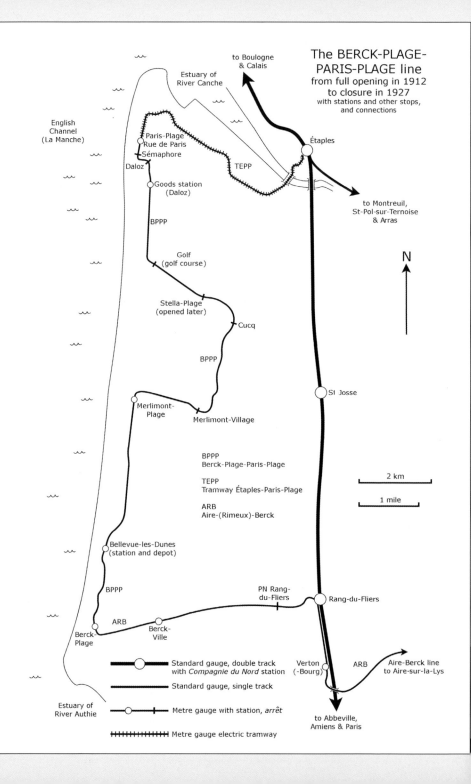

The BERCK-PLAGE-
PARIS-PLAGE line
from full opening in 1912
to closure in 1927
with stations and other stops,
and connections

to Boulogne
& Calais

Estuary of
River Canche

English
Channel
(La Manche)

Étaples

Paris-Plage
Rue de Paris
Sémaphore
Daloz
Goods station
(Daloz)

TEPP

to Montreuil,
St-Pol-sur-Ternoise
& Arras

BPPP

N

Golf
(golf course)

Stella-Plage
(opened later)

Cucq

BPPP

St Josse

Merlimont-
Plage

Merlimont-Village

BPPP
Berck-Plage-Paris-Plage

TEPP
Tramway Étaples-Paris-Plage

ARB
Aire-(Rimeux)-Berck

2 km

1 mile

Bellevue-les-Dunes
(station and depot)

BPPP

PN Rang-
du-Fliers

Rang-du-Fliers

ARB

Berck-
Plage

Berck-
Ville

Verton
(-Bourg)

ARB

Aire-Berck line
to Aire-sur-la-Lys

Standard gauge, double track
with *Compagnie du Nord* station

Standard gauge, single track

Metre gauge with station, *arrêt*

Metre gauge electric tramway

to Abbeville,
Amiens & Paris

Estuary of
River Authie

Tuesdays and Fridays which were market days in Étaples. Services were first and second class only. Some of the services would wait at Étaples for the arrival of main line trains if these were late. In the other direction connections to the main line were guaranteed it there was more than 10 minutes between the scheduled arrival of the tram and the departure of the train. Services increased in the high season, and from 27th June to 30th September 31 each way were scheduled. The first left Étaples at 05.15 and the last at 00.25.

In 1900, 42,950 people visited Paris-Plage, and by 1908 this figure had risen to 187,885. This shows the very rapid growth in the popularity of the resort which was becoming increasingly fashionable. During 1908 the tramway provided more than 180,000 passenger journeys.

From 1912 the line from Berck-Plage to Paris-Plage came to the station in the Rue de Paris. We do not know how many passengers used this connection. As is made clear in the section on the line to Berck-Plage, this service was seasonal and infrequent, and probably the numbers were relatively small (*see below*).

Berck-Plage to Paris-Plage

This rather unfortunate line was poorly conceived, its construction was slow, and its final opening was delayed until 1910. Then, as we shall see in later chapters, it was closed down for World War I only a few years after opening, struggled to get going again, and finally closed in 1927.

The possibility of a line along the coast to link the resorts of Berck-Plage, Merlimont-Plage and Le-Touquet-Paris-Plage had been under discussion from 1891, the year of the opening of the St-Justin, Montreuil to Berck-Plage section of the Aire-Berck line. M. Alfred Lambert, the entrepreneur behind the Aire-Berck line, requested a concession for such a line in that year, with a proposed length of 17 km (10½ miles). M. Lambert was already a part of the *Société des Dunes*, a group developing the area to the north of Berck-Plage, called Plage des Dunes. This area is still the northern limit of development of Berck-Plage. The area was subsequently known as Bellevue-les-Dunes, and also became known as Terminus. M. Lambert was refused the concession in 1891, with the Engineer of the *département* expressing reservations about the viability of the project outside the summer season. The town council of Étaples also opposed the scheme, as it was at that time pressing the case for a rail link from their town to Paris-Plage. However, M. Lambert did obtain permission to build a metre gauge line 2.15 km (1¼ miles) long from Berck-Plage station to Plage des Dunes for the purpose of bringing in materials for his building work.

M. Lambert then offered Étaples a link by horse tramway to his proposed line at Cucq via the hamlet of Trépied, but this did not find favour. Another plan was mooted, to take the proposed line from Berck-Plage to the south end of the bridge across the Canche at Étaples. There it would have met the tramway. This plan would have reduced the length of the proposed line to 13.2 km (8¼ miles). M. Lambert died in 1898. By arrangement with his widow, MM. Itasse and Roy took over the scheme and again applied for the concession in 1900, the year the tramway from Étaples to Paris-Plage was opened. M. Roy was a businessman from Étaples, an owner of a brickworks and a cement factory.

By this time the development at Plage des Dunes was proceeding, with roads laid out, and a hotel and a casino built. A 2 km railway line, probably the one conceded to M. Lambert in 1891, from Berck-Plage to Plage des Dunes, was in use from 1898 to bring passengers to the casino, which was linked with the main Berck casino at the *Kursaal*. There was by now a small passenger building and a siding at Plage des Dunes. However, all was not going well for the developers, now known as the *Société*

The track side of the second station at Berck-Plage. The post office is to the left and the separate goods building is just to the right of the passenger building, with the depot in the distance just to the left of the train. The reason why the train full of passengers is waiting well away from the platforms is not known. Undated.   *Authors' Collection*

The station at Merlimont-Plage, with a train headed towards Paris-Plage. The locomotive is the 0-6-0 Borsig tank engine built in 1910. Undated.   *Éditions Guébin; Authors' Collection*

Immobilière des Dunes, and they faced financial difficulties. They hoped that running their line on from the Plage des Dunes development to Merlimont and Paris-Plage would help them. They agreed in 1901 to sell the 2 km of line and the station at Plage des Dunes to MM. Itasse and Roy, and the transfer took place in 1902.

In 1906, M. Itasse was replaced by M. Berger, a property developer, who became the partner of M. Roy. The line was finally declared of *utilité publique* on 27th April, 1906. A company to build and operate the line was formed, the *Compagnie du Chemin de Fer de Berck-Plage à Paris-Plage*. Money was raised. The original estimate of costs had been 40,000 francs per km, or 760,000 francs in total. It was agreed that the *communes* of Berck, Merlimont and Cucq would between them pay 720 francs per year for 30 years. Various landowners and businesses contributed. Towards the end of 1906, a programme to raise 660,000 francs by selling 6,600 shares of 100 francs each was put in place, but the whole sum to build the line was not raised until 1910.

There continued to be trouble with various landowners, and particularly with the British 'Touquet Syndicate Ltd'. They had offices in London and were developing the golf course at Paris-Plage. The proposed line went across their proposed golf course. In the end the syndicate paid for a short extension of the line to go round, rather than through, part of the course.

Although the first section was already open and work was proceeding on most of the rest, a further sale of shares was mounted in April 1910. It had been agreed to raise an additional 220,000 francs of capital at a special general meeting of shareholders on 22nd July, 1909. The promotional brochure for the share sale is interesting. It emphasises the lack of any public transport along the coast to link the *jeunes plages* of Bellevue-les-Dunes, Merlimont, Golf-Plage (now Stella-Plage) and Mayville, now part of Paris-Plage. The virtues of these new resorts are extravagantly praised. In particular Bellevue is said to be 'becoming the aristocratic neighbourhood of Berck'. The sales pitch emphasises the rapid growth in the number of visitors to both Berck and Paris-Plage between 1900 and 1908. It even claims that the line would be used to bring materials to Paris-Plage for developments because the road and tramway bridge over the Canche at Étaples was not strong enough for such loads. The whole sale smacks of over-optimism with an undercurrent of desperation.

It is easier to see with hindsight what was perceived even by some people at the time, that the business case for the line was very poor. Looking at the map, no-one was likely to travel to Merlimont-Plage by changing trains at Rang-du-Fliers and again at Berck-Plage, or at Étaples and again at Paris-Plage. To make matters worse, the trains on the line were not very frequent, even in the summer. It was always likely that most of the traffic would be trippers from one resort to another on a very seasonal basis.

Building and opening the line

In February 1907, permission was given to proceed with preliminary works. The Engineer of the *département* objected strongly to the use of pine sleepers treated with copper sulphate, in view of the problems these had caused on the Aire-Berck line, and insisted on oak sleepers. By April 1908, rails and sleepers had arrived at the station at Terminus, as Plages des Dunes was now called. Confusingly, the official name for this station when the line was open was Bellevue-les-Dunes. The line was built from this end. There was much criticism from the shareholders about slow progress but the first section from Berck-Plage to Merlimont-Plage opened on 18th June, 1909, according to some reports, on 7th August according to others. The latter date is almost certainly the correct one, since it was the date reported to the shareholders meeting in June 1910, and also the start date of the first timetable. The former date may have arisen from confusion with the date of opening of the next section.

This section from Merlimont-Plage to the station at the Boulevard Daloz in Paris-Plage, by the junction with the Avenue de l'Atlantique, opened on 18th June, 1910. On 30th June, 1910, it was reported to a meeting of shareholders that the final 800 metres to the terminus of the tramway from Étaples in the Rue de Paris would be open by the end of the year. However, this proved even more difficult, with the residents on the south side of the Avenue de l'Atlantique complaining that the works obstructed their access, and they tried to have the work stopped, but failed. This final section opened on 28th July, 1912.

Description of the line

The sand dunes on the stretch of coast that runs from north of the Canche estuary to the Somme estuary form one of the most extensive dune areas in Europe. In places they are 3 km wide. This is the kind of area that the Berck-Plage-Paris-Plage line had to cross. There was and is no coast road, and the roads to the resorts come out individually to the sea even now. This will remain so because the large undeveloped areas are a unique natural environment and are now protected as such. The first continuous north-south road runs 2.5 to 3 km from the coast. Inland from this road is a strip of *marais* (marshland) 2 km deep, with the main railway line from Abbeville to Boulogne running on its inland edge. Beyond are the low hills towards Montreuil. The dunes presented a difficult challenge to those wishing to build and maintain a railway. Experience proved this to be the case. The impermanence of the dune landscape, where features can disappear in a single winter, makes parts of the line almost impossible to trace on the ground 80 years after closure.

The line began at the station of Berck-Plage, which belonged to the Aire-Berck line. It ran in its own path north through Berck to the station at Bellevue-les-Dunes. For just under 1 km, it ran along what is now the Boulevard de la Manche, in its own path with the road running on either side. From Bellevue the line went inland slightly and then straight north, parallel to the sea for 4 km, through the sand dunes, to Merlimont-Plage.

From Merlimont-Plage station, the line turned inland for 2 km along the verge of the road from Merlimont-Plage to Merlimont-Village, then turned north again through the dunes just west of the 'coast' road for 3 km to Cucq. At Cucq it turned towards the sea and ran past the inner end of what is now Stella-Plage but was then almost undeveloped. The line finally turned north, parallel to the sea 500 metres inland, through dunes again, skirting the golf course. This brought it, at 5 km from Cucq, to the south end of Paris-Plage close to the junction of the Boulevard Daloz and the Avenue de l'Atlantique. From here, the last stretch of just under 1 km took it up the verge of the Avenue de l'Atlantique towards the sea. Finally, running in the road, the line took the Rue de Paris, parallel to the sea, to the terminus of the electric tramway from Étaples. The total length of the line as built was 17.2 km (10¾ miles).

Engineering

The single track metre gauge line was constructed with its own formation except for the last section into Paris-Plage. The line was constructed of Vignole rails of 20 kg per metre except for the end section in the road at Paris-Plage, which used rails of 25-30 kg per metre. Presumably, in the light of the comments of the Engineer, oak sleepers were used.

The maximum gradient was 2.5 per cent, and the maximum radius of curvature 100 metres. One of the problems identified for the last section, from Daloz station to the Tramway terminus in the Rue de Paris, was that the Avenue de l'Atlantique was quite steep for a railway, as it went uphill towards the sea over what had originally been dunes. Also, there was said to be quite a sharp turn from there into the Rue de Paris. It is possible therefore that the statements above about the maximum gradient and curvature only apply to the line from Berck-Plage to Daloz (Paris-Plage).

There were no bridges. There were a number of level crossings but as far as we know none had gates. There was a turntable at Berck-Plage, and there were passing loops at Bellevue-les-Dunes, Merlimont-Plage, Paris-Plage (Marchandises) and Paris-Plage (Daloz). There may have been others. There was also a passing loop at the tramway station at the Rue de Paris, but whether this was shared with the trams or whether it was separate we do not know. It was remarked at the time that this arrangement meant that the engine had to haul the train out backwards for 1.2 km to the goods station, where there was another turntable. This seems an odd comment to British observers, for whom the usual single line practice is for tank locomotives to 'run-round' on a loop and then haul the train backwards for the whole length of the line.

Stations and Depots

A list of the stations and other stops on the Berck-Plage-Paris-Plage line is given in *Table Fifteen*. At Berck-Plage the line used the facilities of the Aire-Berck line. There were two stations with substantial buildings, at Bellevue-les-Dunes and Merlimont-Plage. These were handsome two-storey brick stations with brickwork designs and the station name picked out on the ends. Only that at Merlimont-Plage survives, and on that the brickwork is covered up on one side and at the ends. However, the brickwork on the former track side can still be admired. There was a goods station at Paris-Plage about 1 km south of the station at Daloz, which had a smaller but similarly attractive brick building. The initial terminus at Paris-Plage (Daloz) was only temporary and had a small shelter. From 1912, the line used the terminal station of the Tramway from Étaples in the Rue de Paris at Paris-Plage. Daloz was reduced to the status of an *arrêt*.

Table Fifteen
Berck-Plage to Paris-Plage, stations and other stops

Name	Type	Distance km	Altitude m	ft)
Berck-Plage	Aire-Berck (shared)	0	7	(23)
Bellevue-les-Dunes	Station and depot	2.2	9	
Merlimont-Plage	Station	6.1	9	
Merlimont-Village	*Arrêt*	8.3	12	
Cucq	*Arrêt*	10.8	5	
Stella-Plage	*Arrêt**	11.9		
Golf	*Arrêt*	13.4	12	
Paris-Plage (Marchandises)	Goods station†	16.0	6	
Paris-Plage (Daloz)	*Arrêt*#			
Sémaphore	*Arrêt*§			
Paris-Plage (Rue de Paris)	Étaples-Paris-Plage tramway station § (shared)	17.2	12	(39)

Distances - All distances are from Berck-Plage
Heights in feet given only for the line ends
* From 1922 or later
† Only shown on timetables until 1912
# Terminus until 1912
§ From 1912

The path of the former Berck-Plage-Paris-Plage line just behind Merlimont-Village in October 2006, looking towards Paris-Plage. This is 3 km from the sea but still within the belt of dunes.

Authors

The track side of the station at Merlimont-Plage in August 2006. This shows the attractive brick work. The other three sides of the building, including the station name at each end, have been covered over. This was the tourist information centre until recently but is now boarded up. The extension on the right is newer and part of a school. *Authors*

The depot and workshop of the line was at Bellevue-les-Dunes. There was space in the depot for four locomotives on two tracks, with a fire pit on one for two locomotives, but no inspection pit. Workshop facilities were for minor running repairs only, and more major work was contracted out, probably to the Aire-Berck depot at Berck-Plage. There was no covered storage for other rolling stock anywhere on the line.

There were *arrêts* at Merlimont-Village, at Cucq, and at 'Golf', by the golf course. There was also an *arrêt* at the corner of the Rue de Paris in Paris-Plage, called Sémaphore. After 1922 there was also an *arrêt* at Stella-Plage, when this resort had been developed. There were shelters at Merlimont-Village and later at Stella-Plage, and probably at other *arrêts* as well.

Locomotives

A 0-4-0 Corpet locomotive, of very old-fashioned appearance and unusual driving coupling, was brought by the contractors from La Rochelle for the construction of the line. This locomotive also provided a back-up until the company acquired locomotives in 1910. The company acquired two 0-6-0 tank locomotives, one built by *Decauville Aîné à Petit Bourg* in 1908, and the other built by Borsig (Germany) in 1910. The Decauville was not authorized for service until October 1910, when it was given the number 1. The Borsig, given the number 2, may have been authorized for use earlier in 1910 but we do not have a date. It was certainly in service on 18th August, 1910, when it derailed. We do not know how the limited summer service was provided in 1909; perhaps by the 0-4-0 Corpet, or perhaps by a borrowed locomotive.

In 1911, permission to put a further, rented, locomotive in service was refused by the *département*, on the grounds that the regulations for the line required continuous braking, which this locomotive did not have. We do not know the identity of this locomotive. In 1912 the company acquired two 2-6-0 tank locomotives built by the *Société de la Meuse* at Liège (Belgium), with permission to put them into service in October that year. They were numbered 3 and 4.

Table Sixteen		
Technical details of some Berck-Plage-Paris-Plage locomotives up to 1914		
Manufacturer	Decauville	La Meuse
Year(s) of manufacture	1908	1912
Type	0-6-0T	2-6-0T
Company No(s)	1	3 & 4
Year(s) put in service	1910	1912
No. put in service	1	2
Length (m)	6.08	
Weight empty (tonnes)	11.5	20
Weight loaded (tonnes)	15	25
Wheelbase (m)	1.72	
Dia. of driving wheels (m)	0.80	1.00
Boiler capacity (m^3)	1.075	1.700
Boiler pressure (kg/cm^2)	12	12
Heating surface (m^2)	25.85	45
Water capacity (L)	1700	
Coal capacity (kg)	400	
Dia. of valves (mm)	30	50
Dia. of pistons (m)	0.25	0.30
Piston travel (m)	0.32	0.45

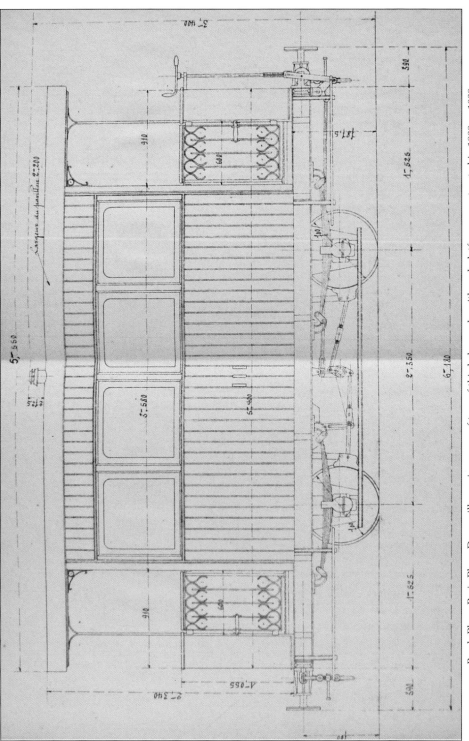

Berck-Plage-Paris-Plage Decauville carriage, one of two of third class only with end platforms constructed in 1908 or 1909.

Technical details of some of the steam locomotives acquired by the Berck-Plage-Paris-Plage line up to 1914 are shown in *Table Sixteen (see page 129)*. The Decauville locomotive seems rather underpowered, and those from La Meuse were clearly larger and more powerful. We do not have any further details of the Corpet and Borsig locomotives. A full motive power list for all the lines in this book is given in *Appendix One*.

Other rolling stock

The company had originally intended to buy two 30 hp 4-cylinder petrol-engined railcars from Decauville. These would have been 5.4 metres long, and would have provided 16 seats in one class, or 12 in two classes, and platform space for 9 standing. This plan was abandoned when Decauville were unable to provide any prolonged guarantees for these.

The passenger carriages were constructed by Decauville in 1908 and 1909, and all had two axles (four wheels). There were four mixed first and second class carriages with a central entrance platform, each for five first class passengers, 10 second class, and space for five standing on the platform. There were two third class carriages with end entrance platforms, each with 16 seats and space for 12 standing on the platforms. Also there were two third class carriages with open sides and curtains known as *tapissières* (from *tapis*, a carpet or rug); these had 20 seats and could take 14 standing. The curtains were of red and white drill. There were two baggage vans (*fourgons*). For goods, the line had two covered wagons, and two high-sided and four low-sided open wagons.

In 1911 permission to put a further carriage, purchased second-hand, in service was refused by the *département*, on the grounds that the carriage was likely to be unstable in use. This was a 2-axle carriage of total length 8 metres, but with only two metres between the axles.

Operations

In respect of the sharing of the station at Berck-Plage, it was agreed that all station services would be provided by the *Compagnie d'Anvin*. The costs would be apportioned with the Aire-Berck line in proportion to the number of trains of each company. In 1910 and 1911 the payment to the Aire-Berck company was 67 francs and 25 centimes. In view of the small number of trains on the Berck-Plage-Paris-Plage line, this seemed a very favourable arrangement for this line. However, the reality was that the trains on the Aire-Berck line always had priority for the use of the station facilities, and the trains on the Paris-Plage line sometimes just had to wait. The Manager of the line took this up with the town council of Berck and then with the *Préfet* of the *département*. In 1911 the town council of Berck agreed to a local tax, added to tickets and goods charges on the line, to help pay for an extra platform at Berck-Plage for the use of passengers on this line.

On opening in 1909, the line operated only from 7th August to 30th September, from Berck-Plage to Merlimont-Plage. The journey time was 20 minutes. Initially seven trains each way were operated on weekdays, with 11 on Sundays and holidays, but the September weather was so poor that the service was reduced to six each way per day. Nevertheless the company reported that more than 10,000 passengers had been carried in this first season.

From summer 1910, the line operated all the way to Paris-Plage (Daloz), and the service continued all year, although it was much reduced in the winter. In 1910, there were eight trains each way in the summer and four in the autumn. In the winter of 1910 to 1911 (*Table Seventeen*), there were planned to be two trains each way per day along the whole line, one in the morning and one in the afternoon, with an additional train in the middle of the day from Berck-Plage to Merlimont-Plage and back. However, all but one train each way was marked ominously on the timetable 'for trial purposes and only until further notice'. It has been stated by one source that in the event only one train ran each way per day in the winters of 1910 and after, so perhaps the other services were axed as threatened. The winter service was entirely composed of mixed passenger and goods trains. There were good connections at Berck-Plage for the trains that did run. For instance, arriving at Berck-Plage on the 10.41 train, the Aire-Berck train left at 11.15 and by changing at Rang-du-Fliers onto the *Nord* main line one could be in Boulogne at 12.18, Amiens at 14.55 and Paris at 16.40. At Paris-Plage, the trams to Étaples were quite frequent, where one could also get the *Nord* trains, on the main line from Paris to Calais, or inland towards Arras. There was a walk of 800 metres to the tram when the line finished at Daloz, but from 1912 the trains went into the terminus of the tramway

Table Seventeen
Timetables – Berck-Plage to Le-Touquet-Paris-Plage

1st November, 1910 to 30th April, 1911

								(1)	(2)
Berck-Plage	dep.	08.10	11.25	14.30	arr.	10.41	14.20	18.24	19.49
Bellevue-les-Dunes	arr.	08.17	11.32	14.37	dep.	10.34	14.13	18.17	19.42
	dep.	08.18	11.33	14.38	arr.	10.33	14.12	18.15	19.41
Merlimont-Plage	arr.	08.34	11.49	14.54	dep.	10.17	13.58	17.59	19.25
	dep.	08.35		14.55	arr.	10.16		17.58	19.24
Merlimont-Village	arrêt	08.43		15.03		10.09		17.51	19.17
Cucq	arrêt	08.51		15.11		10.01		17.43	19.09
Golf	arrêt	08.59		15.19		09.53		17.35	19.01
Paris-Plage	arr.	09.09		15.29	dep,	09.42		17.24	18.50
(Marchandises)	dep.	09.12		15.32	arr.	09.39		17.21	18.47
Paris-Plage (Daloz)	arr.	09.14		15.34	dep.	09.37		17.19	18.45

(1) 1st November to 31st January.   (2) 1st February to 30th April.

May 1914

			(1)				(1)	
Berck-Plage	dep.	07.40	13.35	16.25	arr.	10.15	16.10	19.00
Bellevue-les-Dunes		07.48	13.43	16.33		10.07	16.02	18.52
Merlimont-Plage		08.03	13.58	16.48		09.52	15.47	18.37
Merlimont-Village	arrêt	08.11	14.06	16.56		09.44	15.39	18.29
Cucq	arrêt	08.22	14.17	17.07		09.33	15.28	18.18
Golf	arrêt	08.30	14.25	17.15		09.25	15.20	18.10
Daloz	arrêt	08.45	14.40	17.30		09.10	15.05	17.55
Sémaphore	arrêt	08.48	14.43	17.33		09.07	15.02	17.52
Paris-Plage (Rue de Paris)	arr.	08.50	14.45	17.35	dep.	09.05	15.00	17.50

(1) From 31st May.

By 1st May, 1911, there were four trains each way per day over the whole line, with additional trains between Berck-Plage and Merlimont-Plage. This included one very late service running at 00.30 hrs. This train ran on Sundays and holidays from 25th June to the beginning of October, but every day in August. It picked up passengers from the train arriving at Berck-Plage from Rang-du-Fliers at 00.26, which had in turn picked up passengers from the evening train from Paris at Rang.

In 1910, the fare for the whole length of the line was 1 franc 80 centimes first class, 1 franc 35 centimes second class and exactly 1 franc third class. The open carriages were only used in the summer season. The journey time for the whole line was 1 hour and 4 minutes to Daloz and 1 hour and 10 minutes to the Rue de Paris.

In the winter of 1911-1912 the line only carried an average of three first and 13 second class passengers per month! Something needed to be done and in 1913 permission was obtained to have a combined first and second class compartment in one of the third class closed carriages. This allowed a single carriage train between 1st November and 31st March. By May 1914 (*Table Seventeen*) there were only two trains per day in each direction even at the beginning of the season, one in the morning and one in the afternoon. A third train in the late afternoon and early evening was run from 31st May, but we do not know if any further additional trains were run in the high season.

From the beginning the sand was a major problem. To save costs the dunes beside the line had not been adequately planted with *oyats*. This is the Picardy name for a type of grass used to stabilise sand dunes. Blown about by the wind the sand was always covering the line and great efforts were required to keep it clear, especially in the winter when the winds were stronger. In addition, the sand proved to be a poor base for the ballasted track. Also the blown sand got into the pistons and other mechanical parts of the locomotives and had an abrasive effect, despite constant efforts by the crews to keep the locomotives clean and sand free. The first derailment occurred on 18th August, 1910, when the Borsig locomotive left the track between Bellevue-les-Dunes and Merlimont-Plage at a reported speed of 20 km/hour (12½ mph). Eight carriages and wagons were damaged, but fortunately there were only two people with minor injuries. The Commission of Enquiry came to no definite conclusion as to the cause but some blamed the sand.

Another problem was that cows wandered onto the line especially in the area of Cucq, and in 1911 the company had brought this to the attention of the Mayor. Despite this, on 29th September, 1912, a locomotive was derailed in this area in a collision with a cow. The cow was killed. The owner of the cow claimed that the animal had been able to pass through the barbed wire protecting this part of the line, and pointed to hair on the wire. The company stated that the cow could not have passed through the wire at that point, and that the hair was not hers. Presumably they thought the cow must have been loose at an open level crossing and wandered onto the line there. The cow's owner claimed 500 francs, the company claimed the same sum for damage to the locomotive, and there the matter rested.

From 1911, the town council of Merlimont pursued with the company the possibility of extending the line inland from Merlimont-Village to the station at St-Josse, on the *Nord* main line between Rang and Étaples. This was turned down in 1912 by the *Compagnie du Nord*. This had been a sensible proposal as this would have been the shortest route to Merlimont from the main line.

And so this line, which had come late on the scene, with a poor business case and probably poor management, and which was clearly already struggling, was in no shape to face the disaster of World War I on 2nd August, 1914.

Tramways of Le-Touquet-Paris-Plage

In addition to the electric tramway from Étaples, and the steam railway from Berck-Plage, there were also two 60 cm gauge tramways at Paris-Plage. We mention them here for the sake of completeness, and to avoid any confusion between these and the metre gauge lines. The original proposals included at least four lines, but only two were built.

A self-propelled petrol tramcar on the 60 cm tramway in the Avenue St-Jean at Le-Touquet-Paris-Plage. Undated, but the dress indicates before World War I.
Éditions LL; Authors' Collection

Agreement to build at least one of these lines was reached in 1909. Both lines were probably opened soon after, and operated by the *Société des automobiles sur Rails de Paris-Plage*. The first line began near the Casino and ran the length of the Rue St-Jean to the esplanade, then turning onto the esplanade for a short distance. In this way it linked the Casino and nearby large hotels with the beach along one of the main streets. The length was just over 1 km, and the service was provided by two-axle petrol-driven tramcars. The line crossed the electric tramway to Étaples where the Rue St-Jean met the Rue de Paris.

The second, known as the Tramway du Golf, began at the end of the what was then the Avenue des Anglais (now the Avenue du Général de Gaulle) by the roundabout at the Casino. It followed the Avenue des Anglais as far as the road to Cucq (now the Avenue François Godin), and then along this to the Avenue du Golf, which it turned into and ended close to the Golf Club House. The length was 2 km (1¼ miles). The service on this line up to World War I was also provided by petrol driven tramcars. After the war, closed or open trailer cars, most likely converted from the original power cars, were pulled by an open diesel locomotive.

The second line lasted longer than the first, and the first may not have reopened after World War I. The second is still present on maps of the middle 1920s, but it probably closed in 1925 or 1926.

Dannes-Camier to Ste-Cécile-Plage

This 60 cm gauge horse-drawn tramway ran in the verge of the road from the station at Dannes-Camier, on the main line 8 km north of Étaples, to the small resort of Ste-Cécile-Plage. Originally constructed to take building materials to the resort, it was 3 km long and lasted from 1898 to 1914.

Lines proposed but never built

Bruay to Aire and Fruges

In 1913, detailed plans were produced for a metre gauge electric tramway from Bruay-la-Buissière to Aire-sur-la-Lys. It was also proposed to extend the electrification from Aire along the existing line towards Berck as far as Fruges. This would have involved an enlargement of the facilities at Fruges station, and a rather grandiose design for a new station building. The proposals had not proceeded beyond planning by the beginning of World War I, and were not picked up again after the war.

Dompierre-sur-Authie to Hesdin and Wailly-Beaucamp

As early as 1883, there was a proposal to build a standard gauge line along the Authie valley, inland from the coast main line at Conchil-le-Temple to Auxi-le-Chateau, which was on the standard gauge line from Abbeville to Frévent. It was felt that there was too little industry in the valley to support this.

The western part of the metre gauge *Réseau de la Somme* included a line from Abbeville north through the Forest of Crécy to a terminus at Dompierre-sur-Authie, which opened in 1892. The old station there is now a private house but can still be seen. At Forêt l'Abbaye this line was joined by another from Noyelles. Dompierre is on the boundary between the *départements* of Somme and Pas-de-Calais, the boundary being the River Authie for most of its length.

In 1892 M. Lambert, the entrepreneur of the Aire-Berck line, brought forward detailed plans for two lines which would be linked to the Somme network at Dompierre. One would go north-east across the plateau between the river Authie and the river Canche to Hesdin on the standard gauge line from Étaples to Arras. There would have been stations at Raye-sur-Authie, Guigny, and Lequesnoy, and the line would have been 17 km (10½ miles) long.

The second line would have left Dompierre station and crossed the Authie with the first, then turned north-west along the valley on the Pas-de-Calais side, with stations at Tortefontaine, Douriez and Saulchoy. From Saulchoy it would have turned away from the river to a station at St-Rémy-au-Bois, then climbed onto the plateau between the Authie and the Canche. Further stations were at Campagne-les-Hesdin, Buire-le-Sec and Bois-Jean, before the line joined the Aire-Berck line just east of the station at Wailly. The total length was 26 km (16 miles). An alternative in 1910 took the second line all the way along the Authie valley to Berck. This line would have crossed the main line along the coast just north of the station at Conchil-le-Temple.

None of these lines made progress beyond planning before World War I. After that war they remained on the list, and the plans for the Dompierre-Wailly line were brought out again in 1926. However, no further lines were built in the area, and in 1925 the line from Dompierre to Hesdin was at the bottom of the Departmental Engineer's priority list.

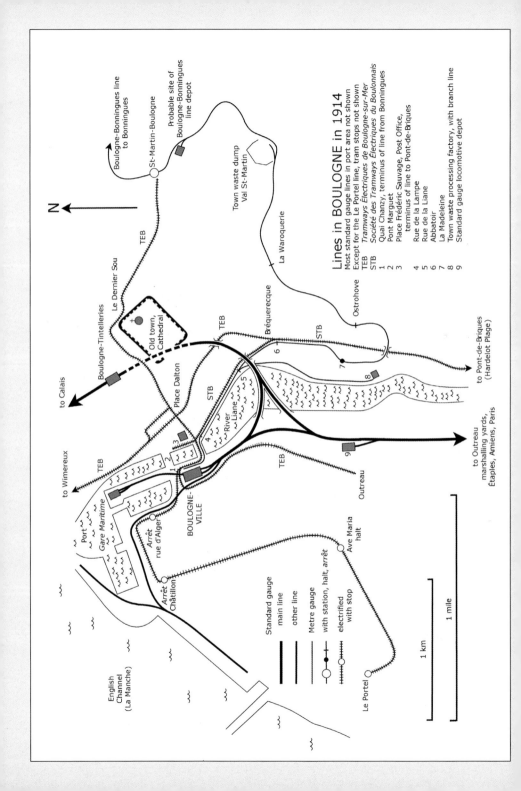

Lines in BOULOGNE in 1914

Most standard gauge lines in port area not shown
Except for the Le Portel line, tram stops not shown
TEB   *Tramways Électriques de Boulogne-sur-Mer*
STB   *Société des Tramways Électriques du Boulonnais*
1   Quai Chanzy, terminus of line from Bonningues
2   Pont Marguet
3   Place Frédéric Sauvage, Post Office,
    terminus of line to Pont-de-Briques
4   Rue de la Lampe
5   Rue de la Liane
6   Abbatoir
7   La Madeleine
8   Town waste processing factory, with branch line
9   Standard gauge locomotive depot

N

to Calais

Boulogne-Bonningues line to Bonningues

Probable site of Boulogne-Bonningues line depot

St-Martin-Boulogne

TEB

Le Dernier Sou

Town waste dump
Val St-Martin

La Waroquerie

Old town,
Cathedral

Boulogne-Tintelleries

Ostrohove

TEB

Bréquerecque

STB

to Pont-de-Briques
(Hardelot Plage)

Place Dalton

STB

River Liane

to Wimereux

TEB

Port

Gare Maritime

Arrêt rue d'Alger

BOULOGNE-
VILLE

Arrêt
Châtillon

TEB

Outreau

Ave Maria
halt

to Outreau
marshalling yards,
Étaples, Amiens, Paris

English Channel
(La Manche)

Le Portel

Standard gauge
main line

other line

Metre gauge

with station, halt, *arrêt*

electrified
with stop

1 km

1 mile

Chapter Four

The Line from Boulogne to Bonningues and Boulogne to Le Portel up to 1914
and related and competing lines and tramways

In 1890, the *Compagnie des Chemins de Fer Économiques du Nord* (CEN) was given permission to build three metre gauge lines in the *département* of Pas-de-Calais. Two were linked, those from Le Portel, a suburb of Boulogne, to the main station in Boulogne, and from Boulogne station to Bonningues-lès-Ardres on the Anvin to Calais line, with plans to run through to Tournehem on that line. These two were often just referred to in documentation, and especially early documentation, as the *Chemin de fer du Portel à Boulogne, Bonningues et Tournehem*. The third line, from Frévent to Lens in the eastern Pas-de-Calais, and completely separated from the others, was opened in 1895 but is beyond the scope of this book.

In practice, the part of the line from Boulogne to Le Portel was operated entirely separately from the part from Boulogne to Bonningues. Until the part of the line from Boulogne-Ville to St-Martin-Boulogne was opened in May 1902, the two parts were not joined. The line from Boulogne to Le Portel was electrified, run as a tramway, and the operation handed over to the Boulogne tramways. We have therefore put the Boulogne to le Portel line in a different section from the rest of the line. From 1914 onwards, discussion of the line to Le Portel is included with the Tramways of Boulogne in Chapter Five.

Boulogne-Ville station and the development and arrangement of standard gauge lines in Boulogne have already been described in Chapter One.

Boulogne to Bonningues

Building and opening

From 1883 onwards various plans for the Le Portel-Boulogne-Bonningues lines were discussed. It seems to have been decided at an early stage that the line from Boulogne to Bonningues must go through the large suburb of Boulogne called St-Martin-Boulogne (or St Martin-de-Boulogne), which is on the hill east of central Boulogne at an altitude of 114 metres (374 ft). Boulogne-Ville station was right by the port and only a few metres above sea level. The straight line distance between the two was 2.3 km (1½ miles), which was too short, and the hill too steep, for the train to take any direct route, unlike the trams of the *Tramways Électriques de Boulogne-sur-Mer*, which from 1901 went almost straight up the hill from central Boulogne to St-Martin. The solution for the railway was to take a circuitous route and this extra journey time was ultimately to prove an economic disaster. The initial discussions centred around two alternative routes leaving Boulogne to the north through Terlincthun. The finally adopted route, however, left Boulogne to the south and then climbed the hill along the

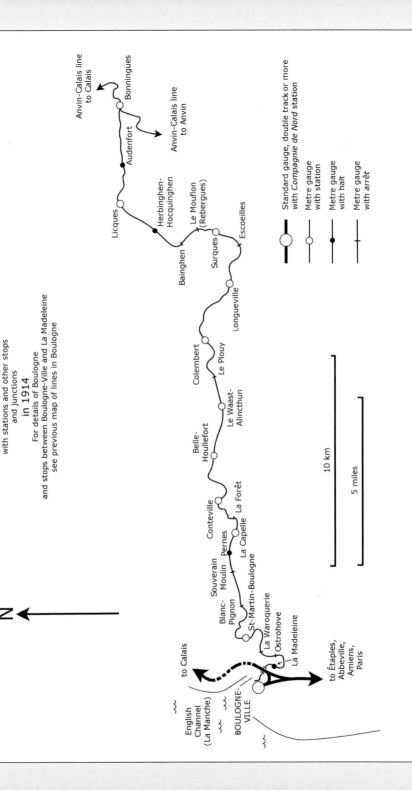

The BOULOGNE-BONNINGUES line
with stations and other stops
and junctions
in 1914
For details of Boulogne
and stops between Boulogne-Ville and La Madeleine
see previous map of lines in Boulogne

N

Anvin-Calais line
to Calais

Bonningues

Audenfort

Anvin-Calais line
to Anvin

Herbinghen-
Hocquinghen

Licques

Le Mouflon
(Rebergues)

Bainghen

Surques

Escoeilles

Longueville

Colembert

Le Plouy

Le Waast-
Alincthun

Belle-
Houllefort

Conteville

La Forêt

Pernes

La Capelle

Souverain
Moulin

Blanc-
Pignon

St-Martin-Boulogne

La Waroquerie

Ostrohove

La Madeleine

to Calais

English
Channel
(La Manche)

BOULOGNE-
VILLE

to Étaples,
Abbeville,
Amiens,
Paris

10 km

5 miles

Standard gauge, double track or more
with *Compagnie de Nord* station

Metre gauge
with station

Metre gauge
with halt

Metre gauge
with *arrêt*

south side of the Val St-Martin. The total distance was 6.1 km (3¾ miles) for the south route as built. It would have been even further at 8 km (5 miles) by the north routes. At the other end, the option of the line going from Licques to join the Anvin-Calais line at Tournehem rather than Bonningues was also discussed.

The line from St-Martin-Boulogne to Bonningues (37 km, 23 miles) was opened on 22nd April, 1900. The section from Le Portel to Boulogne-Ville station (4 km, 2½ miles) was opened on 16th August, 1900 (*see separate section on this part of the line*). The linking section from Boulogne-Ville to St-Martin-Boulogne was opened two years later on 12th May, 1902, making the total length from Boulogne-Ville to Bonningues 43 km (26¾ miles).

Description of the line

The principal line ran in general east-north-east from Boulogne to Bonningues, but like the other lines in this book was quite tortuous in its route, as shown by its length of 43 km (26 miles) for a straight line distance of 30 km (18½ miles). The determinants of this were the same as for the other lines. The line provided a service for the hinterland east of Boulogne, known as the Boulonnais. Once the suburbs of Boulogne were left behind the line ran within what is now the *Parc Naturel Régional des Caps et Marais d'Opale*, and this is still very attractive countryside.

Starting on the east side of Boulogne-Ville station, on the Quai Chanzy, the line had a separate line from the urban tramway across the Pont de la Lampe (also known as the Pont de la Liane (1923 map) or the Pont de l'Écluse (*Baedeker* 1905), and now the Pont de l'Entente Cordiale). It then followed the Rue Pierre Daunou south-east, following the road under the through railway to join the Rue de Brequerecque. At La Madeleine, it left the main road to the west along what is now the Rue André Marie Ampère, but very quickly turned south, where there was a halt called La Madeleine. So far it had run in the road from Boulogne-Ville station, but from here it had its own path. After running parallel with the main road for 300-400 metres it turned east and crossed the main road, the Route de Paris (N1), on a bridge.

The line had started to climb at La Madeleine where the main road goes uphill, and the climb now continued all the way to St-Martin-Boulogne. Turning north and then north-east after the bridge, the line climbed along the south side of the Val St-Martin through Ostrohove and La Waroquerie. Finally it curved west around the top of the valley to complete the climb by joining the Route de Desvres just before its junction with the Route de St-Omer, and crossing both into St-Martin station at 114.4 metres (374 ft).

From St-Martin the line took a long half circle round the St-Martin plateau to the north, before gradually descending to Le Blanc Pignon, at 97 metres (318 ft). This is now very near the motorway junction with the main St-Omer road (N42). The line then ran east along, or close to, the old St-Omer road, now partly replaced by a modern dual carriageway which serves as a bypass to the villages along the way. Just before La Capelle the line regained its own path, at first south of the N42 and then northwards to cross the northern edge of the forest of Boulogne on its way to Conteville. It returned to the old main road at Le Waast-Alincthun station, but then soon again had its own path first one side of the old road then the other. It had also lost height to 52 metres (171 ft) at Le Waast, but after this was soon climbing again to the south-east along the slope of a chalk escarpment. The highest point of these hills is Mont St-Sylvestre at 199.4 metres (654 ft). In the 3 km (1¾ miles) from Le Waast the line

Boulogne Central station (Boulogne-Ville) and the hotel Louvre-Terminus seen across the inner port with the Pont Marguet on the right. The Quai Chanzy is in front of the station and the hotel. A tram is crossing in front of the station going to or from Outreau or Le Portel.
Édition Fauchois, Béthune; Authors' Collection

The same scene in 2006. Both the station and the hotel were destroyed in World War II, and the Pont Marguet has been widened, but the bridge bastions and the bollard are still there.   *Authors*

The station at La Capelle in 2006, now business premises. *Authors*

The Anvin-Calais type 2 station at Bonningues in 2007. This was the junction with the line from Boulogne from 1900, and the lines from Boulogne and from Anvin entered the station from the direction from which the photograph has been taken. The former engine shed and small depot is on the left. *Authors*

The station at Belle-Houllefort in 2006. Now a private house, much of the rendering has been removed to show the underlying brick. *Authors*

The station at Licques. A Blanc-Misseron 0-6-0 *bicabine* tank locomotive is heading a passenger train in the direction of Boulogne. This station is now a private house and the lavatory block in the foreground has been demolished. Postcard postmarked 1904. *Authors' Collection*

The halt at Herbinghen-Hocquinghen in 2006. This is the only recognisable surviving halt building on the Boulogne-Bonningues line.   *Authors*

The crossing cottage at Le Plouy, between Le Waast-Alincthun and Colembert, in 2007. This was one of the places where the line crossed the old main road from Bouloge to St-Omer.   *Authors*

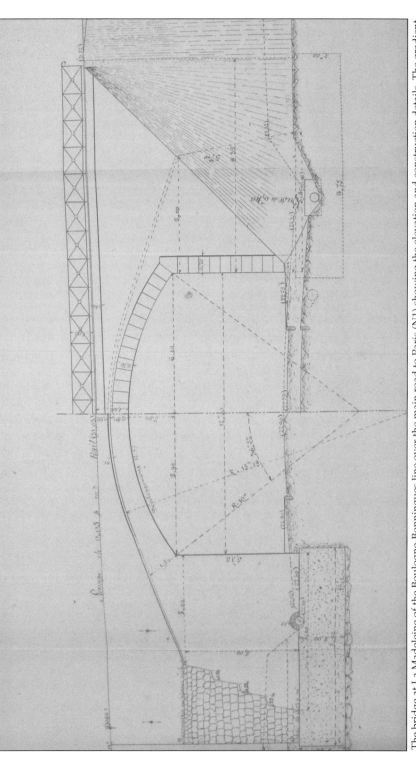

The bridge at La Madeleine of the Boulogne-Bonningues line over the main road to Paris (N1) showing the elevation and construction details. The gradient is obvious with Boulogne to the left and St-Martin-Boulogne to the right.

had climbed to 114 metres (374 ft) at Colembert, and reached the highest point at 136 metres (447 ft) between Longueville and Surques. From here it turned north and gradually descended towards Licques at 67 metres (220 ft), in the valley of the Hem. Licques is a substantial town of the high Boulonnais famous for its chickens, and has a large elevated church which is a major landmark in the area. From Licques the line ran east down the valley. It finally climbed a little again through a cutting to join the line from Anvin which curved in from the right (south) just before the station at Bonningues, a village notable only for its status as a former railway junction.

Engineering

As indicated above, the line to Bonningues ran mostly on its own formation but there were sections alongside roads, each of a few kilometres, between Blanc Pignon and La Capelle and again around Le Waast. In addition, about 2 km ran in the road in Boulogne, from Boulogne-Ville station to La Madeleine. The metre gauge single track used Vignole rails at 21 kg/m except for the road-running section. This probably used tram type rails from Marsillon or Broca at 45 kg/m, because these were the rails used for the longer road running sections of the Lens-Frévent railway built in 1895 by the same company.

In general, the line and station areas in the rural sections resembled those of the Anvin-Calais and Aire-Berck lines. We do not have exact figures for the minimum curvatures for this line, but there were certainly curves down to 100 metres radius. The average gradient, calculated from the height and distance line profile, in the area of Boulogne between La Madeleine and St-Martin was 2.2 per cent, the line climbing 94 metres (309 ft) in 4.3 km (about 2¾ miles). The next steepest average gradient was of 1.8 per cent for 3.5 km (2¼ miles) between Le Waast-Alincthun and Colembert. However, we know that for short distances some of the gradients were greater than this: at the bridge over the Route de Paris at La Madeleine and through the cutting as far as the *arrêt* at Ostrohove, for 460 metres, the gradient was 3 per cent.

Also, as on the other lines, there were frequent level crossings. As far as we know none had gates. There were, in 1901, 150 in total between St-Martin-Boulogne and Bonningues, including private and pedestrian only crossings, and 37 of these were in category 1, on the more important public roads. After leaving the road running section at La Madeleine, 28 were over roads large enough for the crossing to be shown on the 1930 1/200,000 Michelin map.

The line used the road bridge to cross the Liane on leaving Boulogne-Ville station. This bridge had to be strengthened on one side to take the steam line, but not on the other side of the road to take the lighter trams. In the Boulevard Beaucerf, the line also ran in the road under the bridge carrying the standard gauge line to Calais. Both these bridges were destroyed in World War II and rebuilt.

The use of a bridge over the Route de Paris (the N1) at La Madeleine was probably attributable to the need to gain height towards St-Martin rather than to avoid disruption in the road. This bridge was an arch faced with stone and brick, with an opening 7.35 metres high and 12 metres wide. There were metal railings along the top beside the railway. This bridge was also destroyed in the fighting in 1944 but was not rebuilt (*see Chapter Seven*). Between this bridge and the *arrêt* at Ostrohove, an elegant metal footbridge was constructed over the deep cutting. The only other significant bridge on the line was that over the river Hem just east of Audenfort, which was of *tablier métallique* type.

Stations

The stations on the line, and other stops, are listed in *Table Eighteen*. At Boulogne-Ville, the trains to Bonningues stopped in the road outside the station, on the Quai Chanzy, and we have no evidence of any facilities here. Presumably passengers used the lavatories, and perhaps also the ticket office, of the main *Compagnie du Nord* station. At Bonningues the line used the existing station of the Anvin-Calais line. This was a type 2 station; perhaps one of the more imposing type 1 stations might have been provided here if the junction had been foreseen when this part of the Anvin-Calais line opened in 1882, 18 years earlier.

Table Eighteen
Boulogne-Bonningues line, stations and other stops

Name	Type	Distance km	Altitude m	(ft)
Boulogne-Ville	Outside CdN station	0	6	(20)
Rue de la Lampe	*Arrêt (1)*	0.5	6	
Rue de la Liane	*Arrêt (1)*			
Abbatoir	*Arrêt*	1.3	13	
La Madeleine	Halt (2)	1.8	20	
Ostrohove	*Arrêt (3)*	2.8	44	
La Waroquerie	*Arrêt*	3.7	69	
St-Martin-Boulogne	Station	6.1	114	(374)
Blanc-Pignon	*Arrêt*	8.2	97	
Souverain Moulin	*Arrêt*	10.5	102	
Pernes	Halt	11.4	106	
La Capelle	Station	12.6	103	
La Fôret	*Arrêt*	13.4	85	
Conteville	Station	14.8	57	
Belle-Houllefort	Station	17.7	41	(135)
Le Waast-Alincthun	Station	20.8	52	
Le Plouy	*Arrêt (4)*	21.8	63	
Colembert	Station	24.3	114	(374)
Longueville	Station	28.0	120	(394)
Escœuilles	*Arrêt (4)*			
Surques	Station	31.5	110	
Le Mouflon (Rebergues)	*Arrêt*	32.5	109	
Bainghen	*Arrêt (4)*			
Herbinghen-Hocquinghen (5)	Halt	35.1	104	
Licques	Station	37.4	67	
Audenfort	Halt	39.8	55	
Bonningues	AC Type 2 station (6)	43.1	68	(223)

Unless indicated otherwise, all stations and other stops in service from the opening of the line.
All distances are from Boulogne-Ville station, from the distance charts prepared when the line was built.
Heights in feet given only for the line ends, high and low points, and other important stations.

(1) Probably discontinued soon after opening.
(2) Also known on early timetables as La Madeleine-Pitendal.
(3) Marked as halt on some maps by 1935.
(4) *Arrêt* added later, shown on declassification maps 1937.
(5) Herbinghem on some maps of the line.
(6) Junction with Anvin-Calais line.

Between Boulogne and Bonningues, nine proper stations were built. St-Martin was the principal station of the line. The rest were in the rural section from St-Martin to Bonningues. The stations were two-storey with three doors or windows on each side on the ground floor and three windows on each side on the first floor. At one end of the building were two doors on the ground floor and a single window on the first floor; at the other end was one door on the ground floor and a circular embellishment without a window on the first floor. The windows and doors and the circular feature were decorated with raised brick, and there were brick features on the corners and under the gables. The rest was rendered but was brick underneath, as shown at Belle-Houllefort where most of the rendering has been removed. Where there was a goods building this was attached to the end with the circular feature. There was a separate lavatory block at Licques and possibly at other stations. We do not know of anywhere that a lavatory block can now be seen on this line. The stations were thus distinctive from those of both the Anvin-Calais and Aire-Berck lines and were more handsome than those of Aire-Berck.

There were four halts on the line from Boulogne to Bonningues, one in the suburbs of Boulogne at La Madeleine-Pitendal and the others in the rural section. The only halt building that survives in a recognizable form is that at Herbinghen-Hocquinghen, where the single-storey halt building is of similar style to the stations. Maps of 1935 show that Ostrohove had been upgraded into a halt. It had previously only been an *arrêt*. At the *arrêts* , there might have been no facilities, or there might have been shelters. No buildings at *arrêts* have survived.

We do not know how many crossing cottages there were, but one is still there where the line crossed the old N42, then the main road from Boulogne to St-Omer, on the Colembert side of Le Plouy. This has windows with rounded brick arches, compared with flatter arches on the stations, and a circular window at both ends of the roof space, but is otherwise similar.

Station and depot layouts

We have the details of the arrangement of metre gauge lines outside Boulogne-Ville station in 1911, which were probably those from the opening of the line to St-Martin and Bonningues in 1902. Both the line to St-Martin and the line electrified for trams were connected into the goods area of the standard gauge station with transhipment facilities, but there appears to have been no direct link between the metre gauge line and the quays and boats. The plans in 1911 do not show any connection between the steam line and the electric tramway from Le Portel at the north-east corner of Boulogne-Ville station.

We do not have a detailed track plan for the depot or the station at St-Martin. Liquidation documents in 1939 show four sets of points at the station, a 15 tonne weighbridge, and a 3.1 metre turntable. At La Capelle there were four sets of points indicating a passing loop and sidings or another loop, and another 15 tonne weighbridge at the entrance to the station. At Conteville, Belle-Houllefort, and Le Waast there were two sets of points indicating a passing loop. A partial plan of Licques station, in 1902, shows a passing loop and one additional siding or loop. There was a passing loop and a goods yard at the halt at La Madeleine.

At the Anvin-Calais station at Bonningues, which became the junction, the running line on one side of the platform had been removed by 1892. This was re-instated when the Boulogne line opened in 1900, this second line becoming the beginning of the Boulogne line.

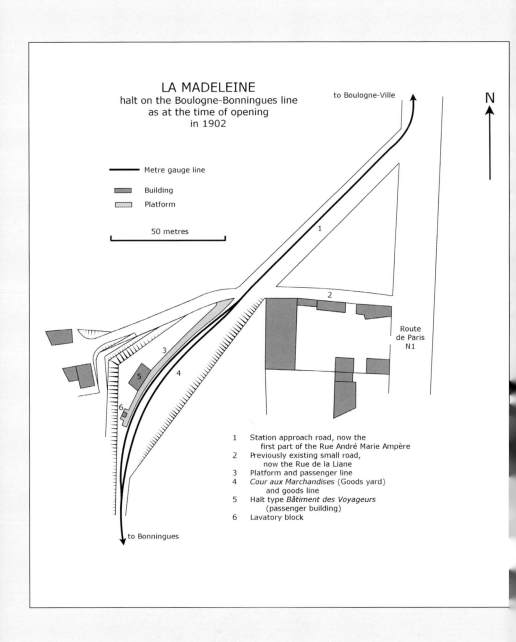

LA MADELEINE
halt on the Boulogne-Bonningues line
as at the time of opening
in 1902

to Boulogne-Ville

N

—— Metre gauge line

Building

Platform

50 metres

Route
de Paris
N1

to Bonningues

1 Station approach road, now the
   first part of the Rue André Marie Ampère
2 Previously existing small road,
   now the Rue de la Liane
3 Platform and passenger line
4 *Cour aux Marchandises* (Goods yard)
   and goods line
5 Halt type *Bâtiment des Voyageurs*
   (passenger building)
6 Lavatory block

Depots and Workshops

The main depot was at St-Martin-Boulogne. This was probably sited on the south side of the Route de Desvres, where the railway left the road. This would locate it between the road and the cemetery, where the Résidence les Trois Fontaines now is. The liquidation documents in 1939 show nine sets of points at the depot.

Industrial links

In 1911 plans were put forward for an industrial line from a junction in the Boulevard Daunou along the Rue de la Liane to the Boulogne town waste processing and incineration plant. There were some small sidings close to the junction, and then a narrow bridge under the standard gauge main line. This road and the plant were then on the right bank of the river Liane, with the plant just downhill from the railway bridge over the Route de Paris at La Madeleine. This line was probably built soon after, and was certainly in use after World War I to take waste onto the principal line and up to the Val St-Martin for dumping. There were certainly other industrial connections but we do not have details. In 1909 the line carried 18,208 tonnes of goods of *petite vitesse*, including 1,258 tonnes of sugar beet.

Rolling stock

Locomotives

A full motive power summary for all the lines in this book is given in *Appendix One*. The steam-powered line from Boulogne to Bonningues was supplied in 1899 and 1900 with four 0-6-0T locomotives of *bicabine* type with skirting to hide the wheels. This was said to be to avoid frightening horses on the road running sections. *Bicabines* have cabins at both ends and can be driven from both ends. These locomotives were numbered 47, 48, 49 and 51, the numbering being in a joint series with other lines run by CEN. They were supplied by the *Ateliers de Construction du Nord de la France de Blanc Misseron*, but were probably built at the *Ateliers de Tubize* in Belgium, owned by the same company.

The depot of the Boulogne-Bonningues line at St-Martin-Boulogne. A Blanc-Misseron 0-6-0T *bicabine* with passenger carriages and a *fourgon* is leaving the depot. The engine shed is on the right with steam vents in the roof and a water point in front, and the carriage shed is on the left. The main running line is in the foreground in front of the post with the direction to Boulogne-Ville to the left and the line headed out to the right into the Route de Desvres towards the main station at St-Martin-Boulogne.   *Collection André Artur*

Blanc-Misseron 0-6-0T *bicabine* CEN No. 48 with a *fourgon* and passenger carriages. Date unknown. The site is probably the Quai Chanzy outside Boulogne-Ville station, with standard gauge stock behind, and the masts of boats in the *Arrière Port*. The train has arrived from St-Martin-Boulogne and Bonningues. *Collection Bram van der Velden*

Characteristics of 0-6-0T bicabine locomotives for Boulogne-Bonningues line
Year of manufacture: 1899 (Nos. 47, 48 and 49), probably 1900 (No. 51)
Max. dimensions: length, 6.89 m; *width,* 2.41 m, *height,* 3.00 m
Weight: empty: 18.7 tonnes; *in steam:* 22.7 tonnes (approx.)
Diameter of driving wheels: 0.84 m
*Wheelbase: total,*1.80 m; *driving wheels,* 1.80 m.
Steam Pressure: 12 kg/cm²
Boiler heating surface: 37.15 metre²
Cylinder diameter: 0.35 metres
Piston travel: 0.36 metres

In October 1910 locomotive No. 51 derailed at Bonningues. This was blamed on the smaller rims of the wheels on the Boulogne-Bonningues locomotives. In September and October 1912 locomotive No. 47 derailed three times on the Anvin-Calais line, once at points entering Tournehem station, once on a siding at Tournehem while collecting a wagon, and once on the open track between Tournehem and Bonningues. In October a wagon of the Boulogne-Bonningues line also derailed on the open track in the area of Zouafques, beyond Tournehem towards Calais, while forming part of an Anvin-Calais train. After the third derailment locomotive No. 47 was jointly examined by representatives of the two lines. Nothing was found, but it was thought possible that the cause was too much load on the middle axle causing problems with the suspension, and that the load should be readjusted towards the outer axles. This was done and the locomotive was put back in service on 10th November. The reporting departmental Engineer found that the probable cause of the derailments at Tournehem station, and of the wagon near Zouafques, was that the rails were slightly too far apart, measuring 1.030 metres between the internal edges. Only the last derailment might possibly be blamed on the locomotive. It is worth noting that the wheelbase of the locomotives of the Boulogne-Bonningues line was, at 1.80 metres, considerably shorter than those of the locomotives in use by the Anvin-Calais company, and this might have made the former more susceptible to derailment if the accuracy of the track gauge was poor.

Passenger carriages

The line was supplied, at opening, with 22 two-axle carriages with end platforms. First class consisted of three carriages with space for 14 passengers, six sitting and eight standing. The first class carriages also doubled as *fourgons*, with baggage space. Nineteen carriages were second class, with space for 32 passengers, 18 sitting and 14 standing. Later there was one mixed class carriage, making 23 in all by 1914. There was no provision for third class passengers, and this is confirmed by the *Chaix* timetables, which both before and after World War I give the fares for only two classes. This is in contrast with the other CEN line in the Pas-de-Calais, Lens-Frévent, and with the Anvin-Calais and Aire-Berck lines, all of which had three classes.

Other Rolling Stock

The line had 52 wagons, some closed, some open, and some flat, but we do not know the distribution at the time of opening. Further wagons were acquired from British Army surplus after World War I. At the time of liquidation in 1939, 13 covered wagons, 15 open wagons, and four flat wagons were offered for sale.

Operations

In 1901 the company employed 10 locomotive crews (driver and fireman) and 15 *Chefs de train* (conductors). Two train sets ran each day, one starting from Licques and the other from St-Martin-Boulogne, and three crews per day were assigned to each train. A reserve crew was based at St-Martin, with the remainder resting or on other duties.

Summaries of the opening timetable from St-Martin-Boulogne to Bonningues in April 1900, of the timetable between Boulogne-Ville and Bonningues of May 1902, and of the timetable between Boulogne-Ville and Tournehem in May 1914, are shown in *Table Nineteen*. The basic pattern is that there were three trains each way every day at every station. One train was based at Licques and one at St-Martin-Boulogne. This accords with the disposition of train crews. In the 1900 timetable, a train returned from Bonningues to Licques in the afternoon, then going back to Bonningues to form the 17.40 to St-Martin. The last train at Bonningues went to Licques for the night and then started from there for St-Martin the next morning. A year later the timings had altered slightly but the significant change was that the afternoon trip from Bonningues to Licques and back had been dropped.

Table Nineteen
Boulogne to Bonningues Summary Timetables

From 14th April, 1900

St-Martin-Boulogne	*dep.*	08.00	11.30		16.30	▲ *arr.* 09.00	14.20		20.30
La Capelle		08.30	12.00		17.02	08.30	13.47		19.55
Colembert		09.23	12.51		17.58	07.31	12.51		19.04
Licques		10.23	13.47	16.43	18.55	06.40	12.01	15.20	18.08 20.20
Bonningues	*arr.*	11.00	14.20	17.00	19.25	*dep.* 11.40	14.55	17.40	19.50

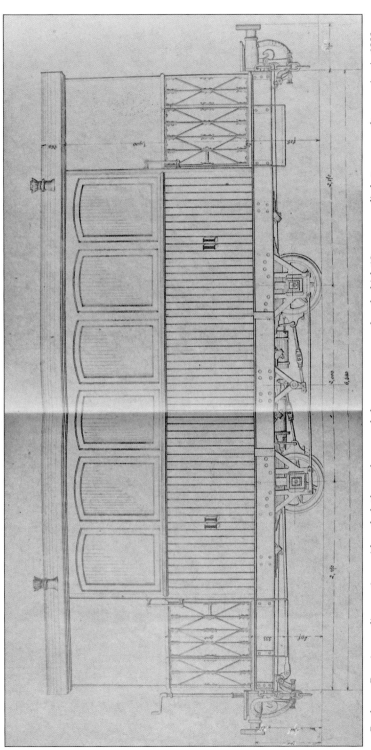

Boulogne-Bonningues line carriage with end platforms for second class passengers only, of which 19 were supplied at or soon after opening in 1900.

From May 1902

Boulogne-sur-Mer	*dep.*		06.17	14.15	17.00	*arr.*	05.45	07.55	12.00	20.05
St-Martin-Boulogne			06.45	14.43	17.28		05.22	07.32	11.37	19.42
La Capelle			07.06	15.04	17.51			07.06	11.11	19.15
Colembert			07.45	15.43	18.32			06.22	10.27	18.32
Licques			08.40	16.50	19.20		05.40	09.45	17.53	20.20
Bonningues	*arr.*		09.00	17.10	19.40	*dep.*		09.20	17.28	20.00

From May 1914

Boulogne-sur-Mer (gare)	*dep.*		08.40	14.25	17.00	*arr.*		08.20	14.00	20.08
St-Martin-Boulogne			09.08	14.53	17.28			07.57	13.36	19.42
La Capelle			09.31	15.14	17.51			07.30	13.09	19.15
Colembert			10.11	15.51	18.32			06.51	12.27	18.32
Licques		05.15	10.55	16.50	19.18		06.18	11.45	17.51	20.20
Bonningues		05.32	11.12	17.10	19.35		06.01	11.25	17.28	20.00
Tournehem	*arr.* 05.42					*dep.*	05.50			

From May 1902 the remainder of the line from St-Martin to Boulogne-Ville opened and was added to the timetable. The timing of the first train of the day from St-Martin became earlier, leaving St-Martin at 05.22 to go down the hill to Boulogne-Ville, then from there at 06.17 and St-Martin at 06.45 to reach Bonningues at 09.00 hours. This allowed the second train from Bonningues to leave at 09.20. The second train from Boulogne was made a lot later, leaving in early afternoon. No train is shown back from Boulogne to St-Martin at the end of the day but there was one, mentioned in discussions on the viability of 'local' trains between Boulogne-Ville and St-Martin. By May 1908 the early morning St-Martin to Boulogne service had been dropped, the train presumably going straight from the depot down the hill to Boulogne-Ville, and the first morning train from Boulogne-Ville had gone back to 08.34. In May 1914, the timings were not much changed, but the first morning train from Licques went to Tournehem, running from Bonningues to Tournehem on the Anvin-Calais line, and then back from Tournehem at 05.50. We do not know exactly when the line fulfilled its original name and ran through to Tournehem once a day, but it was after the timetable of May 1909 and before the locomotive derailment problems at Tournehem began to be reported in Autumn 1912.

In 1897 the *Société des Tramways Électriques de Boulogne-sur-Mer* (TEB) opened a tram route from the Place Dalton to the *'Dernier Sou'* (literally 'the last penny') at the junction of the main road to Calais with that to St-Omer, near the top of the old town. You will not find this name on a modern map of Boulogne but this is still the name of the bus stop at this junction. In 1901, this tram route was extended further up the hill to St-Martin- Boulogne very close to the station of the Boulogne to Bonningues railway. This opening came therefore the year before the opening of the linking section down the hill from St-Martin to Boulogne-Ville. This was a much more direct route from central Boulogne to St-Martin than the railway. We do not know how often this tram ran in 1901, but it is unlikely to have been less than every 20 minutes, which was the frequency in the 1930s. It is therefore not surprising that this affected the viability of the railway for passenger traffic on the section from St-Martin to Boulogne-Ville. By November 1902 the company was applying to the Department to reduce the number of trains on this section, citing trains which regularly ran empty between these stations. The specific trains said to run empty were the 07.55 from Boulogne-Ville to St-Martin and back, the 20.05 on the same route, and the 16.15 from St-Martin to Boulogne-Ville. This was the train which may have become the 17.00 to Bonningues from Boulogne-Ville referred to above. 'Local' trains from Boulogne-Ville to St-Martin and back are not shown on the 'through' timetables that we have seen, and probably the request to withdraw these trains was granted. Further reductions of the service on this section were made later, after World War I (*see Chapter Six*). However, it was not all negative; there was also a request in late 1902 from a hotelier in Belle-Houllefort that extra trains should be put on for Saturdays and Sundays for excursions in the forest of Boulogne. In 1909 the line ran 544 passenger trains and 2,011 mixed trains.

It is probable that the goods traffic on the section from Boulogne-Ville to St-Martin was more important as it connected the port with the rural Boulonnais, but we have no details of this. We have already noted the use of the line after World War I, and probably before, to take waste from the Boulogne town waste processing and incineration plant up to the Val St-Martin for dumping.

When the whole line was opened, from May 1902, journey times between Boulogne-Ville and Bonningues varied between 2 hours 37 minutes and 3 hours. By 1914 the scheduled journey times for the whole line had improved a little to between 2 hours 32 minutes and 2 hours 45 minutes in the direction Boulogne-Ville to Bonningues, and between 2 hours 19 minutes and 2 hours 40 minutes in the other direction. The difference is probably attributable to the net upward gradient starting from Boulogne. It is of interest also that the scheduled journey time up the hill from Boulogne-Ville to St-Martin was 28 minutes but that down the hill 23 to 26 minutes.

Connections with the Anvin-Calais line at Bonningues were reasonable. Based on the timetables for 1914, by leaving Boulogne at 08.40 there was a full connection for stations towards Calais and only an hour later towards Anvin. However, passengers coming from stations between Anvin and Fruges or from the Calais direction had a much longer wait for stations towards Boulogne. Of course, passengers actually going from Boulogne to Calais or Anvin and vice versa could go much more quickly on the standard gauge network, and it was probably considered that from places nearer to Calais, Anvin and Boulogne, passengers would choose to go to the standard gauge network and change. In 1909 the Boulogne-Bonningues line carried 112,946 passengers. For comparison, in 1911 the Aire-Berck line carried 501,208, and the Anvin-Calais line carried 720,474.

Fares

At the opening of the line from St-Martin-Boulogne to Bonningues in 1900, the fare all the way first class was 2 francs 85 centimes, and 2 francs 10 centimes, second class. In the spring of 1914 the fares from Boulogne-Ville to Bonningues were 3 francs 15 centimes and 2 francs 30 centimes respectively, which with the fares from Boulogne-Ville to St-Martin being 30 centimes and 20 centimes respectively shows no change for the original section.

Accidents

As we noted in Chapter Two, the departmental archives retain records of the enquiries held by the *Préfecture* into railway accidents from the trivial to the life-threatening. The extraordinary detail that French administration requires for even the most trivial event remains a source of amusement to us. There were three recurring types of accident: those involving train derailments; those involving horse-drawn carts; and those occurring at level crossings. There were also some that involved serious injury and we will describe two of these below. We will begin, however, with one example of the six derailments recorded in the archives between 1900 and 1926. Although this chapter is principally concerned with this line up to 1914, we have included this later derailment here because of the richness of the detail. This occurred on 22nd June, 1924 between Le Waast-Alincthun and Belle-Houllefort. It took place on a slope, while the train was negotiating a sharp right bend. The report states that train No. 6 had five coaches of second class and one coach of first class and baggage. It was pulled by engine No. 48. The accident happened at 19.14 hours and the leading coach, 567, left the track and travelled 18 metres along the main road, the N42. The 15 passengers were thrown about and a Mme. Hesdin was cut by flying glass. At the enquiry, held a month later, no explanation for the derailment was forthcoming despite submissions by all the staff on the train and by Mme Hesdin. The train and the track were examined and found to be sound. It is, however, worth noting that the train had no speed measuring device fitted and therefore the likeliest explanation for the derailment cannot be confirmed.

The second common category of accident was that involving horse-drawn carts. This is one example of several. On 21st January, 1911, at 06.00, 200 metres from Le Waast-Alincthun station, two carts were travelling in opposite directions on the track adjacent to the railway line. On the approach of a train, the horses reared away and one cart was crushed by the wagons. Luckily the occupants, two girl passengers and the driver, were thrown clear and not badly hurt. The resulting enquiry clearly blames the horses!

It seems clear that many incidents occurred at the numerous level crossings, many of which were merely to provide agricultural access. One example will suffice. This occurred on 10th November, 1900, near the *arrêt* for Souverain-Moulin, at 20.00, and involved a horse and cart. The train was stopped at the crossing and the horse became nervous. The train manager got down and led the frightened animal across. Nothing else happened but this event inevitably led to a full enquiry and resulting piles of paper.

Turning from the trivial to the tragic, on 22nd June, 1911, an extra summer train was travelling from St-Martin-Boulogne to Belle-Houllefort and had just reached the section of track alongside the N42. Two 20-year-old men were walking along the road and, finding they were late for their appointment in la Capelle, and seeing the train going in their direction, decided to grab a lift. The first one jumped onto the open platform of carriage 556, but the second one missed his footing and his right leg became trapped under the carriage. The train was stopped and the young man taken to hospital by a doctor who happened to be driving by. His right foot had to be amputated. The enquiry found no fault with the train crew but it took the opportunity to preach a sermon on the safe use of railways. The verdict was that since both young men had suffered so much already, no further action would be taken. The fact that the injured man was the son of the mayor of Boulogne may have had an effect, but to say that would be cynical!

Finally, an accident to remind us that drunkenness is not a new problem. On 19th January, 1911, at 19.00, a train was travelling from Pernes halt to the *arrêt* for Souverain-Moulin. The driver saw a man lying with his feet on the track. The light was poor, and not seeing the man in time, applied the brake too late to prevent the man's feet being cut off. The victim was 59 years old, lived at la Capelle and worked in St-Martin-Boulogne. He had left work at 17.00 that evening and had been drinking heavily. A friend had left him to sleep it off further from the track. It is not clear how he got himself onto the line.

Stévenard, édit., Boulogne-sur-Mer

A TEB tram to St-Martin-Boulogne just after leaving the stop at the *Dernier Sou* (shelter just behind the tram), with Boulogne Cathedral in the old town in the background. Postcard postmarked 1910.   *Éditions Stévenard; Authors' Collection*

The station at Le Portel, also showing the lavatory block identical to that at Licques but differently orientated to the track. The tram shows the single buffer compatible with rolling stock on the Boulogne-Bonningues line. The single trolley pick-up and double overhead wiring can be clearly seen. Postcard written in 1911.   *Édition des Nouvelles Galeries; Authors' Collection*

45   LE PORTEL. — La Gare. — LL.

Edition des Nouvelles-Galeries. — Le Portel

Boulogne to Le Portel

Building and opening

The line was built by CEN as part of the line to Bonningues. In March 1900 plans were agreed to electrify the line from Boulogne-Ville to Le Portel. According to some reports, the *Société des Tramways Électriques de Boulogne-sur-Mer* (TEB) had already, from 1897, opened a line past Boulogne-Ville station as far as Châtillon, so it is likely that electrification was only needed from there to Le Portel. The section from Le Portel to Boulogne-Ville station (4 km, 2½ miles) was opened on 16th August, 1900. The opening timetable shows that, from the beginning, trams ran through to the TEB terminus at the Place Dalton in the lower town by the main market place. This implies that TEB were responsible for running the line, in conjunction with the other Boulogne tramways, from that time, but the line was not formally handed over to TEB for operations until May 1902. It also means that the line must have been electrified before the opening. TEB also had a line to Outreau which went round in front of Boulogne-Ville station on shared track with the line to Le Portel.

In 1900 there was a proposal to extend the line at the Le Portel end, by making a loop along the Rue d'Outreau to the church and then back along the Rue Carnot to the station. This came to nothing. In 1907 the *Société Hardelot* proposed an industrial line 9 km long from the station at Le Portel, via Equihen, to Le Choquel, on the line of the then proposed tramway from Pont-de-Briques to Hardelot Plage, which was opened in 1911. We do not know the industrial purpose of this line, but in any case the *département* refused permission to proceed.

Description of the line

The tramway to Le Portel as built by CEN started from the Quai Chanzy, outside Boulogne-Ville station (*see map page 136*). From here it went north around the west side of the Bassin à Flot (now the Bassin Napoléon) and then turned west along the Boulevard Châtillon to where the baths of Capécure used to be. These baths were provided for fishermen. From here it turned south. It was built with an accompanying road, the Boulevard du Chemin de Fer, from Châtillon to just south of the cemetery. The Boulevard du Chemin de Fer is now more or less part of the Rue Auguste Huguet and the upper part of the Boulevard Jean Jaurès. South of the cemetery the line turned south-west along its own formation before turning north-west for a short way into the station on the north-east side of the centre of Le Portel. The former path of the railway is now the Boulevard de la Liberté as far as the Rue d'Outreau, while the last section into the station is now the Rue Chateaubriand. The line from Le Portel as far as Boulogne-Ville station was 3.8 km (2¼ miles) long. Having started near sea level at Boulogne-Ville station, the line started uphill at Châtillon and reached a maximum height of 62 metres (203 ft) at the halt of Ave-Maria, before descending gradually to the terminus at Le Portel at 33 metres (108 ft).

At the other end, at Boulogne-Ville station, the line joined the electric tramway from Outreau which was always part of the TEB urban network, and the two ran together on one line across the Pont de la Liane and on to the Place Dalton. On the Quai Chanzy and across the bridge the steam line to Bonningues ran in parallel. This was not joined to the electric line in the Le Portel direction in 1911, but was joined later. There was no connection at the east end of the Pont de la Liane, and the steam line was not electrified, until 1927 or 1928. Both the steam and the electric line also extended south along the Quai Chanzy to a transhipment siding in the main station goods yard.

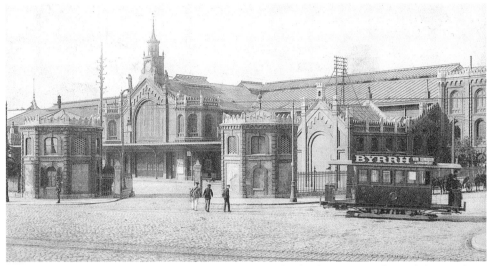

Boulogne-Ville station with a tram going to Le Portel. This line went in front of the Hotel Louvre-Terminus; the tramway to Outreau has just branched off behind the tram, where the men are standing, to follow the line of the kerb behind. Postmarked 1906.

Éditions LL; Authors' Collection

The station at Le Portel, the terminus of the electric tramway from Boulogne. No date but the dress style indicates before World War I. The tram has a passenger trailer.

Éditions Stévenard/ Authors' Collection

Engineering

The line to Le Portel ran in the road to Châtillon, and on the edge of the road to just south of the cemetery; the rest of the line ran in its own formation. Probably the same rails were used for road and off-road sections as had been used for the Boulogne-Bonningues line. The electrification was undertaken with overhead wiring on metal supports and supplied at 600 volts dc. The trams used a single trolley pole to access the supply. There were two overhead wires, one for each direction, so that trams did not need to de-trolley at passing loops. On the hill up from Châtillon to the halt at Ave-Maria, there was a bridge over the Rue d'Henriville. There is still a bridge there, but probably not the original, taking the Rue Auguste Huguet over the other road. The original bridge carried the roadway of 5 metres and the tramway on the verge of 2.6 metres, with a pavement on the other side. The total width was 10.1 metres. This was carried on steel girders resting on abutments faced in brick and stone, with an oblique opening 6.6 metres wide for the Rue d'Henriville.

Stations

Because of the original designation of the line, distances were measured from Le Portel.

Le Portel to Boulogne-Ville line, stations and other stops

Name	Type	Distance km	Altitude m	(ft)
Le Portel	Station	0	33	(108)
Ave-Maria	Halt	1.2	62	(203)
Châtillon	Arrêt	2.7	7	(23)
Rue d'Alger	Arrêt	3.3		
Boulogne-Ville	Outside CdN station	3.8	6	(20)
(Croisement Rue de la Lampe) (TEB)		(4.0)		
(Place Dalton)	(TEB central terminus)	(4.3)		

Distances – All distances are from Le Portel station
TEB   Société des Tramways Électriques de Boulogne-sur-Mer

The station at the terminus at Le Portel was sited just at the end of what is now the Rue Chateaubriand, where it meets Rue Carnot (D236E). The station was typical of the Boulogne to Bonningues line, except that the photographs show a window on the first floor at the opposite end to that with two doors on the ground floor. Tantalisingly, the photographs do not show if the circular feature is on the other end. The photographs do, however, show a lavatory block at Le Portel similar to that at Licques, but with the roof ridge at right angles to the track, whereas at Licques it was parallel to the track. There was a halt, Ave-Maria, with a Petite Gare (small station), situated approximately where the Rue Rosa Luxembourg now meets the Boulevard de la Liberté. There were arrêts at Châtillon, and at the Rue d'Alger, beside the Bassin à Flot (now the Bassin Napoléon).

Rolling stock

The line was operated by four electric power cars numbered 801 to 804. These weighed 5.88 tonnes empty and the motors were of 70 hp. They were manufactured in 1900 and the first three were authorized to be put in service from 1st August, 1901. We presume that, between the opening in August 1900 and August 1901, TEB used trams from other lines. Each tram could accommodate 36 passengers, eight seated in first class, eight seated in second class, and 20 standing on the open platforms at the ends.

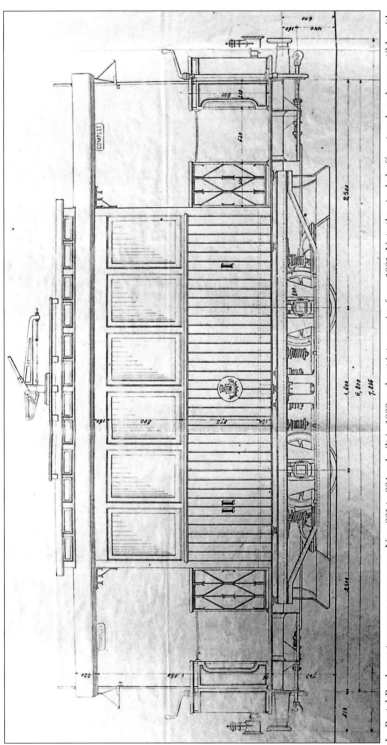

Le Portel-Boulogne tramway power cars Nos. 801 to 804 as built in 1900 and put into service from 1901. Note the single buffer at each end compatible with the rolling stock of the Boulogne-Bonningues line.

OUTREAU (P.-de-C.) – La Petite Gare E. S.

The halt at Ave-Maria, in the *commune* of Outreau, on the tram line from Boulogne-Ville to Le Portel. This is identical with halts on the Boulogne-Bonningues steam railway.

Collection André Artur

The gateway into Boulogne-Ville station and the Quai Chanzy. The two standard gauge lines to the Gare Maritime (*left out of the picture*) are leaving the station just behind the further gatehouse, and there are other standard gauge lines on the quay with wagons. The tram lines to Le Portel (*left line*) and Outreau (*right*) diverge in front of the gateway. The terminus of the Boulogne-Bonningues steam line is just round the corner. The picture also shows the Pont de la Lampe in the middle distance, and beyond that the old line of the river Liane. Postcard written in 1918.

Authors' Collection

La Route de Wimereux par grosse Mer

The tramway from Boulogne to Wimereux, and the coast road, on the edge of Boulogne on a
stormy day; looking towards Wimereux. Undated.   *Authors' Collection*

The Pont Marguet at Boulogne from the side of Boulogne-Ville station, and on the right at the
other side is the Place Frédéric Sauvage and the main Post Office. In front of the Post Office a
tram with baggage van is waiting to depart from the terminus of the tramway from Boulogne to
Pont-de-Briques. Undated.   *Authors' Collection*

38   BOULOGNE-SUR-MER. — Le Pont Marguet. — LL.

The line also had six trailer cars. Some were closed, and could take 26 passengers, 12 seated and 14 standing, and some were open trailer cars taking 34, 26 seated and eight standing. There was at least one second class trailer car with baggage facilities.

Operations

As already noted, the line was electrified, and operated by TEB, from opening in August 1900. It was run in common with the rest of the Boulogne urban network, with the trams running through between Le Portel and the Place Dalton, the terminus of the TEB lines. The trams for the Le Portel line were, however, fitted with a single buffer at each end compatible with the rolling stock of the rest of the line to Bonningues. This enabled the trams to pull trucks to and from Le Portel, although it is uncertain how often this facility was used. The tram to Le Portel ran five times an hour up to World War I. In 1900 the fare from the Place Dalton to Le Portel was 20 centimes. In 1909 the tramway to Le Portel ran 47,504 services, a total distance of 172,801 km, and carried 700,784 passengers.

Tramways of Boulogne

Building and opening the lines

The first network of tramways to be built in Boulogne was conceded to the *Tramways Électriques de Boulogne-sur-Mer* and the inner network of five lines was opened in 1897. The network was based on the Place Dalton in the centre of the lower town by the Church of St-Nicolas. From here lines ran to the Casino (now the site of the Nausicaa Aquarium), to the Dernier Sou just above the Old Town, to the Abattoir at Brequerecque (where it almost met the Boulogne-Bonningues line from 1902 on), to the Moulin-Neuf at Outreau, and to Châtillon. The last two lines ran past the Boulogne-Ville station.

In 1901 the line to the Dernier Sou was extended up the hill to St-Martin-Boulogne, with a terminus in the Route de St-Omer, just by the station of the steam railway to Bonningues. The line to the Casino was extended to Wimereux, a seaside resort 5 km (3 miles) north of Boulogne. The total length of the network was 13 km (8 miles). There were transhipment facilities at Capécure on the west side of the central station on the line to Outreau. The depot was in the Boulevard Beaucerf, next to the bridge. Until the late 1920s TEB generated their own electricity here.

As already noted in the section on the line to Le Portel, the *Tramways Électriques de Boulogne-sur-Mer* formally took over the running of this line from May 1902, but had been running it from the opening in 1900.

Engineering and Rolling Stock

The lines were of metre gauge with overhead electrification at 600 volts DC. Most were laid in the roadway. Broca rails were used for the road sections and Vignole rails for the rest. Lines were double on the line to Wimereux as far as the Casino and on the line to St-Martin as far as the Dernier Sou but were otherwise single. Overhead wires were double except on the line to Outreau beyond the transhipment facilities at Capécure.

We do not know how many powered tramcars the network possessed up to World War I. However, we do know that the tramcars had two motors each of 35 hp, and that they would take 18 passengers seated and 12 standing. There were also a number of trailer cars.

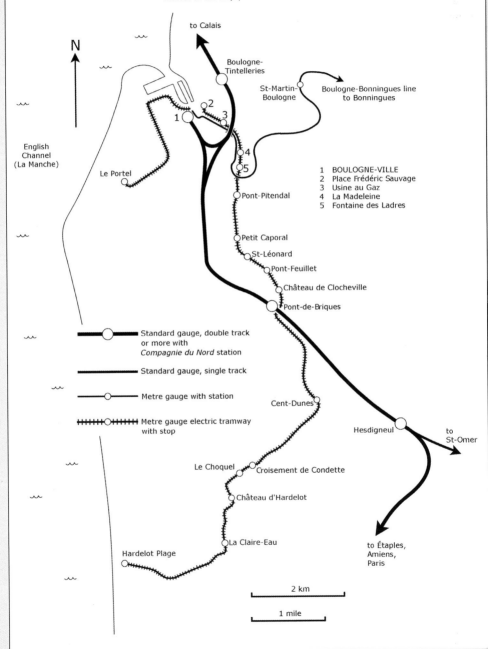

The Tramway from BOULOGNE to PONT-DE-BRIQUES and from PONT-DE-BRIQUES to HARDELOT PLAGE

as at the time of opening in 1911

Parts of the Boulogne-Bonningues line and the Boulogne-Le Portel tramway are shown, without all the stops, for orientation

to Calais

N

Boulogne-Tintelleries

St-Martin-Boulogne

Boulogne-Bonningues line to Bonningues

English Channel (La Manche)

Le Portel

2
1
3

4
5

Pont-Pitendal

1 BOULOGNE-VILLE
2 Place Frédéric Sauvage
3 Usine au Gaz
4 La Madeleine
5 Fontaine des Ladres

Petit Caporal

St-Léonard

Pont-Feuillet

Château de Clocheville

Pont-de-Briques

Standard gauge, double track or more with *Compagnie du Nord* station

Standard gauge, single track

Metre gauge with station

Metre gauge electric tramway with stop

Cent-Dunes

Hesdigneul

to St-Omer

Le Choquel

Croisement de Condette

Château d'Hardelot

La Claire-Eau

Hardelot Plage

to Étaples, Amiens, Paris

2 km

1 mile

Tramway from Boulogne to Pont-de-Briques
and from Pont-de-Briques to Hardelot Plage

The first network of Boulogne tramways has been described above. From 1903 another group started to bring forward proposals for a second network. These proposals were for four or five new lines, but in the end only one of these lines was built. Since this line has two distinct sections with very different histories, it could justifiably be regarded as two lines. The first and more successful section was from Boulogne to Pont-de-Briques and the second section ran from Pont-de-Briques to Hardelot Plage. The first section was just an urban tramway, but the second section was a line of substantial length connecting Boulogne to a major resort. This section is a bit of a mystery. It has been listed in a few compilations (in one, incorrectly, as a standard gauge line), but almost nothing has been written about it. More surprising still is that, until we found a few for this book, we had never seen the line on any postcards of the time. This is in marked contrast to the tramway from Étaples to Le-Touquet-Paris-Plage, likewise providing access to a popular holiday resort, and similarly the Boulogne tramways to Wimereux and Le Portel. In view of the already successful service to Wimereux and Le Portel, no doubt providing the same service to Hardelot Plage would have seemed a safe economic bet. This line was built later than the others and perhaps the shortage of pictures reflects its relatively short life.

Building and opening the line

On 14th December, 1908, it was agreed with the new group, the *Société Anonyme des Enterprises et Transport*, that this line should be built. The line was declared to be of *utilité publique* and conceded by the state to the town of Boulogne on 4th February, 1909, without any financial guarantee or support. Boulogne, in turn, came to an agreement with the *Société Anonyme des Enterprises et Transport*. It was built between 1909 and 1911 and opened for service on 1st April, 1911. On 6th May, 1911, the management of the line was transferred from the *Société Anonyme des Enterprises et Transport* to the *Société Anonyme des Tramways Électriques du Boulonnais*. In spite of the fact that it had already been opened, there was a Public Enquiry into the siting and number of stops on the line in 1912, which the town thought were too many; and perhaps this indicates, at best, local interest, at worst, local opposition.

Description of the line

The first section of the line stopped just short of the *Compagnie du Nord* main line (Boulogne to Paris) at the level crossing by the station at Pont-de-Briques, and the other began on the other side of the level crossing. We have not seen any discussion of why the decision was made to arrange it this way. Probably the *Compagnie du Nord* did not want the tramway joining the road in crossing the level crossing. They had allowed the tramway from Calais to Guînes to do this at Calais-Fontinettes (*see* Chapter Two), but this had been agreed many years before when traffic was lighter. Both sections were of single track and metre gauge.
  The first section of the line from Boulogne to Pont-de-Briques was built as an urban tramway with the rails set in the roadway. The original plans were for the line to start outside the north side Boulogne-Ville station, that is round the corner from the

terminus of the steam railway to Bonningues. The line would then have crossed the Pont Marguet before turning south along the Quai Gambetta. In the event, the line started from the Place Frédéric Sauvage on the Quai Gambetta, just south of the east end of the Pont Marguet. We do not know why this change was made. It may have been because the *Tramways Électriques de Boulogne-sur-Mer*, who ran the line to Le Portel and owned and ran the line to Outreau, objected to another line adjacent to or crossing theirs close to Boulogne-Ville station; or it may have been because the *département* had decreed that trams must proceed at no more than walking pace across the bridge.

Leaving the Place Frédéric Sauvage, the line followed the Boulevard Daunou, and then the Rue de Brequerecque and Route de Paris (then the N1) through La Madeleine. It ran alongside the steam line to Bonningues until this line left the N1. The *Compagnie des Chemins de Fer Économiques du Nord* (owners of the Boulogne to Bonningues line) agreed terms for the new tramway to join its line for the passage under the bridge of the *Compagnie du Nord* main line in the Boulevard Beaucerf. Here also the *département* had decreed that any trams must proceed at walking pace. Likewise the *Tramways Électriques de Boulogne-sur-Mer* agreed terms for the new line to cross its line at the east end of the Pont de la Liane. The new line crossed the final section of the existing *Tramways Électriques de Boulogne-sur-Mer* line from the Place Dalton to Brequerecque in the Place Henri Henneguelle. This was where the city abattoirs used to be.

The line continued to follow the old main road south to Paris, passing under the bridge of the Boulogne to Bonningues line between La Madeleine and Pont Pitendal, and then south-west through St-Léonard as far as Pont-de-Briques. Here a turn south along the Rue de la Gare took it to the north-east side of the main line level crossing at Pont-de-Briques station. There were two inclines on the first part of the line, one in La Madeleine, and the second and higher (nearly 40 metres) between Pont Pitendal and St-Léonard.

The tramway from Pont-de-Briques to Hardelot Plage in the Route d'Audisques at Pont-de-Briques, looking towards Hardelot.   *Photo Combier Macon, Éditions C.L.; Authors' Collection*

Stévenard, édit. Boulogne-sur-Mer

The arrival of a tram from Pont-de-Briques at Hardelot Plage. The tram appears to have an open trailer car at the further end and a closed one at the nearer. Undated.

Éditions Stévenard; Authors' Collection

The second section of the line began on the south-west side of the main line level crossing at Pont-de-Briques station. Almost at once it turned south-east along the Rue du Docteur Brousse and then, leaving Pont-de-Briques, it followed what is now the D940 (then the GC113). It climbed to a height of 65 metres at the point where it left this road and followed a minor road along the south side of the forest known as *Les Garennes*. This brought it to its the maximum height of 85 metres above the centre of Condette Village. The tramway then went downhill to the Château d'Hardelot. From here it went south to the junction with what is now the D113, just south of lake known as la Claire Eau. It then turned west into Hardelot Plage. The terminus was quite close to the sea in the road leading to the Place de la Concorde, at a height of 12 metres above sea level. The first section from Boulogne to Pont-de-Briques was 5.42 km (3¼ miles) long, and the second from Pont-de-Briques to Hardelot Plage was 9.53 km (6 miles), making the whole 14.95 km (9¼ miles).

Engineering and Track Layouts

The whole of the first section to Pont-de-Briques was constructed in the roadway. Parts of the second section were in the roadway, including just under 1 km at the Pont-de-Briques end, and a section in Hardelot Plage near the terminus. The rest was built on the verge of the road. The overhead electrification was with a double wire suspended on brackets from posts. The double wire implies a trolley type pickup, like the other Boulogne tramways. The line was probably electrified at 600 volts dc, again like the others in Boulogne, but we do not have any definite information. There were run-round loops at both ends of both sections. There were nine passing loops on the first section. On the second section there were passing loops at Audisque, at the road junction above Condette, and at the Château d'Hardelot. At Pont-de-Briques a siding was provided into the goods yard of the station of the *Compagnie du Nord*, with transhipment facilities. This implies at least the intention to provide a goods service to Hardelot Plage, but we have no confirmation that this was ever achieved other than for passengers' baggage.

Stops

As far as we know these were all tram type stops in the road, without buildings, or only with shelters. There were probably buildings at the Boulogne end of the first section and the Hardelot end of the second section but we have no details of these. There might have been a building at the stop on the second section called Condette, at the point nearest to the village centre, since this was one of the few places where goods could be handled on this line (*see Operations*). There was a kiosk and shelter at Pont-de-Briques for the use of passengers on both sections of the line.

The original plans for the first section list 25 stops including the termini, and 19 of these were request stops. However, in May 1912, a year after the opening and perhaps after the public enquiry into the siting of stops, the *département* decreed that trams must only stop to pick up or put down passengers at a smaller number of stops which they would approve. There were ten of these from Boulogne to Pont-de-Briques and seven from Pont-de-Briques to Hardelot Plage (*see map page 164*).

Depots and workshops

We do not know where the trams were kept and serviced, but presume this must have been undertaken separately for each section. The timetables indicate that on the section from Pont-de-Briques to Hardelot Plage the trams must have been kept overnight at or near Pont-de-Briques. On the other section they must have been kept at or near the centre of Boulogne, since the first departure and the last arrival were at the Place Frédéric Sauvage.

Rolling stock

We do not know with how many trams these lines started operations. Only two would be needed to operate the first section, and two to operate the second section in the high season. Extra power cars would be needed to cover maintenance and breakdowns, and probably each section had four, as had the Boulogne to Le Portel Tramway.

The maximum width allowed for the rolling stock was 1.90 metres (6 ft 3 in.) on the first section. The company applied for an extra 0.10 metres (4 in.) for the second section to make the seating more comfortable, but we do not know if this was granted. There were 16 seats in each power car. There was standing room allowed for 20 people, of which 9 were on the front platform and 11 on the back. This allowed room for the driver in the front. In accordance with French law at least two seats had to be provided for *mutilés de guerre* (those disabled by war), or the old or infirm. There was discussion with the town council whether these could be extra to the 16 seats, with the council at one stage pointing out that in Paris they squeezed 25 seats into the same space anyway. We do not know the outcome of these negotiations, but even in the 1930s Boulogne trams still had only 16 or 18 seats.

The company also obtained permission to use open-sided trailers. These had 36 seats, and could take six standing. These had to have curtains to keep out the sand when crossing the dunes near Hardelot, and could only be used in July, August and September between 08.00 and 19.00 hours. The conditions imply that these were only for use on the second section in the high season.

Operations

Before World War I trams ran on the first section between Boulogne and Pont-de-Briques every half an hour, leaving each end of the line on the hour and the half hour. The service ran from 06.30 to 21.00 and the full length journey took 20 minutes.

Trams ran on the second section from Pont-de-Briques to Hardelot Plage at least six times per day each way. The full length journey took 35 minutes. In the summer season up to 20 services per day could be provided but when there were 16 or more per day the company reserved the right not to run all the advertised services unless there was the demand. Only eight connections per day were guaranteed at Pont-de-Briques for the service on to Boulogne, with a connection time of five minutes; however, with a half-hourly service anyway a missed connection in this direction did not involve too long a wait.

Through baggage services were provided between Boulogne and Hardelot Plage five times per day in each direction. The company must therefore have used baggage vans (*fourgons*) or trailers with baggage space for these services on both parts of the line. We do not know if the staff moved the baggage from one tram to the other over the level crossing at Pont-de-Briques, or if passengers had to do this themselves. Baggage could only be handled at Boulogne, Pont-de-Briques, Condette and Hardelot Plage. Some of the documents also refer to capacity to handle other types of goods (*marchandises*) at these four stops, but we do not know to what extent this was used.

Tramway from Wimereux to Aubengue

This metre gauge electric tramway was conceded to M. Lonquety in June 1906. In March 1910 the concession was transferred to the *Société du Tramway du Pont de Wimereux à Aubengue*. The tramway began just on the south side of the bridge over the river Wimereux at Wimereux, where the end was alongside the loop forming the end of the tramway from Boulogne. It ran in the roadway along what was then the GC119, now the D940, for 1.9 km (1¼ miles) to the racecourse at Aubengue. There were double overhead wires and the tramcars were probably similar to those of the Tramways of Boulogne. The line was opened on 18th September, 1909.

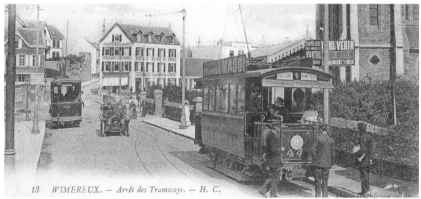

13   WIMEREUX. — *Arrêt des Tramways.* — H. C.

The terminus at Wimereux of the tram line from Boulogne, with power car No. 44 of TEB waiting to leave for Boulogne. Behind, to the left, a tram on the line from Wimereux to Aubenge (TAW) is also waiting to depart. Postcard postmarked 1914, but the photograph must have been taken earlier because the two lines, joined in June 1913, are not joined in this picture.   *Authors' Collection*

The tramway ran from the middle of May to the middle of October, and possibly also at Easter. From 08.00 to 19.00 there were trams at least every two hours, but at busy times they could run up to every 20 minutes. The journey took 15 minutes each way. In May 1913 it was agreed that the line should be operated by the *Société des Tramways Électriques de Boulogne-sur-Mer*, and the following month the tracks were joined to the end of the Boulogne-Wimereux tramway at the south side of the bridge at Wimereux. Operations ceased at the end of the 1915 season, without the approval of the local councils. The company blamed lack of staff due to mobilisation for the war.

Lines proposed but never built

Bonningues to Desvres and Wissant to Colembert

In 1886, after the opening of the Anvin-Calais line, but while the Aire-Berck line was still under discussion, options were considered for providing a railway service to the Boulonnais. At that time the *département* favoured two linked lines. The first would have run from Bonningues, on the Anvin-Calais line, via Licques and Colembert, to Desvres on the Boulogne-St-Omer standard gauge line. There was an option to run this on south to join the planned Aire-Berck line at Enquin-sur-Baillons. The second line would have started at Wissant, and run south along the coast to Ambleteuse, then inland to Marquise, to join the other line at Colembert.

Wimereux to Wissant

By 1891 the above plans for Wissant to Colembert had been abandoned, and detailed plans were produced for a metre gauge line from the standard gauge station at Wimereux, just north of Boulogne, up the coast past Cap Gris Nez as far as Wissant. This would have run alongside the coast main line from Wimereux as far as Aubengue. Then it would have gone out to the coast at Pointe aux Oies. Stations were planned at Aubengue, Ambleteuse, Audresselles, Audinghen, Tardinghen, and the terminus at Wissant, at 19 km (11¾ miles). This received an unfavourable report from the Engineer of the *département*, and it was abandoned.

Aubengue to Ambleteuse

In 1894 it was proposed to build a metre gauge tramway from the station at Aubenge, on the main line between Boulogne and Calais, to the bridge at Ambleteuse on the coast. This would have reached the coast at Pointe aux Oies, and then followed the road, now the D940, north to the bridge over the river Slack just short of Ambleteuse, a distance of just over 4 km (2½ miles). This was more or less a piece of the previously proposed Wimereux to Wissant line. This was never built. Maps of 1930 show a 'secondary line' from the area of the station at Aubengue to the Pointe aux Oies, finishing in the same area as the tramway from Wimereux to Aubengue. This was a standard gauge or metre gauge line built by the British Army in World War I. From 1940 this became part of the German standard gauge network running north from the main line at Aubengue (*see Chapter Seven*).

Chapter Five

World War One

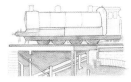

Although events had been building up towards war since the assassination of the Archduke Ferdinand in Sarajevo on 28th June, 1914, World War I formally began for France on 2nd August, 1914.

The area of the lines described in this book was never occupied by the Germans, but it was closely involved in the war as one of the major areas of communication and supply. Following their invasion through Belgium, the German army moved rapidly south towards Paris, with the French army and the British Expeditionary Force (BEF) retreating before them. They were finally stopped at the Battle of the Marne in September 1914, having almost reached Paris.

There followed what has been called 'The race to the sea'. Neither side got ahead and the armies dug in and the war of movement became a war of stalemate. The northern part of this front ran from just west of Ostend in Belgium through the north of Belgium and the eastern parts of the *départements* of Nord, Pas-de-Calais, and Somme. The Allies (Britain, France, and Belgium) thus held the major ports of Northern France, but not the major part of the coal mining and industrial area of north-east France. Once the armies had dug in, the Western front did not change position much until 1918, in spite of many costly battles. Despite advances in spring 1918, ultimately the Germans were steadily pushed back. The war ended with the signing of the Armistice in a railway carriage in Compiègne forest on 11th November, 1918.

Railways in World War I

With the dispositions described above, it was inevitable that the railways of the Nord, Pas-de-Calais and Somme would play a vital role in supply and communication for the Allied armies, particularly the British, who for most of the war held most of the front line north of the river Somme. In the static phase of the war from 1915 to spring 1918, the Western front was less than 100 km (63 miles) from the west coast of the Pas-de-Calais, and the easternmost point of the network which is the subject of this book, at Aire, was less than 40 km (25 miles) behind the lines.

As part of general mobilisation at the beginning of the war, the French Government had placed all railways in the country under military control, although the railways generally continued to be run by the regular personnel. The French army plan specified 10 *Sections de Chemins de Fer de Campagne* to provide personnel for railways in the vicinity of the army, or those needed abroad. Each of these consisted of up to 1,500 personnel with equipment and support, for instance, up to 90 locomotives per section. Nine sections were for standard gauge railways and were drawn from the main French railway companies, but the *Dixième* (10th) section was dedicated to metre gauge railways, with the personnel and equipment drawn from metre gauge companies all over France. These sections were called up as required.

The south end of the main line bridge over the River Canche at Étaples showing the damage caused to the end arch by enemy bombing on 31st May, 1918, and repairs carried out by the 297th (Railway) Company (RE). British 0-8-0 tender engine ROD (Railway Operating Division) number 1177 is hauling a troop train south; soldiers can be seen with their legs hanging out of the wagon doors. *IWM Q47359, reproduced with permission*

British and French Railway Transport Officers (RTOs) on the platform at Étaples main line station in March 1917. The notice above the head of the British Officer is in English and reads: 'A wise old owl lived in an oak, The more he saw the less he spoke, The less he spoke the more he heard, Soldiers should imitate that old bird!' *IWM Q1680, reproduced with permission*

War timetables had already been drawn up. These allowed for up to 144 train movements per day (one train every 10 minutes) on doubled standard gauge track. At first this was not achieved, but was later at times exceeded. One movement per hour was reserved for troop trains. One train or more per day on each line was a *train journaliers*, for small parties of troops, government officials, and 'civilian passengers if there is room'. The British involvement with the railways in the area behind the British lines has been well and extensively described by Colonel Henniker in his book *Transportation on the Western Front 1914-1918*, which was first published in 1937 as part of the history of the Great War based on official documents.

During the war of movement in 1914, with the German army advancing deeply into France, the port of Boulogne was evacuated. Once the static front had established itself, British troops and supplies arrived in an increasing flow, mainly through the ports of Dunkirk, Calais, Boulogne, Dieppe and Le Havre. Close liaison was needed between the railway personnel and British soldiers with responsibility for keeping troops and supplies moving.

By 1916, with the build up to the 'big push' (the Battle of the Somme), there were four British Armies, numbered from the north, the Second, the First, the Third and the Fourth. The main line of communication to the Second, the furthest north, was the railway from Calais to St-Omer and on to Béthune, which was double track and a main line. Further south were the single lines running inland from Hesdigneuil on the coast main line to Lumbres and then Arques on the main line near St-Omer, and from Étaples to Arras via Montreuil, Hesdin and St-Pol. From St-Pol a line ran to Béthune. Both these served the First army, with the Étaples to Arras line also serving, eastward only, the Third army; this army had a return route via Frévent and Abbeville. The coast main line from Paris via Amiens provided from Abbeville to Calais (via Noyelles, Rang, Étaples, and Boulogne) a *rocade* (in military usage, a transverse route) linking the ports and the western ends of the routes going inland towards the front line.

From 1916 to 1918 Field-Marshal Earl Haig established his General Headquarters (GHQ) in the *École Militaire* (Military School) in Montreuil. This is commemorated with a statue of the Field-Marshal on his horse 'Miss Ypres' in the *Grande Place* in Montreuil. He took up residence in the Château de Beaurepaire, 3.5 km to the south-west. Also in 1916, Sir Eric Geddes, who had previously worked in London with Lloyd-George when the latter was Secretary of State for War, was appointed Director General for Transport, France, and given the rank of Lt Colonel in the Engineering and Railway Staff Corps. He set up his Headquarters in huts in the grounds of the Château de Monthuis, 4 km west of Montreuil, which became known as 'Geddesburg'. He was responsible for standard gauge and 'light' railways, roads, and canals, but not 'mechanical transport' (presumably motor road vehicles). 'Light' railways in British Army usage at that time meant 60 cm gauge, and metre gauge railways were included for practical purposes, and many statistical purposes, with standard gauge. The major railway support close to the front line in the static phase of the war was provided, as is well known, by an extensive network of 60 cm gauge lines, but that is another story.

In the area of interest for this book, a major British Army base had been established at Calais by May 1915, with other facilities in the vicinity. Regulating Stations (*Gares regulatrices*), where single commodity trains were sorted into mixed trains to forward to the railheads, were established for the north of the British Army at Outreau (Boulogne), and Vendroux and Les Attaques (Calais), and for the south at Abbeville. There were supply railheads at Montreuil (2), Lumbres and Desvres, as well as many more nearer to the front line.

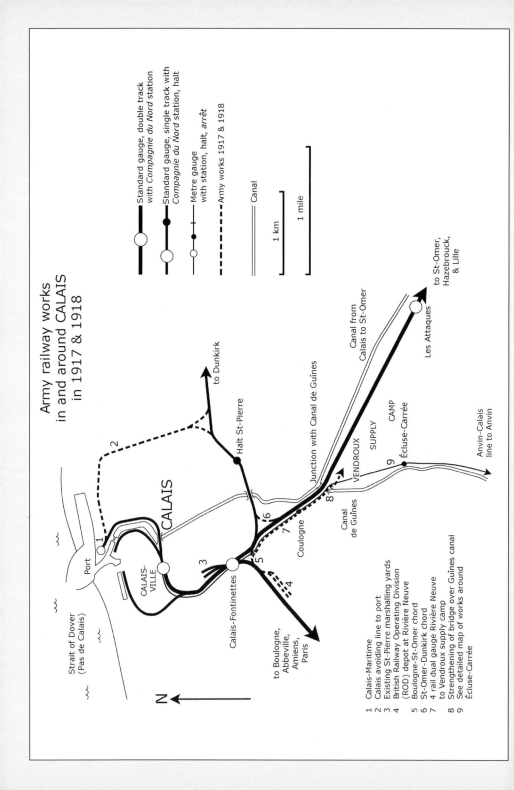

Army railway works
in and around CALAIS
in 1917 & 1918

Standard gauge, double track
with *Compagnie du Nord* station

Standard gauge, single track with
Compagnie du Nord station, halt

Metre gauge
with station, halt, *arrêt*

Army works 1917 & 1918

Canal

1 km

1 mile

N

Strait of Dover
(Pas de Calais)

Port

CALAIS-
VILLE

CALAIS

Calais-Fontinettes

to Boulogne,
Abbeville,
Amiens,
Paris

to Dunkirk

Halt St-Pierre

Junction with Canal de Guînes

Coulogne

Canal
de Guînes

VENDROUX

SUPPLY

CAMP

Écluse-Carrée

Canal from
Calais to St-Omer

Les Attaques

to St-Omer,
Hazebrouck,
& Lille

Anvin-Calais
line to Anvin

1 Calais-Maritime
2 Calais avoiding line to port
3 Existing St-Pierre marshalling yards
4 British Railway Operating Division
   (ROD) depot at Rivière Neuve
5 Boulogne-St-Omer chord
6 St-Omer-Dunkirk chord
7 4 rail dual gauge Rivière Neuve
   to Vendroux supply camp
8 Strengthening of bridge over Guînes canal
9 See detailed map of works around
   Écluse-Carrée

Some Railway Companies of the Royal Engineers already existed in 1914. In keeping with the greater involvement of the British Army with railway construction, maintenance, and operation from late 1916, many more Railway Companies were formed in 1917. Some were formed in Britain, and others in France from soldiers with railway skills transferred from other units.

Railways in the Pas de Calais in 1917 and 1918

The appointment of Sir Eric Geddes in 1916 recognised the importance of transport, and especially railway transport, in the effort to win the war. There followed an agreement in 1916 for the British Army to run their own railways, and in December 1916 a further agreement for the British Army to import wagons and engines for these lines. The British Army Railway Operating Division (ROD) operated extensively on the railways in the north of France in 1917 and 1918, and ROD locomotives are frequently seen on photographs of this period with the letters ROD and the number prominent on the locomotive or tender. It also led, by 1918, to the building and operating in Nord-Pas-de-Calais and Somme of military railways exclusive to the British Army known as 'British Army Railways'.

An increase in the rate of railway building and upgrading followed, culminating in plans for an enormous effort in 1918. The works described later in this chapter, on standard gauge and on metre gauge lines, refer in large part to the War Diaries of the Railway Companies of the Royal Engineers (RE) and that is our main source of contemporary quotes. In reading this chapter, please note that the companies of the Royal Engineers were numbered consecutively regardless of their speciality. Therefore reference, for instance, to the 296th Railway Company does not mean that there were more than 296 railway companies, but that there were more than 296 companies of which the 296th happened to be a railway company. Canadian and Australian railway troops were also available. The skilled workers of the Engineers were employed on major works supported by much larger numbers of less skilled workers. These included the Belgian Labour Force, the Chinese Labour Force, the Egyptian Labour Force, and German prisoners of war.

The ROD had a major base at Rivière Neuve, just outside Calais by the line to Boulogne and close to the chords to the St-Omer and Dunkirk lines. Sidings and a workshop for the ROD were also constructed at the Vendroux supply camp in 1917. The situation was further complicated, and the pressure increased, when on 21st March, 1918, the German army attacked on the Somme from south of Arras to south of St-Quentin. By the conclusion of the offensive on April 5th they had almost reached Amiens, and the railway yards near Amiens were vulnerable to shell-fire. On 9th April, 1918, the German army attacked in the north. By the end of the offensive on the 30th April they had advanced nearly 24 km (15 miles) westward, forming a huge bulge in the Allied lines known as the Lys pocket, since it straddled the River Lys. Ypres (Ieper) to the north of the Lys pocket held, but only just, as did Arras to the south. The German army had captured Merville close to the east side of the Nieppe forest, and were 4 km (2½ miles) from the important railway junction at Béthune, and 8 km (5 miles) from that at Hazebrouck. Both these came under shellfire, as did the slightly more distant Aire-sur-la-Lys (at 14 km, 9 miles), Isbergues and Berguette. The British First army was supplied through the St-Omer-Béthune and St-Pol-Béthune lines, fed by the lines from Hesdigneuil-Arques and Étaples-St-Pol. These lines joined at Fouquereuil and by the middle of April this was also only 8 km (5 miles) behind the line and also subject to regular air and artillery attack.

The No. 1 Group Railway Construction Company of the Royal Engineers were much occupied repairing damage from bombing and shellfire in the Béthune, Isbergues and Berguette areas, and there was also bomb damage further west. On 16th May, 1918, station sidings at Aire were cut in four places by bombs but were repaired within 24 hours. Air forces were rapidly developing on both sides, threatening lines further west still. On the night of the 30th/31st May, 1918 the main line bridge at Étaples was partly destroyed by bombing.

The Allies expected further attacks in the north, and indeed the German army intended these. They were never carried out following reverses in the Somme area and near the Marne in July and August 1918. The loss of the railway junctions at Hazebrouck and Béthune would have caused grave difficulties to the Allies, and could have led to the loss of the Channel ports. This German advance in the north was a further stimulus to maximise the use of all railways in the Pas-de-Calais, both along the coast and leading inland, and to build and operate further railways as required.

It also led to the development of a plan (known as Plan Z), which was of course at the time highly secret, for an orderly withdrawal to the line of the River Somme, should this become necessary. This plan does give useful information as to how the British Army used the railways in the withdrawal area, which included all the then unoccupied part of the Pas-de-Calais. The list of proposed demolitions in this plan is also an indication, sometimes the only one we have found, that certain structures and facilities existed. It is difficult, with our possession of hindsight, to accept that in the spring of 1918 the Allies had no certainty of rapid victory; rather they thought it likely that they were about to lose, or at least suffer further serious reverses in a war which might then go on for many more years.

Standard gauge railway works in and near to the Pas-de-Calais

This is not a comprehensive list but includes those works close to the metre gauge lines or otherwise of relevance to this story. They are only a small part of the enormous effort, by both the French and the British, which went into the development of railways in northern France in 1917 and 1918. Many previously single lines were doubled, and junctions improved, for instance by providing flyovers to replace crossings. Many chords were built to complete triangular junctions. Some 'avoiding lines' were built to take railways around towns. Many sidings and marshalling yards were constructed, but a full list of those not related to the metre gauge systems is beyond the scope of this book. In the peak year for railway works, 1918, the Royal Engineers constructed 709 miles of new lines and sidings, and reconstructed 589 miles, of standard and metre gauge. The majority was standard gauge, but 47 km (29 miles) of metre gauge line was constructed in 1918.

At Calais, chords were constructed at Rivière Neuve between the Boulogne line and the St-Omer line. This, or a successor, is still in place. Another chord was placed between the St-Omer line and the Dunkirk line. In July 1918 an avoiding line was constructed directly into the port; this line roughly followed the route of the present motorway access to the car ferry port.

South of Boulogne, a flyover was installed at Hesdigneuil. This was at the junction of the main line and the line to St-Omer via Lumbres. The section to Desvres was doubled. In 1918 the section from Affringues, west of Lumbres, to Arques was doubled. This included the construction of a lattice girder bridge over the river Aa for the second line east of Lumbres. In April and May 1918, extra passing loops were installed on the remaining single track section between Affringues and Desvres, with a hospital siding at Affringues. The line inland from Étaples to Montreuil, Hesdin, St-Pol and Arras had been doubled as far as St-Pol in 1917 or before, probably by French railway troops. The line from St-Pol to Arras was doubled by Royal Engineers between January and June 1917. In 1918 the British Army also built a standard gauge line from Hesdin, on the Étaples-St-Pol line, to Frévent on the Abbeville-St-Pol and the Doullens-St-Pol lines.

A chord between the coast main line from the Abbeville direction and the Arras line at Étaples was constructed before 1918. The bridge over the Canche for the main line at Étaples was one of the most vulnerable points for air attack, and usually carried at least 100 trains per day in each direction. Since Étaples was being frequently bombed in the spring of 1918, it was decided to construct a second bridge and line to the east of the existing one, from the main line south of the river to join the Étaples to Arras line on the north side. This was also known as the Étaples avoiding line. On the night of the 30th/31st May, 1918, the existing bridge was heavily attacked. Part of the southernmost arch was destroyed by a bomb at 2.00 am, but was repaired within 24 hours by the 297th Railway (Bridging) Company of the Royal Engineers (*see photograph page 172*). In any case, the new bridge and avoiding line were just ready and trains from the south were transferred onto this from 3 am on 31st May.

During 1918, the coast main line was quadrupled between the beginning of the Étaples avoiding line at St-Josse and Port le Grand near Abbeville. From St-Josse to Quend, which is just south of the River Authie and therefore just in the Somme *département*, the work was carried out by the British Army. Much of the route can easily be traced on satellite images. Mostly it ran alongside the existing *Nord* lines, but in places, for instance at Rang-du-Fliers, they were separated, to avoid demolition of buildings. At Rang, combined standard gauge and metre gauge workshops and sidings were built between them (*see later in this chapter*). South of Verton the two new lines were crossed by the Aire-Berck line on a bridge. The embankment on which the line from Aire approached this bridge from the east has been cut back and it is probable that the bridge was widened to take the two extra lines.

Further south the French army was also busy. From Quend to Port le Grand the main line quadrupling work was carried out by French railway troops. Another French line, the *Ligne de Cent Jours*, starting from Noyelles not very far south of Quend, has been well described in *Railways of the Baie de Somme* (Philip Pacey, The Oakwood Press, 2000). This book also describes the connections at the south end of the main line quadrupling at Port le Grand. In April 1918 it was agreed to extend the Acheux-Candas line, built earlier in the war, westwards to Conteville on the Abbeville-Frévent line, and this was completed by July. In April 1918, work also began on a line from the coast main line just south of Conchil (between Rang and Quend) to Conteville to link with the line to Candas. In addition to sidings at Conchil, a triangular junction with the coast main line, and more sidings, were constructed just north of the river Authie and the line then crossed the Authie into the Somme *département*.

German prisoners of war excavating a cutting 'during the construction of the locomotive depot at Rang du Fliers' on 25th June, 1918. Despite the original caption, this appears to be the cutting of the additional two standard gauge lines, built as part of the main line quadrupling just to the east of the new locomotive depot.   *IWM Q10337, reproduced with permission*

The north end of this cutting in October 2006, filled with bushy scrub.   *Authors*

Metre gauge railways in World War I

Colonel Henniker in his book sums up the metre gauge railways of Northern France thus:

> They were not trunk lines of heavy construction, such as are found in India and elsewhere, but light steam tramways often running along roads and crossing rivers by the road bridges. While several small independent lines might be linked together to form a miniature system, each such system was isolated, with no connection with any other system, and the component parts might be under different managements, each with its own type of locomotives and rolling stock. For reasons such as the height of the buffers above rail level and the type of coupling in use, the stock of one system could not as a rule be used to supplement the stock of another system.

Colonel Henniker is hardly fair to the Anvin-Calais and Aire-Berck lines, which were well engineered and had permanent way independent of the roads. They also had stock and other systems which were compatible with each other. However, his overall assessment was that the metre gauge railways made little contribution to the war effort except for three to four months in 1918.

He goes on to describe the system which is the subject of this book, which he simply calls the Calais-Anvin line. He also describes the system in the Hazebrouck-Bergues area, the Flanders system, and finally, the very extensive Belgian system. The line from Hazebrouck to Hondschoote had been conceded to M. Alfred Lambert (the entrepreneur responsible for the Aire-Berck line) in 1891 and was opened in 1894, with its branch to Bergues, and run by the *Compagnie des Chemins de Fer des Flandres* with assistance from the Anvin-Calais company. The line on from Hondschoote to Bray-Dunes-Plage was also expected to be conceded to M. Lambert, but he could not obtain the necessary financial guarantees and the line was opened in 1903 by another company. The line from Bergues to Bollezeele was opened the day after war was declared in 1914. From the end of summer 1914, civilian traffic was suspended between Hondschoote and Bray-Dunes and from 1915 to 1918 the line was run by the aforementioned *Dixième Section,* with assistance from the Anvin-Calais company. From the winter of 1914-1915, the whole line from Hazebrouck to the coast was managed by a collaboration between the *Compagnie des Chemins de Fer des Flandres*, and the *Dixième Section*, with Anvin-Calais help.

By 1918 all stations on the Anvin-Calais, Aire-Berck and Boulogne-Bonningues lines were under the control of the British Army Traffic Officer (Metre Gauge) at Berck.

A list of all the works of which we are aware, undertaken on the metre gauge systems in the western Pas-de-Calais in 1917 and 1918, is given in *Appendix Two*. French sources state that the British Army laid 47 km (29 miles) of new metre gauge track in 1918, of which 20 km (12½ miles) was the Tournehem-St-Momelin line. Apart from this, the additional works were largely sidings for ammunition and other supplies.

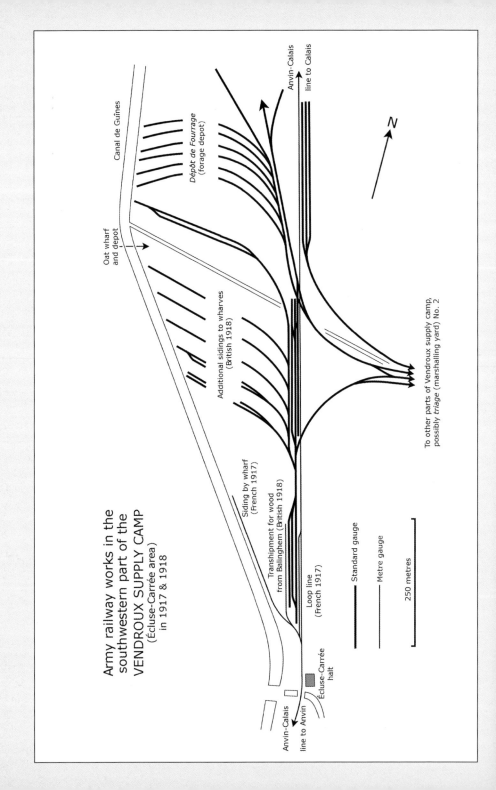

Army railway works in the southwestern part of the VENDROUX SUPPLY CAMP (Écluse-Carrée area) in 1917 & 1918

Canal de Guînes

Oat wharf and depot

Dépôt de Fourrage (forage depot)

Additional sidings to wharves (British 1918)

Anvin-Calais

line to Calais

N

To other parts of Vendroux supply camp, possibly *triage* (marshalling yard) No. 2

Siding by wharf (French 1917)

Transhipment for wood from Balinghem (British 1918)

Loop line (French 1917)

Standard gauge

Metre gauge

250 metres

Anvin-Calais

line to Anvin

Écluse-Carrée halt

Calais Area

The British Army established unloading and supply facilities in Calais from early in the war. Work was undertaken by French railway troops to improve rail communications, and a chord was built at Rivière Neuve between the line from Boulogne and the line from St-Omer. This was probably the chord which still exists between these lines just south of Calais-Fontinettes station. This chord must have crossed the Anvin-Calais line, probably on the level.

From January 1917, after the British Army had taken over responsibility for military railways in the British sector, the 298th Railway Company (RE) were based at Rivière Neuve, which is by the line from Calais to Boulogne, just on the Boulogne side of Calais-Fontinettes station. From then until May 1919, they undertook work between Calais and Dunkirk and between Calais and St-Omer, including military extensions from these lines. Rivière Neuve was very close to what is now the Channel Tunnel Terminal.

Much of the work in 1917 and 1918 was part of the establishment of huge supply dumps and workshops between Pont-de-Coulogne and Audruicq, along the axis of the main railway from Calais to St-Omer. A major ammunition depot was placed at Audruicq. However, the largest depot, a general *camp de ravitaillement* (supply camp) was established at Vendroux. This was between the canal from Calais to St-Omer and the canal to Guînes, which branched off just south-east of Pont-de-Coulogne. The railway from Calais to St-Omer ran just south of the canal to St-Omer, and the Anvin-Calais line left this just east of the bridge over the origin of the Guînes canal and followed this to Guînes. The Vendroux depot was therefore beside both railways and both canals, and was close to the port of Calais and the main lines to Boulogne and Amiens, to St-Omer and Hazebrouck, and to Dunkirk.

We have not seen a detailed map of the whole of this depot, but a French plan from 1919 marks it as extending 2 km (1¼ miles) along both railways from the origin of the canal to Guînes, and extending onto the land between the main line to St-Omer and the canal. It also extended onto the land between the Anvin-Calais line and the Guînes canal as far as Écluse-Carrée, and this canal was also used for supplies to and from the camp. Now this is an area of housing but before World War I there were very few buildings on the canal side. We do not have any detailed railway plan for the depot, except for the Écluse-Carrée corner. We have seen a photograph of the junction from the main St-Omer line into No. 4 *triage* (marshalling yard), and in April 1918 the 2nd Battalion Canadian Railway Troops working with prisoners of war laid 17 miles of track in the camp and constructed the junction for No. 6 *triage*. There were reported to be 43 miles of railway within this camp. There is no place called Vendroux now, except for a farm with this name on the site of the depot.

On 11th June, 1917, the 298th Railway Company reported that alterations to the connections to sidings at Coulogne, Calais-Fontinettes and Calais had been completed. This work included the 'interlacing' of the Anvin-Calais metre gauge line. In this connection they reported that this had made it necessary to strengthen the bridge at the junction of the Guînes and St-Omer canals. This had been carried out at night to minimise the effect on traffic. French documents after the war refer to the British Army making 1.7 km (1 mile) of the Anvin-Calais line into 4-rail dual gauge in order to improve the access for the standard gauge to the Vendroux depot. The dual track began at km 90.056 (from Anvin). This was at the point about 220 metres on the Anvin side of where the Anvin-Calais line left the main line just east of the origin of the Guînes canal, and would mean that the dual gauge followed the

Phot.-Édit. O. LEFEBVRE, Calais

187. *Environs de Calais* — COULOGNE - Le Pont de Fer à la jonction des canaux de Saint-Omer et de Guînes

The junction of the Guînes canal (*foreground*) with the canal from Calais to St-Omer (*beyond the bridge*). The bridge carried the double track standard gauge main line from St-Omer to Calais (*left*), and the single track metre gauge line from Anvin to Calais, which diverged from the main line to the right of the bridge. Postcard written in 1908. By June 1917 the metre gauge line had been made dual gauge and the bridge had been strengthened.

Éditions O. Lefevre, Calais; Authors' Collection

Looking up the incline which led the Anvin-Calais line up to join the standard gauge main line from Calais to St-Omer on the bridge, in January 2007. In 1917 this section of the Anvin-Calais line was made dual gauge and it is almost certain that this incline carried the last part of the dual gauge so that the standard gauge could form an additional access to the Vendroux supply camp, which was behind the photographer. *Authors*

Anvin-Calais line for a short way before leaving it to the east to enter the supply camp. There is other evidence that a standard gauge line entered the Vendroux supply camp there. At the other end the dual gauge would then have run to the beginning of the chords to other lines, in the Rivière Neuve area, between Coulogne and Calais-Fontinettes. This would make three standard gauge lines available over this section between the chords and the supply camp. In the contingency plans for withdrawal in July 1918, the bridge over the Guînes canal is listed for demolition. It is described as having two steel openings of 17 feet each, with two side masonry arches of 6 feet each, carrying a metre gauge and three standard gauge tracks, which again accords with this dualling of one of the lines.

In early 1917, French railway troops installed sidings and a loop line at Écluse-Carrée, including a siding 190 metres long alongside the canal to Guînes. Écluse-Carrée was, at this time, at the south-western corner of the Vendroux supply camp. Documents of April 1918 refer to plans for transhipment facilities to metre gauge, and a metre gauge locomotive depot and triangle, at Vendroux, 'to proceed subject to French approval'. In May 1918 the 298th Railway Company received a requisition for a metre gauge line 'for dumping purposes' at Vendroux and work proceeded on sidings for this. In August the company took part in transhipping materials and doing other works at the 'metre gauge dump' at Vendroux, and work to provide hutting for the transhipment depot was put in hand. Plans drawn up at the end of 1917, and agreed in April 1918, show new transhipment sidings just to the Calais side of Écluse-Carrée. These are within the area regarded as being part of the Vendroux supply camp. Whether these were the same works as those undertaken in August we do not know. At the same time, in April 1918, permission was given to construct two sidings to form a loop line at Balinghem, with the connection to the Anvin-Calais line at the Calais end. The plan was to load timber needed for the Vendroux camp at Balinghem, and tranship it at Écluse-Carrée.

The halt building at Écluse-Carrée in 2007, and the path of the Anvin-Calais line, looking towards Calais. The major part of the Vendroux supply camp of World War I was behind the halt to the right, but the metre gauge sidings and transhipment area were to the left of the line between it and the canal.   *Authors*

The wharf of the oat depot of Vendroux supply camp, on the Guînes canal between Écluse-Carrée and the junction with the canal from Calais to St-Omer, looking away from Guînes. A standard gauge siding of the supply camp is coming to the wharf from the right. The Anvin-Calais line is a short distance to the right.

The plans also show an extensive standard gauge network in the corner of the Vendroux camp nearest to Écluse-Carrée, with multiple lines built, and more planned, between the metre gauge line and the canal (*see map page 180*). This would be in the area of the canal wharves. We wonder if these wharves were identified by their main commodity, since the only one we can name is the 'oat wharf' of which we have a photograph. There were two crossings of the metre gauge line by the standard gauge. At least one continued in use after World War I, and in 1921 was the site of a collision between an Anvin-Calais train and a standard gauge locomotive of the *Compagnie du Nord*.

Lumbres

The 262nd Railway Company (RE) constructed track to the Royal Engineers Park at Elnes, just south of Lumbres and sidings on the site, commencing work on 20th March, 1918. The work was completed on 10th April in spite of delays in the delivery of telegraph poles. The site was by the existing route of the Anvin-Calais line, and the work is stated to have been metre gauge. However, British Army maps show standard gauge sidings to this site, which was in the area of the paper factory, to which the branch was made dual gauge in 1913.

Aire-Berck

Transhipment sidings were constructed at Attin by French railway troops in 1917. These were sited just north of Montreuil where the metre gauge line towards Aire left the standard gauge line towards Étaples.

General upgrading Anvin to Calais and Aire-Berck 1918

As early as January 1918, the 7th Railway Survey and Reconnaissance Section (RE) were asked, amongst other tasks, to report with diagrams on the metre gauge systems in northern France. Unfortunately, we have not found a copy of this report. This strongly suggests that the British Army were already considering the greater use of these lines even before the German advances of March and April that year. On 31st March a Captain and Lieutenant of the 110th Railway Company (RE), who were based at Aire, 'commenced getting particulars on MG railways in the area.' They had been asked to report 'as to their use for military purposes, and to specifically report on the sections Aire to Anvin, Anvin to Montreuil, Aire to Lugy and "Lombre to Gournau"' [*sic*]. Presumably this had been taken down over a poor telephone line.

A note has been made earlier in this chapter of works at Vendroux extending into 1918. These works were listed and mapped in documents of 27th April, 1918, with other projects 'sanctioned or under construction'. These documents date from just after the German advances of early April into the Lys pocket which threatened Hazebrouck and Béthune. As well as a number of standard gauge projects, and the works at Rang-du-Fliers described later, these documents refer to 'improvement at several stations and transhipment points on the Calais/Anvin metre gauge system', to proceed subject to French approval. The British Army phrase 'Calais/Anvin system' included both the Anvin- Calais and the Aire-Berck lines. Much of the work consisted of additional sidings at and between stations, and additional passing loops. On the Anvin-Calais line some of the passing loops at stations reinstated the second running line loops removed in 1892 (*see Chapter Two*).

In late April 1918, the 296th Railway Company (RE) had moved to Rang-du-Fliers. On 1st May, the company HQ and half the company moved to Beaurainville 'to work on the Anvin-Calais & Aire-Berck metre gauge railway systems'. Beaurainville is in the Canche valley south-east of Montreuil on the standard gauge line to St-Pol and Arras. Light Railway Workshops (a 60 cm gauge repair and maintenance depot) were also re-established here in early May, having been removed from Berguette (east of Aire) in March because of the German advance. This facility was run by Canadian Railway Troops. From Beaurainville and Rang-du-Fliers the 296th Railway Company sent out working parties between 4th May and mid-September 1918 to work on the Anvin-Calais and Aire-Berck lines. The specific works are listed in *Appendix Two*, which makes clear the extent of these works, and few stations were not upgraded in some way. Between 27th July and 31st August a chord was added at Gourgesson Junction, so that trains could proceed directly between Anvin and Aire without having to reverse, and a loop line and new water supply were added just north (on the Aire side) of the triangle. New sets of sidings independent of existing stations were also constructed. These were at Guémy, south-west of Tournehem, which were probably built to support traffic on the Tournehem-St-Momelin line (*see later in this chapter*), and at Crecques, between Thérouanne and Aire to the west of Mamtez (where there had just been an *arrêt*). Some of the works were to support industrial facilities established or exploited by the Armies along the routes.

The Anvin-Calais type 2 station at Tournehem, postmarked 1932, with goods building, passenger building and toilet block. Although this is the road side, a siding is crossing the road in the foreground. This is probably one of the additional sidings built by the British Army in 1918. *Authors' Collection*

Canadian journalists visit a Canadian Railway Construction Company 'near Rang du Fliers' on 21st July, 1918. The line on the right is metre gauge with lighter rails and more widely spaced sleepers. Probably this is looking north towards Rang with the Nord main line somewhere to the left, and the standard and metre lines to the right are the approach to the locomotive repair depot (*see page 188*). *IWM Q9124, reproduced with permission*

Anvin

As already indicated, by 1918 the whole of the line from Étaples to Arras via St-Pol had been doubled. Anvin, as the southern terminus of the Anvin-Calais metre gauge line, became an important transhipment centre in 1918. There was also a British Army hospital centre at Anvin, with its own sidings (probably standard gauge, completed in July 1918), and there were tank depots nearby in the valley of the Ternoise at Teneur and Erin.

In May 1918, men of the 110th Railway Company (RE) commenced work on a temporary 'broad gauge' (i.e. standard gauge) to metre gauge transhipment station at Anvin, and this work was completed in early June. On 13th June, 1918 the 262nd Railway Company (RE) commenced work on a metre gauge transhipment depot at Teneur, on the standard gauge line west of Anvin. Work on this must have included extending the metre gauge line alongside the standard gauge the 2 km (1¼ miles) to Teneur . By 3rd July two loops had been completed at Teneur, but on 10th July the scheme was cancelled, and work was resumed next day on a new scheme. On 17th July the Teneur transhipment depot was held up waiting for French turnouts (points), probably for the standard gauge sidings. By 28th August the transhipment facility was '98 per cent' complete and was handed over to another group.

On 26th June, the same company started work on a metre gauge *triage* at Anvin, and track and 20 turnouts were unloaded on the site. On 10th July, this work was awaiting a standard gauge/metre gauge diamond crossing but the whole *triage* was complete by 7th August.

Rang-du-Fliers

In late April 1918, project documents, comprising a plan for 'broad gauge and metre gauge repair shops and triage on the up side of the line', were said to be 'under consideration'. By 9th July, these 'standard gauge and metre gauge locomotive repair shops' were listed as 'in hand or approved'. Photographs of 26th June, 1918, show the work in progress. Work on this proceeded in parallel with that to quadruple the main line. The new lines here were built away from the existing *Companie du Nord* lines. This was probably done to avoid built-up areas. The two additional British Army standard gauge lines passed the repair shops on the other side from the *Nord* lines.

We do not know for certain who did the work on the main line quadrupling in this area, but it was probably the 12th Battalion, Canadian Railway Troops. We do not know who did the work on the repair shops. The 119th Railway Company (RE) spent from 30th May to 10th August, 1918 at Rang, but the records do not say what work they did there. A series of photographs shows a visit by Canadian journalists to Canadian troops, including the Railway troops at Rang, on 21st July, 1918. Canadian Railway troops were also running the 60 cm gauge repair shops at Beaurainville on the Étaples to Arras line at this time, and they were also visited.

We have not seen any maps showing the Rang repair shops but the site is easily identified from the contemporary photographs of the construction in glorious June weather. The chimneys of the Rang sugar refinery about half a mile away can be clearly seen. This factory still stands, although it is empty and the chimneys have gone. Also on the contemporary photographs the cottage of the crossing keeper of the *Compagnie du Nord*, where there was the level crossing for what was then a local road and is now the D303, can be clearly identified. This puts the repair shops just to the south of this road. Now the crossing cottage has been demolished but the site is easily identifiable. On the

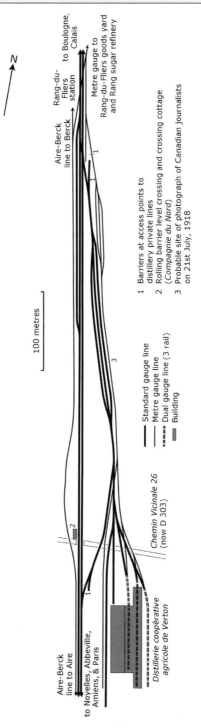

RANG-du-FLIERS STATION
to the DISTILLERY of VERTON in 1923

The distillery was on the site of the combined standard and
metre gauge repair shops built by the British Army in 1918
and probably the trackwork and possibly the buildings
were those of 1918

N

100 metres

Aire-Berck
line to Aire

to Noyelles, Abbeville,
Amiens, & Paris

Chemin Vicinale 26
(now D 303)

*Distillerie coopérative
agricole de Verton*

Rang-du-
Fliers
station

to Boulogne,
Calais

Metre gauge to
Rang-du-Fliers goods yard
and Rang sugar refinery

Aire-Berck
line to Berck

———— Standard gauge line
———— Metre gauge line
===== Dual gauge line (3 rail)
▓▓▓▓ Building

1 Barriers at access points to
   distillery private lines
2 Rolling barrier level crossing and crossing cottage
   (*Compagnie du Nord*)
3 Probable site of photograph of Canadian journalists
   on 21st July, 1918

Construction work at the locomotive depot at Rang-du-Fliers on 26th June, 1918. The chimneys of the sugar factory at Rang-du-Fliers can be seen in the distance to the right. The additional two lines for the quadrupling of the main line are just out of sight to the right.

IWM Q10339, reproduced with permission

Construction work at the locomotive depot at Rang-du-Fliers on 26th June, 1918. Metre gauge line is being laid on the left and there are stacks of metre gauge line on the right. Just below right of the tall tree on the left is the crossing cottage where what is now the D303 crosses the *Compagnie du Nord* main line.   *IWM Q10341, reproduced with permission*

site of the repair shops there is now a modern building. However, on this site in 1923 there was the Cooperative agricultural distillery of Verton. This appears in the accounts of the Aire-Berck line after World War I, as the *Distillerie Rang-du-Fliers*. In 1922 this distillery also installed weighbridges at three locations near the Berck end of the line.

In 1923 the distillery applied for extra track-work. The plans of the track as it was in 1923 show the site of the distillery, with three 3-rail dual gauge sidings, two entering the building. It is likely that the track at that time was wholly or partly that left by the British Army. There is quite a high chance that part or all of the building used by the distillery was also that of the British Army. The track plans also show the layout on the approach to this building from Rang-du-Fliers, with the metre gauge line on the east side of standard gauge lines, identifying the probable site of the photograph of the Canadian journalists on 21st July, 1918.

There were standard gauge sidings in the part of this area nearer to Rang until quite recently, and they are shown on maps of only 15 years ago. There are still signs of these sidings, both on the ground and on satellite photographs, with earthworks for the quadrupling of the main line just to the east. The Rang repair depot was, by August 1918, on the demolition list for the withdrawal plan. It is said to have been in use from August 1918, for light repairs only.

Boulogne-Bonningues

There is very little evidence of use of this line by the British or the French army in World War I, even in 1918. This is perhaps surprising in view of the importance of Boulogne as a supply port and the route of this line straight inland. Perhaps the excellent standard gauge routes from Boulogne and the steep gradient taken by the metre gauge line were deterrents to its use. There was, however, one project, of which we have more detail than usual, from two different sources, which allow us to follow through the accomplishment of a small project during World War I. In November 1917 the British Army requested permission to build a siding 85 metres long at the *arrêt* at La Waroquerie, for supplies to the Ostrohove Camp, close to this *arrêt*. The points would be at the Boulogne end, on a slope, and security points would be needed. The British Army proposed to fill the wagons on the Quai Chanzy and have them hauled to La Waroquerie at night. The road was too steep for their lorries to get up. The company, *Chemins de Fer Économiques du Nord*, commented that the siding must be 4 metres from the through line, and not the 3.2 metres proposed, to allow enough room for the platform for passengers between the two, and this area must be spread with hardcore. The sidings at the Quai Chanzy were fully used, and the Britsh Army must put in an additional 100 metres of siding there, at their own expense and with their own labour. However CEN would maintain this, and charge the British Army. There were enough wagons, and six would be provided on the Quai Chanzy at 6 pm every day for loading. CEN would haul them full to La Waroquerie at 07.00 the next morning, and leave them on the siding. They would have to be emptied and ready for pickup by midday. CEN would charge the British Army for the rent of the wagons, and the *grande vitesse* tarif from Boulogne-Ville to St-Martin, a distance of 7 km. Reporting in December, the local departmental Engineer remarked that the gradient at the Boulogne end of the siding was 2.9 per cent, and a security spur should also be provided.

We have no further details of work on the Quai Chanzy. On 22nd January, 1918, an officer of the 112th Railway Company (RE) met a French sub-Lieutenant of the *5° Génie* (Engineers) at Ostrohove Camp, to discuss the occupation of land for the siding. The work was sanctioned and by the middle of February the siding had been completed. At a site meeting on 18th February, the British Army Director of Metre Gauge lines requested certain alterations, additions and locking arrangements. These were agreed, and completed by 7th March. Presumably the men in the camp then got their supplies!

Tournehem-St-Momelin

In May 1918, the British Second Army in the north requested additional lines. One was what became the standard gauge Watten-Socx (or Watten-Soex) line. This line actually began at least 4 km (2½ miles) south of Watten station, close to St-Momelin. It ended close to Socx, south of Bergues, where it joined the main line north from Hazebrouck to Bergues and Dunkirk. The other pressing request by the British Second Army in spring 1918 was for a metre gauge link between a junction at Zouafsques, close to Tournehem on the Anvin-Calais system, and another east of St-Momelin, near the end of the line from Herzeele and Bergues.

The British Army had a railway depot at St-Momelin at least from April 1917. This was the date when the 7th Railway Survey and Reconnaissance Section (RE) became responsible for this depot (amongst others). As this was before the building of the Watten-Socx line, this must have been based on the metre gauge line from St-Momelin to Herzeele and Bergues. The Tournehem-St-Momelin line was built in the spring and summer of 1918. The main part was built by the Belgian Labour Force, probably under the direction of Belgian railway engineers. The whole link was 20 km (12.5 miles) long. This linked the metre gauge systems all the way through from the west coast of the Pas-de-Calais to Belgium. In the event of further German advance this would enable the evacuation of metre gauge rolling stock westwards. However, by the summer the tide had turned, and this additional line made it possible for the network to carry supply trains all the way from Calais, Rang, Montreuil, and other points on the main line, to the front, which was now moving rapidly back eastwards.

Not very much is known about this line except for the works at the eastern, St-Momelin, end. At that end there was a crossing of the standard gauge Watten-Socx line, transhipment sidings with that line, the junction with the St-Momelin to Herzeele line, and a new marshalling yard in the area of the junction. Most of the works at that end were undertaken between June and August 1918 by the 2nd Battalion Canadian Railway Troops, who were working on the Ferme Bleue station and sidings of the Watten-Socx line. Most of what evidence now remains of this line, which is not much, is in the Watten area and at the St- Momelin end, in the Nord *département*. For this reason a more detailed discussion of this line belongs with a full description of the Flanders metre gauge network, and of British Army railways of World War I. The junction with the Anvin-Calais line was at Zouafsques, on the Calais side of the *arrêt* there. There is little to see in this area now. We know that the Tournehem-St-Momelin line was still being maintained by the British Army in March 1919, but it was lifted later in 1919.

Berck-Plage-Paris-Plage

Finally, we have to discuss the sad fate of this line during World War I. Opened not many years before the war, it was already struggling and providing mainly a summer service for trippers along the coast (*see Chapter Three*). The line was closed at the beginning of the war. Presumably this was because it served no possible military purpose, or had any supply role. It would therefore have been seen as a waste of resources. Some reports have said that the line was lifted and relaid after the war. A dispute after the war (*see Chapter Six*) shows that only a short section was lifted, and other parts were damaged and repaired. The dunes between Berck and Merlimont were used by the British Army for tank training and other purposes. The two newest and best locomotives, 2-6-0 tank engines built by *Ateliers de la Meuse* (Belgium) and delivered in 1912, were requisitioned by the army in 1916 and transferred to the eastern Somme network near the Somme front. Both were destroyed by shellfire at Albert on the same day in 1918.

Civilian travel in World War I

Once the front lines had settled into their long term positions in 1914, various zones were defined with regulations for travelling within or between these. The railway timetables ('*Chaix*') for the *Chemin de Fer du Nord*, and the *Chemin de Fer de l'Est* contained details of these. These timetables included, as they also did in peacetime, the timetables of lines of other companies operating within their area. The timetable for the *Nord* network for 1st July, 1917, includes a warning that the timetable is only in force 'until further notice' and that 'These services may be modified or even abruptly suspended if military necessity requires'. At this time, France was divided into zones with different levels of security. The 'Zone of the Armies' was defined as all of France north of the southern boundaries of the Somme and Oise *départements*. Within the 'Zone of the Armies', the 'Reserved Zone' was the area north and east of a demarcation line marked out by the stations of Abbeville, Rang-du-Fliers-Verton, Étaples, Hesdigneuil, Boulogne and Calais; but not including these towns. The 'Non-reserved Zone' was to the south and west of this line. As can be seen, all of the Pas-de-Calais was in the Reserved Zone except for the strip along the coast to the west of the main line from Calais to Paris via Boulogne. In front of the Reserved Zone was the Advanced Zone, close to the front line. The boundary of this was defined by each army group, who also controlled all travel, including civilian travel, within this zone. Thus it is apparent that the whole of the Anvin-Calais line except that in the Calais suburbs, the whole of the Boulogne-Bonningues line except that in the Boulogne suburbs and the whole of the Aire-Berck line from Rang-du-Fliers to Aire, were in the Reserved Zone.

Within the Reserved Zone, travel was permitted freely within the *Canton* where the person lived. For adjacent *Cantons* a permanent identity card or a *sauf-conduit* was required. Other travel within the Reserved Zone, or to enter or leave the Reserved Zone, required a *sauf-conduit*. All papers for travel in the Reserved Zone were issued by the military authorities. There were special arrangements for urgent travel within the zones. The regulations also required that on arrival at stations on the demarcation line, all passengers should leave the train and have their papers checked by the *Commissaire*. In some circumstances passengers could only buy tickets to the edge of the Reserve Zone, buying onward tickets at the station on the demarcation line after their papers had been checked. For example, a passenger from Paris to Hucqueliers via Rang might only be able to buy a ticket to Rang, and would be subject to a further check at Rang, after which they could buy the ticket to Hucqueliers.

Complaints about this surfaced in the Montreuil newspaper *Le Telegramme* of 19th June, 1918. The article complained especially about checks at Rang-du-Fliers-Verton. Even though those coming from Berck had been checked by a soldier at the ticket office, and by the *gendarmerie* on the platform at Berck-Plage, there were also checks at Rang by the military and the police for those travelling in both directions. Service personnel were allowed to stay on the train but civilians had to walk to the station building for the checks, which could be up to 500 metres from the far end of the metre gauge platform. Often this led to the civilians missing the train as it left without them. One lady going to Berck reported leaving a case containing 14,000 francs of valuables on the train that left without her. She was later re-united with her valuables at Berck. The paper, recognising the need for security at this critical junction, had pleaded for the checks to be carried out on the train.

Civilian Services on Metre Gauge Lines in World War I

Services for civilians were probably reduced from the beginning of the war, and were certainly reduced more towards the end. This reduction in services may reflect the increasing use of the lines for military purposes, especially towards 1918. Other contributing factors could have been lack of staff due to army mobilisation and the removal of rolling stock for use on other systems nearer the front. A summary of the services from 1st July, 1917, is shown in *Table Twenty*. By this time the Anvin-Calais line had two trains per day at every station, and three between Bonningues and Calais, but only one service each way went the whole length of the line. The waiting times at Fruges in both directions were long, in the Calais to Anvin direction more than four hours. The probable working pattern indicates that different trains provided the service each side of Fruges, even though the train numbers in the timetable are the same. There was an additional early morning train from Fruges to Anvin and back on Saturday for market day in Fruges. The advertised service trains crossed at Lumbres in the morning and at Tournehem in the early evening.

The Aire-Berck line had one train per day along the whole length of the line, beginning at Berck-Plage in the early morning and returning there in the evening. Another train provided a service to Berck-Plage in the other direction but only from Fruges. This train left Fruges in the early morning and returned in the evening. In contrast to the Anvin to Calais service, these really were through services with relatively short dwell times at connecting stations along the route. There was also a middle of the day service from Berck-Plage to Montreuil and back, an early morning service from Fruges to Aire and back, and four additional services from Berck-Plage to Rang-du-Fliers and back. The advertised service trains crossed at Montreuil in the morning and at Beussent in the early evening. There would, however, have been many other train crossings with goods services and military services on both these lines.

We do not know for certain how these patterns were worked. Assuming joint working between the two lines the pattern could have been worked with six locomotives and carriage sets, three based at Fruges, two based at Berck-Plage, and one based at Bonningues. This would not have required much cross-working between the two lines, only that the early morning service from Fruges to Aire and back would be worked by the same train set as the later two services from Fruges to Anvin and back. The effective integration of the two lines for operational purposes from the 1890s has already been noted in Chapter Three, and in 1917 the timetables for both lines continued to be published under the title *Chemin de Fer d'Anvin à Calais*. This pattern would have left many locomotives free for other work including military trains.

Compared with the May 1914 timetables, the main difference in July 1917 is a reduction of one through train each way per day on both lines, with less extra services between Berck-Plage and Rang-du-Fliers. With this pattern it was still possible to travel from any station on either line to any other station on either line within one day, but only with long waiting times for some of the changes.

One train per day ran each way on the Boulogne-Bonningues line. This must have been stabled at Licques and started from there at 05.15 to go to Bonningues. It then left Bonningues at 05.50, arriving at Boulogne Central station at 08.50. It departed from Boulogne at 13.30, and got back to Bonningues at 16.50. It then returned to Licques, arriving at 18.35 hours. This service could be run by one locomotive and set of coaches, but we do not know what arrangements were made in case of breakdowns or the need for servicing. In view of the over-riding military requirements and direction of operations, the backup was most probably provided from locomotives on the Anvin-Calais line.

With this pattern, it was not possible to change on the same day from stations between Boulogne and Licques to stations on the Anvin-Calais line in the direction of Fruges and Anvin but there was a connection in the Calais direction. Because the only train to Boulogne left Bonningues at 05.50, it was not possible to travel from any part of the Anvin to Calais line to stations beyond Licques. For all journeys there might have been the option, depending on the timetabling on the standard gauge lines, to undertake some of these journeys on the same day changing at one of the *Compagnie du Nord* stations and then back onto the metre gauge elsewhere. Predictably the convenience of civilians was of low priority at this critical time.

In July 1917, the tramway from Ardres-Pont d'Ardres ran twice daily in each direction, compared with five times daily in 1914. The electric tramway from Étaples to Paris-Plage ran 18 times per day with the first departure from Étaples at 07.00 and the last from Paris-Plage at 20.00 hours. This is the same as the maximum summer timetable for 1914. We do not know why this service was preserved in this way. There are a number of possible reasons. One is that the electric trams would not have been of any use to the military elsewhere. Another is that Étaples was a major British Army base with extensive base camps and a major base hospital. The size of the Étaples British Military Cemetery on the road to Boulogne testifies to this. In addition, Paris-Plage may well have been an important place for rest and recreation.

Table Twenty
Summary Timetables 1st July, 1917

Anvin to Calais

Anvin	dep.	(07.20)	11.35	18.00	▲arr.	(06.50)	11.00	17.00	
Fruges	arr.	(08.00)	12.18	18.44	dep.	(06.05)	10.15	16.15	
	dep.		08.15	14.00	arr.		11.54	20.55	
Rimeux-Gournay			08.36	14.21			11.29	20.40	
Lumbres	arr.		09.57	15.43	dep.		10.32	19.33	
	dep.		10.30	16.04	arr.		09.50	18.36	
Bonningues		04.53	11.36	17.09		08.53	17.43	21.09	
Calais-Ville	arr.	06.32	13.18	18.45		07.05	15.55	19.25	

( ) Saturday only (market day in Fruges)

Aire to Berck

Aire	dep.		08.00				15.25		
Fruges	arr.		09.50				17.00		
	dep.	05.14					17.20		
Rimeux-Gournay		05.32					17.39		
Montreuil	arr.	07.15					19.22		
	dep.	07.52			13.58		19.50		
Rang	arr.	08.40			14.45		20.35		
	dep.	08.45		09.25	14.00	14.55	16.00	20.42	22.55
Berck-Plage	arr.	09.00		09.42	14.15	15.10	16.15	20.57	23.19

Berck-Plage	dep.		06.30	07.25	12.00	13.15	14.39	16.20	20.45
Rang	arr.		06.46	07.45	12.15	13.30	14.54	16.37	21.03
	dep.		06.55		12.30			16.52	
Montreuil	arr.		07.42		13.14			17.41	
	dep.		08.30					18.13	
Rimeux-Gournay			10.30					20.25	
Fruges	arr.		10.56					20.40	
	dep.	05.15	12.35						
Aire	arr.	07.00	14.20						

Boulogne to Bonningues

Boulogne-Ville	dep.		13.30		arr.	08.51	
St-Martin-Boulogne			14.15			08.21	
Licques		05.15	16.30			06.18	18.35
Bonningues	arr.	05.35	16.50		dep.	05.50	18.15

In September 1917, the Anvin-Calais company proposed, supported by the *département*, that a goods train from Ardres to Calais should become a mixed train from Guînes, leaving Guînes at 07.45 and arriving at Calais at 08.23. It was said that this would replace a morning service that had been lost because of the need to increase goods trains at the expense of passenger services. It was particularly needed because many Calais citizens had sought refuge in the *communes* between Ardres and Guînes from the threat of bombing in Calais. These refugees clearly wished to return to Calais to work or to check on their homes. This request was passed on to the *Commissaire Militaire du Réseau du Nord* in Paris. The proposal was implemented and eventually the mixed service was extended so that it started from Ardres.

On 31st May, 1918, the *département* supported a request already made by M. Level, as Director of the *Chemin de fer d'Anvin à Calais*, that certain passenger services should be withdrawn and replaced with goods trains. This was at the request of the British Army for the important transportation of supplies and gravel. The proposed withdrawals were the middle of the day through trains between Ardres and Fruges; the Saturday morning trains between Fruges and Anvin; the middle of the day trains between Berck-Plage and Montreuil; the early morning trains between Fruges and Aire; and one of the two trains per day each way between Ardres and Pont d'Ardres. In addition the 16.20 from Berck-Plage would run 30 minutes earlier from Montreuil to Fruges. In justification for this, it was noted that no-one changed at Montreuil from the connection with the *Compagnie du Nord* train anyway. This change would leave at least one train in each direction every day at all stations, but only one between Fruges and Ardres and Ardres and Pont d'Ardres. There would be no change in the service between Ardres and Calais. It must be noted, however, that since the services withdrawn included the 14.00 from Fruges to Ardres and the 08.08 from Ardres to Fruges (ex-Calais at 07.05) there was no through service on the same day beyond Fruges in either direction on the Anvin-Calais line. In supporting the proposals the *département* noted that 'The retained passenger trains will still be sufficient for the needs of the public, whose travelling must be reduced to that strictly necessary in the interests of national defence; and in any case the reasons given were a matter of military planning and have priority over all other considerations'.

Finally in mid-July 1918 further changes were announced. As a result one train from Berck-Plage to Rang-du-Fliers and back in the mornings would no longer run. Because of changes in connections at Anvin, the 10.15 and the 16.15 from Fruges, returning from Anvin at 11.35 and 18.00 respectively, would be replaced by a single train leaving Fruges at 12.23 and returning from Anvin at 15.18. After the German advances in Spring 1918, the main Arras-Amiens-Paris line was cut and further north, the major centres just east of Aire were threatened. During this period many refugees used the Aire-Berck line to travel from Aire to Rang-du-Fliers, where they joined the coast main line to escape to safer parts of France.

British Army use of the Metre Gauge lines

We think that in respect of lines in the western Pas-de-Calais, Colonel Henniker's assessment of the metre gauge lines, that they only contributed significantly for three to four months in the Spring of 1918, under-estimates the role of these lines, and that there is evidence of a major military function in 1917 and possibly earlier. By 1917 the civilian services were considerably reduced. This does not in itself prove military use; it might for instance be attributable to reduced availability of personnel, or rolling stock, or fuel, because of use in the war effort elsewhere. Need to increase military use was not directly cited as a reason for reduction of services until Spring 1918. However, the provision in 1917 of some additional transhipment facilities, particularly those at Attin near Montreuil on the Aire to Berck line, argues strongly for significant military use by 1917. The contingency plan for withdrawal, in the Spring of 1918, envisaged one day's general supplies and one day's ammunition, enough for a company at each location, being delivered to 14 stations between Z day (the beginning of the withdrawal) and Z+2. The revised list of railheads for this plan submitted in August 1918 included Bonningues and Lumbres on the Anvin-Calais line, Licques on the Boulogne-Bonningues line, and Thérouanne and Dennebrœucq on the Aire-Berck line. These supplies would be brought by seven trains of general supplies from Vendroux, and four trains of ammunition from Audruicq, the ammunition presumably transhipped at Vendroux or Pont d'Ardres onto the metre gauge lines. After the war the Anvin-Calais line, the Aire-Berck line and the Boulogne-Bonningues line attributed current poor timekeeping to the 'intensive use' and poor maintenance of their locomotives during the war.

Doubt has been cast as to whether the Tournehem-St-Momelin line was ever used. We have only one piece of indirect evidence of such use. On 24th August, 1918, the 3rd platoon of the 112th Railway Company (RE) moved to Attin (near Montreuil), where the metre gauge line to Aire and Anvin leaves the standard gauge line. On the morning of the 26th August the rest of the company left Beaurainville and moved to St-Momelin, stopping on the way at Attin. It is likely that this move took place by metre gauge train via Rimeux-Gournay and Tournehem. If the company had travelled either by road, or by standard gauge train, it is unlikely that the larger part of the company would have joined the smaller part at Attin which is further away from St-Momelin, for either of these modes of transport, than is Beaurainville. In any case it is unlikely that the line was not used. It was finished by July or August 1918 and was still in place and being maintained by the British Army at the end of March 1919. This is not in favour of an unused and neglected railway.

Chapter Six

Between the Wars
1918 to 1939

In this chapter, we continue the story by looking at the fate of the lines already described earlier. We begin by looking at the results of World War I and the lines' subsequent recovery. We will follow their progress to the beginning of World War II on 3rd September, 1939. The individual lines will be covered in a slightly different order. As will be seen, their fortunes varied considerably, but even the most fortunate became less viable as 1939 approached. The major reason for this was the rapid increase in road transport: buses for passengers and lorries for freight. Although these had existed before World War I they had been less reliable, less affordable and less available. The rapid development of road transport at this time had been facilitated by developments in military transport during the war. In the period of this chapter, reliability improved, prices came down and oil was cheap and increasingly available. With the flexibility of road transport to provide a service anywhere, local railways, which had been a great improvement when the alternative was walking or horse-based, were clearly going to be threatened. At the end of the chapter, we look at the measures taken by the French Government of the 1930s, particularly 'Coordination', which were in part a response to the increasing competition between road and rail. These measures contributed to the demise of some lines and increased the problems of others.

The aftermath of World War I

Although the lines described in this book were not in the zone of fighting in World War I, the war had a considerable effect upon them. At the time of the Armistice in 1918, the rolling stock and especially the locomotives had been overused and under-maintained. Under the military authorities, stock was requisitioned and sent where needed. Although the organizational problems were worse in the battle zones further east, there were significant problems of recovery and return to normality for these lines too.

We offer one anecdote to illustrate some of these problems and to give an idea of the amount of paperwork that must have been generated in France in 1919. We have chosen to entitle it 'A Little Wagon Lost in France'. The story begins on 10th May, 1919, when the officers responsible for industrial reconstruction at Arras ask the Chief Engineer, based in another office in St-Omer, for a valuation of a particular wagon NVE Z4 in use on the Anvin-Calais line. That is his full name but we can be familiar and call him Nord Z4. Thus, the hero of our story makes his first appearance. All we know about him is that he weighed 3,500 kg and had survived the war, but that he and 19 friends now needed some repairs. They were therefore sent to the repair shops at Lumbres. Three weeks later a letter from Arras states that, since neither Nord Z4, nor possibly his friends, belong to them, the Anvin-Calais line must await the decision of the Ministry of Public Works in Paris on the correct liquidation of stock. On 26th May, 1919, a letter from the Chief Engineer puts a

14 - RANG-du-FLIERS P.-de-C. - La Gare

The forecourt of the Compagnie du Nord station at Rang-du-Fliers, called Rang-du-Fliers-Verton, in the 1920s or 1930s. The *buvette* is on the right with the line from Berck arriving out of sight behind it.   *Éditions Capron-Vallois; Authors' Collection*

The same view in October 2006. The station is now called Rang-du-Fliers-Verton-Berck.
                                                              Authors

value of 2,650 francs on him. Things are looking good for the little wagon, but we must not be hasty. A further letter then informs everyone that Nord Z4 and his 19 friends actually belong to the Guise-Hirson line and they must start the process all over again. The fifth letter in the saga is from yet another office, in Valenciennes this time. This informs Arras that Nord Z4 and his number are known to them but it is not their concern. The buck is passed back to M. Level and the Anvin-Calais line. The end of the story is lost in the mists of time. Did he work happily for many more years for M. Level? Or was he sent somewhere else? He could not have been sent back east to the Guise-Hirson line, because this was now standard gauge. And what happened to his 19 friends?

British Army lines

As early as December 1918, M. Level (of the Anvin-Calais and Aire-Berck lines) was asking the *département* of Pas-de-Calais if it was necessary to maintain the lines installed by the British Army on his networks. In December 1919, the Minister for Public Works in Paris had laid down conditions for the transfer of railways constructed by the British Army. On 26th March, 1920, the Chief Engineer for bridges and highways of the *département* of Pas-de-Calais reported on 'payment for lines and installations recently transferred from the English [*sic*] Military Authority', with recommendations for lines to be incorporated into the network of lines of *Intérêt Local*.

Metre gauge lines

Anvin-Calais and Aire-Berck

In respect of the Anvin-Calais and Aire-Berck lines, the Engineer reported on 26th March, 1920, that the English had only carried out works 'of small importance'. Various sidings and transhipment facilities had been constructed. On the Anvin-Calais line these totalled 4 km in length, and on the Aire-Berck line 4.2 km (about 2½ miles each). The report mentions 13 locations on the Anvin-Calais line and 14 on the Aire-Berck line, with a recommendation for repossession. The list mostly corresponds with that detailing works on these lines in 1917 and 1918 (*see Appendix Two*). It includes all works on the Anvin-Calais line from Tournehem to Anvin except for the works at Wirquin. Since the works at Wirquin were the construction of a loop linked to a factory siding it is possible that the factory took this over. The list does include works at Lumbres supporting the Royal Engineers report of 1918 that they had constructed metre gauge track and sidings there. The list does not include any works between Écluse-Carrée and Calais. On the Aire-Berck line the list does not include the works at Wailly, Beussent and Engoudsent or the two sets of sidings at Crecques. Interestingly, it does include works at Attin, even though the only works there that we know of were said to have been undertaken by French troops in 1917. The cost of repossession of the 8.2 km of lines on the Anvin-Calais-Aire-Berck system, based on a previously agreed price of 44 francs per metre for metre gauge track, increased by 10 per cent for additional costs, came to just under 400,000 francs.

On 8th October, 1921, *M. le Préfet* of Pas-de-Calais ordered the transfer of just under 300,000 francs from the special account for the 'liquidation of material and stock of railways and transport ceded to the French Government by the British Governmentt. This went to the general account for the purchase of 10.765 km (6¾ miles) of laid metre gauge track and 25.5 tonnes of track in stock. The purchases were all on the Anvin-

L.P. 19 - ANVIN - P.-de-C. - Passage à Niveau

Edit. Leclercq   Reproduction interdite.

The level crossing with raised barriers at Anvin just east of the station, shared by the standard gauge line from Étaples to Arras and the beginning of the metre gauge line to Calais, taken in the 1920s or 1930s.   *Éditions Leclercq; Authors' Collection*

The track side of the later station at Berck-Plage, with modernised platforms, probably taken in the 1920s or 1930s.   *Authors' Collection*

Calais and Aire-Berck lines but the list of locations had changed slightly from the list of 26th March, 1920. On the Anvin-Calais line, Anvin was now omitted but Ouve (-Wirquin) included. On the Aire-Berck line Rang-du-Fliers and Bahot had been omitted but Beussent and the RE Park at Thérouanne (in addition to Thérouanne itself) had been included. The works at Attin remained on this list, and were the most extensive, totalling 1.37 km (nearly 1 mile) of track work. However the main reason for the change of length of laid track was that *appareils* (points and other complex track work) were now included. The main reason for the lower price was that the laid line was now priced at 26.40 francs per metre. The stock track was priced at 468 francs per tonne.

In 1920 it was agreed that the Anvin-Calais line could include the sidings at Écluse-Carrée in their system. In 1921 a further decision was made to maintain the facilities built by the 5th (railway) Division of the French army at Écluse-Carrée (sidings) and at Attin-La Paix Faite (transhipment facilities). We do not know how this decision squares with the decision, mentioned above, to include Attin with British Army lines. Possibly both British and French had done works in the Attin area. The transhipment facilities at Attin continued to be used by the *département* and a private contractor until at least 1935. The sidings at Écluse-Carrée, which bordered the canal, were in use until at least 1933, as a transhipment facility for sugar beet from the Anvin-Calais line to barges bound for the *Distillerie de la Lys*. Both these transhipment sites were also used in 1943 by the German authorities to move material inland, probably for the 'V1' programme (*see Chapter Seven*).

The British Army construction in 1917 of the 4-rail dual gauge between Rivière Neuve and the entrance to the Vendroux supply camp led to some tetchy correspondence in the 1920s. The Anvin-Calais line complained in 1923 that the sleepers, which were originally of oak when the line had been built, had been replaced by pine sleepers at the time of dualling. These pine sleepers were now rotting. No doubt in 1917 the British Army had more pressing problems than whether their sleepers would rot in six years time. Another problem arose in 1924. The *Compagnie du Nord* had to pay rent to the Anvin-Calais line for the cost of accommodating their standard gauge lines on the Anvin-Calais track-bed. This caused much friction and in 1924 the *Companie du Nord* wrote to the *département* complaining of this, saying that 'the situation could not be allowed to continue'. Finally, also in 1924, 34,000 francs was allocated to the Anvin-Calais line, apparently for new sleepers. We presume that the standard gauge was removed from this section of track during the works to replace the sleepers.

Berck-Plage to Paris-Plage

The Berck-Plage-Paris-Plage line had particular problems with recovery from the war, partly because it had been closed for the duration of hostilities. These difficulties were intimately connected with the ultimate fate of the line and are detailed in the section on the last phase of the life of this line later in this chapter.

Tournehem to St-Momelin

Of the fate of the Tournehem-St-Momelin line less is known. As noted in Chapter Five, the line was being maintained by the British Army at least to the end of March 1919, but it was lifted not long after. This is perhaps surprising since in 1919 the Anvin-Calais, Aire-Berck and Hazebrouck-Hondschoote-Bergues lines had all came under the management of a new joint company (VFIL, *see below*) and the ex-military Tournehem-

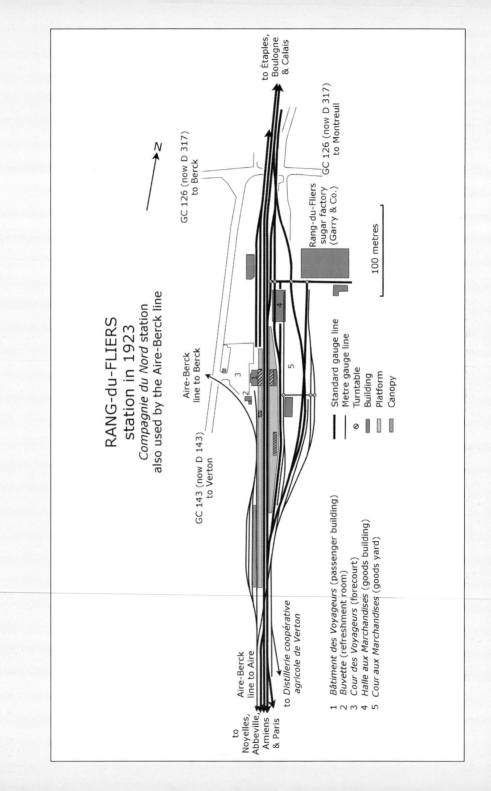

RANG-du-FLIERS
station in 1923
Compagnie du Nord station
also used by the Aire-Berck line

to Étaples,
Boulogne
& Calais

N

GC 126 (now D 317)
to Berck

GC 126 (now D 317)
to Montreuil

Rang-du-Fliers
sugar factory
(Garry & Co.)

100 metres

Aire-Berck
line to Berck

GC 143 (now D 143)
to Verton

to *Distillerie coopérative
agricole de Verton*

Aire-Berck
line to Aire

to
Noyelles,
Abbeville
Amiens
& Paris

Standard gauge line
Metre gauge line
Turntable
Building
Platform
Canopy

1 *Bâtiment des Voyageurs* (passenger building)
2 *Buvette* (refreshment room)
3 *Cour des Voyageurs* (forecourt)
4 *Halle aux Marchandises* (goods building)
5 *Cour aux Marchandises* (goods yard)

St-Momelin line would have seemed a useful link between the lines. Perhaps the problem was that the only way to link the whole network was through the intermediate St-Momelin-Bergues-Herzeele line. This line belonged to the *Société Général des Chemins de Fer Economiques* and perhaps they were not interested. An additional disincentive for VFIL may have been that the resulting line would have been aimed at longer distance travel and the metre gauge railways were satisfying a more leisurely and local style of transport. A further problem could have been that the ex-military lines were without logic in terms of civilian services, and they had no civilian infrastructure.

Rolling stock

By the end of World War I rolling stock was, as has already been noted, widely scattered and often not on the line which had owned it before the war. In addition, because of the pressures on the service and the intensive usage of some of the stock, standards of maintenance had slipped. This applied particularly to locomotives. Even as late as 1925 the Anvin-Calais and Aire-Berck lines blamed locomotive problems on this, and the Boulogne-Bonningues line, also in 1921, attributed their problems with lateness on the hill up from Boulogne to St-Martin to this cause. Some lines acquired locomotives and other rolling stock after the war as *Prise de Guerre* (captured - all German material west of the Armistice line was regarded as in this category), or ceded or abandoned by the German authorities. Further details of problems with rolling stock after the war, and of stock acquired, are given in the sections on each line later in the chapter.

Anvin to Calais and Aire to Berck
(including the Tramway from Ardres to Pont d'Ardres)

It has already been noted in Chapters Two and Three that the Anvin-Calais and Aire-Berck lines were effectively jointly managed by the *Compagnie du Chemin de Fer d'Anvin à Calais* from soon after the full opening of the Aire-Berck line in 1893. In 1919 the two formally joined together, with the tramway from Ardres to Pont d'Ardres, which they had managed since its opening in 1902, as part of the *Compagnie Générale des Voies Ferrées d'Intérêt Local*. This rather confusingly named company is usually abbreviated to VFIL in British literature, but more often CGL in French works. In this book we have used the abbreviation VFIL. Later the company also gave some of the rolling stock the designation CGL rather than AC, for Anvin-Calais, or ARB, for Aire-(Rimeux)-Berck. The other line incorporated into this company in 1919 was the *Chemins de Fer des Flandres* (Hazebrouck-Hondschoote-Bergues), which had been opened by M. Lambert, entrepreneur of the Aire-Berck line, in 1894. Between 1920 and 1930, VFIL acquired a large collection of other metre gauge and standard gauge lines in Pas-de-Calais, Nord, Oise and Aisne. A full list of the lines they acquired is given on page 131 of *Minor Railways of France* by W.J.K. Davies (Plateway Press, 2000).

These lines were the most successful of the steam metre gauge lines in the area of this book, and reached 1939 as a reasonably secure concern. This is attributable to the good original engineering of the lines, and to the management by VFIL, particularly the early use of diesel railcars. These lines, and VFIL, continued to be associated with the name of Level, although by now this was probably a son or even grandson of the Émile Level who had opened the Anvin-Calais line in 1881. Many of the lines acquired by VFIL were those in which the Level family had already long had an interest, as is

Ateliers Nord Belge 2-6-0 tank locomotive, 24 tonnes unladen weight, at Berck-Plage in 1951. No number is shown but since it is marked PDC (Pas-de-Calais) it is most likely to be one of those built in 1909 and acquired by VFIL from the Guise-Hirson line in the early 1920s.

M. Rifault; Collection Bernard Guéret, formerly BVA

One of the two Société Winterthur (SLM) 2-10-0 tank locomotives, 42 tonnes unladen weight, Nos. 51 and 52, built in 1911 and acquired by VFIL from the Guise-Hirson line in the early 1920s. Seen at Lumbres for scrapping in 1955.   *M. Rifault; Collection Bernard Guéret, formerly BVA*

shown by the list of lines in the 1901 operating regulations issued over the name of M. Level. The front pages of these list eight lines, of which seven were started by M. Level or M. Lambert, and of which seven became part of VFIL between 1919 and 1930.

Despite the formation of VFIL, the Aire-Berck company continued to have separate annual meetings of shareholders at least until 1952, and almost certainly until closure in 1955, with annual reports presented to these relating only to the one line. It is almost certain that the Anvin-Calais company did the same.

Stations

Stations had originally been lit by paraffin lamps. By the 1930s most still were. Pressure was put by *communes* for their stations to be given electric light, especially since most other houses and businesses in the *département* were supplied with electricity by this time. The Chief Engineer of the *département* declined to help with this, saying that it was up to VFIL and the *communes* concerned. VFIL were clearly reluctant to spend money on this. Hucqeliers council offered to meet 50 per cent of the cost for their station, and probably other *communes* did too. As far as we know all stations were eventually lit by electric light.

Industrial links

It has already been noted in Chapters Two and Three that before World War I weighbridges were installed at some stations for the weighing of sugar beet. In 1924 a weighbridge was installed at Acquin for the Say factory at Pont d'Ardres. In 1927 one was installed at Journy, even though one was already there for the Say factory from 1905, and this may have been a second one for another company. Between 1922 and 1926 weighbridges were also installed at a further eight stations on the Aire-Berck line, and at Coyecques two were installed, by different companies, at opposite ends of the goods area. At the Aire end of the line two were installed by the Béghin refinery at Thumeries. In the central part of the line near Rimeux-Gournay most were for the Say factory at Pont d'Ardres. One was for the Garry sugar factory at Rang-du-Fliers. However, the three nearest the Berck end of the line were installed by the Agricultural Cooperative distillery at Verton, all in 1922. In 1923 this distillery applied to build extra metre gauge access to its works at Verton. This distillery is of interest because as far as we know it was set up after World War I and even before 1923 had extensive metre gauge and standard gauge track work, with some dual gauge lines within the works building. This building was on the site of the combined metre and standard gauge locomotive repair works built by the British Army in 1918, and probably the track work, and possibly also part of the building, dated from that time (*see page 188*).

VFIL Steam locomotives

Technical details of steam locomotives acquired by the VFIL up to 1939 are shown in *Table Twenty-One*. For the sake of convenience the last steam locomotive acquired by these lines, formerly No. 3 of Berck-Plage-Paris-Plage, and put into service by VFIL in 1941 or 1942 as No. 13, is also shown in this table. A full motive power list for all the lines in this book is given in *Appendix One*.

SLM Winterthür (Switzerland) 2-10-0
41.66 tonne steam locomotives Nos. 51 and 52
as built for the Guise-Hirson line in 1911
and put into service on the Anvin-Calais-Aire-Berck lines in 1922

Collection Jean Willig

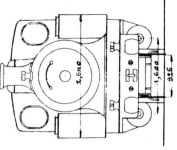

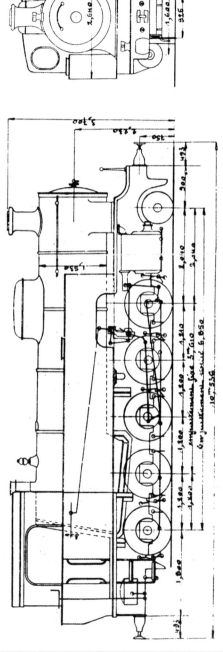

Table Twenty-One
Technical details of VFIL steam locomotives acquired from 1919

Manufacturer	ANB *	SLM	Henschel	SACM
Year(s) of manufacture	1909 & 1924	1911	1917	1924
Type	2-6-0T	2-10-0T	0-6-0+0-6-0T	2-6-0T
Works No(s)			15 161	7381
Company No(s)	23-25, 120,121,126	51 & 52	161	13 †
Year(s) put in service	1922 & 1924	1922	1931	1941/2
Number put in service	6	2	1	1
Length (m)	8.52	10.54	11.56	7.89
Height (m)	3.42	3.70	3.65	3.40
Width (m)	2.59	2.66	2.70	2..31
Weight empty (tonnes)	24	41.66	45.3	22
Weight loaded (tonnes)	31	53.86	54.5	27.85
Wheelbase (m)	4.43	6.85	(2.50 each 6)	4.15
Driving wheelbase (m)	2.54	4.81	7.00	2.45
Dia. of driving wheels (m)	1.06	1.07	0.90	0.90
Boiler capacity (m³)	3.500	4.400	5.730	2.000
Boiler pressure (kg/cm²)	14	12	14	12
Heating surface (m²)	65.51	131.40	82.71	56.50
Water capacity (L)	3,200	5,600	4,500	2,850
Coal capacity (kg)	1,200	1,000	1,400	1,000
Dia. of valves (mm)	100			
Dia. of pistons (m)	0.36	0.44	0.40	0.32
Piston travel (m)	0.46	0.52	0.45	0.42

* Identical to Nos. 20 and 22, see *Table Two*
† Originally No. 3 Berck-Plage-Paris-Plage, in service from 1924

After World War I, VFIL acquired locomotives and other rolling stock from the Guise-Hirson line. During the war this line had been behind the German lines and had been converted by the German army to standard gauge. It linked at Hirson with the German army 'strategic lateral railway' (*rocade*) from Lille to Metz. After the war the French authorities decided that this line should remain standard gauge, and the metre gauge rolling stock was therefore available.

By 1921, VFIL had acquired five locomotives from the Guise-Hirson line, three 2-6-0 24 tonne tank engines built in 1909 at the *Ateliers Nord* (Belgium) and two 42 tonne 2-10-0 tank engines built by SLM Winterthür (Switzerland) in 1911. A report in 1921 gives the state of these engines, and says that they were already either in the depot, or working on the Anvin-Calais or Aire-Berck lines. The 24 tonne locomotives are numbered Nos. 2, 3, and 6, which were probably their Guise-Hirson numbers. They all required work, including boiler refurbishment for two. They were valued at between 15,000 and 30,000 francs, with the one in the worst state requiring 40,000 francs of repairs. They were identical to Nos. 20 and 22, in use on the Anvin-Calais and Aire-Berck lines since 1906 and 1910, and were given the Nos. 23 to 25. Of the 42 tonne locomotives, one, No. 52, had already been repaired at the VFIL depot at Lumbres at a cost of 3,432 francs, had received boiler approval, and was ready for work. This locomotive was valued at 70,000 francs. The other, No. 51, required further work and was valued at 65,000 francs. In 1922 the use of these between Lumbres and Bonningues was approved, and the road bridge of *tablier métallique* at

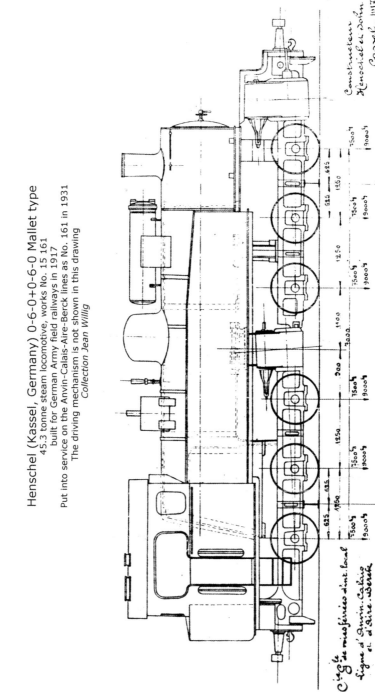

Henschel (Kassel, Germany) 0-6-0+0-6-0 Mallet type
45.3 tonne steam locomotive, works No. 15 161
built for German Army field railways in 1917
Put into service on the Anvin-Calais-Aire-Berck lines as No. 161 in 1931
The driving mechanism is not shown in this drawing
Collection Jean Willig

Acquin had been strengthened for this purpose. Presumably other bridges on the lines were later similarly strengthened, and these 2-10-0 locomotives were definitely at work for sugar beet trains in the season from November 1924.

VFIL also acquired for use on these lines two locomotives reported to be *prise de guerre*. The first was a Henschel (Germany) 0-6-0+0-6-0 of Mallet type. This had been built for German army metre gauge field railways, and was numbered 161. In November 1930 the company requested permission to use this locomotive and this was granted in January 1931, for use on the sections Anvin-Guînes and Aire-Montreuil. The context suggests that this was the first request for permission to use this locomotive and if this is correct we do not know its history between 1918 and 1930. It was built by Henschel in 1917 with the works number 15 161, one of a series of 20 numbered 15 150 to 15 169, unloaded weight 45 tonnes and loaded weight 54 tonnes. Despite its length the Mallet design enabled it to tolerate curves down to a radius of 40 metres. With a maximum speed of 30 kph, the consumption of 236 kg of water and 32 kg of coal per train km gave a range at this speed of 19 km before taking on water and 56 km before re-coaling, but we do not know what weight of train this allowed. The other captured locomotive was a Jung 0-6-0T, built in 1897, which was used on the line from Ardres to Pont d'Ardres. We have no other information about this locomotive.

VFIL also acquired three more 2-6-0 tank locomotives of 24 tonnes built in 1924 by *Ateliers Nord* (Belgium). These were identical with Nos. 20 and 22 to 25 from the same works built in 1906 and 1909, and were numbered 120, 121 and 126.

VFIL Carriages and Goods wagons

VFIL obtained from the Guise-Hirson line 12 bogie passenger carriages in various states of repair, two of which had been converted into ambulance coaches during the war, and two baggage wagons.

Also obtained from the Guise-Hirson line were 22 covered wagons (two serviceable), 19 high-sided wagons (nine serviceable), 21 low-sided or flat wagons (14 serviceable), and a mobile crane. One of these may have been Nord Z4, whose story has already been told (*see page 197*). Twenty-nine further goods wagons were expected from Guise-Hirson later.

VFIL Petrol and Diesel railcars

VFIL began trying out railcars with internal combustion engines in the early 1920s. Technical details of railcars acquired or built by VFIL up to 1939 are shown in *Table Twenty-Two*. In 1924 and 1925 two Renault-Scemia two-axle petrol-powered railcars were put in service, and were given the numbers RS1 and RS2. The first, owned by VFIL, had the drive on one axle only. The second, owned by the *département*, was driven through both axles. Both had 45 hp 4-cylinder petrol engines and could seat 25, with up to 15 standing. At least one was tried out initially on the tramway from Ardres to Pont d'Ardres. In 1926 both were in use between Anvin and Fruges, covering 120 km per day. Their use on this section allowed the re-establishment of a third daily train between Anvin and Lumbres. The running expenses were less than 2 francs per kilometre, comparable with a steam train on this line, but they could only be used for passengers and small parcels. Therefore if used

One of the later bogie coaches at Acquin, probably for scrapping, in 1955. This is probably one of those acquired by VFIL from the Guise-Hirson line in the early 1920s.

M. Rifault; Collection Bernard Guéret, formerly BVA

on sections with heavy goods traffic their use might require separate steam trains for goods to be run. The Departmental Engineer reported that the trials had been entirely successful, and recommended the purchase of at least one more railcar for use on parts of the Aire-Berck line. VFIL refused to consider the extra expense at that time, even on the basis of a loan from the *département*. Between 1933 and 1935 these two railcars were refurbished at the VFIL works at Lumbres and fitted with diesel engines. One was shortened, given a 65 hp Unic diesel engine, and renumbered CGL 11; the other remained the original length, was given an 85 hp Berliet diesel engine, and took the number PdC (Pas-de-Calais) 101; this was the one originally, and probably still, owned by the *département*. We know from the accident records that CGL 11 was in use on the Ardres-Pont d'Ardres line in 1934 and in 1936 and it is probable that this was the regular passenger vehicle on this line from 1934 up to World War II.

Table Twenty-Two
Technical details of VFIL railcars acquired 1923 to 1934

Manufacturer	Renault-Scemia	Renault-Scemia	VFIL	VFIL
Year(s) of manufacture			1932	1933 & 1934
Type	2 axle	2 axle	2 axle	2 axle
	(4 wheels)	(4 wheels)	(4 wheels)	(4 wheels)
Company No(s)	RS1 *	RS2 †	ARB 2 #	ARB 3-5
	(CGL 11)	(PdC 101)		CGL 6-7
Year(s) put in service	1924	1925	1932 or 33	1933 & 1934
No. put in service	1	1	1	5
Length (m)	9.40	9.40	9.30	9.30
Height (m)	3.30	3.30	2.75	2.75
Width (m)	2.60	2.60	2.70	2.70
Weight empty (tonnes)	9.30	10.00	8.00	8.50
Weight loaded (tonnes)	12.80	13.50	11.00	11.00
Wheelbase (m)	3.60	3.60	3.75	3.75
Dia. of wheels (m)	0.80	0.80	0.72	0.72
Drive	1 axle	2 axles	1 axle	1 axle
Weight of adherence (kg)	6,500	13,500	4,000	4,000
Engine			de Dion JMH	Unic M24
Fuel	petrol	petrol	petrol	diesel
Power (hp)	45	45	65	65
Transmission	prob. mech.	prob. mech.	mech.	mech.
Driving positions	Both ends	Both ends	One end	One end
Speeds (kph)			at 2,000 rpm	at 2,000 rpm
Reverse			10	11
1st gear	10	10	11	11.5
2nd gear	16	16	18	20
3rd gear	22	22	34	34.5
Direct drive	40	40	54.5	56
Capacity seated	24	25	28	29
Capacity standing	15	15	12	11
Baggage compartment	one end	one end	at rear	at rear
Post compartment	other end	other end	none	none

*   Owned by VFIL. Refurbished 1933-35 with 65 hp Unic diesel, shortened, given No. CGL 11.

†   Owned by the *département*. Refurbished 1933-35 with 85 hp Berliet diesel, given No. PdC (Pas-de-Calais) 101.

VFIL also built CGL 1, no further details of this vehicle.

Two-axle diesel railcar CGL No. 11 at Lumbres, probably for scrapping, in 1955. This was originally the petrol driven Renault Scemia RS1 built in 1924, and was rebuilt with a diesel engine and shortened in 1933-1935.   *M. Rifault; Collection Bernard Guéret, formerly BVA*

The depot at Fruges in 1953 with 2-axle diesel railcar ARB No. 3. The locomotive is probably an Ateliers Nord Belge 2-6-0 tank built in 1909.   *J. Bazin; Collection Bernard Guéret, formerly BVA*

One of the diesel railcars built at the VFIL works at Lumbres in the 1930s waits at Rimeux-Gournay junction in 1953. It is heading towards Calais or Berck-Plage; the lines diverge 200 yards to the right.   *J. Bazin; Collection Bernard Guéret, formerly BVA*

The Anvin-Calais type 1 station at Ardres, beginning of the line to Pont d'Ardres, in 1953. The 2-axle railcar with staff is ARB No. 5.   *J. Bazin; Collection Bernard Guéret, formerly BVA*

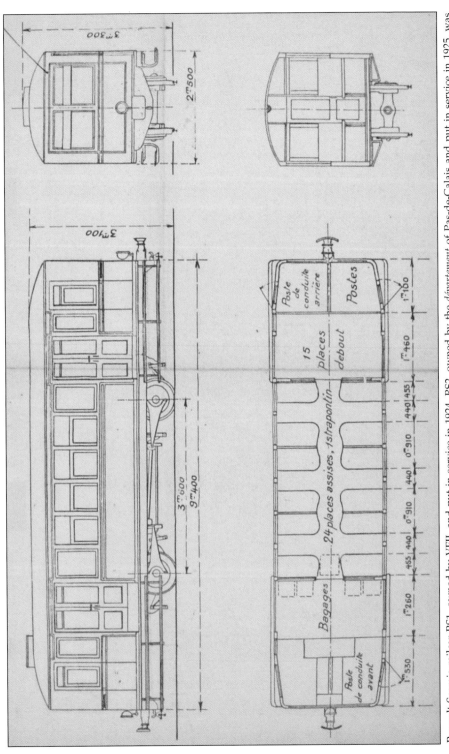

Renault-Scemia railcar RS1, owned by VFIL and put in service in 1924. RS2, owned by the *département* of Pas-de-Calais and put in service in 1925, was different in technical respects but appeared the same.

From the 1930s the VFIL Lumbres works began to produce their own diesel railcars for the Anvin-Calais and Aire-Berck lines. These were 2-axle railcars and looked rather like the sort of model one might make from a shoe box, with holes cut out for the windows, and wheels added! Nonetheless they served these lines well, right up to closure in 1955. Seven were produced, numbered 1 to 7. All seven were unidirectional in the sense that they could only be driven from one end, although they did have a reverse gear. They were small enough to go on the manual turntables available at stations at the end of journeys. Nos. 3 to 7 were all built to the same design, from 1933 onwards, and were fitted with 65 horse power Unic diesel engines. There were 29 seats and the unladen weight was 8.5 tonnes. No. 2, built in 1932, had, at least initially, a de Dion petrol engine, and was different in other minor respects, notably that there were 28 seats, and that the unladen weight was 8 tonnes. The window configuration was different, the four windows between the front and back doors were of equal size, whereas on Nos. 3 to 7 the window just behind the front door was smaller. Finally, Nos. 3 to 7 had a slope on both ends of the roof of the body, but No. 2 only had a slope at the front. No. 2 may have been built on the chassis of vehicle No. 31 (a passenger carriage) of the Flanders network. We do not have any details of No. 1 as it was originally built. However, it is almost certain that No. 1 was the railcar rebuilt in 1955, and now owned by the *Chemin de Fer de la Baie de Somme* as their No. M31 (*see Chapter Eight*). Even the rebuilt railcar shows that originally it must have been very similar to Nos. 2 to 7. Nos. 2 to 5 were given ARB numbers, that is specific to the Aire-(Rimeux)-Berck line, whereas Nos. 1, 6 and 7 were designated CGL, that is generic for VFIL. The photographs of these railcars show that, at least after World War II, the designation bore no relation to where they used. Nos. 2 to 5 were in service by 1934, and probably the others were too.

Departmental regulations on lighting in 1935 noted that CGL1 and CGL2 each had a Marchal headlamp of 50 candlepower, without dimming or dipping capability. Other railcars of VFIL on the Anvin-Calais-Aire-Berck lines had a Ducellier headlamp of 50 candlepower with the ability to dim to three candlepower. A red light also had to be shown on the front of railcars 2.60 metres from the ground and 0.80 metres to the right of the midline.

As far as we know the VFIL works at Lumbres built no more railcars for these lines. They did, however, go on to build a whole series of two-axle and bogie railcars for other metre gauge and standard gauge lines. The works were conveniently situated for the latter beside the standard gauge *Compagnie du Nord* line at Lumbres.

Operations

The timetable for the Anvin-Calais line for May 1919 (*see Table Twenty-Three*) shows a service still much reduced from that before World War I. The service was split at Fruges and there was no possibility of travelling the whole length of the line on the same day. There was one train each way between Fruges and Anvin, and likewise one between Fruges and Calais-Ville. There was one more train from Lumbres to Calais-Ville and back to Bonningues, and one train from Calais-Ville to Ardres but not in the other direction. We presume that these were mixed trains and that they were goods only for part of their journeys. We have found more definite instances of this during and around the wars, and this is the only way this timetable could work.

Diesel railcars ARB Nos. 3 to 5 and CGL Nos. 6 & 7
built at the VFIL works at Lumbres in 1933 & 1934
Collection André Artur

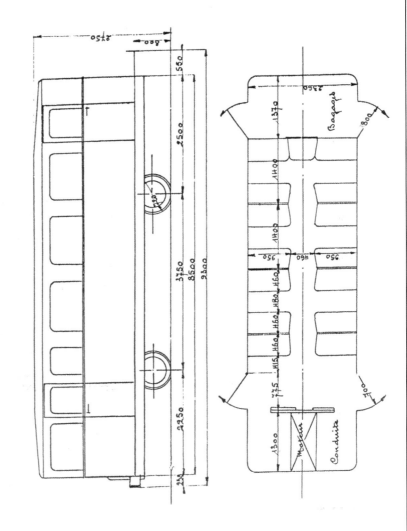

Table Twenty-Three
Anvin to Calais
Summary Timetable from 7th May, 1919

Anvin	dep.			18.50	▲ arr.	09.13			
Fruges	arr.			19.42	dep.	08.27			
	dep.	07.56			arr.		20.12		
Rimeux-Gournay		08.18					19.57		
Lumbres	arr.	09.39			dep.		18.45		
	dep.	10.17	15.40		arr.		18.08		
Bonningues		11.19	17.08				17.12		21.18
Ardres		12.09	18.08				16.25	19.03	20.32
Guînes		12.35	18.37				15.55	18.42	20.05
Calais-Ville	arr.	13.02	19.04		dep.		15.18	18.05	19.30

In December 1919, application was made for an increase in the allowed delay of the departure of what was by now the 19.12 from Anvin for Fruges. The *Compagnie du Nord* train from Arras brought most of the passengers changing for stations towards Fruges, and was due at Anvin at 19.02. However, in October 1919, the train from Arras had been late 23 times and more than 30 minutes late seven times. Application was therefore made for the Fruges train to be allowed to wait up to 50 minutes, rather than the previous 30, to assure the connection. The Anvin-Calais company pointed out that the four crews providing the mixed train service out of Fruges were already working days of between 13 hours 46 minutes and 16 hours 33 minutes, although probably they worked alternate days, with only two crews on any one day. These working hours could not be increased and therefore any additional waiting for the last train at Anvin must be limited to at most once per month per crew.

It is clear from the documents accumulated in the archives over many years that, with the relatively infrequent service and the number of connecting services, both within the VFIL Pas-de-Calais network and with the *Compagnie du Nord*, it was still not possible to please all of the people all of the time. One example from the 1920s will suffice. In Spring 1922 there was a vigorous complaint from Fauqembergues about the connections at Lumbres with the *Compagnie du Nord* service going towards St-Omer. This, it was claimed, made it impossible to travel from Fauquembergues to St-Omer and back in a day, whereas before the war it had been possible, and the pre-war service should be re-instated. Both the Departmental Engineer and the company (VFIL) responded to this. The Engineer conceded that one problem had been lateness of trains, leading to missed connections. This was due to the poor state of the locomotives after the war. However, with improvements at the Lumbres workshops reliability was better and the problem was rapidly coming to an end. The engineer helpfully pointed out that it was possible to go from Fauquembergues to St-Omer and back in a day, even though this only gave you less than an hour there, from 12.39 to 13.35, the time when everything was shut for lunch! It was possible to get to St-Omer at 07.20 and leave at 13.35 but only on Saturday, which was market day in St-Omer. On market days the Anvin-Calais train left Fauquembergues extra early to connect with the St-Omer train at Lumbres. The main problem identified by both the Engineer and the company was that the *Compagnie du Nord* had changed their timetables so that the morning trains towards St-Omer and towards Boulogne no longer crossed at Lumbres, the St-Omer train being much earlier than before, at 06.39 hours. The Boulogne morning train did not leave Lumbres until 08.38. To meet the St-Omer train every day would mean the train leaving Fruges at 04.50 every day. The company pointed out that the longer daily hours would mean doubling the train

Paul Boulanger, impr.-édit. Fruges

The Anvin-Calais type 1 station at Fruges. Postcard written in 1919. Note the *Estaminet* (café) *de l'Univers* to the right. This was nearer to the station than the estaminet 'A LA DESCENTE DES MECANICIENS' (*see photograph page 63*), and may have been built later.

Éditions Paul Boulanger, Fruges; Authors' Collection

L'Avenue de la Gare at Fruges, as above, in April 2006. The station has been replaced by a modern college, but the *Estaminet de l'Univers* is still there on the right, with the same name.

Authors

crews for this train set, and that they had in any case made a loss on the Anvin-Calais line of 388,801 francs in 1920 and 305,414 francs in 1921. The people who should restore the pre-war status quo were the *Compagnie du Nord*. We do not know how all this was resolved, or what were the comments of the *Compagnie du Nord*, but in later timetables there was no very early train from Fruges to Lumbres on any day of the week.

On 19th May, 1925, the *département* reported on the lateness of trains on the Anvin-Calais and Aire-Berck lines. Although the situation was worse during the sugar beet season, there were often significant delays at other times. These were attributed to the fact that the whole service was provided by mixed passenger/goods trains. It was therefore often necessary to shunt in the stations. In addition it was necessary to deliver parcels, which were also carried on the mixed trains. It was in the nature of lines of *Intérêt Local* that staff were scarce, and the writer of the report could not see any way around these problems. The other problem was with rolling stock, especially locomotives, which even now in 1925 (and despite the comments of the Departmental Engineer in 1922 that this problem 'will rapidly disappear') was being blamed on intensive use and poor maintenance during the war. Finally the sugar beet season from November 1924 to January 1925 had involved moving an unusually abundant harvest, but the two new 2-10-0 tank engines had helped greatly.

Despite these problems, and the limited timetable shortly after World War I, the service improved quite quickly, but on the Anvin-Calais line did not return to that provided in Spring 1913 (*see Table Four in Chapter Two and Table Twelve in Chapter Three*). The Anvin-Calais timetable for autumn 1936 is shown in the *Table Twenty-Four*. Among other things, this shows how complex some of these timetables had become, with some services based on, or modified for, market days, weekends, and holidays. Unlike before World War I there was only one train shown as going the whole length of the line in each direction, and this waited more than an hour at Fruges on most days. There was in effect another through train from Calais to Anvin. This is the 06.32 from Calais-Ville, which is shown as stopping at Lumbres; but another train went on from Lumbres. The service pattern strongly suggests that this was in fact the same train going on, but in any case this was effectively a through service. There was no second through service in the other direction. There was one additional service from Bonningues to Calais-Ville and back, and two from Fruges to Anvin and back, every day. There were also one or more additional trains every day between Guînes and Calais-Ville. The service was based on trains at Fruges, but with one train based at Bonningues and one at Guînes. We have already noted in Chapter Two that a locomotive shed had been provided at Bonningues by 1913. By this time a shed and a *dortoir* (dormitory) for staff had been provided at Guînes.

In 1930 the Anvin-Calais and Aire-Berck lines abolished the third class and changed to first and second class only. We have already noted that the Ardre-Pont d'Ardres and Boulogne-Bonningue lines only ever had two classes. We do not know why the other lines changed at this time. However, it must have facilitated the introduction of more diesel railcars a few years later. None of these had any facilities for more than one class, and they were second class only. First class would have been available on steam-, or later diesel locomotive-hauled trains with passenger carriages.

On the Aire-Berck line the autumn 1936 timetable (*Table Twenty-Five*) shows two trains over the full length of the line every day, with at least three trains per day each way at every station. However there were long waiting times at Fruges, 2½ hours in the case of the 06.50 from Berck-Plage. There was only an additional train from

Table Twenty-Four

Anvin to Calais – Summary Timetable 4th October, 1936

Anvin to Calais

Station		(1)MV	(2)	(3)	(4)		MV	(5)MV	(6)	(7)			(8)	(8)
Anvin	dep.								10.25	10.25	17.00		19.51	
Fruges	arr.								10.59	10.59	17.34		20.25	
	dep.								12.24	12.24	17.40			
Rimeux-Gournay	dep.		07.13	08.23	08.53				12.35	12.35	17.50			
Lumbres	arr.		07.24	08.34	09.26				13.19	13.19	18.25			
	dep.	07.06	08.08	09.18		10.19	13.00		13.48	14.20	19.23			
Bonningues		08.03				10.54	13.34		14.42	15.17	19.57			
Ardres		08.34				11.22			15.21	15.56	20.34			
Guines						11.42		14.13	15.45	16.18	20.51	18.53		20.53
Calais-Ville	arr.					12.04		14.42	16.09	16.42		19.17		21.17

Calais to Anvin

Station		(9)	(10)	(11)	(12)	(13)	(14)	(6)	(7)	(5)MV					(8)
Calais-Ville	dep.	05.53	06.15	06.32	06.32			10.34	10.34		16.59	18.12	19.40		
Guines		06.19	06.41	07.00	07.00			11.04	11.04		17.21	18.38	20.05		
Ardres			07.05	07.16	07.16			11.26	11.26		17.37		20.30		
Bonningues			07.33	07.38	08.48*			12.08	12.08	13.28	18.03		20.55		
Lumbres	arr.			08.12	09.22			13.04	13.04	13.55	18.37				
	dep.					09.36	09.36	13.49	14.18		19.05				
Rimeux-Gournay	arr.					10.31	11.11	14.34	15.07		19.50				
Fruges	arr.					10.41	11.21	14.44	15.12		20.00				
	dep.	07.42	08.02			11.31	11.31	16.03	16.03					18.36	21.32
Anvin	arr.	08.16	08.36			12.05	12.05	16.37	16.37					19.10	21.57

* Arrives at Bonningues 07.38
MV Mixed train (Marchandises/Voyageurs)

(1) Thursdays only (market day in Ardres)
(2) Wednesdays only
(3) Except Wednesdays
(4) Saturdays only (market day in Fruges)
(5) Saturdays unless a holiday, in which case Thursdays
(6) Except Saturdays all year, and except Sundays and Feast days from 21st June to 20th September
(7) Saturdays all year, and Sundays and Feast days from 21st June to 20th September and 14th August
(8) Sundays and feast days only
(9) Mondays, Wednesdays and Saturdays, also Friday 14th August and Tuesday 10th September
(10) Tuesdays, Thursdays, Fridays and Sundays, except Friday 14th August and Tuesday 10th September
(11) Except Fridays
(12) Fridays (market day in Lumbres)
(13) Except Thursdays
(14) Thursdays only (market day in Fauquembergues) (waits 41 minutes at Fauquembergues).

L. P. 5 - ARDRES - P.-de-C. - La Gare, ligne d'Anvin à Calais inaugurée en 1882

The Anvin-Calais type 1 station at Ardres. postcard written in 1934. This was also the beginning of the tramway to Pont d'Ardres.   *Collection Jean Willig*

The road side of Hucqueliers station in the 1920s or 1930s. The goods building is on the left, the *buvette* is on the right.   *Éditions G Dewidehem; Authors' Collection*

L. P. 4 - HUCQUELIERS - P.-de-C. - La Gare

Edit. G. Dewidehem   Reproduction interdite

Berck-Plage to Montreuil and back on market day in Montreuil. All this was supplemented, even in this low season, by 10 to 12 additional trains between Berck-Plage and Rang-du-Fliers. This all represents only a slight reduction in service compared with Spring 1914. The overall service is clearly based at the depots at Fruges and at Berck-Plage.

Table Twenty-Five
Aire to Berck
Summary Timetable 4th October, 1936

				(1)	(2)MV		
Aire	dep.			08.40	12.28	14.22	19.06
Fruges	arr.			09.52	14.03	15.34	20.18
	dep.	05.50		11.34		16.41	
Rimeux-Gournay		06.06		11.50		16.57	
Montreuil	arr.	07.27		13.11		18.18	
	dep.	08.04	12.10	13.30		18.53	
Rang	arr.	08.35	12.51	14.02		19.25	
	dep.	08.38	12.54	14.04		19.27	
Berck-Plage	arr.	08.50	13.08	14.16		19.38	

			(2)MV		(1)		
Berck-Plage	dep.			06.50	08.56	12.04	17.20
Rang	arr.			07.02	09.08	12.16	17.32
	dep.			07.04	09.10	12.18	17.37
Montreuil	arr.			07.35	09.42	12.50	18.04
	dep.			08.09		13.45	18.09
Rimeux-Gournay				09.31		15.12	20.02
Fruges	arr.			09.46		15.22	20.15
	dep.	05.48	06.58	12.16		16.16	
Aire	arr.	07.00	08.30	13.28		17.28	

MV Mixed train (*Marchandises/Voyageurs*)

(1) Saturdays (market day in Montreuil)
(2) Fridays (market day at Aire)

Note: Eleven additional trains per day Rang to Berck (10 on Saturdays). Twelve additional trains per day Berck to Rang (11 on Saturdays).

As can be seen from the timetables, by 1936 the service was mainly provided by passenger only trains, but there were a small number of mixed trains on both lines. Average line speeds had also increased, reducing the actual travelling time from Calais to Anvin to 4½ hours. The problem lay in waiting times for connections at Fruges. On the Aire-Berck line, the total travelling time would have been less than four hours if the waiting time at Fruges and at Montreuil could be eliminated. The introduction of mainly passenger only trains and the increased line speeds are attributable to the introduction of the diesel railcars. These times represent an average line speed, including short stops, of more than 20 kph (12½ mph), which compares with at best 18 kph (11½ mph) in the early days of these lines.

Clearly the company felt that long waiting times at Fruges were a reasonable pay-off for maximising the choice of connections. During the morning between the arrival of the train from Berck at 09.46 and the departure of the train for Calais at 12.24, it was possible to arrive from any station on either line and change to another train for any station on either line, with a longest wait of 2 hours and 38 minutes (from Berck, towards Calais). In the afternoon between the arrival of the 13.34 from

Anvin and the departure of the 17.40 to Calais it was also possible to come from any station and change for any station. The longest wait in this case was 2 hours and 57 minutes (changing from Anvin, towards Berck). It was also possible to make some of these changes at Rimeux-Gournay junction. This might possibly avoid some fares, when changing from Berck towards Calais and vice versa, but at the price of waiting longer on a station that, unlike Fruges, had no nearby café.

In 1936 the service from Ardres to Pont d'Ardres ran four times per day in each direction, with a fifth service on Thursdays, Saturdays and Sundays. The service was provided by diesel railcar or steam train. The timetable indicated different journey times for each, 13 minutes for railcar and 22 minutes for steam.

During the 1920s passenger numbers on the Aire-Berck line were at their best ever, over 550,000 in most years. During the 1930s passenger numbers declined, to about 380,000 in 1938. Goods traffic also fell. In spite of making an operating loss in the later years of World War I, the Aire-Beck line returned to a reasonable profit in the 1920s. Profits, however, never returned to their pre-war levels. By 1930 costs were rising, but were reduced from 1932 with the introduction of more diesel railcars. At the same time, however, receipts per train kilometre were also falling, with lower passenger numbers, so that during the 1930s operating profits declined. By the beginning of World War II the line was just about breaking even.

Level crossings and accidents

Level crossings continued to be a source of accidents. Whereas before World War I these had mostly been with horse and carts, now motor vehicles were usually involved. We have already noted that the line speeds of diesel railcars were faster than those for steam-hauled trains. In addition the railcars were said to have weaker horns than the steam whistles. It might be expected that this combination of features would lead, in the 1930s, to an increased number of accidents at un-gated level crossings. Another factor, however, was the increased speed of road vehicles, and not all of the trains involved were railcars.

Two particular level crossings were a problem in this period. The first was at Verchin, between Fruges and Anvin. The line crossed the GC71 (now the D71E) by the eastern entrance to the station approach. There were banks on two corners, 2½ metres (8 feet) high, and these hid approaching trains from the road. In March 1932 a local paper reported a case at the *Tribunal correctional* (Magistrates Court) at Montreuil. The piece was headed 'The Danger Spot at Verchin' and refers to 'this notorious level crossing which frequently causes serious accidents and which, being un-guarded, constitutes, because of poor visibility, a real public danger'. In the accident on 5th March, 1932, the car driver, a merchant from a nearby village, had 'ventured' onto the crossing after slowing down and sounding his horn. A railcar had then 'arrived at high speed'. The driver of the railcar had already been involved in a previous hearing into another less serious accident. In this later accident the mother-in-law of the car driver had been killed and it was the unfortunate motorist who found himself pursued for causing her death, and by the company for damages. The newspaper, clearly sympathetic to the motorist, comments that the Court had shown sound justice in acquitting the defendant and dismissing the company's claim.

In June 1932, after this and another accident, the Mayor of Verchin tried unilaterally to impose a speed limit of 5 kph at this crossing, and an earlier warning of approach by trains. The Departmental Engineer responded by reminding him that the regulations could only be changed by the *Préfet* of the *département*. He also noted that these already said that motorists should slow down to 15 kph, 100 metres from an unguarded level crossing. It had been alleged that lorry drivers could not hear the more feeble sound of the horn of a railcar over the sound of their engines. The company's response was that there were adequate warning signs of an approaching level crossing and this should be sufficient.

The second level crossing causing problems was at Brêmes, about 0.5 km west of the station at Ardres, where the line crossed the main road, then the GC231 (now the D231). In an accident on 8th August, 1938, a lorry coming from Ardres hit the back of a diesel railcar coming from Calais. Four passengers in the railcar were injured, two seriously. The investigators clearly blamed the lorry driver, since the railcar had given due warning of approach and had been 'fully engaged' on the crossing before the lorry arrived. Attention was drawn to the regulations of 1917, stating that trains have priority at un-gated crossings, and that it was up to the road vehicle driver to ascertain that the line was clear before proceeding. Nevertheless, there had been four accidents here between 1927 and 1938, some involving serious injury to the road users. Although the allowed speed at a crossing was up to 35 kph for a railcar, compared with a maximum of 15 kph for road vehicles, it was recommended that railcars should slow down to 15 kph at this crossing, without interfering with their priority. The warning signs should also be improved.

Given all these problems with motor vehicles at level crossings, it is perhaps ironic that, in 1930, the Mayor of Bonningues had drawn attention to a different problem with two level crossings in his *commune*. This was that, where the Anvin-Calais line crossed the GC225 (now the D225), and where the Boulogne-Bonningues line crossed the GC223 (now the D223), the level was raised and this caused severe jolting when motor vehicles crossed rapidly. The Departmental Engineer reported that work had already been undertaken on one of these crossings and would be put in hand for the other. Given the later problems detailed above, one wonders now if it might not have been better to leave these early 'speed bumps' as they were.

Although the tramway from Ardres to Pont d'Ardres was only 6 km long it had its share of accidents particularly at one level crossing. This was where the N43, the main road from Calais to St-Omer crossed the line, by the *arrêt* at Les Tilleuls. The first accidents were, as elsewhere, with horse-drawn farm carts, but as motor vehicles became more common and speeds increased, so did the accidents.

On Christmas Day 1929, a horse-drawn cart was hit by a train on this level crossing. The lady carter was injured and the report lists her injuries, none too serious. The horse took off to Ardres! The enquiry, having laboriously checked that the hooter was sounded adequately, placed the blame firmly with the lady farmer and the horse.

The next reports were of accidents involving cars and these continued to surface throughout the early 1930s. The problem came to a head, however, on 23rd November, 1934, when five people were killed when their car was hit on the level crossing and caught fire. At the resulting enquiry a pronouncement was made that something must be done 'to protect car drivers from their own folly'. As a result, M. Level, President and administrator of VFIL, was called to the enquiry. After much blustering that traditionally trains had right of way and any delay would upset his passengers, he agreed to stop his trains before venturing onto this level crossing. He seemed to obtain agreement that this site should be the only level crossing to have this special treatment.

Tramways of Calais (including Calais To Guînes)

The Calais tramway network continued to operate between the wars. In 1932 the *Société Anonyme des Tramways de Calais et Extensions* complained that a bus operator in Guînes had applied to run a bus service between Guînes and Calais, but had started this without authorization, which was threatening their entire tram service with 'ruinous consequences'. However, in reporting to the Chief Engineer of the *Département*, the local Engineer pointed out that the *Société* were in a weak position since they were themselves running unauthorized bus services between Calais and Ardres, and between Calais and St-Omer. The local engineer did not think it possible to refuse the request of the bus operator to run this service, but recommended that there should be no public financial support, and that these buses should not transport passengers between points within Calais itself, in view of the monopoly granted to the tramway company within the conurbation.

On 6th June, 1939, the Mayor of Calais, having been advised by the town council, and the *Société Anonyme des Tramways de Calais et Extensions*, agreed that line B of the tramway network, that is from the Place d'Armes in the old town to Guînes, should be declassified. The *Société* would not seek compensation for this, but would be granted the concession to operate buses instead. These would start from the north side of Calais-Ville station, but then otherwise follow the tram route to Guînes. The *Société* would also be responsible for removing the track and the overhead wiring, and for restoring the roads. In practice this only meant removing these structures from Guînes as far as what is now the Place Albert 1er, where Line B joined the other lines of the network. The formal decree of declassification, with substitution by a bus service, followed on 18th February, 1940. This meant that between Guînes and Calais the Anvin-Calais line was from 1939 competing with a bus service. The rest of the Calais tramway network arrived at the beginning of World War II intact.

A tram and trailer car on the Calais-Guînes tramway, headed towards Calais, in the Chemin des Régniers at Pont-du-Leu. Undated, but probably 1920s or 1930s.

Éditions Reant, Lille; Authors' Collection

Berck Plage to Paris-Plage

We have already noted in Chapter Five that the service on this line was suspended at the beginning of World War I. We also noted that according to some reports the whole line was lifted for the track to be used elsewhere, but that events after the war show that this was not the case. The two La Meuse locomotives of 1912 had been requisitioned and destroyed near the front line in 1918.

We have included here considerable detail of the claims and counter-claims for war damage between the British Army, the *département* of Pas-de-Calais, the *Compagnie du Chemin de Fer de Berck-Plage à Paris-Plage*, and the Ministry of Public Works, Transport and the Merchant Navy in Paris. These illustrate the competing and often conflicting interests of the parties, and the complexity of some of the issues, even away from the front line. They also illustrate again the scale of the problem of clearing up after the war. It is only too easy to imagine all of this multiplied right across northern France and Belgium.

In June, 1919, a Major of the Royal Engineers, acting on behalf of the British Director General of Transportation, prepared a report on the state of the Berck-Plage to Paris-Plage line. This report followed a claim for damages from the *Compagnie du Chemin de Fer de Berck-Plage à Paris-Plage* for 'damage caused to their line and supposed to have been caused by British Troops' (our re-translation of the official French translation of the original document in English). The report states that the section from km 3.321 to km 3.629 had originally been lifted by the French, and had been re-instated by the British using material from the section from km 4.022 to km 4.329; this latter section should therefore be re-instated by the French. The section between km 4.590 and km 5.102 had been lifted by the British and stored by the side of the line. The gap here was 513 metres or 47 rails each 10.95 metres long. The British Army accepted responsibility for material now missing from this stock at the side of the line, and for six rails damaged in lifting the other section mentioned above. However, there were still 78 of the required 100 rails at the site, but only six of the required 611 sleepers. Most of the joint plates were still there but the bolts and screws had gone. The line distances were measured from Berck-Plage and all these locations were in the section between Bellevue-les-Dunes and Merlimont-Plage.

From 1st May, 1917, the British Army had paid a rental fee for the use of wagons and for the line between Merlimont-Plage (at km 6) and Merlimont-Village (at km 8). When they took it over they had much work to do to clear the line of invading plants and sand. Further along, the line between Cucq and Paris-Plage appeared to have been used by the civilian population as a through route and trees had grown on the line between km 11 and km 13. On 5th February livestock had been seen getting onto the line through breaches in the fencing between km 10 and km 11. This damage seemed minor considering that this part of the line had been left practically untended for more than four years.

The report found no evidence that damage to telephone wires, kilometre and 100 metre posts, and information boards, were attributable to British troops. It was pointed out that the telephone poles were small and the area exposed to the full force of the west and south-west winds. The piling up of sand on the track could not be attributed to movements of or destruction by British troops. In some places where British troops had been manoeuvring, women had been seen digging up the bushy undergrowth, apparently to make fires. The Major's report closes by asking if the company would accept settlement of their claim on the basis that the British would pay for the missing material, and for the replacement of the track and ballast, where the army had lifted them, from km 4.590 to km 5.102.

A further claim by the company, for damage to the station buildings at Merlimont-Plage, was noted to be the subject of separate negotiation with the Claims Commission of the British Army. The report was delivered to the *Colonel Commissaire Militaire* of the *Réseau du Nord* on 18th June, 1919, and shortly afterwards to the Manager of the Berck-Plage-Paris-Plage company at their offices in Béthune.

On 18th July, 1919, the Ministry in Paris wrote to the Chief Engineer of the *département*. The Ministry referred to a claim made by the *département* for materials for repairing the Berck-Plage to Paris-Plage line. The claim of the *département* was for 1.05 km of track of 20 kg/metre rails. The distance had been altered in ink to 2.1 km. They were requesting joint plates, 9 *appareils* (probably points), and 14,000 sleepers. The Ministry referred to previous submissions on this subject, and could only offer 566 metres of 20 kg/metre track, 9 *appareils*, 654 sleepers, 463 bolts and 2,712 large rail fixing screws. The Ministry also requested clarification of the original request.

In replying to this on 24th July, 1919, the departmental Chief Engineer pointed to an earlier document, of 7th May, 1919. This had stated that the British Army had installed in the dunes, along the coast, and in the area immediately around the line, an air force camp, a tank training school, an artillery training school which included the line in its firing range between the stations of Bellevue-les-Dunes and Merlimont-Plage, and various other camps spread throughout the area. As a result of this, the line had become commonly used as a through route for men, horses, lorries and even tanks. All this had caused serious deterioration to the track. A number of rails had been broken or buckled by artillery shells or training bombs dropped by aircraft, and 'an important piece of wrecking had occurred producing a dismantling of the track brought about in a violent manner by the English army, breaking the bolts on the joining plates and twisting the screws holding the rails to the sleepers, between the positions at km 4.584 and km 5.108, that is a length of 524 metres' (our translation, this section being underlined in the original for emphasis). He added that the sleepers from this dismantling had been thrown by the side of the line and had disappeared bit by bit. Here was the explanation for whole difference for the rails, and for the other materials, a portion virtually equal to that which had been requisitioned. The departmental Engineer then goes on to elaborate at great length what is needed to reopen a line after five years' abandonment.

The departmental Engineer goes on to claim that the general refurbishment of the line had already been accepted by the Ministry in a decision of 27th May and that the only difference in the amount of materials concerned the bolts and screws. He then lists again the claimed materials, including 175, 12 metre lengths of Vignole rail of weight 20 kg/metre, 14,000 treated oak standard sleepers 1.8 metres long, and this time another 532 treated oak sleepers of length from 2.0 to 2.6 metres, which would presumably be for points. He also requested that if possible there should be 2,000 special washers for the joint plate bolts (type 'Grover') and 150 wedges with their special screws (type 'Barberot'). Finally he adds that the work had already started one month before and that it was highly desirable for the materials to be sent without delay, otherwise the work would need to be slowed down or even stopped.

The Ministry replied on 2nd August, 1919. They noted that the material claimed in excess of that already allocated was firstly for the replacement of the 524 metres of line removed by the British Army, which they accepted had been rendered unusable by the passage of tanks and lorries, and the explosion of shells on the firing range; and secondly for a general refurbishment of the line, a majority of bolts being rusted and many sleepers being rotten.

The station at Merlimont-Plage, with a train headed towards Berck-Plage. The tank locomotive, hauling the train backwards, is the 0-6-0 Borsig built in 1910. Postcard postmarked 1926.

Éditions Lefevre; Authors' Collection

VFIL No. 13, SACM 2-6-0 tank locomotive of 22 tonnes unladen weight, at St-Just-en-Chaussée on the Oise network in 1960. Originally built in 1924 and No. 3 on the Berck-Plage-Paris-Plage line, and acquired by VFIL for the Anvin-Calais-Aire-Berck lines in 1941 or 1942 as No. 13, this locomotive is now preserved at MTVS Valmondois.

B. Rozé; Collection Bernard Guéret, formerly BVA

The *Direction Générale des Transports militaire* (this probably refers to the British Army Directorate General of Transportation) had commented that the supplies for which they were responsible remained exclusively limited, in terms of the laws of 30th December, 1917, and 10th January, 1919, to material required for the repair of destroyed lines, or the reconstruction of dismantled or requisitioned lines. The only materials which could be supplied were, in the first place, a quantity of material to restore the requisitions made by order of the Director of Railways, French General headquarters, that is 566 metres of rails, 9 *appareils*, 654 sleepers, and the necessary bolts and screws for these, in accordance with the law of 10th January, 1919; and in the second place, material corresponding to the line destroyed, that is 484 metres length of complete running track, in accordance with the law of 30th December, 1917. This material had been ordered for delivery to the contractor, a M. Boulicault, at Bellevue-les-Dunes station.

It seems probable from all of this that the British Army removed the section of track around km 5 in order to allow tanks and lorries to cross without damaging the track, and that there is no good evidence of damage from bombs or shells. It also seems clear that the opportunity was not lost to put the case for the *département* and the company as positively and perhaps dramatically as possible. One could take the view that the company had done quite well, receiving considerably more than the British Army had reckoned was due, including the *appareils*. On the other hand one can feel somewhat sorry for the company. The line had been forcibly closed for five years, depriving them of the revenue on which they probably depended for maintenance in what was undoubtedly a particularly hostile environment.

This was not, however, the end of the matter. In a further letter of 3rd June, 1921, the *département* on behalf of the company refers to a previous letter 27th November, 1920. Both of these letters request compensation for war damages for the line in the sum of 1,382,000 francs. The main headings are for track (865,564 francs), rolling stock (392,000 francs), and buildings (71,100 francs). The figure for rolling stock includes the two locomotives destroyed in 1918, and that for buildings includes repairs to Bellevue-les-Dunes station. The claim also includes 3,142 francs in fees for preparing the dossier. Extensive legal arguments followed. The letter states that the works were in progress at that time. We know that the line was reimbursed for the replacement of the two locomotives, but we do not know the outcome of the rest of the claim.

Rolling stock

A specification for locomotives to replace those destroyed in 1918 was agreed in 1921. However the backlog of orders after the war was such that they were not delivered until 1924. They were 2-6-0 tank engines of 22 tonnes built by SACM, and were numbered 3 and 4, to replace those of same numbers which had been destroyed. By the time they were delivered the service was such that they were not needed. No. 3 was loaned either to the brickworks at Attin near Montreuil, or the quarry at Engoudsent. No. 3 then returned to the Berck-Plage-Paris-Plage line for a few weeks before closure of this line at the end of summer 1927. Then it possibly went (or returned to) the quarry at Engoudsent. It was sold in 1931 to MM. Albert and Felix Leroy, who had a saw-mill at Attin, some sort of works at Recques, and possibly also the Engoudsent quarries. This locomotive later worked as No. 13 on the Anvin-Calais-Aire-Berck lines, from 1941 or 1942 to 1947. The only surviving steam locomotive of any of the lines in this book, it can now be seen at the Museum at Butry-sur-Oise (*MTVS Valmondois*). A full history of this locomotive is given in Chapter Eight. No. 4 was probably sold to the cement factory at Beffes (Cher). We do not know any further history for this locomotive. Technical details of No. 3, which were also those for No. 4, are given in *Table Twenty-One*.

Operations

The service was resumed on 20th July, 1920, having been interrupted for nearly six years. One document states that the service restarted in summer 1919 but this date seems unlikely since arguments were still going on about repairs at that time. It is even surprising that the service was able to resume in 1920, as war damage was said to be still being repaired in 1921. Some sources say that the service was only for tourists in the summer season after the war. However, it is probable that the winter service was not completely suspended until the winter of 1922. This reduced expenses and allowed the employment of seasonal staff. It is alleged that some of these did not know the engines or the line and that this resulted in an increase in accidents. Once the winter service was suspended, it was never resumed.

The timetable for summer 1921 is shown in the *Table Twenty-Six*. This shows only two trains in each direction each day, one in the middle of the day and one in the early evening. Receipts were said to be good in August but poor, with running at a loss, in July and September.

Table Twenty-Six
Berck-Plage to Le-Touquet-Paris-Plage
Summary timetable July to September 1921

		(2)	(1)	(2)	(1)			(2)	(1)	(2)	(1)
Berck-Plage	dep.	12.30	12.45	17.00	17.45	arr.		14.45	15.00	19.15	20.00
Bellevue-les-Dunes		12.37	12.52	17.07	17.52			14.38	14.53	19.08	19.53
Merlimont-Plage		12.49	13.04	17.19	18.04			14.26	14.41	18.56	19.41
Paris-Plage	arr.	13.30	13.45	18.00	18.45	dep.		13.45	14.00	18.15	19.00
(Rue de Paris)											

(1) 1st July to 9th September   (2) 10th September to 30th September

In 1901 annual receipts had been estimated at 45,900 francs. By 1925 receipts were only 36,381, and in 1926, 39,013 francs, despite a sharp devaluation of the franc after the war. A report said that 'Wealthy people who spend time at Paris-Plage do not go to Berck on the train but in their car, and vice versa people of modest means who live at Berck do not often make a journey to Paris-Plage which is too expensive a resort'.

In spite of the suspension of the winter service, management and maintenance costs continued in the winters. Clearing sand from the line continued to be a major problem. It was reported that landowners between Bellevue-les-Dunes and Merlimont-Plage had been paid compensation after the war, so that they could replant the dunes damaged by the British tanks with *oyats* (dune stabilising grass), but that some had spent the money on other things.

From 1922 the town council at Merlimont complained about the reduction in the number of trains, which was limiting the number of bathers coming from Berck and Paris-Plage and affecting business in the resort. In 1922 an extra morning train from Merlimont-Plage to Berck-Plage and back was run as a trial for the summer only on

Wednesdays and Saturdays for the markets, but it is uncertain how long this lasted. The original agreement to build the line had included an undertaking by the company that at least three trains each way per day would be run in the summer season. Up to 1927, the number remained at two.

Closure

In 1926 the *Société Général des Tramways de Rohan* entered into negotiations to buy the line but these came to nothing. In 1927 the town council of Le Touquet (Paris-Plage) requested the suppression of the line.

In the event, 1927 was the last operating season, with the last scheduled passenger trains running on 30th September. In August 1928 a committee to close the line was assembled. Over the next few months the closure was supported by the councils of Cucq and Berck, although in supporting the closure Berck requested instead a large *boulevard* between Berck and Paris-Plage. Only Merlimont held out for the line to remain open. Closure was announced on 26th December, 1928. The line was used once more, for two months in the spring of 1929, by contractors working on the golf course between Paris-Plage and Stella-Plage.

On Christmas day 1929 the President of the Republic signed the decree declassifying the line. The decree specified the buyout of the line by the *département* of Pas-de-Calais for 330,000 francs, to be paid in two instalments in 1930. In vain the company protested that the line had cost 1,280,000 francs to build. During 1930 a demolition company from Rheims purchased the most important items including the two remaining locomotives, the 0-6-0 Borsig tank and the 0-6-0 Decauville tank. The subsequent fate of these locomotives is not known.

The main station buildings, at Bellevue-les-Dunes, at Merlimont-Plage, and the goods station at Paris-Plage, caused problems. As soon as they were empty they were subject to vandalism. The station at Merlimont-Plage was purchased by the town council in November 1930 to make into a school. The goods station at Paris-Plage was demolished in 1936. While discussions were taking place about the future of the station at Bellevue-les-Dunes, now also known as Berck-Terminus, squatters moved in, two couples in the main building and another couple in the annexe. Gradually the building deteriorated and in the end it was sold in 1937 for 960 francs, for the value of the bricks, tiles and woodwork. Demolition followed.

In 1935 the Chief Architect of the *Département*, in a report on the future of the station at Bellevue-les-Dunes, had suggested that some or all of the line could be used as a motor road, the existing inland road between Berck-Plage and Paris-Plage being 'defective and subject to accidents'. In retrospect it was fortunate that the proposed boulevard along the coast between Berck-Plage and Paris-Plage was never built, as it would have led to irresistible pressures for development right along this part of the coast. However the Boulevard de la Manche, formed in north Berck-Plage from the path of the railway and the lateral roads, may have been the beginning of this road. There is now a road nearer the coast linking the resorts of Merlimont-Plage and Stella-Plage, but the dune areas between Stella-Plage and Paris-Plage, and those between Berck-Plage and Merlimont-Plage, have become highly protected areas of scientific interest and natural beauty.

The tramway to Paris-Plage in the Rue de la Gare at Étaples. Étaples station is behind the photographer. Undated but the dress indicates 1920s or 1930s.

Éditions Fauchois, Béthune; Authors' Collection

A tram with baggage van and open trailer car crosses the bridge over the river Canche at Étaples towards Paris-Plage. Postcard postmarked 1925.   *Authors' Collection*

Tramway from Étaples to Paris-Plage

This tramway continued to operate successfully throughout the period of this chapter. However, more than half the services were replaced by buses during the 1930s. This did not augur well for its longer survival. In 1926 the bridge at Étaples was completely rebuilt in concrete, on a different site nearer to the sea, which required the tramway to take a different route from the end of the bridge into Étaples.

In 1930, 20 services each way per day were scheduled, but this could increase up to 32 in the high season. However, in 1928 it was reported to the annual meeting of the company that, because of bus competition, passenger numbers had fallen steeply from 399,544 in 1926 to 277,734 in 1927. In 1936 the tramway company themselves made the case to run part of their services using buses. The case essentially was that they had reduced costs for the trams, but these could not be reduced below 1.35 francs per km run. Buses could be run for 0.79 francs per km. Therefore they proposed to run 100,000 km, nearly half their annual distance, using buses. The buses would be used primarily in winter. This was provisionally approved. Two buses were put in service, one Unic with 29 places and up to six standing, and one Panhard with 25 places and up to five standing.

By October 1936 the timetable in the *Indicateur Chaix* was headed *Tramway Électrique et Autobus d'Étaples à Paris-Plage*, although on the papers the company was still known by its traditional name, referring only to the tramway. For the winter of 1936 all services, 20 per day each way except market days, were by bus. There was an extra bus service each way in the mornings on market days in Étaples. The buses followed the route of the tramway, using the same stops, but after the tram terminus in the Rue de Paris went to and from the nearby covered market.

28   *LE TOUQUET-PARIS-PLAGE. — La Gare des Tramways.*

The later station in the Rue de Paris at Paris-Plage. A tram is waiting to leave for Étaples, pulling an open carriage and a baggage wagon. Tramway personnel are in attendance. Undated.   *Authors' Collection*

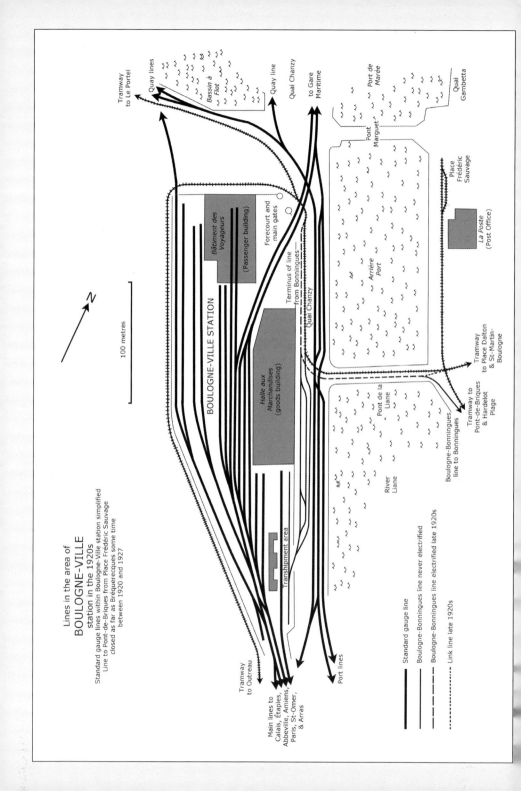

Lines in the area of
BOULOGNE-VILLE
station in the 1920s

Standard gauge lines within Boulogne-Ville station simplified
Line to Pont-de-Briques from Place Frédéric Sauvage
closed as far as Bréquerecques some time
between 1920 and 1927

100 metres

Tramway to Le Portel

Quay lines

Bassin à Flot

Quay line

Quai Chanzy

to Gare Maritime

Port de Marée

Quai Gambetta

Pont Marguet

Arrière Port

Place Frédéric Sauvage

La Poste (Post Office)

Forecourt and main gates

Bâtiment des Voyageurs
(Passenger building)

BOULOGNE-VILLE STATION

Terminus of line from Bonningues

Quai Chanzy

Halle aux Marchandises (goods building)

Transhipment area

Pont de la Liane

River Liane

Boulogne-Bonningues line to Bonningues

Tramway to Pont-de-Briques & Hardelot Plage

Tramway to Place Dalton & St-Martin-Boulogne

Tramway to Outreau

Main lines to Calais, Étaples, Abbeville, Amiens, Paris, St-Omer, & Arras

Port lines

Standard gauge line

Boulogne-Bonningues line never electrified

Boulogne-Bonningues line electrified late 1920s

Link line late 1920s

In 1937 the *département* again approved the use of buses for the whole or partial replacement of the trams as the company required. In the summer of 1937 there were 13 trams and 19 buses each way every day. As before the winter services were all buses. In 1938 and 1939 there more than 30 services per day from 1st July to 30th September, but the trams only ran 12 times per day, and only ran between 9th July and 31st August; outside that the services were all buses. So the tramway reached World War II mainly as a bus service, with the trams restricted to six or seven weeks in the holiday season.

Boulogne to Bonningues

In Chapter Four we saw that this line was already struggling, especially on the section up the hill from Boulogne-Ville station to St-Martin-Boulogne. Although it continued with some success for 17 years after World War I, part of the line and all the passenger services had closed before World War II.

After World War I, the line received 28 additional goods wagons, from British Army surplus. There were various problems with the locomotives, blamed on lack of maintenance during the war. In April 1921, two instances of trains being late on the hill up from Boulogne to St-Martin-Boulogne were reported, one a delay of 25 minutes and another of 30 minutes. The first was attributed to minor problems with the locomotive (No. 48), the second to lack of steam pressure on the climb up the hill.

In 1922 the *département* ordered a 19 tonne (25 tonne loaded) 0-6-0T locomotive from Corpet-Louvet, of La Corneuve (Seine), for the Boulogne-Bonningues line. The price was 108,000 francs. We are not sure when this was delivered but it was said to be in service by 1925, with the number 1. An 0-6-0T locomotive was also acquired, in 1924, from Piguet of Lyon-Anzin, but we have no other details of this. It was given the number 23. Both of these locomotives were put up for sale in 1939 after the closure.

Operations

From July 1919 (*see Table Twenty-Seven*) there were two trains per day at every station, compared with only one over most of the line in 1917. Two trains per day also went down the hill from St-Martin to Boulogne-Ville station and back. However there was still only one train per day that went the whole length of the line. The evening train towards Boulogne stopped at St-Martin, but passengers could still get into central Boulogne from there on the tram. The evening train towards Bonningues stopped at Licques. Before World War I there had been three trains per day over the whole length of the line, with the late train going to Bonningues and then back to Licques. Also the early morning through train from Licques to Tournehem on the Anvin-Calais line, and then back to Boulogne, which had run before the war, was not reinstated. In October 1919 the company received a request by the town council at Licques to reinstate the late service from Licques to Bonningues and back. The company said that very few people changed from the Calais train at Bonningues at this time of day, and that reinstating the service would cost 13,000 francs per year, so they refused.

Table Twenty-Seven
Boulogne to Bonningues
Summary Timetable from 1st July, 1919

Boulogne-sur-Mer (gare)	dep.		11.15	17.00	▲ arr.	08.51	16.30	
St-Martin-Boulogne	arr.		11.45	17.30	dep.	08.21	16.00	
	dep.		12.00	17.38	arr.	08.15		20.00
La Capelle			12.26	18.04		07.49		19.34
Colembert	arr.		13.10	18.48	dep.	07.08		18.53
	dep.		13.15	18.53	arr.	07.03		18.48
Licques	arr.		14.00	19.38	dep.	06.18		18.03
	dep.	05.15	14.15		arr.	06.10		17.55
Bonningues	arr.	05.35	14.35		dep.	05.50		17.35

In 1923 the councils of Colembert and Bainghen again pressed to have the third daily service restarted. The company response was that in 1919 two per day had been agreed because of financial pressures. Now, there were additional problems, including the imposition of an eight hour working day, an increase of pay rates, and an increase in the price of coal. The councils also asked that if the third train could not be provided, then the last, which since 1919 had been changed to leave Boulogne at 14.00 hours, should be put back to 17.00. The company said that it had to leave Boulogne at about 14.00 in order to meet the 17.15 to Lumbres and Fruges and the 17.30 to Calais at Bonningues.

During the 1920s, the line put on extra trains on race days between St-Martin and the *Hippodrome de l'Inquéterie*. This was between Blanc-Pignon and Souverain-Moulin, on the other side of the N42 from the railway. This is approximately where the 'Auchun' hypermarket is now. It is characteristic of the bureaucracy that all extra trains such as these had to be approved by the *département*, with a new application for every race meeting.

From 1928, timetables were introduced with only one train per day between Boulogne-Ville station and St-Martin, which was in the middle of the day. There were still two trains per day in both directions at every station from St-Martin to Bonningues, but the last train was still early, being the 13.50 from Boulogne-Ville. There were additional trains between St-Martin and La Capelle or Colembert, but only on certain days of the week. In supporting the application for the changes, the sub-divisional Engineer of the *département* makes much of the fact that the morning departure from St-Martin will be brought forward from 10.05 to 08.30, so that it can arrive at Bonningues at 10.45 and connect with the 11.00 train from Fruges to Calais. He makes nothing of the fact that the Boulogne-Ville to St-Martin service has been reduced.

From 1929 it was approved for part of the service to be provided by buses between Boulogne and La Capelle. In the *Indicateur Chaix* of July 1930 (*see Table Twenty-Eight*) the buses are shown together with the trains. There was now only one train each way per day over the whole length of the line from Boulogne-Ville to Bonningues. A second train from St-Martin to Licques and back was run on Sundays and holidays only. Extra services between St-Martin and La Capelle were provided on particular days. Other services, including the regular morning service from Boulogne to Bonningues and back, are provided by bus. The buses all started and finished at the *Place Frédéric Sauvage* in Boulogne, which was much more convenient for passengers. In addition, although it had long been the case that it was better to get the tram to St-Martin from the Place Dalton or Boulogne-Ville station than to use the steam train on this section, this option was now shown on the timetable.

Table Twenty-Eight
Boulogne to Bonningues
Summary Timetable July 1930

		(1)	(2)	(3)		(4)	(5)
Boulogne-sur-Mer (face gare)	dep.				13.40		
Boulogne Place Dalton		(08.30)	(10.45)	(11.15)	(14.15)	(17.45)	(20.20)
St-Martin-Boulogne		08.45	11.00	11.30	14.30	18.00	20.45
La Capelle		09.07	11.22	11.52	14.54	18.22	21.07
Le Waast-Alincthun		09.34			15.24		
Colembert		09.47			15.41		
Longueville		09.57			15.53		
Licques	arr.	10.27			16.25		
	dep.				17.00		
Bonningues	arr.				17.20		

		(3)	(6)	(2)	(1)		(4)		
Bonningues	dep.							17.45	
Licques	arr.							18.05	
	dep.				10.45			18.20	
Longueville		06.20			11.15			18.59	
Colembert		06.32			11.25			19.15	
Le Waast-Alincthun		06.40	06.46		11.39			19.29	
La Capelle			07.25	11.53	12.03		18.35	20.00	21.15
St-Martin-Boulogne			07.50	12.15	12.25	12.25	19.00	20.25	21.40
Boulogne Place Dalton			(08.15)	(12.30)	(12.45)		(19.15)	(20.45)	(22.00)
Boulogne-sur-Mer (face gare)	arr.				12.55				

Notes:
   Times in brackets are from and to the Place Dalton by electric tramway (Tramways of Boulogne) changing at St-Martin
   Additional services by bus to and from the Place Frédéric Sauvage in Boulogne; mostly from La Capelle, two from Le Waast on a Saturday only, one from Bonningues starting in the early morning and returning in the morning. Also one early morning bus Licques to Bonninges, returning mid-morning.

(1) Sundays and feast days only
(2) Sundays and feast days only, from 1st June to 11th September only
(3) Saturdays only
(4) Sundays and feast days only, from 1st June to 20th September only
(5) Sundays and feast days only, from 1st June to 31st August only
(6) Wednesdays only

Partial closure

   The above shows that this railway was clearly in a vicious circle of declining revenue, leading to service reduction leading to further decline in revenue. Then the introduction of bus competition led in turn to further decline of revenue. On 31st December, 1935 the *département* bought back the concession for the line from the *La Compagnie des Chemins de Fer Économiques du Nord* (CEN). 'Coordination' (*see later in this chapter*) may also have played a part in the decision of the *département*, with a leaning towards buses, but we have no direct evidence of this.
   The line was closed completely between the Val St-Martin, at km 4.52 from Boulogne-Ville station, and Colembert, at km 23.9, that is 19.38 km (12 miles) out of the total length of 43 km (26¾ miles). This included the closure of the main depot at St-Martin-Boulogne. The beginning of the closure in the Val St-Martin was 1.6 km short of the station at St-Martin. Up to this point the line was given to the town of

8. - LICQUES (P.-de-C.). — La Gare

The station at Licques taken from the road to Lumbres. There are goods wagons in the station but this was probably taken after the line closed for passenger services in 1936, and the waiting bus is probably the replacement service. *Éditions Pollet, Lille; Authors' Collection*

The road side of the former station at Licques in August 2006. The goods building is to the left but the lavatory block to the right has gone. *Authors*

Boulogne, initially for three years from January 1936. As already noted, there was a metre gauge line, belonging to the town, from the Boulogne waste treatment plant and incinerator, on the right bank of the Liane below La Madeleine, along the road on the right bank of the Liane until it met the Boulogne-Bonningues line in the Boulevard Daunou. The line from there via La Madeleine to the Val St-Martin had been used for many years to take town waste to the Val St-Martin, where there were already sidings at a waste dump just before km 4.52. The town continued to do this, after the closure, up to April 1944. The line from the Pont de la Lampe (Pont de la Liane) to the Val St-Martin was re-classified as an industrial railway. We do not know what locomotives were used for this work, but they were not any of the ones operating on the line to Bonningues, since all these were offered for sale in 1939.

The rest of the line from Colembert to Bonningues remained open for goods only. This was probably to allow the continuation of the delivery of sugar beet from the eastern Boulonnais to the factory at Pont d'Ardres. The operation of the section from Colembert to Bonningues was handed over to VFIL, who already ran the Anvin-Calais line with which this section connected at Bonningues.

The line from Val St-Martin to Colembert was declassified, probably in 1938. In July 1939 the *département* offered for sale those parts of the line between Val St-Martin and Colembert which were not in the road or on the road verge. With some exceptions, the sale included the rails, points and all buildings and other effects, and tenders for purchase were invited. It would have been expected that these parts of the line would have been lifted. However, when in 1942 the German military authorities wanted to reopen this part of the line (*see Chapter Seven*), it was found that only a small part had been lifted and other parts had been covered over with tarmac. This suggests that these sales never happened.

Also in July 1939 the *département* offered for sale all the rolling stock of the line, including all six locomotives, 23 passenger carriages, 32 goods wagons and five lorries. All these were parked at the depot at St-Martin-Boulogne, with the depot tools and effects, and all moveable effects from the stations at St-Martin, La Capelle, and Belle-Houllefort. On 7th May, 1940, the local Engineer reported to the *département* on the state of things, although he was unable to make a full inventory as the depot building was occupied by a motorised army unit. All the tools and effects had disappeared, except for those too large or heavy to move. The locomotives were there but all valuable metal such as copper had been removed. The wagons were completely demolished and the wood removed. Of the five lorries only one remained. He further reported that information received indicated that the goods were all very worn and that the theft and pillaging had begun before the outbreak of hostilities. He considered that the remaining goods could only be sold as scrap metal. It is interesting that the passenger carriages are not mentioned in this document, and it is possible that these had been sold, and perhaps also some of the wagons.

Such was the state of things when three days later the German forces invaded France. In reviews of locomotives available to VFIL for the Pas-de-Calais lines only a few years later (*see Chapter Seven*) there is no mention of the locomotives original to the Boulogne-Bonningues line. In these circumstances it is reasonable to assume that the Engineer's recommendation was accepted and that they were all scrapped. The sugar beet trains, including those on the Colembert-Bonningues section, were hauled by VFIL 24 tonne 2-6-0 Nord-Belge or 42 tonne 2-10-0 Winterthur locomotives.

Tramways of Boulogne (including the line to Le Portel)

In 1927 a plan was brought forward to make better use of the metre gauge track in the area of Boulogne-Ville station (*see map page 234*). The steam railway to Bonningues and the electric tramway from the Place Dalton to Le Portel and Outreau had up to then separate tracks on the Quai Chanzy. They were joined at the north end only, but then ran in parallel along the Quai and over the Pont de la Lampe before going separate ways on the east side of the bridge, the tramway to the Place Dalton and the railway along the Boulevard Daunou. The plan was to join the steam line across to the tramway at the east end of the bridge and electrify it, so that trams could use both lines on this section, speeding up the service to Le Portel and Outreau. We have already noted that by this time only two passenger trains per day were using this part of the Boulogne-Bonningues line, and this was reduced to one in 1928. The plan was approved in August 1927, and may have been put forward with the knowledge of the further reduction of services between Boulogne-Ville station and Boulogne-St-Martin.

In the 1930s the *Tramways Électriques de Boulogne-sur-Mer* had 31 power cars, each with two motors of 35 hp. These could take 18 seated and 12 standing passengers. There were two closed passenger trailers of 30 places, and eight open trailers of 36 places, of which three were those owned by the town of Boulogne for the line to Pont-de-Briques. In addition there were four similar power cars, four trailers with 32 places, two covered wagons, six open wagons, four flat wagons and two baggage cars with second class accommodation, all belonging to the *département* and allocated to the line from Boulogne to le Portel.

Depot, workshops and other buildings

The depot and workshops were situated in the Boulevard Beaucerf, between the Abattoir and the standard gauge railway bridge. Facilities included offices, warehouses, a repair shop with two inspection pits and a paint shop, and a generating station. Some rolling stock, probably the goods wagons, was kept at the transhipment facilities at Capécure, in the port area, and some at Le Portel.

In 1928 the company applied for permission to buy their electricity from outside, and convert the generating station into a garage for 12 buses. They said that it was not worth upgrading the ageing equipment. The annual consumption was about 1 million kilowatt/hours, with a peak consumption up to 600 kilowatts at busy times; for instance, when the offices closed at 7 pm and heavily loaded trams were climbing the hill to St-Martin. They proposed buying electricity from the *Compagnie Générale Boulonnaise d'Électricité*. A presentation to the town council warned of the dangers of becoming dependent on another organization for power, pointing out that this *Compagnie* was *une filiale* of the *Société Béthunoise de Lumière et d'Energie*, which was itself *une filiale* of the *Compagnie des Mines de Bruay*. The example of Hull in Yorkshire was quoted, which being as close to the Yorkshire mines as Boulogne was to those of the Pas-de-Calais, had chosen to continue to generate its own electricity for its trams. However, the company had their way. We are not sure when, but by 1939 the depot contained an electricity sub-station with transformers, and a garage for 12 buses.

There were a number of waiting rooms, kiosks and shelters around the network. In 1930 the Mayor of Le Portel requested an *arrêt* where the line to Le Portel almost met the Rue d'Outreau (D235). This is where this road now meets the Boulevard de la Liberté. This was only 200 metres from the terminus, and there is no indication of a stop at this point on later maps. However the paperwork indicates that the *arrêt* was authorized.

Operations

In 1926 the company complained to the town council about independent bus operators, who were taking their passengers, and threatening to turn their operating profit into a loss. There was direct competition to Le Portel, to St-Martin, and to Wimereux. The town council refused financial help to the tramways, but agreed to try to get the independent operators to concentrate on the many places around Boulogne where there was no tram service. However, around this time, or certainly soon after, the tramway company started running their own buses to supplement the tram service; hence the request in 1928 to garage 12 buses at the depot.

By the 1930s buses run by the tramway company were regularly supplementing the trams. In winter the service ran trams from 07.00 to 20.00 hours. There were trams every 20 minutes to and from Le Portel and St-Martin, with additional services around lunchtime. To Pont-de-Briques, Wimereux, and Outreau, there were two services per hour, but to Outreau there was no service in the off-peak or on Sunday mornings. These were supplemented by bus services. There were two or three buses per hour between Boulogne, Place Frédéric Sauvage, now a bus station, and Le Portel. There were also morning and lunchtime buses between Boulogne and Wimereux, and Boulogne and Pont-de-Briques. On summer afternoons trailers were added to tram services to Le Portel and the service was increased to three times per hour to Pont-de-Briques. Bus services to Le Portel were also increased to four an hour and were provided hourly to Wimereux in the afternoons.

In all the trams travelled 650,000 km (400,000 miles) per year and the whole service would have required at minimum 14 power cars, four trailers, and six buses. The company did in fact have considerably more than this. At the end of the 1930s, 2,100,000 passengers per year were carried on the trams and 850,000 on the buses. A total of 300 tonnes per year of post, parcels and packages were carried between Boulogne and Le Portel.

Readers will recall from Chapter Four that in 1913 the *Tramways Électriques de Boulogne-sur-Mer* took over the operation of the line from Wimereux to the racecourse at Aubengue, and that operations had ceased at the end of the 1915 season, without the approval of the local councils. In 1919 the *département* gave formal notice that operations must restart in the 1920 season in accordance with the *Cahier des Charges*. We do not know for how long this service continued. There is no mention of it in the reports of activity of the Boulogne tramways in the late 1930s, and it must have closed by then. From 1920 the *Tramways Électriques de Boulogne-sur-Mer* also took over the running of the line to Pont-de-Briques.

Boulogne to Pont-de-Briques and Pont-de-Briques to Hardelot Plage

The company responsible for these lines, the *Tramways Électriques du Boulonnais*, was in severe financial difficulties after World War I. The loss was 17,000 francs in 1918 and 86,000 francs in 1919. Readers will recall from Chapter Four that of four or five lines planned as part of the second network, to be developed by the *Tramways Électriques du Boulonnais*, this was the only line built. Having only opened in 1911, the company had little opportunity to recover its costs and secure its financial position before the war. The service was completely suspended from 1st May, 1920. The town of Boulogne was only willing to assist under conditions which were impossible to achieve, and the company's property was sequestered.

HARDELOT-PLAGE (P. d. C.). - l'Arrivée du tramway. — E. H. C.

The arrival of a tram and trailer car from Pont-de-Briques at Hardelot Plage. The power car has 'Tramways Boulonnais' on the front. Undated.   *Authors' Collection*

The running of the line as far as Pont-de-Briques was handed over to the *Tramways Électriques de Boulogne-sur-Mer* who ran the other Boulogne tramways (the first network). From 1920 trams of the first network, run by the *Tramways Électriques de Boulogne-sur-Mer*, were given permission to run to Pont-de-Briques. After long talks, the service on the second section of the line from Pont-de-Briques to Hardelot Plage was resumed from 1st July, 1922, but only ran for three months each year, from 1st July to 1st October. This position was formalised during 1923 and 1924. The sequestration of property was lifted from 12th August, 1924. By 1925 businesses in Hardelot Plage were complaining bitterly about the effects of lack of service for the other nine months of each year. However, even when running for only three months per year the deficit in 1924 was 27,000 francs, and an appeal to the *département* for funds was turned down on the recommendation of the Chief Engineer.

The first section of the line from Boulogne to Pont-de-Briques was, after long negotiations, handed over in 1927 to the town authorities of Boulogne, who would have absolute rights to determine its future running. This transfer was to be permanent and free, and all assets were to be transferred. From 1st January, 1929 the town authorities formally handed over the line to the *Tramways Électriques de Boulogne-sur-Mer*, who had now been running it from 1920, with a new agreement on costs and conditions. The *Tramways Électriques de Boulogne-sur-Mer* agreed to be responsible for the operation of the line from the terminus of their line No. 2 at the Abattoir in the Rue Coquelin-Bréquerecques to the main line level crossing at Pont-de-Briques, with a through service provided from the Rue Victor-Hugo (Place Dalton) over line No. 2. This implies that the service on the section from the Place Frédéric Sauvage to the Abattoir at Bréquerecques had been or was about to be abandoned, and that the lines were joined at the Place Henri Henneguelle in Bréquerecques. We do not have a date for these changes but it may well have been in or soon after 1920 when the *Tramways Électriques de Boulogne-sur-Mer* first took over the provisional operation of the line. That this happened well before 1929 is supported by the detailed 1927 plans for the link between the Boulogne-Bonningues railway and the tramway at the east end of the Pont de la Lampe, which do not show the line from the Place Frédéric Sauvage into the Boulevard Daunou.

The *Tramways Électriques de Boulogne-sur-Mer* took over three open-sided trailer cars from the other company, but apart from this, ran the line using its own rolling stock. It was agreed to provide at least 12 services each way per day, considerably less than before World War I when it had been every half an hour. The fare from Boulogne (Abattoir) to Pont-de-Briques was to be 35 centimes.

The second section from Pont-de-Briques to Hardelot Plage was conceded once again to the *Tramways Électriques de Boulogne-sur-Mer*, in April 1928, but in 1929 the town authorities transferred the concession to the *Compagnie Générale Boulonnaise d'Électricité*. At some time before 1938, quite possibly many years before, the service ceased altogether. On 4th February, 1938 the line from Pont-de-Briques to Hardelot Plage was formally declassified by Decree of the President published in the official Journal of the Republic. In December 1938 a report confirmed that the whole of the line had been lifted and the roads and verges restored.

SNCF and the Coordination Committees

In 1938 the major standard gauge railway companies were joined together across France to form the *Société Nationale des Chemins de Fer Français* (SNCF). This was, and is still, effectively a nationalised railway company subsidised by the French treasury. In the first instance SNCF was granted the concession to run the French railways until 1976. The SNCF quickly started large scale closures of passenger services. Some of these were temporarily reversed after the German occupation in 1940, because of the military requirements of the occupying forces, and the scarcity of petrol and diesel fuel to run road vehicles.

The formation of SNCF was part of a more general review of public transport in France which had begun in the early 1930s. This arose out of increased competition, especially for local services, between railway companies often running at a loss, and bus companies, rapidly increasing and often extending without controls. The National Economic Council was asked to take evidence on these problems and advise. In 1934 they recommended that each Region should have a coordination committee to advise on which transport mode or modes should provide local and long-distance passenger and goods services. As set up the Coordination Committees represented local and national railways and road operators, but did not include users, as the Council had recommended. Closures of *Intérêt Local* lines, usually of metre gauge, and especially of the roadside tramway type, were widespread in the 1930s and by 1937 France had lost nearly half of its *Intérêt Local* lines. Replacement was with buses for passengers and lorries for goods, but some lines remained open for goods only, especially those used for transport of sugar beet to the factories. Commentators have observed that *départements* already had powers to close uneconomic lines, and doubt to what extent, if at all, the coordination committees speeded a process already under way.

Whatever the effect of the committees, the majority of closures of metre gauge lines in France occurred between 1930 and 1960, with a lull during World War II. In the area of interest of this book, the closure in 1935 of passenger services on the Boulogne-Bonningues line, but with retention of sugar beet services between Colembert and Bonningues, would be typical of closures of this period. However, we do not know if in this case coordination played a part. The history of the line suggests that it was in any case already failing in the face of road competition.

Chapter Seven

World War Two to the end

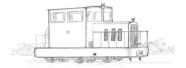

As we have seen in Chapter Six, the two core lines of the Pas-de-Calais network, Anvin-Calais and Aire-Berck, reached 1939 just about breaking even, despite the increasing pressure of competition from road transport. The two urban tramway networks, those of Calais and Boulogne, were surviving quite well. However, in 1939 another disaster was to strike northern France, leading to another period of damage, over-use and under-investment for these railways.

In this chapter the experience of the metre gauge railways and tramways in the western Pas-de-Calais during and after World War II is described. The information about the war period itself is patchy and the subjects covered have been determined by the availability of archive material. The experience of the Boulogne Tramways under German occupation is covered more extensively than other tramways because this period is described in detail in a report prepared by the Boulogne Tramways in order to claim reparations after the war. This is the only line in our area for which such a detailed report is available.

World War II

France declared war on Germany on 3rd September, 1939. This was the same day as the United Kingdom declared war, and for the same reason, that the German Government did not respond to an ultimatum to withdraw from the invasion of Poland, commenced on 1st September.

A considerable British Expeditionary Force was established in Northern France, with Headquarters at Arras, to supplement the French forces defending France. On 10th May, 1940, the German forces attacked France, Holland and Belgium, and despite fierce resistance swept through Northern France, taking Boulogne on 25th May, Calais on 26th May, and Paris on 14th June. French and British Army units held out for a time on the line of the river Somme. In the north, Calais was fiercely defended, leading to the destruction of most of the town centre. British and French troops trapped in the north were evacuated in large numbers from the beaches near Dunkirk at the end of May. The French Government under Marshal Pétain made peace on 17th June, retaining some control over part of France from their new centre of government at Vichy. The north and west, including all the Channel and Atlantic coastline, and the eastern border areas all the way down to the Swiss border, came under direct German military rule. The north and east including the *départements* Nord and Pas-de-Calais were included in a zone of special control ruled directly by the German High Command in Brussels. The boundary of the special zone was the river Somme, and for at least a year no French citizen was allowed to cross this line in either direction; they were trapped where they were when it was set up. Along the coast was a 'red zone', where restrictions were even tighter, and it was said that French law no longer applied at all.

During the summer of 1940, large German forces were assembled in northern France with a view to the invasion of Britain, but this was abandoned after the failure of the German Air Force to establish air superiority (the 'Battle of Britain'). From 1942 onward, the Todt organisation was building the coastal defences against invasion by Allied forces (the 'Atlantic Wall'), and from 1943 Northern France was the main area for the construction of launching sites for the 'V1', 'V2' and 'V3' weapons. All this led to heavy aerial bombardment, intensified in the spring of 1944 as part of the campaign to convince the German Government that the expected Allied landings would take place on the beaches of the Pas-de-Calais or Nord *départements* between Berck and Dunkirk. In anticipation of this, the German authorities ordered the evacuation of most of the population of the coastal towns in spring 1944.

The French population had a hard time between 1940 and 1944, particularly so in the north. Forced labour either in France or elsewhere was common and it was difficult to maintain local services. There was much courageous resistance, but any act of resistance was likely to be met with the taking of hostages by the German forces, and if the people responsible were not handed in by the local population the hostages were often shot. Many young French people were made to work for the German authorities in France or elsewhere under the STO (*Service du Travail Obligatoire*). During the German occupation 1,043 French citizens of Nord-Pas-de-Calais were shot and more than 5,000 sent to concentration camps, of whom half did not return.

Following the Allied landings in Normandy on 6th June, 1944, most of Northern France was liberated in September, with Allied armies returning to Arras on 1st September. They reached Brussels and Antwerp on 4th September and by the end of the month most of northern France and Belgium was free of German occupation. The main thrust of this advance initially swept past the Atlantic Wall and the ports of the Pas-de-Calais, which were left to be liberated later. However, the ports were necessary for supply as the troops advanced eastward. Boulogne was liberated by Canadian troops supplemented by British armour and special weapons. The attack on Boulogne on 17th September was preceded by heavy bombing of the port area and the defences. By 22nd September the town had been liberated, including the nearby forts by the coast. However, the port area, the railway yards and the central station were destroyed. The defenders had also destroyed all the bridges over the Liane. Many ships had been sunk in the harbour during or in the months before the attack, but the port was reopened by 10th October, unloading 11,000 tons of goods per day, and became the French end of the Pipeline under the Ocean (PLUTO) for petrol and oil.

Calais was liberated by the same forces between 27th and 30th September, again preceded by heavy bombing. During 1944 the German authorities flooded the *marais* to the south and east of the town, as part of measures to repel the expected invasion. Because of this the initial attacks were from the west. Most of the centre of Calais had already been destroyed in the fighting of 1940, but further damage was done during heavy fighting at the time of the liberation.

In Article 13 of the Armistice of 22nd June, 1940, the French Government agreed that in the territory occupied by the German army, all military and industrial facilities, including railways, must be handed over without damage. It was also agreed that the French Government would work with the German High Command to undertake any work necessary to make these facilities serviceable, and to make materials and personnel available to this end.

Standard gauge and other lines

In 1940 the German armed forces built a standard gauge line from the coast main line at Aubengue, between Boulogne and Calais, to Slack and then up the valley of the Bazinghen river almost to Wissant. This line had a spur to the Pointe aux Oies, where there was or had been a line constructed by the British Army in World War I. There was another spur at La Caleuse, and according to some maps another at les Dunes de Slack just south of Ambleteuse. These were used mainly to mount railway guns capable of firing across the Channel. Later the line was used for the construction of the Atlantic Wall. There was a station at Warcove, and from there a metre gauge line ran west to Framezelle (or Framzelle) on Cap Gris Nez. There were also narrow gauge lines, probably 60 cm gauge, west from Calais to the east side of Cap Blanc Nez.

Anvin-Calais and Aire-Berck (including the Tramway from Ardres-Pont d'Ardres, and remaining services on the Boulogne-Bonningues line)

This network, as all other railways in the zone of occupation, came effectively under German military control. We do not have the details of how this control was exercised, or of the command structure. Important matters had to be referred by the officials of the *département* to the office of the *Oberfeldkommandantur* (OFK) (Senior field headquarters) No. 670 in Lille. We also know that there was a German station commander at the station at Rang-du-Fliers, but this may only have been the case at important stations and junctions such as Rang.

German military use

The German armed forces made extensive use of the metre gauge network during the war. The *Marine Verpflegungsamt* (MVA) (Naval Supply and Maintenance organization) took over part of the Lumbres works in 1942 or before to maintain locomotives requisitioned from these lines for their own use. The MVA also had a headquarters and staff office in Lumbres.

We do not have a complete list of works undertaken by or for the German forces on these lines. However, we know that, in addition to the work on the Boulogne-Bonningues line (*see below*), some metre gauge construction works were undertaken. In May 1942 the Chief Engineer at Arras approved the placement of points at Berck-Ville station to serve a branch line constructed by the Germans. It is clear from his comments that even personnel from the upper levels of French railway management were not allowed to know too much. He clearly had only been told that the line in question went north 'in its forbidden part to the area of the aerodrome which it appears to serve'. The airfield at Berck was probably constructed in World War I by the British as an RFC/RAF base, but was used by the German air force in World War II, and was bombed by the RAF. By Spring 1943 there was also a branch line of the German agricultural organization at Verchin, with a projected maximum goods traffic of 750 tonnes per day. In October 1943 VFIL also claimed for rails, points and other materials for the station at Elnes, just south of Lumbres, in connection with the Avot paper factory.

Around this time the German authorities issued a notice in German and French warning that any interference, by those who were not part of railway administration, in the working of the railways or their installations or telephones and telegraphs was forbidden and would be punished. This was signed by the Supreme Commander for armed forces traffic management in Brussels.

An interesting illustration of the increased use of both roads and railways at this time came in December 1942. In November VFIL had sought approval to run two extra goods trains in the sugar beet season, one between the Fruges area and Lumbres and one between Ardres and Lumbres. These trains both used gated level crossings, one over the N28 at Fruges and Lumbres and one over the N42 at Lumbres, but were running outside the normal hours when the crossing gates were manned. In the previous winter there had been an accident involving a German lorry on the level crossing at Fruges when the crossing had been unmanned, and OFK 670 in Lille had decreed that when trains ran out of hours at these crossings a railway worker from the nearest station must attend and operate the gates. However, it was now proposed to the *Péfecture* and OFK 670 that it would be acceptable, when the level crossing was unmanned out of hours at night, to put up a notice by the road on either side, saying

UNBEWACHTER BAHNÜBERGANG
Passage à niveau non gardé
[unguarded level crossing]

This arrangement had previously been approved on the Aire-Berck line, but on this occasion the notices would be accompanied by a St Andrew's cross furnished with *cataphotes* (reflectors). We do not know the outcome of this proposal. However, other warning signs in German, probably from ungated crossings, can be seen built into the roof of the shelter at Renty, which say *Achtung. Eisenbahn in Betrieb* (warning - railway in use).

The roof of the *abri* (shelter) at the former *arrêt* at Renty, on the Anvin-Calais line, in 2007. The roof is made from level crossing warning signs in French (*Attention au Train*) and in German (*Achtung - Eisenbahn in Betrieb*).
Authors

Boulogne-Bonningues

Readers will recall from Chapter Six that the Boulogne-Bonningues line had been closed entirely from Boulogne to Colembert in 1935, but that the line from Colembert to Bonningues had been retained for goods services, particularly in the sugar beet season. In September 1942, the Chief Engineer in Arras reported to the MVA at their office in Boulogne on the state of the line from 'Le Portel' to Bonningues. This followed a letter from the MVA to M. Level, Director of VFIL, instructing him that the line should be brought back into use all the way from Boulogne to Bonningues. The Engineer reported that the line from Le Portel to the Val St-Martin was in the hands of the Boulogne Tramways, who were running the electric trams to Le Portel, and the Town of Boulogne, who were using the line to deliver town refuse to the Val St-Martin for dumping. From Val St-Martin, which was km 4.52 from Boulogne-Ville station, to the station at Colembert at km 24.0 the line was disused. Most of the disused line had not been lifted. Only seven short sections, maximum length 400 metres, and 1,542 metres in total, were missing. Most of the lifted sections were at level crossings. In addition there were short sections where the rails had been covered over with tarmac. These would have to be exposed, but one section would have to be reconstructed on the verge. There were 1,200 metres of usable rails in the depot, but another 1,900 metres would be required, with chairs, screws, jointing plates, and bolts. Also required were 15,000 sleepers, ballast, and 10 point levers and rods. Most of the point levers were found to be missing, and the rods twisted, and it was recommended that the points be dismantled and refurbished. The sleepers included those for the replacement rails, and others needing replacement along the track, which were about 25 per cent of the total. Work was also undertaken on the section from Bonningues to Colembert, including strengthening the bridge at Audenfort. The total cost of reinstating the line was 2,650,000 francs. There was no usable rolling stock. The reinstatement of the line would be in the hands of and at the expense of the German authorities, who should discuss the running of the line with VFIL and the Tramways of Boulogne.

The line was reinstated and used by the German forces from November 1942, beginning with a service of two trains per day for workers for the German forces. On 7th April, 1943, a serious accident occurred between La Capelle and Belle-Houllefort. Workers of the MVA detached a rake of wagons from a train and they ran back down an incline and collided with another train, causing considerable damage. Both trains had numbers, so the service must have been well re-established.

On 15th May, 1943, a departmental Inspector reported to the Chief Engineer that he had that day been called to a meeting with a senior inspector of the MVA at Lumbres. The MVA had stated that they had to have two trains per day from Lumbres to St-Martin-Boulogne for the transportation of materials and personnel. They demanded that the previously agreed timings be continued. There would be 15 wagons of materials to be transported to Boulogne every day. In addition, from 7th June, 10 supply trains per month from Lumbres to St-Martin-Boulogne would be required by the German Navy. These would have to be faster and for this purpose the MVA would install a telephone between St-Martin and Bonningues with assistance posts spaced out along the line, at La Capelle, Belle-Houllefort, Colembert or Surques, and Licques. It would be the responsibility of VFIL to provide the train crews to ensure running of these services.

The pattern of these services, and indeed the presence of the MVA in Lumbres, makes it likely that the German authorities were using the Bonningues to Boulogne route as an alternative supply route for their forces in Boulogne. The main Calais-Boulogne-Étaples line along the coast was vulnerable to aerial attack, and by 1943 such attacks were becoming increasingly common. We have had two reports, one from a contemporary witness, Rémy Marquis, that the German forces had a transhipment siding in a tunnel in *La Montagne*, the steep chalk hill at Lumbres. M. Rémy Marquis worked on the Anvin-Calais line from the end of 1943 to January 1947 as a *Cantonnier* (plate layer) and then as a *Chef Cantonnier*, based at Acquin. The hill at Lumbres is close to the path of the Anvin-Calais line and just beside the Avot paper factory at Elnes, which had standard gauge sidings using the metre gauge formation from Lumbres station in a 4-rail dual gauge section. It is known that the German forces made extensive use of this factory during World War II, and there were two accidents on the dual gauge section involving standard gauge wagons being used by the German forces.

According to these witnesses, supplies for the Navy were brought in by standard gauge from the direction of St-Omer. After transhipment in the tunnel, metre gauge supply trains were sent to the Navy at both Boulogne and Calais. Bombing of this area by Allied forces was frequent. Eventually the entrance to the tunnel was blocked after a raid which completely demolished the paper factory at Elnes, and killed around 200 people. At every raid at least one bomber was shot down by anti-aircraft fire, particularly from one emplacement at Setque on the hill on the other side of the valley, until this gun was itself put out of action by aerial attack. This transhipment tunnel was well separated from the 'V1' storage tunnel at Wavrans, further along the same hillside (*see later in this chapter*).

Rolling stock

By the spring of 1943 (and quite possibly before) the demands of the German authorities, and other pressing needs, had led to a crisis in rolling stock and manpower. The records associated with this are of interest because they give information about the over-riding military requirements and priorities of the time, and because the reviews of available rolling stock clarify what had happened to some of the pre-war stock of the lines.

At the time of a meeting at Tournehem on 10th April, 1943, the MVA had two 24 tonne locomotives in service, one (No. 23) working regularly between Calais and Lumbres and probably based at Guînes, and one (No. 24) between Lumbres and Colembert, based at Lumbres. Another (No. 22) was under repair, to be completed in a few days, and a fourth (No. 120) was awaiting repair, all by the MVA. The German authorities also had one 24 tonne locomotive, based at Fruges, working the agricultural branch line at Verchin. MVA were demanding two 18 tonne locomotives at once, one for works at Colembert, and one for the Avot factory at Elnes near Lumbres. As already noted, this paper works with dual gauge sidings was probably near underground transhipment facilities. MVA wanted to have two 24 tonne locomotives working Bonningues to Colembert by 12th April, and to have in all six by 1st May. During May it was reported that there were 'multiple problems' (probably derailments) with the 24 tonne locomotives on the reopened Colembert to St-Martin-Boulogne section of the Bonningues to Boulogne line, and MVA swapped one 24 tonne locomotive for No. 1, one of the 18 tonne locomotives with enlarged water tanks, which was then based at Berck.

As a result of all this, in the early summer of 1943, VFIL applied to the *département* for new, reduced civilian timetables, which led to a prolonged review of the situation by the Chief Engineer of the *département* in June. At this time VFIL owned 31 locomotives for the Anvin-Calais and Aire-Berck lines, including Ardres-Pont d'Ardres and the goods service from Bonningues to Colembert. These were:

	in service and reserve	used for sugar beet season	rapidly repairable	probably not repairable	totals
16 T				4	4
18 T	9		2		11
21 T	6				6
24 T		6	1		7
42 T		2			2
45 T				1	1
Totals	15	8	3	5	31

Of these the MVA had by this time taken, or were about to take, all six serviceable 24 tonne and two 18 tonne locomotives. This left 13 in service, including reserves for breakdowns and maintenance, and only the two 42 tonne locomotives for the sugar beet season. The distribution of the 13 was probably as follows:

	Based at	Used for		Based at	Used for
18 T	Berck	2 regular service	21 T	Guînes	1 regular service
		1 reserve			1 reserve
	Lumbres	1 local work, available		Fruges	2 in service
		1 reserve			1 available
		1 to Fruges 4 days per week			1 reserve
	not known	1			
Totals		7			6

There were also two railcars in service, one diesel and one converted to use a gas generator (*gazogène*). One of these was based at Bonningues and one at Ardres. There were seven more in reserve, but these could not be put in service because of shortage of fuel, and could not be converted to gas because of shortage of materials and time. These nine railcars accord with the nine known to be in service before the war; two from Renault-Scemia and seven constructed at VFIL Lumbres.

There are some anomalies in the list of steam locomotives compared with those the lines were known to have had before and after the war. The lines were known to have had one 16 tonne Corpet, and ten 18 tonne locomotives, eight SACM and two Pingueleys. There were six 21 tonne Corpets. There should have been the 22 tonne SACM acquired in 1941 or 1942 (No. 13). The seven, 24 tonne locomotives would be from among the eight from Ateliers-Nord-Belge, two acquired before World War I and six after. The two 42 tonne locomotives were the two of 2-10-0 ex-Guise-Hirson (Winterthür) and that of 45 tonnes was the 0-6-0+0-6-0 Henschel mallet. The extra 18 tonne locomotive was probably the Henschel from the Ardres-Pont d'Ardres tramway. The locomotives listed as probably not repairable were reported to need at least six months work and 'some will probably need to be written off'. Half of all the locomotives were said to be very worn because of their age, intensive use since the beginning of the war, and poor maintenance.

The departmental Engineer concluded that with the number of locomotives in reserve the reduction from 15 to 13 would not be too bad in the short term. Because many of the trains were mixed passenger and goods, the service reductions proposed by VFIL would reduce the general goods capacity by 300 tonnes per week and there was no prospect of this being transported by road. The longer term would have to encompass the sugar beet season beginning in the autumn of 1943 and then even this small reduction could cause problems. The service reductions were therefore opposed by the *département*. In the previous season, 1942-1943, season a record 103,000 tonnes of sugar beet had been transported, 15,000 tonnes on scheduled trains, and 88,000 tonnes on special trains. Of this, 66,000 tonnes had been hauled by the six 24 tonne locomotives now not available, and 22,000 tonnes by the two 42 tonne locomotives. Sugar beet was regarded as a strategic harvest by the French and the Germans. We do not know how the situation was resolved but probably the German forces had greater priorities than sugar and they would have had their way.

Difficulties of getting their own work done at the Lumbres works added to the problems that VFIL were experiencing with rolling stock in 1943. In April 1943 they complained that works by the Germans (MVA) had priority over their own works at all times. The works the Germans were demanding were on the engines and other rolling stock which they wished to use for their own services. Work on wheel maintenance, for example, on the VFIL locomotives would be stopped to allow those for the MVA to be undertaken. In addition MVA workers had priority on all machine tools. Sometimes there were as many as 80 MVA workers at Lumbres. In addition VFIL workers were required to work on the locomotives used by MVA, including the work on wheels and tyres, and all boiler works.

At a meeting on 15th May, 1943, Inspector Gross of the MVA gave powers to VFIL to have workers of the German organization under their control, recognising that the duality of the service could only have bad results for everyone. Conversely it was agreed that the German managers could have VFIL workers employed in their section and under their control. In order to encourage VFIL workers and to increase their rewards, a daily supplement would be paid directly to these workers by the MVA. VFIL only paid them 6 francs per hour. In addition the MVA were organizing several teams of skilled workers to ensure the maintenance of the line from Bonningues-Boulogne, and recruitment of these was in progress. The main purpose was to eliminate the causes of the previously frequent derailments.

In August 1943 the *département* reported a further reduction in available locomotives. Only nine were now available compared with 10 required at minimum to keep running the part of the service for which VFIL were responsible. One additional factor was that in four months, three locomotives had been damaged by machine gun fire during aerial attacks. As a result of all this the civilian passenger services had been reduced by half in July. Nine locomotives were awaiting repair and the materials were not available. At the end of August the MVA demanded another 30 covered wagons for their own use. They now had six locomotives, one railcar, four passenger coaches, four baggage vans, 56 covered wagons, and 30 open wagons.

Other German services

It is clear from the rolling stock documentation that by the spring of 1943 the German authorities were running, in addition to the services on the Boulogne-Bonningues line, regular services for their own purposes on other parts of the Anvin-Calais-Aire-Berck network. At the meeting with VFIL on 15th May, 1943, Inspector Gross of the MVA passed on the order of OFK 670 that the services required by MVA must be secured, even at the cost of civilian services, and if necessary also of those serving the German agricultural administration.

In the light of all the above, *M. le Préfet* of the *département* wrote to OFK 670 in Lille in the middle of July to say that the 'extremely critical situation of the metre gauge network of the coastal area calls for urgent decisions'. He also requested payment of the sum, now stated to be 13 million francs, spent to reopen the line from Colembert to Boulogne. However, another factor was added to the situation from late July, making it worse.

'Special projects' - The 'V1' programme

It had already been reported in June 1943, as part of the discussion on reduction of civilian services, that the ability to transport goods from Anvin towards Fruges on the Anvin-Calais line had been reduced for many months because the transhipment facilities at Anvin had been blocked by the occupying forces to serve 'defence works' in the canton of Heuchin. Then on 28th July, 1943, M. Level, at the Head Office of VFIL in Paris, wrote to M. Fontana, Chief Engineer for Bridges and Highways for the *département*, in Arras. M. Level wrote to bring to the attention of the Chief Engineer that VFIL had been contacted by the *Eisenbahnbetriebsamt* (Railway traffic administration) in Calais and told that the company would have to transport, for the needs of the German army, 70,000 tonnes of material, divided between the following routes:

Anvin to Fruges	10,000 tonnes
Écluse-Carrée to Zutkerque or Guémy	20,000 tonnes
Aire canal quay to Coyecques	10,000 tonnes
Montrueil to Hucqueliers	20,000 tonnes
Montreuil to Rumilly	10,000 tonnes

These deliveries were to be commenced soon and were to be completed within 100 working days. The plan would be developed in the course of a meeting with German representatives. The company also pointed out to the *département* the extra difficulties this program would cause particularly once the sugar beet season started. A further letter in August confirms that this program to move 70,000 tonnes is in addition to and separate from the existing MVA programme and that the six 24 tonne locomotives in use exclusively by the MVA would not be available for this programme. The programme is now said to be for completion by end December 1943.

It is apparent that the amounts to be transported are all 10,000 tonnes or multiples thereof, that the departure points are all transhipment points to metre gauge, either from canals (Écluse-Carrée, Aire) or standard gauge railways (Anvin, Montreuil), and that the destinations are all inland in rural areas. All the departure points are those transhipment facilities closest to the delivery points, minimising the metre gauge journey. It is also of interest that there was never a station at Guémy, which is between Tournehem and Bonningues, but sidings were constructed there by the British Army in World War I, and it is likely that the selection of this delivery point indicates that at least one of those sidings was still usable.

From 30th October, 1943, the grip of the German forces on the metre gauge railways increased with a decree from *Sonderführer (Z)* (Special Chief) Linkenbach at the OFK 670 in Lille announcing the future mode of management of the *réseau côtier* of VFIL. Unfortunately the letter to the company detailing these changes is not with the letter to the *département*, but they were to be discussed further at a meeting to be held in the MVA office at Lumbres on 4th November, and we do have the record of this meeting.

The meeting on 4th November was attended by Special Chief Linkenbach (OFK 670 Lille); two senior inspectors of the MVA based at Lumbres, Herr Hesse and Herr Gross; Herr Wolter, senior inspector of construction from the staff office of Colonel Schmalsläger; and Herr Brügmann, an employee of the German Government in the construction service No. 1 based at St-Omer. The French had four representatives and were led by M. Fontana, Chief Engineer for bridges and highways for the *département*. At the beginning of the meeting the instructions of OFK 670 of 29th October, 1943, for changes in control of the lines, were implemented. This gave greater German presence in the Commission controlling the lines, which now consisted of Herrn Linkenbach, Wolter,

Brügmann and Gross, and MM. Fontana and Poignant, the latter being the new inspector of operations based at Lumbres. These changes were said to have been requested also by the 'Air Force construction service' and the management of VFIL.

The representatives of the Air Force (who we believe were Herrn Wolter and Brügmann) and of the Navy once again stressed the importance of giving absolute priority to transportation for the armed forces. Herr Wolter insisted particularly on the programme being efficiently carried out, over a long period, to the end of the 'special construction project'. This was the programme of transportation brought to attention of a previous meeting at Lumbres on 16th September, 1943, and again in a later letter. This programme concerned the following quantities and routes:

Pont d'Ardres to Journy	240 tonnes per day
Aire-sur-la-Lys to Coyecques	480 tonnes per day
Attin to Hucqueliers & Rumilly	480 tonnes per day
Anvin to Fruges	480 tonnes per day

There is an interesting misunderstanding here resulting from working in more than one language. The above figures are from the German language notes of the meeting, which are the originals. The French is a translation, in some places a rather confused one. The German writer has numbered the four lines, as follows:

1. 240 To Täglich auf der Strecke Pont Ardres - Journy, (etc)

The French translator has mistaken the numbering for the French indication for thousands, in which one thousand in French is 1.000. The French version therefore lists the quantities as:

1.240 tonnes par jour sur la ligne Pont d'Ardres - Journy (etc)

That is to say 1,240 tonnes per day, the other quantities becoming 2,480, 3,480 and 4,480 tonnes respectively. In any case, compared with the end of July the amounts have changed somewhat. The routes are in general the same as before, except that Pont d'Ardres to Journy has replaced Écluse-Carrée to Zutkerque or Guémy. However Pont d'Ardres is another standard gauge or canal transhipment point. The quantities are again in exact ratios.

The VFIL representative from Paris was charged with producing, within three days, a new timetable, in which the trains necessary to overcome the transportation problems of the air force must be introduced as regular scheduled goods trains. This must be presented through the OFK representative for approval of the Commission of control. All other trains for military destinations must be notified by 17.00 hours the day before to the VFIL inspector of operations at Lumbres, also a member of the Commission of control. Herr Wolter went on to say that the demands of the air force first raised at the beginning of August and since repeated several times, including at a discussion at OFK in October, had not brought any positive result. He raised doubts whether VFIL could or would follow commands given them, since the volumes to be transported by 'le petit train' had not been delivered.

VFIL replied that up to the present they had not had sufficient rolling stock, especially locomotives, or personnel, especially engine drivers. The VFIL representatives went again at length through all the problems with locomotives and personnel, now worse than in the spring. Various dispositions were made to improve the flow of material for repairs to locomotives to VFIL, but these matters remained under German control. At the end Herr Linkenbach addressed the VFIL people and invited them 'to trust themselves to the task assigned to them in a loyal fashion and secure as good as possible a service within the means at their disposal'. He also asked the military personnel to support VFIL and to be understanding of interruptions in deliveries bearing in mind the difficulties with rolling stock and personnel. The Commission of control would address and fix those problems which could be overcome.

We have not found the records of some of the meetings which preceded this one, nor of any after this. One senses a tense meeting with an air of some desperation on both sides: the Germans perhaps sensing by this time that the war could be lost and the French perhaps secretly reluctant to support a programme whose purpose they must have suspected. Both sides were obviously under intense pressure.

There can be little doubt that this transportation programme was for the delivery of materials to 'V1' launching sites. This book is not the place for an extended review of the 'V1' programme, and readers are referred to the Bibliography for this chapter. However, a few key facts are needed to support the conclusion reached above. Launching sites for the 'V1' were surveyed in summer 1943 from western Belgium to the Cotentin peninsula. Sites were all at least 12 miles from the sea to avoid naval bombardment or sea-borne raids. Construction workers supervised by the Todt organisation or the Luftwaffe were brought to the sites at the end of July 1943, and by early August there were 40,000 workers. Conscripted French (STO), Belgian and Dutch labourers were used and billeted in towns and villages close to the sites. Some French civilian firms were called in to help. The programme relied heavily on the railway network to bring construction materials close to the sites.

The first wave of sites was constructed beginning in August 1943 and were known as 'heavy' sites. They had more extensive concrete buildings and storage buildings in a ski shape. Although at first Allied intelligence did not know what they were for, they were identified quite early from French resistance reports and aerial photography, and called 'ski' sites. By the end of December 1943, 69 of 96 planned sites had been completed but more than half had been subjected to bombing and 10 destroyed. From late 1943 or early 1944 the German authorities began a second wave of 'light' sites, better camouflaged and with fewer buildings and other works. These were often near farms, or in woods. French and other foreign workers were not used for these for security reasons. It was almost exclusively these sites, 80 in all by June

The curved entrance to the 'V1' storage building ('ski' building) at the former 'heavy' 'V1' launching site at the hamlet of Bellevue, *commune* of Herly, in 2007. This site was probably supplied with materials via the Aire-Berck or Anvin-Calais line.   *Authors*

Storage tunnel for 'V1' flying bombs, built into the chalk at Wavrans-sur-Aa, close to the former Anvin-Calais line, in 2007. *Authors*

1944, which started the launch programme from the middle of that month. Bombing was intensified in 1944 but with less success against the 'light' sites, not all of which were identified by Allied intelligence. The launch programme continued until the sites were over-run by the Allied armies. There are detailed records of bombing raids because Mayors were required to complete a pro-forma for each raid in their *commune* and return this to the office of the *Préfet* of the *département*.

There were also backup sites and surface and underground storage facilities. In August 1943 the 155th FLAK Regiment of the Luftwaffe was formed to run the programme and undertake the launches. The western part of the Nord *département*, and the Pas-de-Calais north-east of a line from Cap-Gris-Nez to near Frévent was the responsibility of the 1st *Abteilung* (battalion) based at Lumbres. South-west of this line the rest of the Pas-de-Calais and part of the Somme *département* was the responsibility of the 2nd battalion.

The quantities of materials specified at the end of July 1943 must have related to the construction of 'heavy' sites and suggest one site each near Fruges, Zutquerque, Guémy, Coyeques and Rumilly, and two sites near Hucqueliers. The quantities stated in early November may have related partly to 'light' sites and some of the previous sites may have been completed. The figures suggest one site near Journy, and two near Hucqeliers and Rumilly, Coyeques, and Fruges.

There is a close match, particularly for the July 1943 figures, with heavy sites known to have been started before November 1943 and which are usually closest to the destination station named. The most likely sites relating to these transportation programmes are shown in *Table Twenty-Nine*. For all the sites in this table, stations on the Anvin-Calais-Aire-Berck network were closer than any standard gauge station. However the station of delivery suggested by the documents is not always the closest station on the Anvin-Calais-Aire-Berck network. Where this is the case it is shown by an asterisk by the station in the table. There are three candidate sites for supply from Fruges. For Lisbourg, stations on the Aire-Berck line were closer but not much. There is no obvious second 'heavy' site near Coyecques, but Lisbourg is a possibility.

Zutkerque is not on these lines, or any railway, but the probable site was between Zutkerque and Zouafques, which is on the Anvin-Calais line, and this was the nearest station for this site. It is quite likely that the nearest station was not always used. Availability of loading and unloading capacity on the route compared with others, and ease and availability of road communications between the site and the

Table Twenty-Nine
'V1' 'heavy' launch sites started before November 1943 and probably or possibly served by transportation of materials on the Anvin-Calais-Aire-Berck lines

Name of site (commune)	Location	Station (delivery point)	Distance (km)	Notes
Zutkerque	Bois de Cocove	Zouafques	2	First bombed 21.12.1943. Abandoned April 1944.
Journy	Hameau de Haut Pannée/ Forest of Tournehem	Guémy ?* ? later Journy	5 0.75	First bombed 11 .1.1944 Destroyed by bombing April 1944
Audincthun	Bois Quartier	Coyecques	2.	First bombed 24.12.1943
Wicquinghem	Bois de la Bouloye	Hucqueliers	3.5	
Clenleu	Bois Remipré	Hucqueliers	4.0	
Renty	Bois de Renty	Rumilly	3.3	First bombed 22.12.1943. Evacuated 1944
Radinghem	Bois de Radinghem	Fruges	2.5	First bombed December 1943. Work slowed down
Ruisseauville	Ferme de l'Abbaye	Fruges	3.5	First bombed 22.12.43
Lisbourg	Hameau Le Groseillier	Fruges* or Coyecques*	5.5 9	First bombed 24.2.1944
Herly	Hameau de Bellevue	Rumilly* or Fruges*	4.5 8.5	First bombed 6.2.1944.

* Indicates station not the nearest to the site.

unloading point were probably factors. So there can be no final conclusion as to exactly which sites were supplied from where without a list, which is unlikely to be available because of the secrecy surrounding the programme.

Two storage tunnels for 'V1s' were constructed in the chalk hillsides near Lumbres by the Todt organisation in 1944. One of these, at Wavrans-sur-Aa (*see walk 3, Chapter Eight*), is three metres wide and goes 25 metres into the hillside, and is lined with concrete.

The 'defence works' in the canton of Heuchin, which were reported to be blocking the transhipment facilities at Anvin in June 1943, were probably the storage facility known to have been constructed at Bergueneuse, less than 2 km from the centre of Heuchin. This consisted of three tunnels in a quarry area on the south-west slope of Le Rouge Mont, which is identified on present maps only as Le Mont, just east of Bergueneuse. Until April 1943 German engineers thought that this might be a 'V2' launching site, but this plan was abandoned when it was decided to build a launch site at Wizernes, the site now known as La Coupole. The tunnels at Bergueneuse were then used for 'V1' storage. The site was linked to the railway system. We are not sure if there was a branch line from the standard gauge Étaples-Arras line at Anvin 2.5 km away, or a branch from the Anvin-Calais line. The latter is more likely, in view of the comments about the transhipment facilities at Anvin in 1943, and since this line was less than 400 metres from the site. The entrance to one tunnel is visible now from the minor road at the foot of Le Mont at Bergueneuse. It resembles that at Wavrans.

Bombing of the 'V1' site at Haute Pannée near Journy damaged the station at Journy, less than 1 km away, during the first bombardment of this site on 11th January, 1944. On 23rd January, 1944, the first and very inaccurate bombing of the site at the Bois de Séchier near Rebecques cut the Aire-Berck line on the high ground between Mametz and Creques, more than 2 km away. On the night of the 24th June, 1944, there was very heavy bombing at Rimeux, where there was a 'light' 'V1' site, and the hamlet was almost totally destroyed. M. Rémy Marquis, as a *Cantonnier* on the Anvin-Calais line, was called on frequently to repair some of this damage. He recalls a particularly long break, of 200 metres, in the line between Rimeux-Gournay and Assonval. This was most likely after the attack on Rimeux.

Summary of German use 1943-1944

Some further information about German military use of the Anvin-Calais-Aire-Berck lines in 1943 and 1944 comes from a claim for reimbursement for the loan of rolling stock to the German forces which was submitted to the Authorities in Paris in June 1945.

Days of use	Locomotives and railcars	Coaches 2 bogies	Coaches 2 axle	Fourgons	Wagons
Dec. 1942 to Dec. 1943	1,010	746	358	779	13,538
Jan. to Sept. 1944	881	706	351	952	12,295

This suggests rather less use of locomotives than the reports of the crisis in 1943 suggest. The monthly figures for locomotives only show the use of the equivalent of three locomotives in most months, of four in November and December 1943 and of five in the first four months of 1944. This report is also of interest in that the daily hire rate charged by the company in 1944 was 53 per cent higher than that in 1943. This must have reflected the rate of inflation against the franc at the time.

Other war damage

We have already noted damage to the track from bombing of nearby 'V1' launching sites. We do not have a complete inventory of other damages to these lines during World War II, but there were no doubt many of these. We have already noted damage to three locomotives by machine gun fire from aircraft in 1943. On one occasion in 1943 a scheduled mixed train on the Anvin-Calais line was shot at by a low-flying aircraft. Locomotive No. 5 was damaged, and a young woman civilian travelling on the train was killed. No doubt there were other casualties. M. Rémy Marquis was in a train on the Bonningues-Boulogne line in 1944 when it was attacked by a low-flying aircraft at Herbinghen. On that occasion the locomotive was damaged but no-one was hurt.

In September 1943 heavy bombardment of the area around Berck-Plage station led to severe damage to eight bogie coaches. In addition 160 glass windows were broken and 60 opening windows damaged. A complaint in a newspaper in December 1943, that glass panes in some coaches were still missing, was followed by a report to the *préfecture*. The plain glass had all been replaced quickly but special wood for the opening sections had been difficult to find. However all had now been replaced. One must suspect that the newspaper report had made sure this would happen quickly. The damage to the railway infrastructure at Calais and Boulogne is discussed, with details of reconstruction, in the section dealing with events after World War II.

Problems with soldiers

It is to be expected that armed forces, especially forces of occupation, would cause problems by their behaviour from time to time. In one such incident, on 8th March, 1944, the train from Rang to Berck had been delayed to wait for a train from Paris which arrived at 18.00 . Three German soldiers 'who did not appear in a normal state' took their places on the train to Berck with a number of parcels. When the train was about to leave, they objected on the grounds that they were missing a suitcase. When the train nevertheless began to leave, one of them drew a revolver and threatened to shoot the train crew, who then stopped the train. The matter was referred to the German station master who intervened but was unable to resolve the matter. The military police were informed and after enquiry by them the train was able to proceed without further incident at 19.25. In reporting the incident to the *département*, the company asked that the units of the German armed forces be reminded not to interfere in the running of the railways and that the soldiers responsible should be identified. At the bottom of the report someone at the *département* has made a handwritten note that the German station master and the military police were powerless to act without further information and that there was nothing further to be done.

Civilian services

It must be presumed that services ceased for a while during the German invasion of France in May and June 1940. The summary timetables for October 1940 are shown in the *Table Thirty*. These were at the time of maximum restriction on travel for those civilians who remained in the restricted zone of northern France, and when the coastal area was totally forbidden except by permit. The remaining services available without restriction are confined to the section Fauqembergues to Ardres on the Anvin-Calais line, and the section between Aire and Hucqueliers on the Aire-Berck line. These are weekly services to support market days and all well inland. The only daily service is the one that ran twice daily from Ardres to Pont d'Ardres. We have no details of other services which were undoubtedly run for the German authorities for their own personnel and for French personnel who were required at work nearer the coast and given permits to do this.

Table Thirty
Summary Timetables 21st October, 1940

Anvin to Calais		(1)	(2)	(3)			(2)	(3)	(1)
Anvin	dep.					▲ arr.			
Fruges	arr.					dep.			
	dep.					arr.			
Rimeux-Gournay									
Fauquembergues			11.05				08.35		
Lumbres	arr.		11.55			dep.	07.45		
	dep.	06.00		13.50		arr.		09.14	13.09
Bonningues		07.08		15.03				08.05	12.01
Ardres		08.15							11.00
Guînes									
Calais-Ville	arr.					dep.			

(1) Thursdays only (market day in Ardres). (2) Thursdays only (market day in Fauquembergues). (3) Fridays only (market day in Lumbres).

Aire to Berck		(1)	(2)	(1)			(2)	(1)	(1)
Aire	dep.		11.56			▲ arr.	09.49		
Delettes			12.57				08.48		
Dennebrœucq		09.07							13.23
Fruges	arr.	09.45				dep.			12.45
	dep.			15.35		arr.		10.15	
Rimeux-Gournay				15.55				09.58	
Hucqueliers				17.05				08.48	
Montreuil	arr.					dep.			
	dep.					arr.			
Rang	arr.					dep.			
	dep.					arr.			
Berck-Plage	arr.					dep.			

(1) Saturdays only (market day in Fruges). (2) Fridays only (market day in Aire)

Ardres to Pont d'Ardres

Ardres	dep.	05.30	18.10	▲ arr.	08.00	19.10
Pont d'Ardres	arr.	05.51	18.30	│ dep.	07.38	18.48

There is photographic evidence in M. Claude Wagner's article *Le Train de Guînes* of a more regular public service provided by diesel railcars and steam-hauled trains in 1941. He says that because of the almost total destruction of Calais-Nord (the part north of the canal by the central station) in May 1940 many of the population moved to Guînes or the surrounding villages and many travelled to Calais once or more per week. His grand-father, aunt and uncle were among those who moved out. Since the Tramway from Calais to Guînes did not run after 1939, dependence on the Anvin-Calais line increased.

We know from the rolling stock crisis of 1943 that by that time more priority was again being given to military uses of these lines, and that less engines were available. In particular, because of fuel shortages, only two railcars, one diesel and one *gazogène* (fitted with a gas generator), were in use. One was based at Bonningues and one at Ardres. The summary timetables for May 1944 are shown in *Table Thirty-One* and *Table Thity-Two*. On the Anvin-Calais line there was an early morning train from Bonningues to Calais, and one back in the early evening, every working day; and there was another service from Ardres to Calais and back every day. There was also a service from Lumbres to Fruges and back every day. Other than these, services were less than daily, being only twice a week between Anvin and Fruges and three times per week between Lumbres and Bonningues.

Table Thirty-One
Summary Timetable May 1944

Anvin to Calais

		(1)		(2)	(3)		(4)	(5)	(6)	(2)
Anvin	dep.			11.05						21.40
Fruges	arr.			11.58						22.34
	dep.					14.00				
Rimeux-Gournay						14.23				
Lumbres	arr.					15.46				
	dep.				13.25					
Bonningues		05.40			14.40					
Ardres		06.40	10.40		15.35		15.35	19.40	20.31	
Guînes		07.15	11.06		16.10		16.10	20.08	20.59	
Calais-Ville	arr.	07.57	11.40		16.53		16.53			

		(1)	(2)		(4)	(3)		(2)	(5)	(6)
Calais-Ville	dep.				09.00	09.00	12.20		18.15	18.15
Guînes		05.35			09.45	09.45	12.57		19.00	19.00
Ardres		06.05			10.16	10.20	13.20		19.36	20.40
Bonningues						11.17			20.16	21.20
Lumbres	arr.					12.25				
	dep.		08.10							
Rimeux-Gournay			09.44							
Fruges	arr.		10.05							
	dep.	08.12					16.47			
Anvin	arr.	09.06					17.41			

(1) Working days only.
(2) Monday and Thursday only.
(3) Monday, Thursday and Saturday only.
(4) Tuesday, Wednesday and Friday only.
(5) Tuesday, Thursday and Friday only.
(6) Monday, Wednesday and Saturday only.

Table Thirty-Two
Summary Timetable May 1944

Aire to Berck

		(3)	(4)	(5)	(6)
Aire	dep.		12.13		14.40
Fruges	arr.		14.24		16.45
	dep.	05.00		13.10	
Rimeux-Gournay		05.23		13.33	
Montreuil	arr.	07.41		15.32	
	dep.	08.36		16.40	
Rang	arr.	09.35		17.44	
	dep.	09.41	13.50	17.58	19.30
Berck-Plage	arr.	09.59	14.08	18.03	19.48

		(4)	(5)	(6)	(3)	(1)	(2)
Berck-Plage	dep.		06.15	12.40	14.26	17.50	18.55
Rang	arr.		06.23	12.58	14.45	18.08	19.14
	dep.		06.40		14.52		
Montreuil	arr.		07.37		15.49		
	dep.		08.10		16.40		
Rimeux-Gournay			10.33		18.59		
Fruges	arr.		10.54		19.20		
	dep.	07.55	11.39				
Aire	arr.	10.03	13.47				

(1) Working days only
(2) Sundays and Feast days only
(3) Wednesday and Saturday only
(4) Friday only
(5) Monday, Wednesday and Saturday only
(6) Tuesday and Sunday only

On the Aire-Berck line, services between Aire and Fruges ran only three times per week. Between Fruges and Berck-Plage there were two trains each way on two days per week and one each way on a third. In addition there were two services each way every day between Rang and Berck-Plage. Trains ran between Ardres and Pont d'Ardres (not shown in these tables) twice a day on three days per week only. With the return of fighting to the area in September 1944, all services must have ceased again for a time. In any case, it is unlikely that the service between Guînes and Calais could have continued after the flooding of the *marais* by the Germans during part of 1944.

Table Thirty-Three below shows some figures for activity and profitability for the Aire-Berck line for the years 1938 to 1946. We do not have equivalent figures for the Anvin-Calais line but they are likely to have been similar. It is probable that some or all of the use by the German armed forces is not included. Passenger numbers were markedly reduced in 1940 and 1944 but through the middle of the war were better than pre-war levels, probably because of the lack of alternative transportation. By 1946 passenger levels were almost back to the best between the wars, which had been approaching 600,000 per annum in the 1920s and early 1930s. Goods suffered more and never recovered to pre-war levels. The coefficient of exploitation is the expense per train kilometre divided by the income per train kilometre and is a crude indicator of operating profit. A low number represents a good profit, increasing numbers from 100 up represent an increasing loss. The results show that this line was just breaking even before the war, but made a loss during and immediately after the war.

Table Thirty-Three
Aire-Berck line - Activity and profitability 1938 to 1946

Year	No. of Passengers	Goods (petite vitesse) tonnes	Coal and coke tonnes	Coefficient of exploitation (per cent)
1938	383,249	156,250	14,498	100
1939	325,792	110,415	19,032	98
1940	122,932	94,131	25,016	107
1941	250,329	80,048	15,596	133
1942	429,137	56,094	11,503	129
1943	411,890	42,228	14,084	104
1944	112,512	26,529	8,057	155
1945	410,577	42,187	15,299	160
1946	509,912	57,648	17,700	116

Tramway Étaples-Paris-Plage

We have already noted in Chapter Six that, by the summer of 1939, trams were only running 12 times per day for six or seven weeks, and that the whole of the rest of the summer service, and the whole of the winter service up to the winter of 1938/1939, was provided by buses. Nonetheless, the timetable from 2nd October, 1939, provided for seven services every day, and two extra on market days in Étaples. All these were trams. Presumably the buses, and probably the bus drivers as well, had been requisitioned for the French armed forces. The tram service was suspended in 1940 at the time of the German occupation.

Ordinary services never resumed. However, from April 1942, the tramway was used by the occupying forces, mainly to transport materials to Le-Touquet-Paris-Plage for the construction of the coastal fortifications. In November 1943, the Mayor of Le Touquet reported to the *département* that this had damaged the rolling stock, but that this work had been completed and now the line was being used to carry workers for German projects, living in Le Touquet but working further away. There was also an unofficial use by French civilians in return for a tip to the *wattman* (tram driver)! So far the German authorities had done all this at their own expense, but now they were asking the town to pay the wages of three tramway staff, two drivers and a chief mechanic. The Mayor objected to this. There had been no public transport at all between Le Touquet and the station at Étaples since 1940. He wanted to re-establish a bus service, despite the grave shortage of oil and tyres, and the risk that the German authorities would demand most of its use. The Chief Engineer of the *département* recommended that the Mayor be supported in refusing to pay for the tramway staff, and in trying to set up a bus service. The outcome of all this is not known.

After World War II all services were provided by bus. The fate of the rolling stock is unknown. The Chief Engineer of the *département* repeatedly tried to contact the Managing Director of the *Compagnie du Tramway d'Étaples à Paris-Plage* to discover their intentions for the future of the track. By September 1948 Gaz de France wanted to use part of the road verge occupied by the track to lay a gas pipeline. Having given the company due notice and received no reply, *M. le Préfet* decided in January 1949 that the path of the line should be considered freed from any obligation to the company. He informed the Managing Director that the company were considered to have permanently abandoned the operation of the line, and that the ground was freed for other use. Formal declassification followed in 1953.

Tramways of Boulogne

In 1939 the bus service was suspended because all the drivers were mobilised. Some service was maintained on all the tramways using staff exempt from call-up and some staff who were due to retire but agreed to stay on. From the time of the German invasion of May 1940, the service stopped because of some damage to the tracks and extensive destruction of the overhead wiring, much of it around the port. The workshops were also damaged but the rolling stock was almost intact.

The lines to Le Portel, to St-Martin, and to Pont-de-Briques were repaired. The German authorities refused permission to repair the line to Wimereux because it went along the open coast, and there were insufficient materials to repair the line to Outreau. Between June and August 1940, 79,000 francs were spent repairing the lines but despite many approaches to the *Oberfeldkommandantur* (OFK 670) in Lille, the German authorities would not give permission for the lines to be re-opened. From September 1940, frequent bombing raids by the RAF partly destroyed the repaired lines again. In 1940 and 1941 the German Navy and the Todt organisation removed rails, overhead wires and other materials from some of the lines. In September 1941, on the orders of the German Navy, the German firm Holzmann cut the line to Wimereux by the casino, and joined it to a new line from the port for the transport of materials to construct a defensive barrier on the beach. The same month the German Navy were taking overhead wiring for use with the transformers they had requisitioned from the tramway depot and set up at the Bassin Loubet.

In January 1942, the German authorities ordered that the lines to St-Martin-Boulogne and Pont-de-Briques should be re-opened. Both were re-opened in June 1942 after repairs costing a further 130,000 francs. A number of stops on each line were suspended to save electricity. During the repairs the German Navy had said that they would pay a monthly bill for the transport of German military personnel and other German nationals, but later they said that these people should be carried free and any bill sent to the Organization of the *Voies Ferrées d'Intérêt Local* (VFIL) in Paris. The tramways were, however, also allowed to carry French civilians on these lines.

The line from Boulogne to Wimereux was put back in service in February 1943, and that from Châtillon (which is on the Le Portel side of Boulogne-Ville station) to Le Portel in August 1943. Both were for the exclusive use of the occupying forces. The line to Wimereux remained in service until the beginning of June 1944. Le Portel was heavily bombed by the RAF on the 4th, 8th and 9th September, 1943. This closed the line to Le Portel again. It re-opened on 1st December but was found to be unserviceable and finally closed later in December 1943. Despite all the problems, the trams travelled in total nearly 23,000 km over the line to Wimereux in 1943 and nearly 15,000 km in 1944. However, they only travelled 969 km on the line to Le Portel, all in 1943.

During the period June 1942 to May 1944 the Tramways of Boulogne billed the *Voies Ferrées d'Intérêt Local* in Paris just over 1,800,000 francs for German military use of their lines, but only 52 per cent of this was reimbursed. The Tramways, in claiming reparations after the war, said that 33 per cent of use of the lines to St-Martin and Pont-de-Briques was by German forces. This heavy use had forced them to put on extra services.

The Boulogne port area was bombed for 24 hours on 5th and 6th June, 1944. In addition to a desire to deny use of the port to the German forces, this was probably part of the plan to convince the German High Command that the invasion would be on the *Côte d'Opale* (Pas-de-Calais) and not in Normandy. The Normandy D-Day landings began in the early morning of 6th June. Following heavy bombing by the RAF on 15th June, 1944, with much further destruction of the tramway infrastructure, all tram operations again came to an end. More damage followed, particularly during the battle to liberate Boulogne in late September. In all, six power cars, three trailers, and some wagons were destroyed. By the end of the war there were 27.7 km (17 miles) of overhead wire to be replaced, 12 km of it on the line to Wimereux, and 4.14 km of Broca rails (for roadways) and 0.74 km of Vignole rails were also required. The bridge across the Liane carrying the two tram lines had been destroyed. The final claim submitted by the Boulogne tramways for reparations after the war was 3,372,000 francs.

After the war

It was after World War II that the rapid rise in availability and use of motor lorries, buses and private cars, soon followed by light motorcycles and motor scooters, put even the more viable lines under increased pressure. During the 1950s and 1960s SNCF closed many standard gauge lines of both *Interêt Général* and *Interêt Local*. Financial pressures and, one suspects, pressures from bus company and motor trade interests also led to the closure of many metre gauge lines during this period. This happened in spite of opposition from the public, and the frequent deterioration of services when the buses took over.

Tramways of Boulogne

In August 1945 the Chief Engineer of the *département* reported that there was great need for metre gauge rails in the port of Boulogne, to replace an important network of metre gauge lines that had run before the war to the sea defence works of the port. This came at the same time as the need to refurbish other lines within the port for the removal of rubble. The 2.7 km of line between Châtillon and Le Portel had been so damaged by bombardment that repair was not worthwhile. A bus service was in place and in any case the Tramways company was in discussion with the town about the replacement of the whole network with trolleybuses. The Chief Engineer recommended that the remainder of this part of the line should be lifted, and the useable rails given, for a payment, to the port authorities. It is probable that this is what happened, and that this part of the line was never reopened.

The rest of the Boulogne tramways were repaired and continued to run until 1951. With the closure of the line to Bonningues in 1935, and then the demise of the Tramways in 1951, Boulogne really ceases to be part of this story. However, we think readers will wish to know a little more of what happened after the war, to relate all this to the Boulogne which we see and visit now. Boulogne-Ville station was destroyed, with most of the rest of the port area, in the bombing and the fighting of 1944. After the war the lines were restored and the station operated using temporary buildings.

In a major restructuring of the Boulogne port area and the valley of the Liane after the War, the Liane river itself was narrowed and straightened. The west bank was cut back, removing a piece of land with destroyed factories. A triangular piece of land more than 1 km long and 0.5 km deep was reclaimed on the east bank between the Boulevard Pierre Daunou, which had been on the edge of the Liane as well as being the route of the line to Bonningues, and the new Boulevard Diderot, a dual carriageway along the river bank. On this new land schools, colleges and sports facilities have been built. Most importantly for the railways the curved bridge linking the old Boulogne-Ville station to the through line in the Calais direction was pulled down in 1962 or 1963. A new *Gare Centrale*, also

The 'new' station at Boulogne, called like the old one Boulogne-Ville, built on the reclaimed east bank of the River Liane on the through line to Calais, in 1962. The cathedral at the top of the old town can be seen on the left.   *Authors' Collection*

called Boulogne-Ville, was constructed in concrete on the southern part of the reclaimed land, on the through line from Paris and Abbeville to Calais. The area of the old abbatoir became part of the new goods yard.

The lines to the port were maintained, as was the line through the site of the old Boulogne-Ville station to the *Gare Maritime*, which was rebuilt. Boulogne remained a regular car ferry port until the 1990s, when the new generation of larger ferries arrived and were too big to use the port. All the Pas-de-Calais ferry traffic then went to Calais. Since 2004 a fast service between Boulogne and Dover for cars and light vans has been restored using a large catamaran. In the last few years the rail link to the *Gare Maritime* through the site of the old station has been cut off, and part of the formation has been used to provide new road access to the ferry port. Rails remain within the station part of the *Gare Maritime*, and there is still a locomotive turntable at the end of the lines close to the mooring point of the fast catamaran.

Tramways of Calais (including Calais To Guînes)

Readers will recall from Chapter Six that the tramway to Guînes had already closed in 1939, before the war. The remaining tramways of the Calais conurbation were extensively damaged in the fighting of 1940, and ceased to operate. At the end of the war the *Société Anonyme des Tramways de Calais et Extensions* reported that all the trams had been destroyed and all the overhead lines were down. The remains had been looted by the occupying forces. Their 12 buses had either been destroyed or taken away by the occupiers.

After the war there were discussions about restarting the tram service but the *Société* were in a parlous financial state and the town was unable to help. In 1946 the

Société appealed for help to get licences for the buses which they hoped they could afford. That there had been no legislation for compensation for war damage for railways of *Intérêt Local* or tramways had not helped. They had been offered new buses, and second-hand London Transport buses used by the American Army, but could afford neither. Faced with the inability of the *Société* to obtain buses, and the problem that there was no urban or suburban service, the town council opened talks with another company to provide a minimum service on a short term basis.

By 1948 the *Société* were able to restore the bus service to Guînes, and some other services, by permission of the *Comité Technique Départementale*, who agreed to allocate the necessary petrol and diesel fuel from the still rationed resources. There were three services each way to Guînes per day, and the services were co-ordinated with the VFIL train service. Finally, on 3rd May, 1949, the Mayor and the *Société* agreed to apply for the formal declassification of all the abandoned tramways and their permanent replacement with buses. The service agreed for the route to Guînes was 20 per day each way as far as Pont de Coulogne, and 5 each way all the way to Guînes. So the Calais tramways had effectively come to an end in 1940, and never restarted.

Anvin-Calais and Aire-Berck (including the Tramway from Ardres-Pont d'Ardres, and remaining services on the Boulogne-Bonningues line)

After World War II these lines picked themselves up and continued to run, moderately successfully, for nearly 10 years.

Stations

We have already noted that Calais, and particularly the old part of Calais north of Calais-Ville station, had been very badly damaged in 1940 and 1944. Few buildings were still standing. When Bryan Morgan visited it in 1954 or 1955 (*The End of the Line*, Chapter Three, *see the Introduction*) the devastation of Calais between the *Gare Maritime* and Calais-Ville station was still there.

Some sources say that Calais-Ville station was destroyed in the fighting of 1940. Others say that this happened in 1944. The truth may be part and part. Some photographs show the change between 1939 and 1944, the latter showing nothing standing. On the other hand photographs taken by British Army photographers in October 1944, show the train shed and large parts of the station still standing, although extensively damaged. The station was pulled down, and temporary buildings were probably used. The distinctive footbridge, allowing access between the roads on either side of the station without going into the Boulevard Jacquard, survived the war. The Anvin-Calais line continued to use the same bay platform, and a photograph in 1953 shows a train in this platform with the footbridge behind. After the closure of the Anvin-Calais line in 1955, the station was rebuilt in concrete with the entrance from the bridge over the lines to the *Gare Maritime* at the Boulevard Jacquard. The footbridge was demolished in this rebuilding. The former metre gauge bay platform at the far end of the station is now standard gauge, and the platform has been straightened, but the position is still identifiable from the buildings in the background.

Calais-Ville station in 1939 and 1944, the latter showing apparently complete destruction of the station.   *Éditions Fauchois, Béthune*

Calais-Ville station on 12th October, 1944, looking east, taken by a British Army photographer. The train shed and some of the buildings are still standing, but extensively damaged, and the track is ripped up at the far end of the platforms.   *IWM B10761, reproduced with permission*

Diesel locomotive No. 301 waits to leave with a passenger train in the bay platform at Calais-Ville station in May 1953. Although headed towards Fruges, this locomotive in general only went as far as Bonningues. The old station has gone but the distinctive footbridge was still there.

J. Bazin; Collection Bernard Guéret, formerly BVA

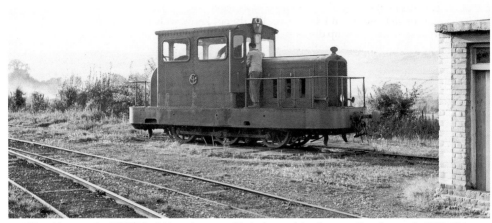

Diesel locomotive VFIL No. 301 on the turntable in front of the depot at Bonningues in 1953. This locomotive is now owned by the *Chemin de Fer de la Baie de Somme*, with the same number.
J. Bazin; Collection Bernard Guéret, formerly BVA

One of the former CF Dordogne diesel locomotives (VFIL Nos. 650 to 652) at Wailly-Beaucamp station in 1953 with a passenger train. The train is headed in the direction of Fruges but is probably only going to Montreuil. *J. Bazin; Collection Bernard Guéret, formerly BVA*

Rolling stock

In 1948 the VFIL works at Lumbres constructed a 6-wheel diesel locomotive on the chassis of an 0-6-0 steam locomotive. We do not know which locomotive was used for this. A Willème 180 hp diesel engine was fitted, and the locomotive was given the number 301. In 1949 three diesel locomotives, built at the works of *CF de Périgueux* between 1946 and 1948, were bought from the *CF de la Dordogne* which had recently closed. These were given the numbers 650 to 652. The VFIL works at Lumbres built two other 6-wheel diesel locomotives but these went straight to the Flanders network and as far as we know were never used on the Anvin-Calais-Aire-Berck lines.

VFIL took the opportunity of the closure of other lines to purchase additional diesel railcars, all with two bogies, for these lines. From the *CF de la Dordogne* they acquired, in 1949 or 1950, two Billard A80D1 railcars, built in 1938, and numbered 608 and 610, and a third without its motor as a trailer (Ra 606). In 1951 a Billard A80D2 (No. 704), built in 1939, came from the *CFD de la Vendée*. Finally, in either 1951 or 1952, two Billard railcars of type A150D6, built in 1947, came from the *Tramways d'Ille et Villaine*. With these came three R210 trailers numbered Ra 20 to 22.

CGL No. 1, one of the original railcars built at Lumbres in the 1930s, was rebuilt with rounder contours in 1954-1955, to match the Billard railcars transferred from other lines. It is said to have been returned to service only in February 1955 and to have been used for only eight days before closure on 1st March, 1955! Previously in the chestnut brown and off-white livery of railcars of the Anvin-Calais-Aire-Berck lines, in the rebuild it was repainted red and off-white, to match the colours of the railcars which had arrived from other lines. In 1947 steam locomotive No. 13, the 24 tonne SACM built in 1924, was transferred to the VFIL Oise network.

A Billard railcar, probably running part of the service between Berck-Plage and Rang-du-Fliers, at Berck-Plage in July 1954. A longer passenger train is waiting to leave on the left. The photograph illustrates how relatively busy this part of the line still was, at least in the summer, less than a year before final closure.

J. Bazin; Collection Bernard Guéret, formerly BVA

One of the diesel railcars built at the VFIL works at Lumbres in the 1930s waits at Hucqueliers with a Billard trailer in 1953. It is heading towards Berck-Plage.

J. Bazin; Collection Bernard Guéret, formerly BVA

Diesel railcar ARB No. 5, heading towards Fruges, at Bonningues in 1953. The passenger stock on the left is for the Bonningues-Calais service, which was hauled by diesel locomotive No. 301 based at Bonningues.   *J. Bazin; Collection Bernard Guéret, formerly BVA*

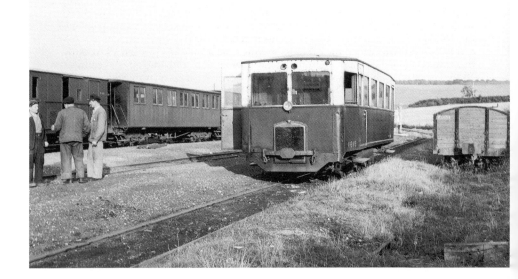

Operations

After the war services were in general less good than before, and fares were rising rapidly. During and after World War II inflation was high. In 1941 the second class fare per kilometre had been 41 centimes, in 1946 it was 2 francs 2 centimes, and by 1950 it was 3 francs 30 centimes. First class fares increased over the same period from 50 centimes to 4 francs 52 centimes per kilometre. Another, perhaps more dramatic, indication of increasing costs, and of inflation and the devaluation of the franc during this period, is that the operating cost for the Aire-Berck line was 10.99 francs per train kilometre in 1939 and 220 francs in 1951.

In May 1945 the service was extremely limited. On the Anvin-Calais line, there was no through service at Lumbres. There was one service daily Monday to Saturday for workers from Bonningues to Calais and back, and another daily from Calais to Ardres and back. Apart from that, services were three times weekly, usually on different days for Anvin-Fruges, Fruges-Lumbres, and Lumbres-Calais. It was never possible to travel the whole length of the line on the same day, and only possible to go from Fruges to Calais with a reasonable connection at Lumbres, on a Thursday. On the Aire-Berck line there were services once each way between Aire and Fruges on two days per week, and twice each way between Fruges and Berck-Plage on three days, but different days. There were up to five additional trains daily between Rang-du-Fliers and Berck-Plage. Between Ardres and Pont d'Ardres there were two trains each way on two days per week. Fuel shortages were the main cause for the poor services, and this affected bus services too which virtually disappeared at this time. Reference to *Tables Thirty-One & Thirty-Two (pages 259 & 260)* shows that services were actually worse in May 1945 than in May 1944. A note with the May 1945 timetable states that places were strictly limited, personal luggage only could be carried on the railcars, and return tickets for railcar services would not be sold.

By 1946 things had improved, but there were loud complaints from Guînes because services to Calais were still only four each way per day compared with six each way before the war. Six hundred people travelled from Guînes to Calais and back on working days of whom 481 bought weekly season tickets. The people of Guînes had already lost their tramway to Calais in 1939, and now the reduction in train service made matters worse. A particular problem was that holders of workers' weekly tickets had to travel on the designated workers' trains or pay a supplement. In 1939 there had been two workers' trains in the mornings, leaving Guînes at 05.55 and 07.10, and two back in the evening, leaving Calais-Ville at 18.10 and 19.40. Now there was only one workers' train in the morning at 07.10 and one in the evening at 18.15. The 19.40 train still ran but was not classified as a workers' train and required the supplementary fare. The company and the *département* responded to these complaints by agreeing that the service was less good than 1939, but said that it met the needs of the customers, and in any case, line repairs prevented additional services. Workers' weekly tickets, which were about two-thirds of second class fares, were also increasing in price in line with fares generally. In 1950 there was a further complaint. Workers at a chemical factory near the halt at Coulogne, 7 km from Guînes, had to pay the rate to Calais-Fontinettes, the next station which was 9 km from Guînes. Following a petition from 18 of the 30 workers involved, supported by the Mayor of Guînes and by the factory, VFIL gave way on this. Nevertheless the records of the closure show that by 1955 many workers had drifted away from the train, although they did return for the last day to pay their respects. They might have transferred to buses, but probably eventually went by car.

Table Thirty-Four – Summary Timetable from 14th May, 1950

Anvin to Calais (VFIL)

Station		(1)	(2)	(3)	(4)	(5)	(5)		MV (6)				
Anvin SNCF		08.25		09.15	11.55	11.55			14.44		17.55	20.25	
Fruges	06.20	08.56	09.15	09.46	12.30	12.26	13.06		15.27	17.15	18.26	20.58	
Rimeux-Gournay	06.40		09.29		12.43		13.20			17.29		21.12	
Fauquembergues	06.57	(7)	09.45		13.00		13.27	(10) (11)		17.46		21.29	
Lumbres SNCF	* 07.30	08.02				13.34	14.11		14.25		18.19	19.15	22.02
Bonningues	05.20	08.42		(8)	(9)	(8)			15.30	17.43	19.58		
Ardres	06.00	09.15			13.18	13.18			16.18	18.28	20.30		
Guînes	06.30	09.33	09.33		13.39	13.52			16.52	18.57	20.52		
Calais-Ville SNCF	07.06	10.01	10.06		14.05	14.18			17.25	19.33			

Station		(12)	(13)	(2)	(13)	*(9)	*(8)	(8)	(7)	*(10)	(11)
Calais-Ville SNCF		08.50	08.50			12.20	12.20	16.10	16.15	18.15	20.20
Guînes	05.41	09.34	09.34			12.46	12.54	16.41	16.50	18.53	20.55
Ardres	06.24	10.06	10.00		12.00	13.03	13.17		17.09	19.16	21.19
Bonningues			06.57	10.49		12.42			17.42	19.55	20.58
Lumbres SNCF	05.45	07.38	08.04	11.50		13.40		14.45	18.22		19.00
Fauquembergues	06.19	08.38		MV (6)	13.02			15.19			19.34
Rimeux-Gournay	06.36	08.55			13.21			15.36			19.52
Fruges	06.52	09.08	10.56	13.00	13.34			15.49	16.59	18.59	20.05
Anvin SNCF	07.23		11.30	13.43					17.30	19.30	

MV Mixed passenger and goods train (*Marchandises / Voyageurs*)   * Workers season tickets valid

(1) To 30th June, 1950.
(2) Thursdays only (market day in Fauquembergues).
(3) From 1st July, 1950.
(4) Except Thursdays (market day in Fauquembergues) and Saturdays (market day in Fruges).
(5) Thursdays (market day in Fauquembergues) and Saturdays (market day in Fruges).
(6) Saturdays only (market day in Fruges).
(7) Not Saturdays between Guînes and Calais.
(8) Saturdays only.
(9) Except Saturdays.
(10) Not Sundays or holidays between Bonningues and Calais 14th May to 17th September.
(11) Sundays and holidays only, 14th May to 17th September.
(12) Daily except Thursday (market day in Ardres).
(13) Thursdays only (market day in Ardres).

Table Thirty-Five – Summary Timetable from 14th May, 1950

Aire to Berck (VFIL)

Station			(1)		(2)		(3)	(4)	(5)	
Aire SNCF	dep.		08.45		13.18	15.15	19.25	19.25		
Thérouanne			09.10		13.56	15.40	20.03	19.50	21.35	
Fruges		05.32	09.57	11.18	15.09	16.30	21.14	20.37	22.20	
Rimeux-Gournay		05.47		11.33		16.45				
Montreuil SNCF	arr.	07.17	(6)		13.03		18.15		(8)	
	dep.	07.40	08.50	09.52	12.23	13.26	18.34		21.16	
Rang SNCF		08.20	09.36	10.31	13.11	14.04	19.13		21.53	
Berck-Plage	arr.	08.34	09.52	10.45	13.27	14.18	19.28		22.09	

Station			(2)		(6)	(1)		(3)	(4)	(5)		(7)
Berck-Plage	dep.		06.20	07.20	08.24		12.12			17.24	19.15	
Rang SNCF			06.36	07.40	08.52	09.48	12.30			17.42	20.30	
Montreuil SNCF	arr.		07.13	08.22	09.30	10.32	13.06			18.18	20.50	
	dep.		07.50				13.30			19.06		
Rimeux-Gournay			09.29				15.02			20.38		
Fruges		06.22	07.02	09.48		12.00	15.15	16.29	17.10	20.40	20.51	
Thérouanne		07.10	08.07			12.48		17.44	17.58	21.27		
Aire SNCF	arr.	07.35	08.42			13.13		18.19	18.23			

At least eight additional services each way between Rang and Berck-Plage, up to 12 summer weekends.
First departure (from Berck-Plage) at 05.37. Last departure (from Rang) at 22.04. Journey time 14 to 16 minutes

(1) Saturdays only (market day in Montreuil)
(2) Fridays only (market day in Aire)
(3) Not Sundays and holidays
(4) Sundays and holidays only
(5) Sundays and holidays only for a trial period 24th September, 1950 to 25th March, 1951
(6) From 1st July, 1950
(7) Saturdays, Sundays and Mondays only, 1st July to 25th September, 1950
(8) Daily from Rang to Berck, Sundays and Mondays only from Montreuil to Rang, 1st July to 25th September, 1950.

From 1948 a number of major stations were not staffed on Sundays. These were selected as those where the crossings of regular trains were not scheduled, which were Fauquembergues, Tournehem, Thérouanne, Hucqueliers and Beussent. Special arrangements were made for the single line tokens (*bâtons-pilotes*) for the sections concerned.

Although services improved after 1945, the through service at Lumbres on the Anvin-Calais line was never restored after the war. Very limited through services were restored at Fruges. The timetables from 14th May, 1950 for these lines are shown in the *Tables Thirty-Four and Thirty-Five*. On the Anvin-Calais line there was one through service per day in each direction between Anvin and Lumbres, and one more from Anvin to Lumbres in the middle of the day except on Thursdays and Saturdays. However, because the daily service left Lumbres for Anvin early in the morning and returned to Lumbres late in the evening, it was not possible to use this to connect to or from Calais at Lumbres. In the direction from Calais to Anvin, it was only possible to travel the whole line by leaving Calais at 08.50 and arriving at Anvin at 17.30, 8 hours and 40 minutes later, having changed and waited at Lumbres and Fruges, and, on a Thursday, also at Ardres. In the other direction it was also possible to travel the whole length of the line on the same day, leaving Anvin at 11.55 and reaching Calais at 17.25, the total journey time would be only 5 hours and 30 minutes with a change only at Lumbres; except on a Thursday or Saturday, with an additional change at Fruges, or on a Sunday or holiday when there was an additional wait or change at Bonningues, arriving at Calais at 19.33. There was only one morning train on which workers season tickets were valid, leaving Bonningues at 05.20 for Calais. On the line from Ardres to Pont d'Ardres there were two trains each way on Mondays and Wednesdays only.

On the Aire-Berck line the pattern was similar but not as bad. The services were broken at Fruges, except for one train per day in the Aire to Berck direction only. This was the 15.15 from Aire, which completed the journey in 4 hours and 13 minutes. In the other direction, taking the 12.12 from Berck-Plage, the journey took 6 hours and 5 minutes because of the change at Fruges. It may be that through services were better preserved on the Aire-Berck line because of the much longer distance between SNCF connections for this line (Aire to Montreuil 75 km, 46½ miles) than those for the Anvin-Calais line (Anvin to Lumbres, 44 km, 27¼ miles, and Lumbres to Calais-Fontinettes,

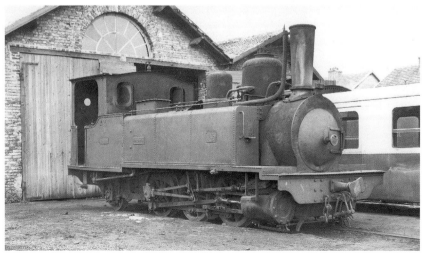

Corpet 0-6-2 tank locomotive ARB No. 45, delivered 1892, of 21 tonnes unladen weight, in front of the depot at Berck-Plage in 1951.   *M. Rifault; Collection Bernard Guéret, formerly BVA*

A passenger train going to Berck-Plage, hauled by one of the former CF Dordogne diesel locomotives (VFIL Nos. 650 to 652), waiting at Rang-du-Fliers in July 1954 for passengers to change from the Paris train on the other side of the platform.

J. Bazin; Collection Bernard Guéret, formerly BVA

Locomotive CGL No. 120, a 2-6-0 tank locomotive of 24 tonnes unladen weight, built at Ateliers-Nord-Belge in 1924, passing Rang-du-Fliers in the direction of Aire with a goods train in 1951.

M. Rifault; Collection Bernard Guéret, formerly BVA

49 km, 30½ miles). There was also a much longer distance between depots for the Aire-Berck line (Fruges to Berck-Plage, 65 km, 40½ miles).

In reality those travelling to or near the ends of the lines would have gone on SNCF. By spring 1952 services on the Anvin-Calais line were completely cut at Fruges. These were the last few months for the Aire-Fruges and Anvin-Fruges sections which closed at the end of August 1952. It is likely that the motivation for the breaking of services after World War II was to save costs by limiting train crew hours and avoiding crews spending the night away from their base. The services were based around the large depots at Fruges, Lumbres and Berck-Plage and the smaller facilities at Bonningues and Guînes.

There was a clear pattern of rolling stock use after World War II. Through passenger services were provided using the 1930s railcars constructed at Lumbres (Nos. 1 to 7), usually alone but sometimes with a coach and a baggage van, and later sometimes with a Billard trailer. These were based at Fruges, Guînes, and Berck. The larger rebuilt Renault-Scemia railcar, No. 101, worked mainly between Berck-Plage and Rang-du-Fliers. This route was later mostly served by Billard railcars and trailers as these were acquired.

Of the diesel locomotives, No. 301 provided passenger services on the section between Bonningues and Calais and was based at Bonningues. The other three, Nos. 650 to 652, hauled passenger trains on the Aire-Berck line mainly between Berck-Plage and Montreuil, and also goods trains. At least one, probably two, and possibly all three were based at Berck-Plage. From 1950, after the acquisition of additional diesel railcars and locomotives, VFIL saved money by a deliberate policy of universal use of diesel traction.

The steam locomotives were mostly used to haul goods trains in the sugar beet season. The seven 24 tonne 2-6-0 and the two 42 tonne 2-10-0 locomotives were the main ones used for this. The remaining steam locomotives were available for goods or passenger use as back-up at busy times.

The Boulogne-Bonningues line

Readers will recall from Chapter Six that the Boulogne-Bonningues line was closed for passenger services in 1935. The section from St-Martin-Boulogne to Colembert was closed completely. The section from Colembert to Bonningues was retained for goods traffic, mainly in the sugar beet season, and under the management of VFIL. Readers will also recall from earlier in this chapter that the line from Colembert to St-Martin-Boulogne was reopened by the German authorities for military use in 1942.

In 1945 a group of Mayors of interested *communes* requested the reopening of the line between St-Martin-Boulogne and Colembert for all traffic, pointing out that the line had already been refurbished and operated by the German armed forces. After the closure of this part of the line in 1935, the bus services had been unsatisfactory, and effectively only La Capelle and Colembert had a service. The Mayors had some support from the *Conseil Général*. VFIL had already reported in November 1944 that the Germans had made extensive use of un-creosoted beech sleepers, and already over-used rails. In addition fighting had damaged the line between La Capelle and St-Martin-Boulogne, especially on the Boulogne side of Blanc-Pignon. Given the heavy fighting in September 1944 when the Canadians took the nearby Mont Lambert, the latter report is not surprising. The Mayor of Boulogne reported in 1945 that the town had stopped using the line from La Madeleine to the Val St-Martin for the disposal of town waste in April 1944, when the German forces had seized the rolling stock and partly lifted the line. Now town waste was being used to reclaim land on the right bank of the Liane, and the longer term plan for the rebuilding of Boulogne proposed a new treatment facility for waste on the left bank. In any case the line could not be used unless the bridge over the main road to Paris, the N1, at La Madeleine, destroyed in the war, was rebuilt. In the light of all this the Chief Engineer of the *département* reported in 1945 that the German forces had only made the line fit for short term use, and that making it fit for the longer term would be costly. There was no available rolling stock to operate the services. In 1946 the Chief Engineer further reported that there were three bus services each way per day between Boulogne and La Capelle, and two each way on Mondays, Wednesdays and Saturdays between Boulogne, Le Waast, and Colembert. He said that 'it seems that the population are satisfied'. This seems surprising. VFIL said that it was already costing 9 million francs per year just to run the goods service from Colembert to Bonningues, and cost may have been the real reason why the request was rejected. The remaining part of the line from Colembert to Bonningues was closed completely in 1948.

Industrial links

We do not have comprehensive figures for sugar beet carriage after World War II. We do know that in an average season about 3,600 tonnes of sugar beet and 850 tonnes of pulp were carried between Guînes and the factory at Pont d'Ardres. Also we know that in each season 3,000 wagons were loaded with sugar beet in the Lys valley between Matringhem and Mametz, probably mainly for carriage to factories near Aire or on the canal system beyond. Further weighbridges for the sugar factories were installed at stations. In 1946 a third was installed at Coyecques, for the cooperative *sucrerie* at Lillers, which would probably have been reached by way of the canal from Aire. This went with the weighbridges for the Béghin factory at

Weighbridge and small office in the former station yard at Coyecques in 2006. This was installed in 1946 for the cooperative *sucrerie* at Lillers. This was the third such weighbridge at Coyecques, each installed for a different company, but this is the only one that remains.   *Authors*

The bridge over the River Aa into the former paper factory at Vedringhem, in 2006. This carried the metre gauge siding, and later, after World War II, the dual gauge siding, into the factory. *Authors*

Thumeries and the Say factory at Pont d'Ardres already in place. A weighbridge and office were also installed at Matringhem for the Lillers factory, where there was also one already for Say at Pont d'Ardres.

We have already noted in Chapter Two that in 1913 MM. Emile Avot et fils, proprietors of the paper and cardboard factory at Elnes, built a standard gauge line to the factory. This was built in 4-rail dual gauge which extended on the Anvin-Calais through line for a distance of 520 metres from the east end of Lumbres station. By the time of closure of this part of the Anvin-Calais line in 1955, the 4-rail dual gauge had been extended to the paper factory at Vedringhem, also then owned by the Avot family. This must have been constructed after World War II. During the war the factory at Elnes was used by the German armed forces. In December 1940, and again in February 1944, trains on the Anvin-Calais line came round the curve just south of the factory at Elnes to find SNCF standard gauge wagons left on the through line by the occupying forces. On both occasions a collision occurred. The sketch maps of both accidents show the dual gauge ending at the factory at Elnes, exactly as on the plans of 1912.

With the extension to Vedringhem the dual gauge track was 4 km (2½ mile) long. After the closure of the Anvin-Calais line in 1955 the standard gauge track remained as a private industrial branch line until a few years before the factory closed in 1975. There now remains a short spur (about 500 metres) of standard gauge track on the path of the Anvin-Calais line from Lumbres towards Elnes, but it is overgrown and disused. There is also evidence of the dual gauge on the turntable on the loop for the metre gauge branch to the paper factory at Wavrans (*see walk 3 in Chapter Eight*).

Other plans after World War II

In 1924, a proposal had already been made to convert the section of the Aire-Berck line between Aire and Thérouanne to standard gauge. Similarly in 1937, a proposal had already been made by Berck-Plage town council to convert the line between Rang-du-Fliers and Berck-Plage to 3-rail dual gauge so that standard gauge trains on the main line could run through to Berck. This had been resoundingly rejected by VFIL and the *département*. In 1946, following a vote in the Pas-de-Calais *Conseil Général*, VFIL looked at the possibility of converting the whole of the Aire-Berck line to standard gauge. VFIL pointed out that the cost for the line alone would be 1.38 million francs per kilometre, and that each standard gauge locomotive of 30 tonnes cost 3.5 million francs. Also that, if operations were to continue during the work, the metre gauge rails would have to be replaced at least temporarily on the standard gauge sleepers. Clearly VFIL did not want to do it.

In 1946 a request was also made by the Inspector General of lines of *Intérêt Local* in Paris for the *département* and the company to look at the possibility of making the lines from Calais to Guînes and from Guînes to Pont d'Ardres standard gauge. Having had a report from the company, the *département* reported to Paris that the metre gauge lines met all the needs of the population and of industry, and that the expenditure could not be justified in view of the financial state of the country. In any case these sections would have to be made dual gauge if metre gauge services from Anvin were to continue to run through to Calais.

In the Montreuil area, there was already a standard gauge branch from Étaples to Arras to the factories at La Paix Faite. In 1946 it was proposed to extend this to Recques station, and to *Les Ballastières* (the gravel pits), which already had a branch from the Aire-Berck line on the Montreuil side of Recques. Nothing came of this either. So in the end no new standard or dual gauge was constructed after World War II. One can speculate whether such projects might have delayed or avoided ultimate closure. Perhaps such improvements between Rang-du-Fliers and Berck-Plage would have kept this line open. The trend, however, in the 1960s and 1970s, throughout France, was to close short and rural standard gauge lines.

Closure

From the late 1940s the Anvin-Calais and Aire-Berck lines faced two major problems, one financial and one administrative. Much of the information about these comes from the annual reports of the Aire-Berck line, since the companies continued to report separately to shareholders. We do not have the reports for the Anvin-Calais line but since they were jointly operated by VFIL it is unlikely that the situation was any different. Measures to reduce costs, such as only using diesel traction except for the sugar beet season, must have been applied to the whole network.

The financial problem was that the Aire-Berck line, and almost certainly the Anvin-Calais line too, continued to make a substantial operating loss after World War II up to 1951, and probably until final closure in 1955. The last operating profit had been made in 1938, and then barely, and in 1947 and 1948 costs per train kilometre were more than 70 per cent in excess of income. This was exacerbated in 1947 by a government decision to reduce prices and therefore receipts by 10 per cent. Buses were cheaper to operate. One suspects that this was partly because they did not pay the full cost of building and maintaining their 'permanent way'. Passenger numbers recovered well after the war, but never recovered to the levels of the 1920s. They were more than 500,000 on the Aire-Berck line in 1946 and 1947 but by 1951 had declined to 418,000. Goods remained at about half the level of the 1920s.

The administrative problem was that in 1948 the *département* tried to take the concession to run the Aire-Berck line away from the company. Again this almost certainly applied to the Anvin-Calais line as well. The *département* used a law of 1947 to apply to Ministers in Paris for the concession to be withdrawn before the end of the contract on the grounds that the company were *'concessionnaires infidèles'* (unreliable concessionnaires). The company contested the allegations vigorously, and presumably the *département* did not have their way since the concession remained with the company until closure in 1955. However, for some time after 1948 they had to run the line without the official endorsement of the *département* for their operating plans. Both the Chief Engineer concerned, M. Fontana, and the *Préfet* of the *département*, M. Phalempin, were against the continuation of the metre gauge lines. With the Government in Paris, they were for 'modernisation', which meant roads, buses, lorries and cars for local transport. The frequent level crossings just held up the increasing road traffic.

Anvin to Fruges and Aire to Fruges

All services east of Fruges, both those to Anvin and those to Aire, closed on Monday 1st September, 1952, the last services having run on Sunday 31st August. The local paper at Aire noted that the services from Fruges to Calais and to Berck would continue, but also said that their closure could be foreseen next. This was the state of things when Bryan Morgan travelled from Calais to Rimeux and then from Rimeux to Rang (*The End of the Line*, see also *Introduction*).

The replacement bus services were much worse. At least to begin with the buses were run by VFIL, who probably saw the opportunity to make economies. We do not have the details for the line from Anvin to Fruges. Between Aire and Fruges, there had been three trains per day in each direction every day, and one extra on market day in Aire. The replacement buses ran twice in each direction, from Berguette to Fruges via Aire and Thérouanne, every day except Wednesdays, when there was no service at all. On Fridays the timings in the morning were changed for the market in Aire. All the buses also went to Fauquembergues, where the Fruges-Calais line was still providing a service. On Mondays, Thursdays and Saturdays, the bus left the Lys valley after Thérouanne, and served the Aa valley between Ouve-Wirquin and Fauquembergues, all on the Fruges-Calais line. These services returned to the Lys valley at Wandonne, two kilometres from Dennebrœucq, and also served Mencas and Matringhem before Fruges. On Mondays, Friday afternoons, and Sundays the bus left the Lys valley after Coyecques, went to Fauquembergues, and returned to the Lys valley only to serve Dennebrœucq and Wandonne. Only on Friday mornings did the service in each direction travel the length of the Lys valley from Matringhem to Aire. All this meant that from Delettes to Dennebrœucq, and for Mencas and Matringhem, there was only a service on three days per week, although all services did call at Wandonne, fairly nearby. No doubt the people who had been served by the line did not think this was progress, although there were some villages between the valleys which now had a bus service and probably did not have one before. After the closure of the whole Aire-Berck line in 1955, replacement services, provided by a different company all the way from Berck to Lille twice per day each way, did run the whole length of the Lys valley between Dennebrœucq and Aire every day.

On 3rd October, 1954, Aire was hit again, since on the that day SNCF closed the passenger services on the standard gauge line from St-Omer to Berguette, so that Aire station had now lost all passenger services on both lines. The standard gauge service, between St-Omer and Berguette via Aire, had not even in 1952 been as good as that on the Aire-Berck line, with only two trains per day each way. However, at least the 08.08 from Aire had guaranteed the connection with the Paris express at Berguette at 08.29, arriving at the Gare du Nord at 12.43 hours. The goods services on the standard gauge line remained open.

Arrival of a steam-hauled train from Berck-Plage at Rang-du-Fliers in July 1954. The tank locomotive is a 2-6-0 of 24 tonnes unladen weight constructed by Ateliers-Nord-Belge, probably No. 120, 121 or 126 built in 1924. *J. Bazin; Collection Bernard Guéret, formerly BVA*

One of the diesel railcars built at the VFIL works at Lumbres in the 1930s on arrival at Fruges in May 1953. From September 1952 this was the end of the lines from Calais and from Berck-Plage. *J. Bazin; Collection Bernard Guéret, formerly BVA*

The pattern of services in early 1955, just before the closure of the rest of the lines, was not much changed from 1952, apart from the loss of the sections from Anvin to Fruges and from Aire to Fruges. The service between Ardres and Pont d'Ardres remained limited to twice daily two days per week but the times had changed since 1952, and the service now began and ended at Pont'd'Ardres.

Fruges to Calais and Fruges to Berck

The remainder of the Anvin-Calais-Aire-Berck network closed on Tuesday 1st March, 1955, with the last trains running on Monday, 28th February. The contemporary local and regional newspaper reports make clear that the closure was widely regretted and opposed. There was also a contrast in the way the closure was marked on different parts of the network.

On the section from Fruges to Calais the last day began with 60 workers, out of the 120 who had used to travel regularly on the line, making a special last journey on the 07.00 from Guînes to Calais. The last train from Calais, a diesel *locotracteur* hauling passenger carriages, departed from Calais-Ville at 18.45 for Bonningues. At each station the driver and 'fireman' of the *locotracteur* made their farewells to the station masters and the level crossing guardians. The Mayor of Guînes, M. Jules Ledoux, and the Departmental Councillor, M. Chatillon, travelled with the final passengers. When the train arrived at Guînes at 19.20 hours, local people gathered on the platform, with children lining the edge holding Venetian lanterns. There was a good turnout despite it being a bitterly cold evening. As the train entered the station it set off 70 *pétards* (explosive fog signals), 'one for each year that the station had been open'. (It would be pedantic to point out that the station had actually opened in 1881, 74 years earlier.) Alighting from the train the Mayor greeted M. Lacquet, the station master, and presented him with a spray of flowers. M. Lacquet is reported to have been fighting back tears, and unable to respond. When the train started off towards Bonningues the travellers sang a sentimental song called 'Le Petit Train' 'admired sadly by the older inhabitants of Guînes, remaining silently on the platform'. The very last train was the 'Micheline' (diesel railcar) which arrived from Ardres at 20.57, greeted by 20 *pétards*. This then went off towards the depot, 'with the shameful placard "out of service"'.

On the line from Fruges to Berck the final day was much more low-key, to the extent that *La Voix du Nord* lamented its passing 'without music and without champagne'. This newspaper wrote a sentimental 'last song for our good tortillard, whose 'pou-pan' (horn sound) so sympathetic, which one loves to hear, now has a tragic and despairing air'. It is worth quoting part of this lament:

> I am an old philosopher and I know this. I served them for more than 60 years and as the hour came for my retirement no-one came to say goodbye. Usually when an old servant goes, you say goodbye, you offer him a memento or a glass of champagne. Me, nothing. They put me in a siding and that's all. Go away, my last friend, leave me to my lonely grief.

Another newspaper took pictures on Berck station of the driver of the last departure, M. Ernest Guéant, posing with his passengers in front of the railcar. Another picture shows the driver of the last arrival from Fruges, M. Jean Chrétien, with his passengers and railcar. This latter railcar was CGL No. 1, then recently returned to service after refurbishment. Both these pictures were taken in daylight. These were not quite the very last trains, however; *Les Petits Train de Jadis (Nord)* has photographic evidence of a later train, a Billard type A150D6 railcar, departing in darkness from Berck-Plage with the explosion of *pétards* and with a sign *'Fin'* fixed to the radiator grill. The earlier trains must have been the last along the main part of the line, and the latter the last service to Rang-du-Fliers, which service is known to have been provided by Billard railcars in the later years.

The closure of the rump of the Anvin-Calais and Aire-Berck lines in 1955 marked the closure of the last metre gauge railways and tramways in the whole of the Pas-de-Calais. The 170 workers had been given only one month's notice of the closure and the loss of their jobs. Some had been taken on as road menders by the *département*, some by *Autocars Citroën*, who ran bus services, and some as lorry drivers for SNCF, who would take over the goods services for the closed lines. However, it was claimed that on 1st March, 1955, most of the workers did not know what they would be doing the next day.

Replacement bus services

From 1st March the bus service between Berguette, Aire and Fruges, which had replaced the Aire to Fruges section of the Aire-Berck line, was itself replaced by a service run by *Autocars Citroën*. This service ran all the way from Lille to Berck via Berguette and Aire. The service ran twice per day in each direction seven days per week, and took about 3 hours 10 minutes for the section from Aire to Berck-Plage, the length of the closed railway. This compares with the best time of 4 hours 13 minutes for the train, shown in the timetable for May 1950 (*see Table Thirty-Five*). In addition another company, *Autobus Marcel Noël*, provided a service between Aire and Dennebrœucq, twice in each direction, on Fridays only, market day in Aire.

There were three further services per day each way between Montreuil SNCF station and Berck-Plage station, provided by *Autocars Citroën*. Another company, *Autobus G. Dumont*, provided a twice daily service (once on Sundays) between Hesdin and Berck-Plage via Montreuil and Rang-du-Fliers, with an additional service on school days from Berck to Montreuil to and from school.

The main sufferers from the replacement bus services for the Aire-Berck line in 1955 were the people who lived in the Valley of the Course and the rest of the line between Rimeux-Gournay and Montreuil. The first morning train towards Berck had left Fruges at 05.26 and arrived in Montreuil at 07.12. This enabled a connection to be made with the 08.54 to Boulogne. The only morning bus left Fruges at 09.10 and reached Montreuil SNCF station at 10.25. This missed the connection; the next train was not until 13.00 hours and too late to shop in Boulogne and return the same day, especially since the last bus from Montreuil towards Fruges left at 16.35, well before the last train from Boulogne which reached Montreuil at 18.30. Worse, the bus did not reach Montreuil in the morning in time for children from the Course Valley and the Hucqueliers area to attend school and college. The same problem arose for people attending Court and other administrative business in Montreuil, which was, and still is, the chief town of the *arrondissement*. The morning bus in the other direction left Montreuil at 07.35, 10 minutes before the arrival of the train from Boulogne. This also meant that fish from Étaples could not be delivered up the valley of the Course on the day of the catch.

The journalist reporting all this in the *Journal du Pas-de-Calais et de la Somme* commented quite reasonably that the little trains had been suppressed in the name of progress, but that services had got worse. The new timetables for the buses had been established in haste to respond to the desire of the *administration préfectorale* who wanted the train service closed, and no account had been taken of connecting with the SNCF services, or of the needs of the people. Of course things did improve in response to pressure, but the whole episode was also another stimulus to the rise of private car ownership, leading to a further long-term decline in the use of public transport.

The additional services between Rang-du-Fliers SNCF station and Berck-Plage station were replaced by *Autobus Boutrie* who, from 1st March, 1955, ran the service 10 times per day in each direction. These were at the same times as the trains had run, and therefore made the same connections at Rang with SNCF main line services between Paris, Boulogne and Calais. SNCF opened an office at Berck-Plage station for the sale of tickets and for the registration of luggage and parcels.

Autocars Citroën also ran the replacement bus service for the Anvin-Calais line. This ran twice per day in both directions between the SNCF station at Calais (Calais-Ville) and the SNCF station at St-Pol-sur-Ternoise, via Guînes, Ardres, Lumbres, Fruges and Anvin. These services ran between Zouafques and Journy (both on the former line) via Clerques and Licques (not on the former line, though Licques had been on the Boulogne-Bonningues line). These services would have had to go through Tournehem and Bonningues, and these are mentioned on the stopping places but not on the timetable. An additional two services per day each way were provided between Calais and Lumbres; these went between Zouafques and Journy via Audrehem, these also necessarily going through Tournehem and Bonningues. Between Journy and Lumbres all services went through Alquines and Quercamps, also not on the line, as well as Acquin, which was. In this way the service was improved compared with the railway for the number of places served, and Licques was brought back into the service.

The bus service took between 3 hours 15 minutes and 3 hours 25 minutes for the section from Anvin to Calais, the length of the closed railway. It is not possible to compare this with the train for the timetable of 1950 (*see Table Thirty-Four*) since by 1950 there were no through services. In 1936 the best time had been 5 hours and 44 minutes (*see Table Twenty-Four, page 220*), but this included waits of 1 hour 26 minutes at Fruges and 29 minutes at Lumbres, which made the actual running time 3 hours and 49 minutes. This was not much more than the bus, and there was no reason why the train should not have achieved this in 1955, if there had been the will. The waits were to facilitate connections, which were less easy with the bus service. The bus service would dispatch and receive parcels at Calais, Fruges and St-Pol. At other places parcels could only be dispatched by arrangement with the conductor on the bus, and then only for reception at Calais, Fruges or St-Pol.

Disposal of assets

Stations and other estate

The buildings and land became the property of the *département*, who either used them or sold them off. Because of the value of town centre sites most of these stations have disappeared. The majority of the rural stations have survived, most as private houses. A full list of these is given in *Appendix Three*, with further information in Chapter Eight.

Rolling stock

There are differing reports of the fate of some of the rolling stock. We are particularly fortunate to have the account of M. Claude Wagner in his article *Le Train de Guînes* (*Chemins de Fer Régionaux et Urbains* (2000) No. 280, page 4). He was a contemporary observer of the closure and provides an account of the disposal of the main items of rolling stock, including a list of steam locomotives assembled at Lumbres for scrapping in 1956. Where there are conflicting reports, his is most likely to be correct.

Steam locomotives

M. Wagner lists 22 steam locomotives assembled at Lumbres for scrapping in 1956. These include five of the original eight SACM 0-6-2Ts of 1880 to 1883 of the Anvin-Calais line, although he says elsewhere that all eight had survived to the closure. One of the five known to be at Lumbres at this time was No. 5 which was unmodified. They also include one of the 16 tonne 0-6-2T Corpets and all six of the 21 tonne 0-6-2T Corpets original to the Aire-Berck line from the early 1890s. It is particularly sad that none of these machines, which had served the lines for more than 60 years (70 plus for the Anvin-Calais locomotives), was saved, although efforts were made to do so.

The only steam locomotive of any of these lines to survive was No. 13, built in 1924. This was undoubtedly saved because VFIL moved it to the Oise network in 1947. It can now be seen at the MTVS museum at Valmondois and a full history of this locomotive is given in Chapter Eight.

We do not know the fate of all the locomotives known to have been owned and used by VFIL on the Anvin-Calais-Aire-Berck lines and not accounted for in the 1956 Lumbres list. Of the six original 16 tonne Corpets of the Aire-Berck line, five are known to have gone elsewhere before 1914, and the sixth is on the Lumbres list.

The locomotives unaccounted for are:

Possibly AC Nos. 2, 3, and 4, 18 tonne SACMs from early 1880s
APA Nos. 1 and 2, 0-6-0T Corpet-Louvets of 1902
Jung 0-6-0T of 1897, acquired after World War I
No. 161, 45 tonne 0-6-6-0 Henschel Mallet, acquired after World War I

Of these, the 45 tonne locomotive (Henschel Mallet) was reported in 1943 to need repairs which would take at least six months, and it was on the list of those which might have to be written off. There is no mention of this locomotive in service after World War II and it was probably scrapped during or soon after the war.

Diesel railcars and trailers

Only one of the original diesel railcars constructed at Lumbres for these lines survived. CGL No. 1, which had been refurbished and returned to service only in 1955, was purchased in 1957 by the *Société Générale des Chemins de Fer Économiques* (SE) for the Somme lines. It is now owned by the *Chemin de Fer de la Baie de Somme* (CFBS) and numbered M31.

Three metre gauge bogie railcars built by VFIL at Lumbres are now also owned by CFBS. These, numbered M41 to 43, were all built in 1936. All originally went to VFIL lines, in Flanders (M41) and Oise (M42 and 43).

The railcars acquired after World War II were quickly disposed of. The two Billard A80 D1s and the A80 D1 trailer went to the *CF de Corrèze* (POC) at their Tulle depot. The Billard A80 D2 remained with VFIL for the Oise network, going to the depot at St-Just-en-Chaussée. The two Billard A150 D6s and the three R210 trailers went to the *CFD du Tarn* at their Castres depot. We do not know the subsequent fate of any of these.

One of the former CF Dordogne diesel locomotives (VFIL Nos. 650 to 652) re-fuelling in front of the depot at Berck-Plage in 1954. A second of these locomotives is half seen at the extreme left.   *J. Bazin; Collection Bernard Guéret, formerly BVA*

Diesel locomotives (locotracteurs)

No. 301, which had been built at Lumbres, and Nos. 650, 651 and 652 bought from the CF Dordogne, were all sold to the CF Ardennes to work from the depot at Rethel. When these lines closed in 1961, No. 301 was sold on to the *Société Générale des Chemins de Fer Économiques* for the Somme network based at the depot at St-Valery. No. 301 is still there, now owned by the *Chemin de Fer de la Baie de Somme*, with the same number.

Of the others, two went to the cement works at Haubourdin near Lille, and the third to the steel works at Isbergues, near Aire-sur-la-Lys. All three were scrapped in 1975.

CFBS also has two 6-wheel diesel locomotives, Nos. 351 and 352, which were constructed at the VFIL works at Lumbres in 1951. These went straight to the Flanders network and were not used on the Anvin-Calais-Aire-Berck lines.

The End

So ends the story of the metre gauge railways and tramways of the western Pas-de-Calais, the last to survive in the whole *département*. The Anvin-Calais line had lasted from 1882 to 1955, longer than many similar enterprises in France. For much of that time it was, with the Aire-Berck line, a thriving concern.

In the end the lines succumbed, like so many others in France and elsewhere, to the familiar story of lack of investment and deteriorating services, coupled with the rise of the internal combustion engine, the bus and the private car. VFIL probably did not over-exert themselves to prevent these closures. The year after the closure of these lines, in 1956, VFIL had renamed themselves the *Compagnie Générale des Enterprises Ferroviares et Routières*. They still had many railway interests elsewhere, but this better reflected their increasing interest in road transport.

It only remains for us to describe, in the next chapter, what can be seen now of these long-closed railways.

The former dormitory building for train crews at Guînes, on the Anvin-Calais line, in 2007.

Authors

The former Anvin-Calais type 2 station at Remilly, in May 2003. The goods building is to the right and the square lavatory block with lead roof can be seen in the foreground on the left.

Authors

Chapter Eight

Exploring the Scene Today

We find it difficult to start this chapter other than with a lament that so little remains of the rolling stock of these lines, and that not only have no sections remained as tourist lines, but also that relatively little of the track bed has been preserved as long distance footpaths or cycle routes. If any of these lines had survived longer the outcome might have been different.

Efforts were made at the time of closure by local enthusiasts to preserve more, but to no avail.

The Track

The whole of the original routes of these lines can be identified using old maps, current large scale maps showing remains, and satellite images, and by walking the ground as far as is possible. Much of the original earthworks, and some bridges and other features, are shown on the IgN (*Institut Géographique National*) 1:25000 (1 cm = 250 m) maps. The older editions are in general more helpful in identifying earthworks and 'other linear features' than the newer ones. We have given the map numbers for some of the features to be seen and for the walks. These maps have four figure numbers followed by either O (*ouest*, west), E (*est*, east), or ET for special tourist maps covering a larger area. The best satellite images of France are at www.geoportail.fr The images can be viewed from a height of 400 km (250 miles) down to 1,500 metres (just under one mile), and adjusted to be photographic images, maps, or any mixture of the two.

Some of the old track bed can be walked. Our suggested walks offer the best glimpses of what little is left (*see later in this chapter*). Regrettably the *département* sold off most of the land soon after the closure of the lines and much is now in private hands. In many places short bits can be walked but sooner or later, usually sooner, comes the locked gate, the barbed wire, and the warning signs; *Propriété privée* (private property), *Défense d'entrer* (no entry), and, most sacred of all in French eyes, *Chasse gardée* (hunting/shooting reserve). Trespassing in France is not recommended, and there are a lot of dangerous dogs about on private properties.

Stations and other buildings

After the closure, stations and the associated land were sold. Most of the stations and their associated buildings have survived. Of those demolished, the majority are in town centres, presumably because of pressure on land use. Most of the stations can be seen easily but a few are hidden up private drives. Most are now in use as private houses, after variable amounts of refurbishment and extension, but almost all are still easily recognisable. When looking at the stations please respect the privacy of the present occupants. A full list of the present status of all the stations and halts and associated buildings at the time of writing (August 2007) is given in *Appendix Three*. *Arrêts* are only listed where there is something to see, which is rarely. The differences between the styles of the stations and halts on the various lines are

The typical Aire-Berck line station at Beussent in the valley of the river Course, in 2006. The extensions to the right are new but the former lavatory block on the extreme right is original. The station is now the *Mairie* (Town Hall). *Authors*

At Thérouanne, the sign in April 2006 still shows the way to the Aire-Berck line station which closed in 1952. *Authors*

discussed in the initial chapters on each line: Chapter Two for Anvin-Calais, Chapter Three for Aire-Berck and Berck-Plage to Paris-Plage, and Chapter Four for Boulogne-Bonningues. Longitude and latitude are given to help those with GPS, and the IgN 1:25,000 map numbers are also shown. There are some interesting additional features. At Guînes there is still, painted on the corner of the building, a very faded notice asking season ticket holders and workers (ticket holders) to present their tickets for inspection. There is also a smaller building, left of the gateway, which was the dormitory block built for train crews. At Bonningues the small depot building survives.

Lavatory blocks vary from line to line. Where they survive these are identified in the station list (*see Appendix Three*). The most appealing are those on the Anvin-Calais line which are square with lead roofs. The best and easiest to see are at Verchin, Rimeux-Gournay and Remilly, but they can also be seen at Bergueneuse and Bonningues. There are no separate lavatory buildings at halts on this line, and we presume that the lavatories, if any were provided, were in the halt building. The lavatory blocks on the Boulogne-Bonningues line were also distinctive, with an open wood pattern above the brick walls (*see photographs of Le Portel - page 156 - and Licques - rear cover*) but none, or at least none that are visible, have survived. Many stations and halts on the Aire-Berck line still have the old lavatory blocks, including the halt at Bahot. These are less attractive, being of brick with a simple pitched roof. They do have a pattern of open brickwork on the upper side walls for ventilation. They can be seen at many stations on the Aire-Berck line, and are particularly easy to see at Moulin-le-Comte and Bahot. Some of the weighbridges installed by the sugar beet processors have survived. Weighbridges in public areas close to stations can be seen at Delettes, Coyecques, and Wicquinghem.

Many stations, for instance Thérouanne and Wailly-Beaucamp, are still in the *Rue de la Gare* (Station Road). The Berck-Plage-Paris-Plage line seems to have preferred the archaic *station* rather than *gare*. Merlimont-Plage station is in the *Rue de la Station*, and the site of the former station at Bellevue-les-Dunes is in the *Rue de la Station des Dunes*. At Thérouanne, the station, which has not been used since 1952, is still signposted from the main road through the town, 500 metres away. In front of the old station, now the casino, at Berck-Plage, the road is named *Rue Alfred Lambert* in honour of the entrepreneur responsible for the Aire-Berck line.

The prize for the most altered station building which has survived in any recognisable form goes to Dennebrœucq (Map 2205E) on the Aire-Berck line, where one wall of the old station has been built into a much larger warehouse/workshop. We missed this completely the first time we visited the site. The second time we met a former Mayor, M. Lapoeulle, who pointed out to us the remains of the station building. He remembered taking the train at this station in 1952. The halt at Audenfort on the Boulogne-Bonningues line just looks like a modern bungalow. We have seen a picture of the halt as it was, looking exactly like that at Herbinghen-Hocquinghen. Since then it has been enlarged, re-roofed, and re-rendered, with all new doors and windows. However, local people assure us that some of the original walls remain within the structure.

The only *abri* (shelter) at the site of an *arrêt* is that at Renty (Map 2205E) on the Anvin-Calais line. On map 2204E, leave the D129 at Renty on the south side of the river Aa. Where the road turns north to cross the river, go straight on and take the next right. This leads to 'La Haute Peine' which is not signposted but is found on the top edge of map 2205E. A quarter of a mile up this minor road is the old track and the *abri* is on the left (east). This was probably built after World War II, and is constructed of shuttered

The station at Dennebrœucq has now been built into an extensive warehouse, but the tops of the three upper windows can be seen above the corrugated iron in the middle of the wall. July 2006.
Authors

The *abri* at the former *arrêt* at Renty on the Anvin-Calais line, in 2007. The roof is made from level crossing warning signs (*see page 247*). *Authors*

concrete on a frame of old rails. The roof consists of old crossing warning signs, mostly in French (*Attention au Train*) but some in German (*Achtung - Eisenbahn in Betrieb*) which clearly date from World War II. Presumably the *abri* was rebuilt after the war using what was available. Coming across this was one of the most evocative discoveries that we made when researching this book. It became possible to picture the local people, having survived the occupation, coming home and setting about restoring their train halt and it is tempting to think that they did enjoy making use of the occupying forces' intimidating notices to reroof their shelter.

The tram depot and generating station of the Tramway from Étaples to Paris-Plage have survived. The depot is at Trépied, just off the D940 south of the roundabout which is now the junction for the main road into Le Touquet-Paris-Plage. On the map this is called the Avenue des Hêtres but on site is called the Avenue de l'Aéroport. This is the old main road to Le Touquet and on the café on the left corner as you enter it there is still the plaque with the road number and distances. The generating station is a short way in on the left and is still faintly labelled 'TRAMWAY ELECTRIQUE D'ETAPLES A PARIS-PLAGE'. The chimney at the back, for the boilers, has gone. The old depot next to it has a new front and is now the departmental road repair depot for Cucq. The 'new' 1910 tram shed is across the road and is now part of a garage and car dealers. From the road at the side its length can be appreciated, and its handsome round windows. At the front, under the '1910' plaque, the garage has over-written the old sign, but under this the sign 'COMPAGNIE DU TRAMWAY' can still be seen. It is interesting that the bus from Étaples to Le Touquet still comes round this way rather than straight along the new main road, with bus stops in both directions outside the old depot.

The long tram shed of the Tramway from Étaples to Paris-Plage, at Trépied, built in 1910, in 2007. Behind the prominent lettering at the front, the sign 'COMPAGNIE DU TRAMWAY' can still be faintly seen. The original depot and generating station are across the road just behind the photographer. *Authors*

The brick arch bridge for the Anvin-Calais line over the Vieux Chemin at Bergeneuse, in 2007. *Authors*

Bridges and other civil engineering

Some of those which survive are described in the walks. Only two road bridges survive, both on the Anvin-Calais line. One is over the Vieux Chemin, a minor road which leaves the west side of the D94 (Rue d'Anvin) 100 metres south of its junction with the D71 in Bergueneuse (Map 2305 O, E 2° 15' 13" N 50° 28' 00"). The other is over the D208 at Bouvelinghem (Map 2204 E, E 2° 02' 31" N 50° 44' 25"). Bouvelinghem is not marked on the map but the bridge is at the south-east corner of the wood marked 'Bois du Petit Quercamps', and the halt is just west of the bridge, accessed by a track which leaves the D208 just north of the bridge. Both bridges are brick arches between sections of embankment, that at Bouvelinghem being the higher and the more overgrown.

There are a number of river bridges, and many smaller bridges over ditches and culverts. The swing bridge over the side canal at Aire-sur-la-Lys, which was shared with the standard gauge line, can be seen 400 metres north-west of Aire station and immediately south-east of the D943E to Boeseghem (Map 2304 E, E 2° 24' 11" N 50° 38' 35"). There is a river bridge over the Ternoise at Anvin, 100 metres north-east of the station (Map 2305 O, E 2° 15' 28" N 50° 26' 48"). From the north side of the level crossing over the D343, still in use for the standard gauge line, the old metre gauge track bed curves away round the back of a café/bar to the river bridge, and then on to the D70. This makes a pleasant short walk of half a mile there and back. We think that the best river bridge to see is that over the Lys just west of Delettes station (Map 2304 O). A visit to this is described in Walk 7.

Rolling stock

Little rolling stock survives from these lines. Almost all of the steam locomotives from the Anvin-Calais-Aire-Berck system were assembled at Lumbres after closure in 1955 and then scrapped. Likewise the passenger carriages were assembled at Acquin for disposal.

Steam locomotives

The only surviving steam locomotive from any of the lines in this book is now at the *Musée de Tramways à Vapeurs et des chemins de fer Secondaires français (MTVS)* at Valmondois. This 22 tonne 2-6-0 tank engine was one of two built by SACM in 1924 for the Berck-Plage-Paris-Plage line as replacements for the two La Meuse engines destroyed in action in 1918 at Albert. By the time they were delivered as Nos. 3 and 4 they were no longer really needed by this line. No. 3 was loaned either to the brickworks at Attin near Montreuil, or the quarry at Engoudsent, or possibly both at different times. Both of these were on the Aire-Berck line. No. 3 then returned to the Berck-Plage-Paris-Plage line for a few weeks before closure of this line at the end of summer 1927. It then went (or returned to) the quarry at Engoudsent and was sold to the quarry in 1931. In 1940 it was transferred to the sugar factory at Trézennes where it was damaged in a bombardment. In 1941, or possibly 1942, this locomotive was bought by VFIL and given the number 13 to work on the Anvin-Calais-Aire-Berck lines. It was moved by VFIL to Noyon on the Oise network in 1947 and then to St-Just-en-Chaussée in 1955 or 1957, where it hauled goods traffic until 1961. The engine was then parked at Jouy-le-Châtel (Seine-et-Marne), then at Verneuil (Marne), and then at the *Chemin de Fer de la Baie de Somme*. Finally in 1990 the owner transferred No. 13 to the Museum at Butry-sur-Oise (*MTVS Valmondois*). The engine has been put back into a presentable state, and has been in steam. Sadly, the museum staff say that now, although in generally good mechanical state, a boiler refurbishment is required which would cost €50,000, and this cannot be afforded. The engine still bears the number 13 but its name is now *Valmondois*, and it can be seen in static display at the museum.

The SACM 2-6-0 tank locomotive, built in 1924 for the Berck-Plage to Paris-Plage line, and later No. 13 on the Anvin-Calais line, at the *Musée de Tramways à Vapeurs et des chemins de fer Secondaires Français* at Butry-Valmondois. This is the only surviving steam locomotive of any of the lines described in this book.   *Collection MTVS, reproduced with permission*

Diesel railcars and locomotives

Only one of the original diesel railcars for these lines has survived. This railcar was purchased in 1957 by the *Société Générale des Chemins de Fer Économiques* (SE) for the Somme lines, and numbered M31. It is now owned by the *Chemin de Fer de la Baie de Somme* (CFBS), with the same number. We have seen photographs of it in use at Noyelles for passengers in 1959, and also in the early days of CFBS in 1972, during works on the line. In Chapter Seven we have stated that this railcar was originally CGL [VFIL] No. 1, built at Lumbres in the 1930s, and refurbished and returned to service only in 1955, just before the lines closed. Whilst there is agreement that this railcar came from the Anvin-Calais-Aire-Berck network, other statements have been made as to its precise origins and history. One is that although this was CGL 1, this was a 1930s rebuild with a 65 hp Unic diesel engine of one of the 1920s Renault-Scemia petrol railcars, RS1. However we think it probable that RS1 was rebuilt as CGL No. 11 with a shortened wheelbase and a Berliet 85 hp diesel engine. Another view is that M31 was originally ARB No. 2, built at Lumbres in 1932 with a petrol engine, possibly on the chassis of vehicle No. 31 of the Flanders network, which may have been a passenger coach. M. Claude Wagner (*Le Train de Guînes*, 2000) states that M31 is the rebuilt CGL No. 1, originally built at Lumbres in the 1930s, and he supports the view that RS1 was rebuilt as the shortened CGL 11. He was an observer at the time of closure and is probably right. That M31 was the rebuilt CGL 1 is strongly supported by a photograph we have seen of the rebuilt CGL 1 at Berck-Plage on the day of closure. This was the only railcar rebuilt in this way, and the photograph shows a railcar of identical appearance to M31. M31 now has a Willème diesel engine, which may have been installed at rebuilding in 1955. Three metre gauge bogie railcars built by VFIL at Lumbres are now also owned by CFBS. These, numbered M41 to 43, were all built in 1936. All originally went to VFIL lines, in Flanders (M41) and Oise (M42 and 43).

Diesel locomotive No. 301, which had been built at Lumbres, and Nos. 650, 651 and 652 bought from the CF Dordogne, were all sold to the CF Ardennes to work from the depot at Rethel. When these lines closed in 1961, No. 301 was sold on to the *Société Générale des Chemins de Fer Économiques* for the Somme network based at the depot at St-Valery. No. 301 is still there, now owned by CFBS, with the same number. Railcars M31, M41, M42 and M43, and diesel locomotive No. 301, have not been in use at CFBS for many years. All are in storage awaiting major rebuilding. For this reason they can only be seen by special arrangement with CFBS staff. CFBS also has two 6-wheel diesel locomotives, Nos. 351 and 352, which were constructed at the VFIL works at Lumbres in 1951. These went straight to the Flanders network and were not used on the Anvin-Calais-Aire-Berck lines. These are in regular use on CFBS.

Walks

It is recommended to use these notes and sketch maps with the IgN 1:25,000 maps (1 cm = 250 m). The map number is given at the beginning of each walk. Longitude and latitude of starts and ends are also given to help those with GPS. We have walked all of these walks and have had no problems with access. Some are designated as footpaths. Others are open and obviously in use by walkers, but we cannot guarantee that these are rights of way.

Walk 1 - Guînes to Pont de Coulogne

Map 2103ET. This is a walk of 3¾ miles (6 km) and 1½ to 2 hours each way and the route must be retraced unless someone picks you up at the other end. It is completely flat across the *marais* of Guînes. The walk falls into three not quite equal sections, the first through farmland, the middle section alongside the Canal de Guînes with the main road on the other side, and the third with some open land but some housing alongside. It is possible to park at either end, or in the middle at the former *arrêt* at Banc-Valois, or the halt at Écluse-Carrée, and do part of the walk from these. A lot of the walk nearer to Calais has the flavour of being on the edge of a major town but there is much of interest to see.

We will describe the walk from the Guînes end. At this end, park at the sports centre at the end of the Rue Leo Lagrange (E 1° 52' 36" N 50° 52' 12"). Walk back up this road and turn left to look at Guînes station. Although boarded up when we last saw it, it is in quite good condition and is the only surviving example of a type 1 Anvin-Calais station building. The courtyard is used for road mending materials, but to the left of the gate as you enter is the old *dortoir* (dormitory) for train crews.

From the sports centre, the old track is signposted as a footpath to Pont de Coulogne. The path runs through the *marais* between fields, trees and drainage ditches until at 1½ miles you come to the next metalled road. This is the D248 at Banc-Valois and to the left it crosses the canal on a bascule bridge to reach the main road from Guînes to Calais (D127). Continue straight across the road. The *arrêt* was on the Calais side of the road. Follow the track between the bungalows until you reach and follow the side of the canal. Before Écluse-Carrée, almost one mile from Banc-Valois, the track leaves the canal again and shortly after this appears to be in someone's front garden. Do not be put off by this but continue on the left of the ditch and you

73 — Environs de CALAIS — Ecluse Carrée sur le Canal de Guînes, construite en 1787, à droite, halte du chemin de fer d'Auvin à Calais

Walk 1. Écluse Carrée, postcard postmarked 1908. *Écluse Carrée* means 'square lock'; in addition to the lifting bridge there were locks into two side canals. The Halt building of the Anvin-Calais line is at the back on the right. *Éditions Lefervre; Authors' Collection*

WALK 1
Guînes to Pont-de-Coulogne

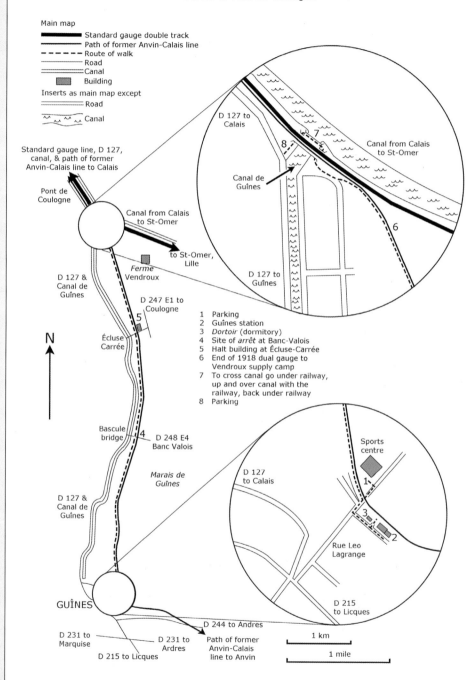

Main map

▬▬▬	Standard gauge double track
▬▬▬	Path of former Anvin-Calais line
- - - -	Route of walk
	Road
	Canal
▨	Building

Inserts as main map except

	Road
∼∼∼∼	Canal

Standard gauge line, D 127,
canal, & path of former
Anvin-Calais line to Calais

Pont de
Coulogne

Canal from Calais
to St-Omer

D 127 to
Calais

8 7

Canal from Calais
to St-Omer

Canal de
Guînes

6

to St-Omer,
Lille

D 127 &
Canal de
Guînes

Ferme
Vendroux

D 127 to
Guînes

D 247 E1 to
Coulogne

5

Écluse
Carrée

N

1   Parking
2   Guînes station
3   *Dortoir* (dormitory)
4   Site of *arrêt* at Banc-Valois
5   Halt building at Écluse-Carrée
6   End of 1918 dual gauge to
    Vendroux supply camp
7   To cross canal go under railway,
    up and over canal with the
    railway, back under railway
8   Parking

Bascule
bridge   4   D 248 E4
             Banc Valois

*Marais de
Guînes*

D 127 &
Canal de
Guînes

D 127
to Calais

Sports
centre

1

3
2

Rue Leo
Lagrange

GUÎNES

D 244 to Andres

D 215
to Licques

D 231 to
Marquise

D 231 to
Ardres

D 215 to Licques

Path of former
Anvin-Calais
line to Anvin

1 km

1 mile

come to a footbridge on the old abutments where the line crossed the side canal. Across the road is the typical halt building at Écluse-Carrée. Écluse-Carrée means literally 'square lock' and it used to be a lock with four gates where the lower side canals crossed the main Canal de Guînes. The lock gates and the old bascule bridge for the road have gone but it is still worth a look. Across the canal bridge, both here and at Banc-Valois, the tramway from Calais to Guînes used to follow the main road.

From the halt follow the track again, with houses between the track and the canal. There is no sign of the sidings and canal to train transhipment facility which used to be here. After half a mile there is a diversion round another old bridge with brick abutments. Cross the small road here and continue along the track. More extensive 'bungaloid' development is on the left but on the right are open fields and the farm ahead right is Vendroux. Ahead you can see the main Calais-St-Omer line on a low embankment. From Écluse-Carrée to the main line and from the canal to well beyond the farm was the site of the vast World War I British Army Vendroux supply camp. As you approach the main line there are some vague signs of earthworks on the right which probably represent the 1916 to 1918 sidings and other works.

On reaching the main line, the track curves left and up to meet it and then follows it across the canal and into Calais. Probably the dual gauge on this section in 1918 came down this slope and into the supply camp (*see Chapter Five*). We have to leave the line here, as we come onto a minor road at the end of the housing. Turn right to the canal. If you do not want to go back, go under the main line beside the canal which you then cross, before passing back under the main line. This brings you out to the D127 and it is possible to park in this area also (E 1° 52′ 22″ N 50° 55′ 21″). The main line railway bridge is beside the junction of the Guînes canal with the canal from Calais to St-Omer.

Walk 1. The bridge at the junction of the Guînes canal (foreground) with the canal from Calais to St-Omer (beyond the bridge), in 2007. The bridge carried the double track standard gauge main line from St-Omer to Calais (*left*), and the single track metre gauge line from Anvin to Calais, which diverged from the main line to the right of the bridge. Originally there were two spans over the canal, now replaced with one, probably on rebuilding after World War II.   *Authors*

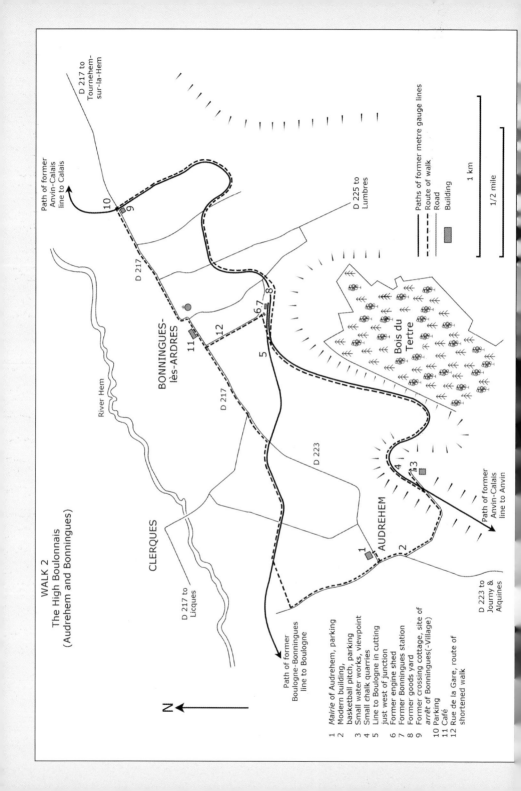

WALK 2
The High Boulonnais
(Audrehem and Bonningues)

N

CLERQUES

BONNINGUES-
lès-ARDRES

AUDREHEM

Bois du
Tertre

River Hem

D 217 to Licques

D 217 to Tournehem-
sur-la-Hem

Path of former
Anvin-Calais
line to Calais

D 217

D 217

D 225 to Lumbres

D 223

Path of former
Anvin-Calais
line to Anvin

D 223 to Journy &
Alquines

Path of former
Boulogne-Bonningues
line to Boulogne

Paths of former metre gauge lines
Route of walk
Road
Building

1 km
1/2 mile

1 *Mairie* of Audrehem, parking
2 Modern building,
  basketball pitch, parking
3 Small water works, viewpoint
4 Small chalk quarries
5 Line to Boulogne in cutting
  just west of junction
6 Former engine shed
7 Former Bonningues station
8 Former goods yard
9 Former crossing cottage, site of
  arrêt of Bonningues(-Village)
10 Parking
11 Café
12 Rue de la Gare, route of
   shortened walk

Walk 2 - The High Boulonnais (Audrehem and Bonningues)

Map 2204E. 2½ hours on the signposts: we think three hours particularly if you are going to linger and look at the views and the stations. Distance 5½ miles (9 km). Vertical height about 60 metres (200 feet). This circular walk has been signposted as the *'Sentier de la ligne d'Anvin'*. A variant is also signposted which is only 3¾ miles (6 km). The full walk includes a very attractive part of the Anvin-Calais line, the junction with the Boulogne line at Bonningues, and later part of the Boulogne line. It also includes a rather tedious section of just over a mile on a main road in the middle; see end of this Walk for suggestions how to avoid this. The going can be wet and muddy.

Park in the centre of Audrehem, in front of the *Mairie* (E 1° 59' 30" N 50° 46' 52"), or on the D223 as you leave the village towards the south, 200 yards after the bend on the main road in the middle of the village (E 1° 59' 30" N 50° 46' 46"); at this point there is a modern building on the left with parking. There is a signpost here to mark the beginning. Follow the track past the basket ball practice ground and up the hill.

Towards the top of the hill, the line of the former Anvin-Calais railway crosses the track up the hill. To the right the line can be picked out as a grassy shelf on the hillside. The path is signposted along the line to the left. It is a great pity that the line to the right is not open all round the hillside to Journy or Alquines-Buisson. What a great footpath this section would make. A tourist railway would be even better! There are good views from this point, but even better views can be enjoyed by walking a little further up the hill to the small water works. There is a seat on the bend on the way up. From here the whole of the lower land around Licques can be seen, with low hills surrounded on all sides by higher downland, and the town of Licques, with its large church, on a small hill in the middle. Follow the track of the railway down the hill towards the old station at Bonningues. The line curves to the right through a cutting where there are small chalk quarries, one of which is still in use. There is a flat area beside the track here and there were probably sidings for the quarries. The right curve continues across an embankment and then the line curves back left across the valley. The rest of the line to Bonningues runs almost straight along the right side of this valley which is beautiful and usually very peaceful. There are abundant wild flowers and, at the right time of year, blackberries and sloes. Just before Bonningues station the line from Boulogne came in from the left, in a cutting. The junction area has been filled in so that now the gradient would be impossible. Old track diagrams (*see page 52*) show the Boulogne line starting from the station on a separate running track from the Anvin line, and probably, originally, it started to go downhill immediately after the crossover just west of the platform. A short diversion into the cutting is interesting, but unfortunately you cannot follow the Boulogne line on from here. Bonningues station is now a private house and the line went straight on into what is now the back garden. The old station building is typical of the Anvin-Calais type 2 buildings but has been extended at the back (track side). You can see, in the garden, the small depot or engine shed (not usually provided at type 2 stations), the side of which can be better seen just down the track to the left. There is also a good example of the lavatory block, typical of this line, with an attractive lead roof. All these can be seen over the hedge or from the road side of the station without entering the private ground. Usually geese waddle in front of the engine shed where there used to be a turntable.

The shorter walk is signposted to the left here which takes you past the engine shed into the *Rue de la Gare*. Turn left down this road and at the end is the D217, the

Walk 2. Beyond Bonningues station the line continued to descend; here it curves to the left beyond the trees and can be seen crossing the field.   *Authors*

Walk 2. The *arrêt* with halt type building, at right angles to the track. Originally a crossing cottage, where the line crossed the D217 east of Bonningues village. On the timetables this was (confusingly) also known as Bonningues, but in other documents it is occasionally called Bonningues-Village. If you are following the signposted walk this is the place to turn left along the road through the village.   *Authors*

main road through the village. Turn left here and you are now once again on the route of the full walk. For the full walk, take the path to the right which takes you round the upper side of the hedge now enclosing the old station area. On the left, past the station is a new bungalow and then a large enclosed area, all part of the old station yard. Beyond this you rejoin the line. This continues down the hill in a series of curves through a small cutting and over a small embankment, with good views of another valley and open downland on the right. On the way, you cross a small road, then the D225 from Bonningues to Lumbres, and then another small road. Finally you come out past some buildings and a farmyard onto the D217 between Bonningues and Tournehem. Here there is a railway building. In a 1914 timetable it is listed as an *arrêt* and confusingly also called Bonningues. However, the building we see now is a typical halt type building, but facing the road not the old track of the railway. It was originally a crossing cottage, but when it became an *arrêt* a ticket window was added to the corner.

The line of the railway continues across the road towards Tournehem, and there is a flat open area here beside the line which is probably another old quarry; however, the sign across the road tells you to turn left along the D217. There follows the often busy section, of just over a mile, through the village. On the right after the double bend there is a café. Just past here on the left the *Rue de la Gare* goes back up to Bonningues station and this is where you come out if you take the shorter option at the station.

At the far end of the village take the left fork which is the D223 to Audrehem. After about 300 yards, the line of the Boulogne railway comes in from the left and you turn right onto it across the fields. About 250 yards after crossing a minor road the line of the railway goes off to the right at a slight left bend, but you continue on the path round this bend and soon you come out onto a larger track where you turn sharp left. At this point you can see Audrehem church; follow the track which becomes a small road back into the village.

The main drawback of this walk as signposted is the road section through Bonningues village. If you do not mind retracing your steps we suggest parking in the open area opposite the railway building where the line crossed the D217 (E 2° 01′ 24″ N 50° 47′ 45″). Walk up the line in the opposite direction to the signposts, to the top where it goes into the field, and then, if you wish, up to the small water works, and then return. You avoid the main road, get all the best views and bits of track in both directions, and you can still see the beginning of the Boulogne line in the cutting at Bonningues station. You also take the climb at an easy gradient, as the railway once did.

Walk 3 - The valley of the Aa, Wavrans to Elnes

Map 2204E. ¾ hour/1½ miles (2.5 km) there and back. Take the D225 south from Lumbres and in Wavrans (1½ miles) turn left. After crossing the river Aa go straight on towards the high down and at the top of a slight rise is a car park (E 2° 08′ 31″ N 50° 41′ 12″). There is an informative map of the walk at the car park.

A new footpath created by the local council follows the hillside just above the former route of the Anvin-Calais railway between Wavrans and Elnes to the north, on the east side of the Aa. Shortly after the last house you will see on the right a concrete-lined tunnel going into the chalk hillside. This was one of two constructed in the Lumbres area in 1944 by the Todt organisation to store 'V1s' safe from

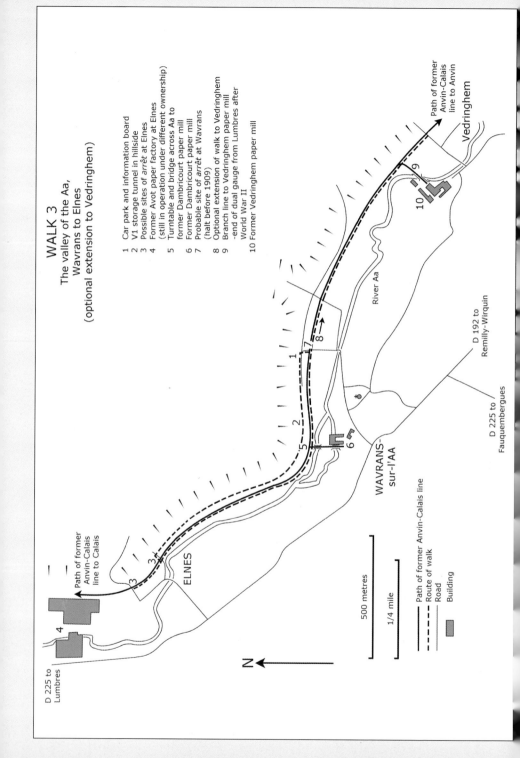

WALK 3
The valley of the Aa,
Wavrans to Elnes
(optional extension to Vedringhem)

1 Car park and information board
2 V1 storage tunnel in hillside
3 Possible sites of *arrêt* at Elnes
4 Former Avot paper factory at Elnes
   (still in operation under different ownership)
5 Turntable and bridge across Aa to
   former Dambricourt paper mill
6 Former Dambricourt paper mill
7 Probable site of *arrêt* at Wavrans
   (halt before 1909)
8 Optional extension of walk to Vedringhem
9 Branch line to Vedringhem paper mill
   –end of dual gauge from Lumbres after
   World War II
10 Former Vedringhem paper mill

Path of former
Anvin-Calais
line to Anvin

Vedringhem

River Aa

D 192 to
Remilly-Wirquin

D 225 to
Fauquembergues

WAVRANS-
SUR-l'AA

ELNES

D 225 to Lumbres

Path of former Anvin-Calais line to Calais

N

500 metres

1/4 mile

—— Path of former Anvin-Calais line
- - - Route of walk
—— Road
▨ Building

Walk 3. Manual turntable on former loop line by the River Aa. The bridge to the former Dambricourt paper mill is on the left, the main path of the line is now the footpath behind the barriers on the right.   *Authors*

bombing attacks (*see photograph page 255*). The new footpath is conveniently near the railway just below. Follow it to its end at Elnes, and return along the line of the railway below. You can cut it short through one of the intermediate connecting paths along the way or, for the more adventurous, paths lead up the steep chalk down to the right. All are shown on the map at the car park.

There are information points in French (and French Braille!) along the way. Returning along the line of the railway, there is a manual turntable on the right on the edge of the Aa, with the remains of a girder bridge across the river. The plaque tells us about the railway, and that the turntable was on a loop, with the track across the bridge leading to the paper factory owned by Dambricourt, one of many businesses using water power in the valley. The plaque only shows one gauge in the diagram, but this was on the section of dual gauge track after World War II (*see Chapter Seven*), and there are slots in the turntable to take both metre and standard gauge track. It is clear from the bridge that the siding was metre gauge only.

When you get back to the road leading up to the car park, you are close to the site of the halt at Wavrans, but it appears to have been demolished. If you wish, the footpath along the old track continues south from the car park as far as Vedringhem, about ¾ mile. The paper mill here, one of those in the Avot group, was the destination of the dual gauge track.

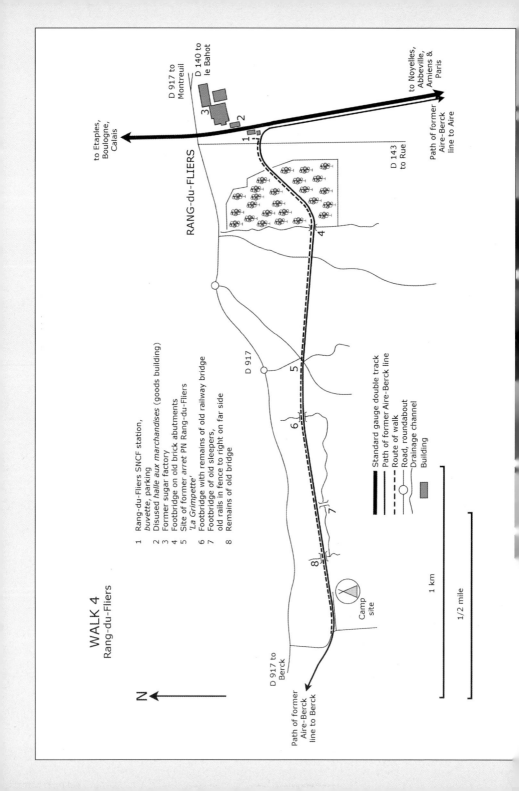

WALK 4
Rang-du-Fliers

N

1 Rang-du-Fliers SNCF station, *buvette*, parking
2 Disused *halle aux marchandises* (goods building)
3 Former sugar factory
4 Footbridge on old brick abutments
5 Site of former *arrêt PN* Rang-du-Fliers 'La Grimpette'
6 Footbridge with remains of old railway bridge
7 Footbridge of old sleepers, old rails in fence to right on far side
8 Remains of old bridge

Standard gauge double track
Path of former Aire-Berck line
Route of walk
Road, roundabout
Drainage channel
Building

1 km
1/2 mile

to Etaples, Boulogne, Calais

D 917 to Montreuil

D 140 to le Bahot

RANG-du-FLIERS

to Noyelles, Abbeville, Amiens & Paris

D 143 to Rue

Path of former Aire-Berck line to Aire

Camp site

D 917

D 917 to Berck

Path of former Aire-Berck line to Berck

Walk 4 - Rang-du-Fliers

Map 2105ET. 1 to 1½ hours/3 miles (5km) there and back. This is a walk across the *marais*, the lush low-lying farmland with drainage ditches which lies between the main line to Paris at Rang-du-Fliers and the sea. It is not as exciting as some of the walks but it is interesting and flat and easily accessible from Berck and some of the other coastal resorts.

Park at the SNCF station at Rang-du-Fliers (E 1° 38' 51'' N 50° 24' 57''). To the left across the main line is the former sugar factory and, nearer, the disused goods building. The Aire-Berck line shared a platform on this side of the station. It passed to the right of the *Buvette* (café), and then crossed the road behind you. Cross the road outside the station and follow the line of the railway, which begins as an asphalted section for 100 yards leading to a modern warehouse on the right. Keeping straight on, the line enters a marshy woodland with drainage ditches each side. Soon it curves right and leaves the wood across another ditch where there is a metal footbridge resting on the brick abutments of the old railway bridge. From here the line is easy to follow straight on through pasture with lots of trees, and some areas of housing backing onto the track.

Shortly after the metal footbridge, the line crosses a small road. Where it next meets a road there is a junction of four roads. On the right, as you come out here, is a road sign *'Impasse de l'Arrêt'*. This is the site of the railway stop called on the timetables *'PN Rang-du-Fliers (Arrêt)'* (level crossing at Rang-du-Fliers). The old picture of a train crossing here calls it *La Grimpette* but we have not found a satisfactory translation of this. *Grimper* means to climb and therefore perhaps this is 'the little climb' – maybe a joke about the flatness of the *marais*? On the far side of the road the line widens out, by a new house on the left, and this was probably the site of the stop with passenger access and perhaps a shelter. Continuing straight on again there is another bridge with not only a metal footbridge but also the old steel girders of the railway bridge still on the brick abutments. Further still the line

Walk 4. The *arrêt* known as PN (*passage à niveau* - level crossing) Rang-du-Fliers, with a train stopped on the crossing. We do not know why this was called *La Grimpette*. Undated, but the dress indicates before World War I.   *Authors' Collection*

Walk 4. The site of the *arrêt* known as PN Rang-du-Fliers in August 2006, looking along the path of the railway towards Berck. The building in the previous picture can be seen on the left. *Authors*

follows a big ditch on the left and there is a footbridge of old sleepers laid on wooden joists supported on brick abutments reinforced with bits of rail. To the right of the bridge on the other side two rails help to hold up the fence and the bank. On the other side a wide path to the left leads up to the farmhouse known as *'Le Tortillard'*. Eventually the line passes a camping and caravan site on the left and after this reaches another road. Beyond this the line towards Berck-Ville is mostly lost in new roads and houses and it is time to quit. Retrace your steps unless you can get some kind person to bring the car round for you.

Walk 5 - Under the walls of Montreuil

Map 2105ET. ½ hour/1 mile (1.5 km) each way, or 3 miles (5 km) continuing round the walls. Most of it is an easy gradient but the total climb is 100 feet. The going is good underfoot at all times of year.

Park the car on Montreuil-sur-Mer station forecourt (E 1° 46′ 06″ N 50° 27′ 58″). The Aire-Berck line ran alongside the standard gauge line on the far side of the far platform. Take the steps up the hill to the right of the now defunct Hotel de la Gare. In the days when most of the visitors to the town would arrive by train, this would have been their first climb. At the top, on the right you will see the old *octroi* which was where visitors arriving would pay the local visitors' tax. Cross the road by the pedestrian crossing and follow the arrows marking three walks. These cross what was the car park for the also defunct Hotel Belle Vue to your right. Follow the path along the back of the block of modern apartments and climb up into the moat that circles the town walls. These fortifications were built by the famous French military engineer, Sebastien de Vauban (1633-1707) around an earlier citadel by his predecessor Jean Errard. Proceed along the path in the moat for a few hundred yards to a fork in the path. The left-hand branch circles an isolated bastion, now merely

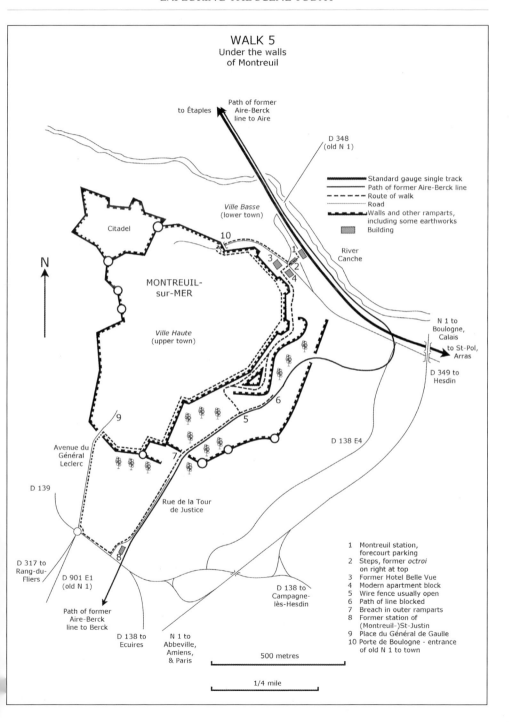

WALK 5
Under the walls
of Montreuil

Path of former Aire-Berck line to Aire

to Étaples

D 348 (old N 1)

Standard gauge single track
Path of former Aire-Berck line
Route of walk
Road
Walls and other ramparts, including some earthworks
Building

Citadel

Ville Basse (lower town)

10

MONTREUIL-sur-MER

1
3
2
4

River Canche

N

Ville Haute (upper town)

N 1 to Boulogne, Calais

to St-Pol, Arras

D 349 to Hesdin

6

5

9

D 138 E4

Avenue du Général Leclerc

7

D 139

Rue de la Tour de Justice

D 317 to Rang-du-Fliers

D 901 E1 (old N 1)

D 138 to Campagne-lès-Hesdin

1 Montreuil station, forecourt parking
2 Steps, former *octroi* on right at top
3 Former Hotel Belle Vue
4 Modern apartment block
5 Wire fence usually open
6 Path of line blocked
7 Breach in outer ramparts
8 Former station of (Montreuil-)St-Justin
9 Place du Général de Gaulle
10 Porte de Boulogne - entrance of old N 1 to town

Path of former Aire-Berck line to Berck

D 138 to Ecuires

N 1 to Abbeville, Amiens, & Paris

500 metres

1/4 mile

Walk 5. The steps up from the forecourt at Montreuil station, which are the start of this walk. At the top on the right is the *octroi* (local tax office). Postcard written in 1915.

Édition Fontaine Segret; Authors' Collection

Walk 5. 400 yards down the hill from St-Justin station, the path of the Aire-Berck line passed through the outer ramparts of Montreuil, where a hole had been unceremoniously blasted. Photograph taken 1915. *Collection Mairie de Montreuil, reproduced with permission*

Walk 5. Montreuil station taken from the top of the ramparts. In the middle across the road from the nearest building, the small building is the *octroi* at the top of the steps up from the station. Postcard written in 1927. *Authors' Collection*

139. MONTREUIL-SUR-MER. — La Gare et les Environs

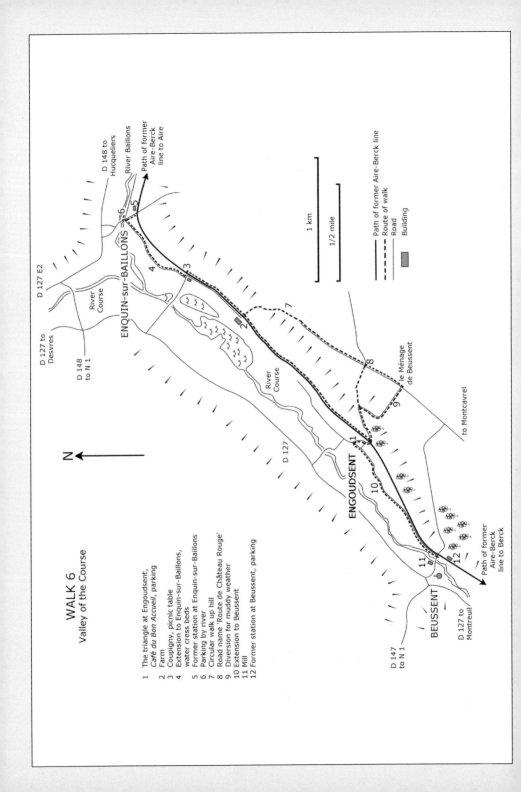

WALK 6
Valley of the Course

1 The triangle at Engoudsent,
   Café du Bon Accueil, parking
2 Farm
3 Coupigny, picnic table
4 Extension to Enquin-sur-Baillons,
   water cress beds
5 Former station at Enquin-sur-Baillons
6 Parking by river
7 Circular walk up hill
8 Road name 'Route de Château Rouge'
9 Diversion for muddy weather
10 Extension to Beussent
11 Mill
12 Former station at Beussent, parking

N

---- Path of former Aire-Berck line
- - - Route of walk
—— Road
▨ Building

1 km

1/2 mile

showing as a sharp hillock covered in trees. In the spring the whole area is covered in primroses and celandines. Completing the circuit of the bastion and rejoining the main path, take the track that turns to the left away from the walls. This track descends steeply and at the bottom it meets the former line from Aire to Berck.

Turn left back toward Montreuil station, through a wire fence, usually left open, and follow the line along an embankment. Once past the steps up to an allotment gate the line of the railway becomes less distinct and may well be impenetrable in summer. After a hundred yards further access is prevented by barbed wire. From here, the line of the railway curved to the right through farmland before breaching the outermost earthworks towards the N39. The railway then turned sharply left to cross the N39 and the standard gauge railway by a crossing on the level to enter the station, as we noted at the start of the walk, on the far side of the standard gauge platform (*see page 99*). Return to the wire fence and follow the line of the railway as it climbs the hill in the other direction towards St-Justin. At one point we pass through the outermost fortifications with the remains of the wall visible on both sides. Obviously the railway builders of old were no great respecters of antiquity! Follow the track until it becomes a metalled road with houses both sides. This is the village of St-Justin and the station is the much modernised house at the end on the left. The line had climbed about one hundred feet from the station at Montreuil and now had a fairly easy passage to Campigneulles-les-Petites, the next station on the way to Berck-Plage.

From here there are two options, either to retrace your steps or to take a circular walk through the town to get back. To do the latter, turn right when meeting the main road just past the 'station'. Walk up the hill to turn right at the roundabout. Follow the road into the largest of Montreuil's three squares, the Place General de Gaulle. As you enter the square you will see a footpath to the right leading up onto the walls. Follow these round to your left and you will soon see below you the path you followed earlier. Further on you will see the station far below. Continue until you reach the gateway through the walls where the main road enters the town. Believe it or not until the late 1950s this road was the N1, the main road from Calais to Paris. This explains why Montreuil was a major staging post from the Channel to Paris and goes some way to explain why Montreuil has always been so dear to English visitors. Go down the hill and you will find the steps down to the station where you started.

Walk 6 - Valley of the Course

Map 2105 ET. Distance along the old railway track from Engoudsent to Coupigny and return just under 3 miles (4.5 km) - about one hour return. Adding the round trip up the hill means an extra half a mile and 140 feet of climbing. Extension Coupigny to Enquins-sur-Baillons 1 mile (1.5 km) return. Extension Engoudsent to Beussent less than 2 miles (3 km) return; both extensions fairly flat.

There is nothing to indicate that these are rights of way but there are no obstructions and we have met people who have walked them regularly over many years. The going is good in all seasons on rough tracks or metalled roads, except for the final descent on the circular walk which may get muddy. This can be avoided by a short road detour.

Arrival and parking: for Engoudsent turn off the D127 at Zérables, cross the river turn right and park in the triangle by the *Café du Bon Accuiel* (E 1° 48' 33" N 50° 33' 08"). To start in Beussent turn off the D127 in Beussent and park in the old station

Walk 6. The station at Enquin-sur-Baillons. This was originally a halt on the Aire-Berck line but was converted into a station with the addition of a goods building before World War I; June 2001.   *Authors*

Walk 6. The valley of the Course near Engoudsent, from the circular walk up the hill. The path of the Aire-Berck line, which formed the first part of the walk, crosses the ploughed field in the middle distance; May 2006.   *Authors*

yard on the right immediately across the river (E 1° 47' 41" N 50° 32' 44"). There is also good parking in Enquin by the river (E 1° 50' 16" N 50° 34' 15").

From the *Café du Bon Acceuil* walk up the hill. The railway crossed this road just above the last house on the right where the road bends left. You can see the line running through a private copse on the right, and there is an old sleeper incorporated in the fence. On the left the line forms a dirt track running between gardens to the left and some banks to the right. It then passes through the edge of a small wood, where it is cut into the hillside, and then out into open fields. At a farm on the left, at one mile, the track becomes semi-metalled. After less than another half a mile, the road takes sharp left turn with farm buildings on the left (Coupigny) and straight ahead is a handy picnic table. The railway ran straight on but is now too overgrown to follow into Enquin. There is a pleasant optional extra here, into Enquin-sur-Baillons. Follow the road left at the picnic table and then right in about 50 yards. This road parallels the old railway which is behind the houses on the right. There are water cress beds on the left. At the crossroads at the end turn right and the old station at Enquin is just up the hill on the left.

For the circular walk, retrace your steps along the line half a mile from the picnic table and at the farm where the semi-metalled road ends turn left on the track up the hill, which bends right as it climbs. It is quite a pull up here but the views along the Course valley are worth it. The line of the old railway is soon clearly visible below. Follow the track until it meets a narrow metalled road. Turn right and keep to the road for half a mile along the hill top until another road comes in from the left; here there is a road name, Route de Château Rouge. On the right a track cuts between fields and fencing. Take this track; beginning as a farm track it soon narrows to a footpath as it drops rapidly back into the valley. It meets a metalled road and by turning right down the hill you get back to the start of the walk. For muddy weather the option is to continue on the metalled road at the top and take the first right.

From Engoudsent you can extend on foot or by car to Beussent, or if you wish, start and finish in Beussent. Take the road left out of the bottom of the triangle at the *Café du Bon Accuiel*. The line of the railway is still on the hill to the left above you but comes down to the road at river level halfway to Beussent. It then hugs the river bank with the road before reaching the station at Beussent. This is now the *Mairie*. As you enter Beussent you will see on your right a mill with a sluice and a mill race, and on the left a fence made with old railway sleepers.

Walk 7 - Delette and the bridge over the Lys

Map 2304 O. ½ hour. This is an easy stroll to see the bridge over the Lys. Distance ¾ mile (1 km) there and back, flat, good going.

Arrival and parking: at Delettes leave the main road along the Lys valley (D157) by the D193 to Erny-St-Julien. Descend through the village and follow the road right soon after crossing the river. The old station is set back from this road on the right after about 200 yards. There is some parking here (E 2° 12' 44" N 50° 37' 04").

The old station is now a private house, much extended, with a garden running down to the river. There is a station clock on the track side (river side) but no name. Left of the station is a public open space down to the river with an old weighbridge; presumably this was the station yard. Follow the path across this open space and the track becomes the line of the old railway. Cross the end of another metalled road. To the right there is a metalled path leading to a footbridge which crosses to an old water mill and the part of the village on the other bank of the Lys. Staying on this

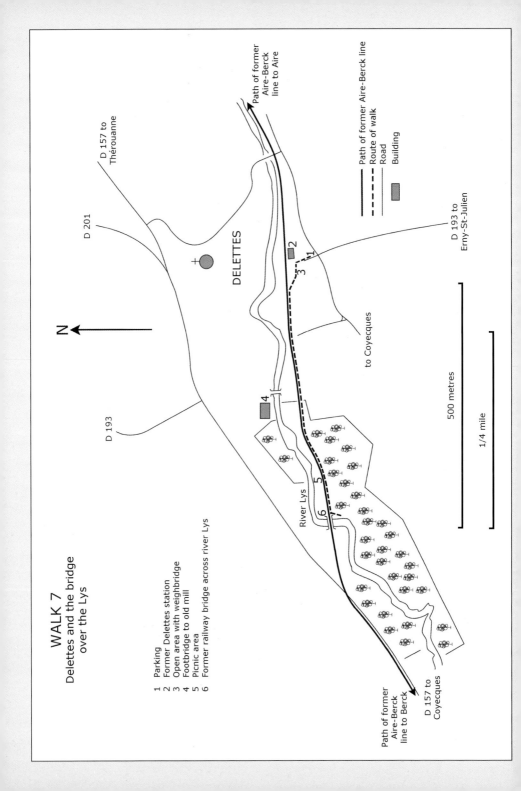

WALK 7
Delettes and the bridge over the Lys

1 Parking
2 Former Delettes station
3 Open area with weighbridge
4 Footbridge to old mill
5 Picnic area
6 Former railway bridge across river Lys

N

D 157 to Thérouanne

D 201

D 193

DELETTES

Path of former Aire-Berck line to Aire

D 193 to Erny-St-Julien

to Coyecques

River Lys

Path of former Aire-Berck line to Berck

D 157 to Coyecques

Path of former Aire-Berck line
Route of walk
Road
Building

500 metres

1/4 mile

Walk 7. The bridge of the Aire-Berck line over the river Lys near Delettes; April 2006.

Authors

side of the river go straight on. This is the line of the old railway. The river bank on the right has been refurbished with picnic tables. The track leads to the old bridge across the Lys. This is private and on the other side the line passes through a garden, although the signs saying that the bridge is dangerous would be more convincing if there were not plants in boxes and a seat on the bridge! The bridge and abutments can best be seen by following the river bank a short way to the left.

Walk 8 - Boulogne and St-Martin-Boulogne

Map 2104ET. 3½ miles (5.5 km): 1½ hours but allow longer if you want to stop and look at things.

This walk explores the route of the Boulogne-Bonningues line from the top of the hill at St-Martin-Boulogne, where the line had its depot and main station, to the site of the old Central station (Boulogne-Ville). It shows very clearly the long climb of this section of the railway when starting from the centre of Boulogne.

It is recommended to park the car at the bottom of the hill, on the Quai de la Poste (E 1° 36′ 05″ N 50° 43′ 22″), get the bus up the hill, and walk down. Alternatively park at the top in the Place J. Moulin at St-Martin-Boulogne (E 1° 37′ 52″ N 50° 43′ 33″), walk down and get the bus up. Either way, while at the bottom walk round the block across the river and back. Facing the river Liane, turn right and cross it by the Pont Marguet. At the far side the fast car ferry (catamaran) terminal is on your right. Ahead is a road and in the angle of this half-left is a bus park, the site of the old Central Station (Boulogne-Ville). The gates of the bus park are on the site of the old station gates, and the standard gauge lines to the *Gare Maritime* came out here and along the quay. You can see the post-war version of the *Gare Maritime* to the right. Turn left along the Quai Chanzy; the tram line to Le Portel and Outreau, and the terminus of the steam line to Bonningues, were on the right of this road. Turn left again across the Pont de l'Entente Cordiale. The lines also crossed the former bridge here, the tram to go straight on at the other side to the Place Dalton, and the railway to turn half right into the Boulevard Pierre Daunou. Across the bridge, turn left again to come back to where you started. By *la Poste* is the Place Frédéric Sauvage,

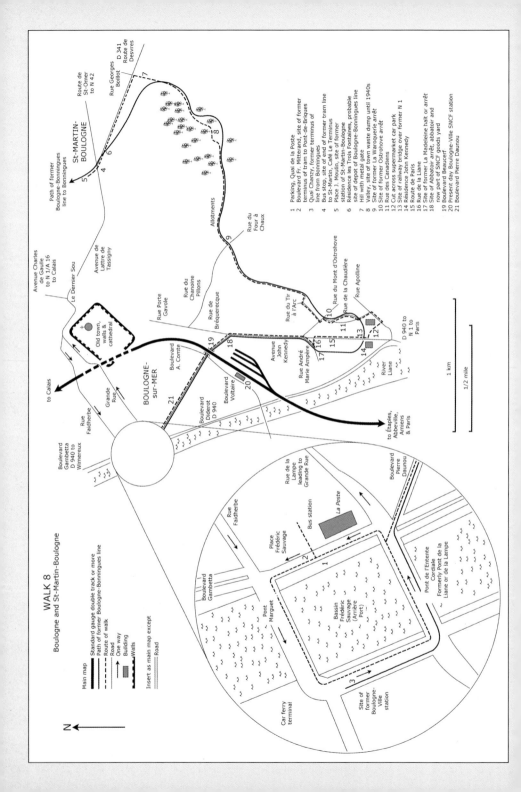

WALK 8
Boulogne and St-Martin-Boulogne

Main map
▬▬▬ Standard gauge double track or more
▬ ▬ Path of former Boulogne-Bonningues line
━━━ Route of walk
═══ Road
→ One way
▦ Building
▨ Walls

Insert as main map except
═══ Road

N ←

1 Parking, Quai de la Poste
2 Boulevard Fr. Mitterand, site of former terminus of tram to Pont-de-Briques
3 Quai Chanzy, former terminus of line from Bonningues
4 Bus stop, site of end of former tram line to St-Martin, Café Le Terminus
5 Place J. Moulin, site of former station of St-Martin-Boulogne
6 Résidence les Trois Fontaines, probable site of depot of Boulogne-Bonningues line
7 Hill with metal gate
8 Valley, site of town waste dump until 1940s
9 Site of former La Waroquerie arrêt
10 Site of former Ostrohove arrêt
11 Rue des Canadiens
12 Cut across supermarket car park
13 Site of railway bridge over former N 1
14 Résidence John Kennedy
15 Route de Paris
16 Rue de la Liane
17 Site of former La Madeleine halt or arrêt
18 Site of Abbatoir arrêt, abbatoir and now part of SNCF goods yard
19 Boulevard Beaucerf
20 Present day Boulogne-Ville SNCF station
21 Boulevard Pierre Daunou

from where the trams to Pont de Briques and Hardelot originally started, with the statue of Frédéric Sauvage. He invented the screw drive for ships.

The bus station is at the side and back of *la Poste*. Catch the No. 4 to St-Martin. This turns inland past the Place Dalton where the Le Portel and other trams terminated, and then follows the route of the old tram line to St-Martin up the hill, round the old town, past the *Dernier Sou* (the bus stop here is still called this, but the road is not), and up the Route de St.Omer to St-Martin. Get off at the top of the steepest bit, where the Route de Desvres leaves the Route de St. Omer; the bus goes on to Mont Lambert. On this junction was, and still is, the Café Terminus, by the end of the former tram line and across the road from the Place J Moulin, which is the site of the former St-Martin station on the steam line to Bonningues. The line crossed the Route de St.Omer in front of the Café.

Take the right fork and follow the Route de Desvres, passing the cemetery on the right. Next on the right is an area of new housing, the *Résidence les Trois Fontaines*, which is the probable site of the depot for the Boulogne-Bonningues line. The line started down the slope to the right after this. Walk straight on for a further ¼ mile, and turn right down the hill opposite the Rue Georges Boillot. Straight ahead is a metal fence which appears impassable but in fact has a small gate in it. Through this the track leads gradually down the hill and after a short distance the line of the railway joins it from the right. Continue to follow the line, as it crosses the head of the valley of St-Martin, where the town used to use the railway to dump its waste, and then contours along through bushy scrub, with the valley on the right, losing height all the time. After a while the line leaves the path and goes away to the left. The path goes down and up across a small side valley, rejoining the line on the other side; here there are earthworks and an electricity sub-station up the hill to the left. After this there are buildings up the hill on the left, and allotments to the right, with views back right

Walk 8. The Café Terminus at St-Martin-Boulogne; postcard written in 1915. Looking straight down the Route de St-Omer, towards the centre of Boulogne, the electric tramway from the Place Dalton is on the left and ends at the corner. The steam railway from Boulogne to Bonningues crosses the foreground into the main station at St-Martin, which is on the right just out of the picture. *Génet, Éditeur; Authors' Collection*

Walk 8. The Café Terminus, now the Café Le Terminus, from a different angle in August 2006.
Authors

Walk 8. The route of the line at La Waroquerie in 2006. The *Val St. Martin* is on the left, and the line curved round to the left through the trees at the head of the valley to St-Martin-Boulogne which is off picture to the left. *Authors*

across the valley to St-Martin, and forward right to the old town with the Cathedral.

Now the line crosses a road. Just before this the oval is the site of the *arrêt* of La Waroquerie, but the information board here does not mention the railway. Continue straight on across the road. The line curves left and then is straight on between trees. At the end of this there is a metalled road, the Rue du Tir à l'Arc, and the path of the railway goes straight on into the drive of a house. Turn right and then left along the road that parallels the line and at the end is a more main road, the Rue du Mont d'Ostrohove. Turn left up the hill and after 30 yards on the left is the end of a narrow garden behind a wall. This is the path of the railway. Cross the road and continue downhill along the Rue des Canadiens. The *arrêt* of Ostrohove was about here. Fork left into the Rue de la Chaudière, and follow this until it rejoins the Rue des Canadiens. This was the line of the railway which then descended straight ahead quite steeply through a cutting. Turn left and, at the end of the Rue des Canadiens, turn right and then take the shortcut to the right across the supermarket car park to the Route de Paris. This used to be the main Boulogne to Paris road, the N1. This was also the route of the trams to Pont de Briques.

At the Route de Paris, turn right and about 50 yards up the hill is the site of the bridge which took the line over this road. On the right is a modern infill house, and on the left the entrance to the Résidence John Kennedy. Continue along the main road over the hill, and on the left, over the top, is first the narrow Rue de la Liane and then the wider Rue André Marie Ampère. Turn left along the former which joins the latter after 50 yards. On the left is a disused factory and just beyond this on the left is the site of the former *arrêt* or possibly halt at La Madeleine. Beyond this on the left is the beginning of a strip of scrubland which maps show as going through to the grounds of the Résidence John Kennedy, but is now impenetrable. This was the route of the railway.

From the Rue André Marie Ampère the line joined the main road and from here to the Central station it was built as a road tramway, running alongside the tramway to Pont de Briques when this was built 10 years later. Follow the main road, now the Avenue John Kennedy, towards the centre of Boulogne. At the Place Henri Heneguelle, fork left into the Boulevard Beaucerf, with the railway bridge ahead down the hill. Now, the goods yard and the new Boulogne-Ville station are on the left, but then, this was the corner of the abbatoir, and the *arrêt* of the same name. Under the railway bridge and straight on is the Boulevard Pierre Daunou which leads to the end of the Pont de l'Entente Cordiale, completing the route of the line into Boulogne. Until after World War II, the Boulevard Pierre Daunou was the east bank of the Liane. All the buildings to the left, and the present Boulogne-Ville station, are built on land reclaimed when the Liane was narrowed and straightened during the rebuilding of Boulogne after the war. The railway bridge on the main line from Paris to Calais is in the same place but formerly the bridges carrying the lines across the Liane, to Abbeville and to the old Central station, began close to this.

Other things to do

Tourist train of the Valley of the Aa

The single track standard gauge line from Arques to Lumbres and further west towards Boulogne has not all been lifted. The *Chemin de Fer de la Vallée de l'Aa* (CFTVA) runs 'Picasso' railcars from Arques to Lumbres, where the Anvin-Calais line used to share the standard gauge station, and where the VFIL main workshops

The station at Lumbres, built for the Compagnie du Nord, later SNCF, in 2007. The platform in the foreground used to be that serving the Anvin-Calais line. A 'Picasso' railcar of the Train Touristique de la Vallée de l'Aa, which now uses the station, is waiting to depart for Arques. *Authors*

and depot used to be. The trains also stop at Wizernes for the museum at the V2 site of La Coupole. In 2007 the trains operated from May to September on Saturdays, Sundays and public holidays only. For further information visit their website at cftva.free.fr or telephone 00 33 (0)3 21 12 19 19 or 00 33 (0)3 21 93 45 46.

Bicycles on rails at Nielles-les-Bléquin

Rando-Rail du Pays de Lumbres is also on the Arques-Boulogne line, based at the station at Nielles-les-Bléquin (map 2204E). This is on the part of the old line between Lumbres and Desvres and is 4½ miles west-south-west of Lumbres. It was open in 2007 from April to September, and they say that booking is essential. For further details visit their website at www.rando-rail.com or telephone 00 33 (0)3 21 88 33 89.

Museum of the Atlantic Wall

The *Musée du Mur de l'Atlantique* (Museum of the Atlantic Wall) is at Haringzelles near Cap Gris Nez. It is signposted off the D940 just south of the junction with the D191 at a roundabout just south of Audinghen (Map 2103 ET, on which the museum is marked). The museum is based in the Battery Todt, named by the Germans in memory of the leader of the Todt organisation who was killed in an air crash in February 1942. The casemate is that of one of the larger gun batteries of the Atlantic Wall, and contains weapons and other memorabilia from World War II. Of particular interest for this book is a heavy standard gauge railway mounted gun, similar to those deployed by the German armed forces on lines in this area before the building of the permanent emplacements of the Atlantic Wall. There are also posters, including ones about hostages and reprisals, which illustrate the harshness of life in occupied France. The museum is owned and run by a Frenchman of Welsh descent, D.C. Davies, and his family.

Postscript

It is now more than 50 years since the last of the lines described in this book closed. Much else has changed in the western Pas-de-Calais during this time. Since the end of the metre gauge lines, the line inland from Hesdigneuil, near Boulogne, to Arques and St-Omer has closed, as has the line from St-Omer to Isbergues. The former served Lumbres, and the latter, Aire. There is now no railway service down the coast from Calais except for the Calais-Abbeville-Amiens-Paris main line. There is also a vast area inland, the area between Calais, Boulogne, Montreuil, and St-Omer, with no railway service. With the widespread closures of lines of *Intérêt Local*, both standard and metre gauge, over the past 70 years, this is now not unusual for rural areas of France.

Motorways have been built along the coast and inland from Calais. Public transport is mainly provided by buses, which are comfortable and modern. In the towns these are not very frequent, and in the country even less so. People rely, as elsewhere in France and many other countries, on the private car, and for goods traffic on vans and lorries.

The major development in railways has been the building of the TGV line from Calais to Lille and on to Paris, Brussels and the rest of the growing French and European network. In the UK we associate this with the opening of the Channel Tunnel in 1994, and the Eurostar services direct from London to Paris, Lille and Brussels. However, and again as elsewhere in France, the TGV line now provides the principal and fastest domestic passenger train services. The TGV can be joined at Calais-Ville, or at Calais-Fréthun. There had already been a station of this name on the line from Calais to Boulogne, but it was rebuilt, sited where the line from Calais to Boulogne crosses the line emerging from the Channel Tunnel. There are platforms for trains on both lines. Some Eurostar services for Paris or London can also be joined here. The TGV line takes the fastest services south-east from Calais. Main line services are also provided on the old main line from Calais to St-Omer and further, and on the coast line through Boulogne. Surprisingly for France, the coast main line south of Boulogne has not been electrified.

The huge French Channel Tunnel terminal for road traffic is sited adjacent to the marshalling yard at Rivière Neuve, south-west of Calais-Fontinettes station. It is interesting that Rivière Neuve was the major depot of the Railway Operating Division of the British Army in World War I.

What of the future? France has already reduced her dependence on electricity generated using fossil fuels. Eighty per cent of electricity is generated in nuclear power stations, and wind generators are rapidly springing up around the coast and countryside. It is to be expected that at some time the coast main line south of Boulogne will be electrified. There is major road congestion, and difficulty parking, at holiday times in the coastal resorts, particularly Berck and Le Touquet (Paris-Plage). If the main line from Boulogne south is electrified, the restoration of some form of electric tramway from the main station at Rang-du-Fliers to Berck-Plage, and from the main station at Étaples to Le Touquet, is likely. This might take the form of a loop from Étaples to Rang, linking Le Touquet, Merlimont, Berck-Plage, the smaller resorts between, and the 'Bagatelle' theme park just north of Berck. In other words, a route not much different from the original three lines forming this loop, but fast, frequent, and electric.

It is also possible that Calais, and Boulogne, may join the growing number of French towns restoring urban and suburban electric tramways. Further ahead is more speculative. Any future for personal or public transport in the rural areas must address the twin problems of oil scarcity and CO_2 emissions. Perhaps rechargeable electric cars and buses will be the answer. But if any of these metre gauge lines had survived into the present era, they would probably now be seen as part of the solution, as for instance in Switzerland. The economies of metal rolling on metal on a fixed track with external electricity supply have not gone away. Of course none of these comments are specific to the area of this book, or to France. As elsewhere, all this might have been foreseen.

Meanwhile the buses struggle and the private car is king. We could not have written this book without ours. And, as for well over 50 years now, the replacement bus still waits for the Paris train at Rang-du-Fliers station.

Appendix One

Motive Power Rolling Stock Summary

Anvin-Calais (AC) up to 1918

Steam Locomotives

Engine	Builder	Type	Wt (tonnes)	Year	Power (hp)	Disposal	Notes
1 Fruges	SACM	0-6-2T	18.5	1880		At Lumbres for scrapping 1956.	In service from January 1882. Enlarged water tanks by 1909.
2 Fauquembergues	SACM	0-6-2T	18.5	1880		Unknown.	In service from January 1882.
3 Guines	SACM	0-6-2T	18.5	1880		Unknown.	In service from August 1881.
4 Calais	SACM	0-6-2T	18.5	1881		Unknown.	In service from August 1881.
5 Ardres	SACM	0-6-2T	18.5	1881		At Lumbres for scrapping 1956.	In service from August 1881.
6 Lumbres	SACM	0-6-2T	18.5	1881		At Lumbres for scrapping 1956.	In service from January 1882. Cab enclosed before 1914.
7 Heuchin	SACM	0-6-2T	18.5	1882		At Lumbres for scrapping 1956.	In service from July 1882. Cab enclosed before 1914.
8 Saint Pierre	SACM	0-6-2T	18.5	1882	8.5	At Lumbres for scrapping 1956.	In service from May 1883. Enlarged water tanks before 1914.
9 Tournehem	Pinguely	0-6-0T	18	1900	12.5	Transferred to Aire-Berck as No. 46 1900.	
10 Rimeux	Pinguely	0-6-0T	18	1900	12.5	To CF d'Allier 1886.	
8 Anvin	Batignolles	0-6-0T	10	1878	8.5	Unknown.	Construction locomotive, other use from 1882.
20	Ateliers-Nord-Belge	2-6-0T	24	1906	14	Unknown.	Bought by Anvin-Calais but put in use initially to Berck.
22	Ateliers-Nord-Belge	2-6-0T	24	1909	14	At Lumbres for scrapping 1956.	Ex-Guise-Hirson No. 1, in use from 1910, purchased 1912.

Tramway Ardres to Pont d'Ardres (APA) up to 1918

Steam Locomotives

Engine	Builder	Type	Wt (tonnes)	Year	Power (hp)	Boiler pressure (kg/m²)	Disposal	Notes
1	Corpet-Louvet	0-6-0T	10	pre-1900		10	Unknown	Acquired 1902. 13 tonnes loaded.
2	Corpet-Louvet	0-6-0T	10	1882		9	Unknown	Acquired 1902. 13 tonnes loaded.
3	Winterthür (CH)	0-6-0T	13	1889		14	To *sucrerie* Say (Pont d'Ardres) - when?	Acquired 1905 from tramways of Geneva. 16 tonnes loaded.
3 Ardres-Pont-d'Ardres	Henschel (D)	0-6-0T	18.4	1912		12	To *sucrerie* Say (Pont d'Ardres) - when?	Works No. 11393. 24 tonnes loaded

Aire-Berck (ARB) up to 1918

Steam Locomotives

Engine	Builder	Type	Wt (tonnes)	Year	Power (hp)	Disposal	Notes
004	Corpet	0-6-2T	16	1890	9	Unknown.	21 tonnes loaded.
31	Corpet	0-6-2T	16			To Réseau Flandres 1894.	Possibly same locomotive as 004. 21 tonnes loaded.
32	Corpet	0-6-2T	16	1891	10	To Réseau Flandres 1894.	21 tonnes loaded.
33	Corpet	0-6-2T	16	1891	10	At Lumbres for scrapping 1956.	21 tonnes loaded.
34	Corpet	0-6-2T	16			To Noyon-Lassigny 1894.	21 tonnes loaded.
35	Corpet	0-6-2T	16	1891	10	Unknown.	21 tonnes loaded.
36	Corpet	0-6-2T	16			To Réseau Flandres 1912.	21 tonnes loaded.
40	Corpet	0-6-2T	21	1892	10	At Lumbres for scrapping 1956.	26.5 tonnes loaded.
41	Corpet	0-6-2T	21	1892	10	At Lumbres for scrapping 1956.	26.5 tonnes loaded.
42	Corpet	0-6-2T	21	1892	10	At Lumbres for scrapping 1956.	26.5 tonnes loaded.
43	Corpet	0-6-2T	21	1892	10	At Lumbres for scrapping 1956.	26.5 tonnes loaded.
44	Corpet	0-6-2T	21	1892	10	At Lumbres for scrapping 1956.	26.5 tonnes loaded.
45	Corpet	0-6-2T	21	1893	10	At Lumbres for scrapping 1956.	26.5 tonnes loaded.
46	Pinguely	0-6-0T	18	1900	12.5	? To Hermes-Beaumont post-WWII.	Previously Anvin-Calais No. 10, transferred 1900.

Private locomotives associated with Anvin-Calais and Aire-Berck

Builder	Type	Wt (tonnes)	Year	Power (hp)	Disposal	Notes
Fives-Lille	0-6-0T		1882		Distillerie of Verton.	From CF Cambrésis.
SLM	0-6-0T		1889		Sucrerie Say (Pont d'Ardres).	From Tramways of Geneva.
Henschel	0-6-0T		1912		Sucrerie Say (Pont d'Ardres).	From APA.

Anvin-Calais-Aire-Berck, from 1919 (VFIL or CGL) (including tramway Ardres-Pont d'Ardres)

Steam Locomotives

Engine	Builder	Type	Wt (tonnes)	Year	Power (hp)	Disposal	Notes
23	Ateliers-Nord-Belge	2-6-0T	24	1909	14	At Lumbres for scrapping 1956.	Nos. 23-25 Ex-Guise-Hirson (Nos. 2, 3 & 6, early 1920s).
24	Ateliers-Nord-Belge	2-6-0T	24	1909	14	At Lumbres for scrapping 1956.	
25	Ateliers-Nord-Belge	2-6-0T	24	1909	14	At Lumbres for scrapping 1956.	
51	Winterthur (CH)	2-10-0T	42	1911	12	At Lumbres for scrapping 1956.	Ex-Guise-Hirson early 1920s.
52	Winterthur (CH)	2-10-0T	42	1911	12	At Lumbres for scrapping 1956.	Ex-Guise-Hirson early 1920s.
120	Ateliers-Nord-Belge	2-6-0T	24	1924	14	At Lumbres for scrapping 1956.	(Nos 120, 121 and 126 identical with Nos. 20 & 22 to 25)
121	Ateliers-Nord-Belge	2-6-0T	24	1924	14	At Lumbres for scrapping 1956.	
126	Ateliers-Nord-Belge	2-6-0T	24	1924	14	At Lumbres for scrapping 1956.	
161	Henschel (D)	0-6-0+0-6-0T	44	1917	14	Probably scrapped 1940s.	Captured WW1, in use from 1931 (?). Works No. 15161. Captured WW1, used for APA.
	Jung (D)	0-6-0T		1897		Unknown.	Originally No. 3 Berck-Plage-Paris-Plage, from sugar factory at Trézennes 1941 or 1942. Now at MTVS Valmondois.
13	SACM	2-6-0T	22	1924	12	To VFIL Noyon (Oise) 1947.	

Diesel railcars

No.	Builder	Type	Wt (tonnes)	Year	Power (hp)	Disposal	Notes
RS 1 (CGL11)	Renault Scemia	2 axle		1924	45	At Lumbres for scrapping 1955.	Initially petrol, rebuilt and shortened 1933/4 as CGL 11 with diesel engine.
RS 2 (PdC 101)	Renault Scemia	2 axle		1925	45	Unknown.	Initially petrol, refurbished 1934/5 as (PdC) No. 101 with 85 hp Berliet diesel engine.
CGL 1	VFIL Lumbres	2 axle		1930s		To Somme network 1957, now CFBS No.M 31.	Rebuilt 1955.
ARB 2	VFIL Lumbres	2 axle	8	1932	65	Unknown, probably scrapped after 1955.	de Dion petrol.
ARB 3	VFIL Lumbres	2 axle	8.5	1933/4	65	Unknown, probably scrapped after 1955.	Unic diesel.
ARB 4	VFIL Lumbres	2 axle	8.5	1933/4	65	Unknown, probably scrapped after 1955.	Unic diesel.
ARB 5	VFIL Lumbres	2 axle	8.5	1933/4	65	Unknown, probably scrapped after 1955.	Unic diesel.
CGL 6	VFIL Lumbres	2 axle	8.5	1933/4	65	Unknown, probably scrapped after 1955.	Unic diesel.
CGL 7	VFIL Lumbres	2 axle	8.5	1933/4	65	Unknown, probably scrapped after 1955.	Unic diesel.
608	A80D1 Billard	2 bogies		1938		CF Corrèze 1955.	From CF Dordogne 1949/50.
610	A80D1 Billard	2 bogies		1938		CF Corrèze 1955.	From CF Dordogne 1949/50.
CGL 26	A150D6 Billard	2 bogies		1947		CFD du Tarn 1955.	From TW Ille et Villaine.
CGL 27	A150D6 Billard	2 bogies		1947		CFD du Tarn 1955.	From TW Ille et Villaine.
704	A80D2 Billard	2 bogies		1939		VFIL Oise (St Just-Froissy) 1955.	From CF de la Vendée 1951

Diesel railcar trailers

No.	Builder	Type	Wt (tonnes)	Year	Power (hp)	Disposal	Notes
Ra 606	A80D1 Billard	2 bogies		1938		CF Corrèze 1955.	Motor removed. From CF Dordogne 1949/50.
CGL Ra20	R210 Billard			1938			CFD du Tarn 1955. From TW Ille et Villaine.
CGL Ra21	R210 Billard			1938			CFD du Tarn 1955. From TW Ille et Villaine.
CGL Ra22	R210 Billard			1938			CFD du Tarn 1955. From TW Ille et Villaine.

Diesel locomotives (locotracteurs)

No.	Builder	Type	Wt (tonnes)	Year	Power (hp)	Disposal	Notes
301	VFIL Lumbres	0-6-0		1948	180	To CF Ardennes 1955.	Now at CFBS.
650	Ateliers CF Dordogne	0-6-0		1946		To CF Ardennes 1955.	Cimenterie d'Haubourdin 1961, scrapped 1975.
651	Ateliers CF Dordogne	0-6-0		1947		To CF Ardennes 1955.	Cimenterie d'Haubourdin 1961, scrapped 1975.
652	Ateliers CF Dordogne	0-6-0		1947		To CF Ardennes 1955.	Aciéres d'Isbergues 1961, scrapped 1975.

Berck-Plage to Paris-Plage

Steam locomotives

No.	Builder	Type	Wt (tonnes)	Year	Power (hp)	Boiler pressure (kg/m²)	Disposal	Notes
	Corpet	0-4-0T	11.5	1908			Sold, fate unknown.	Used for construction.
1	Decauville	0-6-0T		1910			Sold, fate unknown.	15 tonnes loaded.
2	Borsig (D)	0-6-0T	20	1912	12		Destroyed in WW1 1918.	
3	La Meuse (B)	2-6-0T	20	1912	12		Destroyed in WW1 1918.	25 tonnes loaded.
4	La Meuse (B)	2-6-0T	22	1924	12		To Attin/Engoudsent (Leroy) 1924.	25 tonnes loaded.
3	SACM	2-6-0T	22	1924			To cement factory, Beffes (Cher) 1924.	Later VFIL No. 13
4	SACM	2-6-0T						

Boulogne-Bonningues

No.	Builder	Type	Wt (tonnes)	Year	Power (hp)	Boiler pressure (kg/m²)	Disposal	Notes
47	ACNF Blanc-Misseron	0-6-0T	18.7	1899		12	Probably scrapped early 1940s.	22.7 tonnes loaded.
48	ACNF Blanc-Misseron	0-6-0T	18.7	1899		12	Probably scrapped early 1940s.	22.7 tonnes loaded.
49	ACNF Blanc-Misseron	0-6-0T	18.7	1899		12	Probably scrapped early 1940s.	22.7 tonnes loaded.
51	ACNF Blanc-Misseron	0-6-0T	18.7	1900(?)		12	Probably scrapped early 1940s.	22.7 tonnes loaded.
23	Piguet	0-6-0T		1924			Probably scrapped early 1940s.	25 tonnes loaded.
1	Corpet-Louvet	0-6-0T	19	1925			Probably scrapped early 1940s.	25 tonnes loaded.

Electric Trams

Le Portel-Boulogne

No.	Builder	Type	Wt (tonnes)	Year	Power (hp)	Boiler pressure (kg/m²)	Disposal	Notes
801		2 axle	5.9	1900	70			Single buffer compatible with Boulogne-Bonningues.
802		2 axle	5.9	1900	70			
803		2 axle	5.9	1900	70			
804		2 axle	5.9	1900	70			

Other tramways of Boulogne; Tramways of Calais; Étaples to Paris-Plage

No information other than that in the main text.

ACNF Ateliers de Construction du Nord de la France (de Blanc Misseron)
SACM Société Alsacienne de Constructions Mécaniques

Appendix Two

Works on Metre Gauge Lines 1917-1918

Location	Work done	Done by	Dates
Anvin to Calais			
Anvin	Temporary transhipment	110 RC (RE)	29.05.18-07.06.18
	Marshalling yard (*triage*)	262 RC (RE)	26.06.18-07.08.18
	Anvin-Teneur transhipment	262 RC (RE)	13.06.18-28.08.18
Bergueneuse	Additional loop	296 RC (RE)	15.06.18-03.07.18
	Conversion of siding to loop		
Verchin	Additional loop	296 RC (RE)	14.06.18-06.07.18
	Conversion of siding to loop		
Gourgesson Junction	Chord line Anvin to Aire, loop on Aire line	296 RC (RE)	27.07.18-31.08.18
Fruges	3 sidings and crossovers to east of station	296 RC (RE)	22.07.18
Rimeux-Gournay	2 sidings	296 RC (RE)	05.07.18-02.08.18
Fauquembergues	RE Workshops, guard house, 2 sidings	296 RC (RE)	21.07.18-06.08.18
	Water supply	296 RC (RE)	20.08.18
Wirquin	Loop line linked to existing factory siding	296 RC (RE)	14.06.18-27.06.18
Remilly	Reinstatement of loop on running line	296 RC (RE)	12.07.18-20.07.18
Lumbres	Track/sidings to RE park Elnes	262 RC (RE)	20.03.18-10.04.18
Acquin	Reinstatement of loop on running line	296 RC (RE)	06.05.18-18.05.18
	Conversion of siding to second loop		
Journy	Conversion of siding to loop	296 RC (RE)	05.07.18-19.07.18
	Siding extension and crossover		
Guémy	Loop line with 3 looped sidings	296 RC (RE)	01.06.18-03.07.18
Tournehem	Conversion of 3 sidings to loops	296 RC (RE)	11.05.18
	1 additional siding		
Zouafsques	Junction with line to St-Momelin	Belgian?	Spring 1918
Balinghem	2 sidings in a loop	298 RC (RE) ?	early 1917
Écluse-Carrée	2 sidings, and loop line	French 5th Div.	
Vendroux ? Écluse-Carrée	Supply camp sidings and transhipment	298 RC (RE)	01.08.18
Pont de Coulogne	Strengthening Guînes canal bridge	298 RC (RE)	11.06.17
Riviere Neuve	Dual gauge to Vendroux	298 RC (RE)	11.06.17

Location	Description	Unit	Date
Aire to Berck			
Mametz	Siding	296 RC (RE)	27.05.18-17.06.18
Crecques	No. 1 sidings (*raccordement*)	296 RC (RE)	10.05.18-08.06.18
	3 looped sidings		
	No. 2 sidings (*raccordement*)	296 RC (RE)	05.06.18-22.06.18
Thérouanne	Siding with looped second siding	296 RC (RE)	08.05.18-07.06.18
	Loop line and siding		
	Siding with loop west of station	296 RC (RE)	21.06.18-10.07.18
	RE park (?same as above)	296 RC (RE)	28.05.18-15.06.18
Delette	Siding	296 RC (RE)	21.05.18-12.06.18
Coyecques	Siding	296 RC (RE)	04.06.18-17.06.18
Dennebrœucq	Additional loop line and siding	296 RC (RE)	02.06.18-18.06.18
Matringhem	Siding	296 RC (RE)	06.05.18-23.05.18
Verchocq	Siding	296 RC (RE)	30.07.18-23.08.18
Rumilly	Additional loop line	296 RC (RE)	12.05.18-07.06.18
	Water supply	296 RC (RE)	15.05.18
Ergny	Additional loop line and siding	296 RC (RE)	07.09.18-01.11.18
Hucqueliers	Additional loop line and siding	296 RC (RE)	14.05.18-02.06.18
Engoudsent	Concrete factory sidings	296 RC (RE)	14.05.18-02.06.18
Beussent	Additional loop line and siding	French 5th Div.	1917
Recques-sur-Course	Additional loop line		
Attin	Transhipment sidings		
Wailly	Additional siding	296 RC (RE)	28.05.18-14.06.18
Bahot	2 long loops and spur		1918
Verton	Bridge mod. for quadrupling main line		
	2 additional sidings		
Rang-du-Fliers	SG/MG workshops and sidings	Unknown	06.18-08.18
Boulogne to Bonningues			
Ostrohove	Siding for camp	112 RC (RE)	26.01.18-07.03.18
Tournehem to St-Momelin			
Line Zouafques to St-Momelin	Diamond crossing with Watten-Socx line	Belgian Labour Force	Prob. 05.18-08.18
St-Momelin	Triage and transhipment sidings	2 Bttn CRT	03.07.18-28.08.18

RC (RE) Railway Company (Royal Engineers), Bttn CRT Battalion, Canadian Railway Troops.

Location and Present Status of Stations and other Buildings

Name	Type	Location (longitude/latitude)	Present status & use, notes (abbreviations, see p.332)
Anvin-Calais *Map 2305 O Heuchin*			
Anvin	CdN	Rue de la Gare, off D94 just W of jn with D343 S of level crossing at E 2° 15′ 17″ N 50° 26′ 48″	Building disused, freshly painted with windows blocked up, platforms in use by SNCF as *Arrêt*
Bergueneuse	Type 2	Up private drive E off Rue de Teneur (D97), 250 m SW of jn with D71 at Bergueneuse E 2° 15′ 05″ N 50° 28′ 01″	Private house, LB
Équirre * #	Halt	Just S of D71, 150 m W of corner by entrance to Château at Équirre E 2° 13′ 53″ N 50° 28′ 26″	Private house
Verchin	Type 2	Rue de la Gare, W off D71E(Rue Maranville) 100 m S of jn with D93 at Verchin E 2° 11′ 04″ N 50° 29′ 34″	BV demolished, HM & LB remain. Private bungalow on site
Map 2205 E Fruges			
Fruges	Type 1 & depot	N of corner in Rue de la Gare (one way), 200 m W of jn with D928 in Fruges E 2° 07′ 48″ N 50° 30′ 59″	Demolished, now College Départementale de Jacques Brel
Coupelle Vieille	Halt	Just E of D155 (Rue Cavée), 300 m NE of jn with D343 in Coupelle Vieille E 2° 06′ 13″ N 50° 31′ 29″	Private house
Rimeux-Gournay *	Type 2	In small road just N of D126, 500m W of jn with D129E (for Rimeux) E 2° 04′ 43″ N 50° 33′ 08″	Private house, LB. Junction from 1893
Renty	Arrêt	Just to E of minor road to la Haute Peine, right off Rue du Rouchet 200 m E of corner on D129 imm. S of river at Renty E 2° 04′ 43″ N 50° 34′ 42″	*Abri*, level crossing signs making roof
Map 2204 E Lumbres			
Fauquembergues	Type 1	In Rue St-Sebastien, N off D92 100 m W of jn with D928 at Fauquembergues E 2° 05′ 42″ N 50° 36′ 01″	Demolished
Merck-St-Liévin *	Halt	Imm. N of Rue de l'Église and W of river Aa between D225 and village centre at Merck E 2° 06′ 56″ N 50° 37′ 28″	Private house
Ouve *	Halt	In Chemin des Marais N of D341 200 m E of jn with D225 at Ouve E 2° 08′ 05″ N 50° 38′ 51″	Private house
Map 2304 O St-Omer Remilly-(Wirquin) *	Type 2	Just E of D225E immediately S of jn with D192 in Remilly E 2° 09′ 47″ N 50° 40′ 07″	Private house, LB
Map 2204 E Lumbres Wavrans-sur-l'Aa	Halt	Probably W of minor road, and just S of car park, 600 m off D192 in Wavrans Approx E 2° 08′ 32″ N 50° 41′ 11″	Demolished
Lumbres	CdN & depot	In D131 250 m W of jn with D225 at Lumbres E 2° 07′ 11″ N 50° 42′ 03″	Station in use by CdF Touristique de la Vallée de l'Aa. Depot including VFIL works demolished
Acquin	Type 2	S off Rue de la Gare (D208) 250 m W of jn with D225 at Acquin E 2° 05′ 05″ N 50° 43′ 44″	Private café in approach road still in use, with sign on end wall

Station	Type	Location	Status
Bouvelingham	Halt	150 m down track W off D208 just N of old railway bridge at La Coete, halfway between Petit Quercamps and Bouvelinghem E 2° 02' 28" N 50° 44' 24"	Private house
Alquines-Buisson	Halt (atypical)	Imm. N of sharp corner in Rue de la Gare (D216) at Le Buisson E 2° 00' 18" N 50° 44' 29"	Private house
Journy #	Station	At La Couronne, imm. N (HM imm. S) of Route de St. Omer (D206) 500 m SE of jn with D191 N of Journy E 2° 00' 35" N 50° 45' 21"	Private house. Halt type building, HM across road
Bonningues	Type 2 & depot	No. 36 Rue de la Gare, 500 m S of jn with D217 in Bonningues E 2° 00' 49" N 50° 47' 14"	Private house, depot building , LB. Junction from 1900
Bonningues	Arrêt	Imm. S of D217 550 m E of jn with D225 in Bonningues E 2° 01' 23" N 50° 47' 44"	Private house. Halt type building
Tournehem-sur-la-Hem	Type 2	In Rue de l'Ancienne Gare, off D217E 200 m W of corner in D217, 350 m N of jn with D218 in Tournehem E 2° 02' 35" N 50° 48' 39"	Private house, HM & LB demolished
Map 2203 E Gravelines			
Louches *	Halt	Imm. W of D225E (Rue de l'Abbé Pierre) to Louches village, 300 m S of jn with N43 E 2° 00' 57" N 50° 50' 06"	Private house
Junction building for tramway to Pont d'Ardes		Just S of Rue des Moulins 100 m SE of jn with D224, 300 m SW of jn of D224 with N43 at Ardres E 1° 58' 55" N 50° 51' 00"	
Map 2103 ET Calais			
Ardres	Type 1	S side of jn of Rue Léon de l'Acre and Avenue Charles de Gaulle 250 m SW of Ardres centre E 1° 58' 27" N 50° 51' 08"	Demolished
Balinghem	Halt	E side of D228 (Rue du Camp du Drap d'Or) to Balinghem, 200 m N of jn with D231 E 1° 56' 05" N 50° 51' 08"	Private house (atypical building)
Andres *	Halt	770 Rue de l'Église, W side of D248 to Andres, 700 m N of jn with D231 E 1° 54' 33" N 50° 51' 40"	Private house
Guînes *	Type 1 & depot	Right off Rue Leo Lagrange, 300 m NE of jn with D215 near Guînes centre E 1° 52' 36" N 50° 52' 09"	Boarded up, dormitory building left of gateway
Écluse-Carrée	Halt	Just N of D247E1 (Rue de l'Écluse-Carrée), 150 m E of jn with D127 and canal E 1° 52' 55" N 50° 54' 20"	Private house
Calais-les-Fontinettes	CdN	In Rue des Fontinettes, 650 m S of origin from Boulevard Pasteur, Calais-St-Pierre E 1° 51' 00" N 50° 56' 27"	Rebuilt, in use by SNCF
Calais-Ville	CdN	W side of Pont Jacquard, just N of Hôtel de Ville and belfry E 1° 51' 02" N 50° 57' 12"	Rebuilt, in use by SNCF

Ardres to Pont d'Ardres

Station	Type	Location	Status
(Junction building with Anvin-Calais)		(See Anvin-Calais between Louches and Ardres)	
Chemin de St-Quentin	Arrêt	Immediately E of what is now the Rue de St-Quentin 100m N of jn with N43 at Ardres & Café E 1° 58' 57" N 50° 51' 24"	No shelter, adjacent café with old sign on wall is private house.
Pont d'Ardres	CdN	Immediately N of D228 just E of bridge under N43 at Pont d'Ardres E 1° 58' 16" N 50° 53' 31"	In use by SNCF, downgraded to *Arrêt*

Aire-Berck
Map 2304 E Aire-sur-la-Lys

Station	Type	Location	Status
Aire-sur-la-Lys	CdN	Just SE off Square Jean Moulin (roundabout on D194), 500 m E of large church in centre of Aire E 2° 24' 23" N 50° 38' 27"	Business use (Ambulance HQ)

Station	Type	Location	Status/Notes
Recques-sur-Course	Standard	W of D149 to Montcavrel (Rue du Moulin), 800 m from jn with D127 in Recques E 1° 47′ 23″ N 50° 31′ 05″	Private house, LB
Montreuil(-sur-Mer)	CdN	SE off Rue St-Gengoult (D349), just W of level crossing 650 m SW of jn with N1. E 1° 46′ 07″ N 50° 27′ 58″	In use, SNCF
Sat-Justin (Montreuil)	Standard	On right (No 6) Rue de la Tour de Justice, off Chaussée Marcadée (D139), 150 m E of jn with D901. E 1° 45′ 35″ N 50° 27′ 25″	Private house
Campigneulles-les-Petites	Standard	Just S of D145 at minor jn 500 m E of jn with N1 E 1° 45′ 01″ N 50° 26′ 28″	Private house. Name removed since 2002. LB extended
Wailly(-Beaucamp)	Standard	In Rue de la Gare, E off N1 750 m N of jn with D142 in Wailly E 1° 43′ 32″ N 50° 24′ 39″	Private house, LB
(Le) Bahot*	Halt	Imm. E of D140 just N of jn with D142E2 at le Bahot E 1° 41′ 18″ N 50° 24′ 10″	Private house, LB
Vertont(-Bourg) *	Standard	On W of main line 100 m S of level crossing for D140 (Rue de la Mairie/Route de Wailly) at Verton E 1° 39′ 07″ N 50° 24′ 02″	Private house, LB
Rang-du-Fliers-Verton-Berck	CdN	In Rue Jean Moulin (D143) 250 m S of jn with D917 in Rang-du-Fliers E 1° 38′ 52″ N 50° 24′ 57″	In use, SNCF
Berck-Ville	Atypical	Opposite N end of Rue de la Gare, Between Rue Henri Alquier and Avenue du Docteur Quettier, 200 m W of jn with D940 at Berck E 1° 35′ 29″ N 50° 24′ 38″	Larger station building. Demolished
Berck-Plage*	Atypical & depot	E of Rue Alfred Lambert, opposite end of Avenue du Général de Gaulle E 1° 34′ 03″ N 50° 24′ 28″	Rebuilt 1909 in grandiose style. Now casino, bus stat. in yard

Berck-Plage-Paris-Plage
Map 2105 ET Le Touquet-Paris-Plage Berck Vallée de la Canche

Station	Type	Location	Status/Notes
(Berck-Plage)		(see Aire-Berck)	
Bellevue-les-Dunes	Standard & depot	Right side of Rue de la Station des Dunes, 400 m N of jn with Chemin des Anglais at N end of Berck-Plage (Dunes du Terminus) E 1° 34′ 11″ N 50° 25′ 38″	Demolished
Merlimont-Plage	Standard	Rue de la Station, S off Avenue de la Plage (D144E), 2.3 km W of jn with D940 in Merlimont E 1° 34′ 52″ N 50° 27′ 38″	Boarded up, school adjacent. Distinctive brick patterns
(Boulevard) Daloz		Gare Marchandises Near jn of Avenue François Godin (route to Cucq) and Avenue de Verdun, Le Touquet Approx. E 1° 35′ 12″ N 50° 30′ 48″	Demolished
(Rue de Paris – Paris-Plage)		(see Étaples-Paris-Plage)	

Tramway Étaples-Paris-Plage
Map 2105 ET Le Touquet-Paris-Plage Berck Vallée de la Canche

Station	Type	Location	Status/Notes
Étaples	CdN	In Place d'Huckeswagen, 500 m up Boulevard Lefevre d'Étaples, off D939 200 m SE of jn with D940. E 1° 38′ 32″ N 50° 30′ 59″	In use, SNCF, tramway building probably demolished
Trépied	Depot gen. sta. tram shed	First W off D940 300 m S of jn with N39 (roundabout) at S end of bridge over Canche at Étaples Avenue des Hêtres on town map. Avenue de l'Aéroport on site E 1° 37′ 38″ N 50° 30′ 28″	Depot and generating station is departmental road mending depot. 1910 shed across road is part of garage and car dealers
La Fôret	*Arrêt*	SE corner of jn of Avenue de Picardie and Avenue de l'Hippodrome, Le Touquet E 1° 35′ 57″ N 50° 31′ 19″	*Abri* demolished, concrete replica across road
Rue de Paris - Paris-Plage	Atypical	E side of Rue de Paris between Rue de la Paix and Rue Jean Monnet, Le Touquet E 1° 34′ 54″ N 50° 31′ 19″	Became bus station, later demolished

Le Portel-Boulogne-Bonningues
Map 2104 ET Boulogne-sur-Mer

Station	Type	Location	Status/Notes
Le Portel	Standard	SW side of Rue Chateaubriand, just SE of jn with Rue Carnot (D236E) at Le Portel E 1° 34′ 41″ N 50° 42′ 29″	Demolished

Name	Type	Location (longitude/latitude)	Present status & use, notes
Ave-Maria	Halt	N side of Boulevard de la Liberté, just W of jn with Rue Rosa Luxembourg, Outreau Approx E 1° 35′ 27″ N 50° 42′ 37″	Demolished
Boulogne-Ville	CdN	Quai Chanzy between Pont Marguet and pont de l'Entente Cordiale (on E side of former main line station) E 1° 35′ 58″ N 50° 43′ 21″	Main station destroyed 1944; rebuilt in another location
La Madeleine	Halt	Just S of Rue André Marie Ampère just W of jn with Rue Guilmant. Approx E 1° 36′ 43″ N 50° 42′ 37″	Demolished
St-Martin-Boulogne	Depot	Probably Residence les Trois Fontaines, Route de Desvres Probably E 1° 38′ 04″ N 50° 43′ 28″	Demolished
St-Martin-Boulogne	Main sta.	Place J Moulin, N off Route de St-Omer, St-Martin-Boulogne E 1° 37′ 52″ N 50° 43′ 33″	Demolished, now car park with new shops
Pernes	Halt	S side of D237, opposite end of D233E2 to Pernes, in Huplandre E 1° 41′ 32″ N 50° 44′ 02″	Demolished
La Capelle	Standard	W off Rue Marcel Caudeville (D234) 100 m S of jn with D237 in La Capelle-lès-Boulogne E 1° 42′ 22″ N 50° 43′ 52″	Business use
Conteville	Standard	964 Rue du Croquet, in Hamlet of Le Croquet, 800 m S of jn with D233 in Conteville-lès-Boulogne E 1° 43′ 42″ N 50° 44′ 15″	Private house
Belle-Houllefort	Standard	In Rue de l'Ancienne Gare, W off D238 just S of jn with D252 in Belle-et-Houllefort E 1° 45′ 36″ N 50° 44′ 31″	Private house
Le Waast-Alincthun*	Standard	N side of Route des Pichotttes (old N42) between jn with new N42 and road to Alincthun E 1° 48′ 06″ N 50° 44′ 24″	Private house has deteriorated badly
Le Plouy	Halt or Arrêt	2 Rue Profonede, at jn with Route Nationale (old route of N42) at Le Plouy E 1° 49′ 07″ N 50° 44′ 28″	Small building, possibly old halt, much modernised
Le Plouy	Crossing cottage	Route Nationale (old route of N42) opposite jn with D253 between Le Plouy and Colembert E 1° 49′ 45″ N 50° 44′ 32″	Modern roof, otherwise old, atypical windows
Colembert	Standard (?)	On N side of Route Nationale (old route of N42) just E of jn with D252/D251E in Colembert E 1° 50′ 40″ N 50° 44′ 44″	Demolished, now modern housing
Map 2204 E Lumbres			
Longueville*	Standard	Imm. N of N42 at jn with D252, E of Longueville E 1° 53′ 14″ N 50° 43′ 54″	Boarded up, yard used as road depot
Surques	Standard	E side of Route Principale (D215) 400 m NE of jn with D215E at Surques E 1° 55′ 01″ N 50° 44′ 24″	Private house, religious statue on front
Herbinghen -Hocquinghen	Halt	In Route d'Herbinghen, opposite Impasee du Rossignol, 800 m SE of Herbinghen and 600 m NW of jn with D206E 800 m SW of Hocquinghen E 1° 55′ 10″ N 50° 46′ 06″	Building in garden of private house
Licques	Standard	Impasse de l'Ancienne Gare, NE off D191 250 m S of jn with D215 in Licques E 1° 56′ 21″ N 50° 47′ 02″	Private house
Audenfort	Halt	31 Rue d'Audenfort, 300 m S of jn with D217 (café de la Gare No. 33) E 1° 58′ 06″ N 50° 47′ 02″	Completely rebuilt as modern house, adjacent café now private house
(Bonningues)		(see Anvin-Calais)	

Notes and abbreviations

* - Station or Halt has name still visible on building (not noted for CdN/SNCF stations); # - Station or Halt still has clock ; CdN - Compagnie du Nord, standard gauge stations, now SNCF if still in use; LB - Lavatory block present at station (if not shown then not present now; not shown for CdN/SNCF stations)

BV - *Bâtiment des Voyageurs*, passenger building; HM - *Halle aux Marchandises*, goods building; jn - junction.

A Note on Archive Material

The archives of the dealings of these lines with the *département* of Pas-de-Calais are held at the departmental archives at the Centre Mahaut-d'Artois, 1 rue du 19 Mars 1962, BP 965, Dainville, Arras. The archives for the *Chemins de Fer d'Intérêt Local* are in *Sous-Séries* S files 896-1131 & *Sous-Séries* 3S, 13th section, files 2318-2858. Other archives of the *département*, including the newspapers, are held at the Centre Georges-Besnier, 12 place de la Préfecture, Arras.

We have not been able to find most of the archives of the railway companies themselves. There are some documents at the *Centre des Archives du Monde de Travail* (CAMT) at Roubaix. These are all in the section 65 AQ subsection E (*Chemins de Fer*). In file E8 are the annual reports to shareholders of the Aire-Berck company for 1895, 1898-1900, 1909-1911, and 1918-1952. In file E37 are the equivalent reports for the Anvin-Calais company, but only for 1898-1900, and 1912, and the statutes of the company from 1882. In file E82 there are reports of some early shareholders' meetings of the Berck-Plage-Paris-Plage company.

The British National Archives at Kew have railway documents and maps about northern France during and after World War I. The series WO (War Office) 95/ includes general documents and a full but not complete series of War Diaries of the British and Commonwealth railway troops. There are also maps in the WO 153/ series but these are more patchy in their coverage.

The Royal Engineers library at the Royal School of Military Engineering, Brompton Barracks, Gillingham, Kent also have a full but not complete series of War Diaries of the Royal Engineers Railway Companies from World War I. Many of these are duplicates of those in the National Archive (or vice versa). This library has some photographs but none of the lines described in this book. The Imperial War Museum (IWM) photographic archive has many railway photographs from World War I, but only a small number of relevance to this book. The IWM map archive at Duxford also has limited relevant material, but the archive has not yet been fully sorted and indexed.

Bibliography

General
Davies, W.J.K., *Minor Railways of France*. East Harling, Norfolk: Plateway Press, 2000.
Domengie, H., and Banaudo, J. *Les petits train de jadis. Nord de la France*. Breil-sur-Roya: Les Éditions du Cabri, 1995.
Pacey, Philip, *Railways of the Baie de Somme. A Landscape with Trains*. Oakwood Press, Usk, Mon., 2000

The Anvin-Calais line
Le Chemin de Fer à voie Étroite d'Anvin à Calais. *La Nature* (Paris), 1883, pp. 69-70.
Wagner, Claude. Le train de Guînes. *Chemin de Fer Régionaux et Urbains* No. 4, 2000, pp. 4-18.

The Aire-Berck line
Valcq,P. Souvenez-vous....Le Tortillard de Berck à Aire. Les aventures du Tortillard. *Les Cahiers du Pays de Montreuil* 1983, Vol.2, pp. 8-9, Vol. 3 pp. 2-3, Vol. 4, pp. 4-5, and 1984 Vol. 5, pp. 4-5, Vol. 6, pp. 2-3, Vol. 7, pp 2-3.

The Berck-Plage-Paris-Plage line
Gonsseaume, Christian. Le chemin de fer d'intérêt local: Berck-Paris-Plage. *Sucellus. Dossiers archéologique, historiques et Culturels du Nord-Pas-de-Calais* 1995, Vol. 40, pp. 35-39.
Crépin, Guy & Michèle. Naissance et disparition de la ligne de chemin de fer d'intérêt local de Berck-Plage à Paris-Plage. *Sucellus. Dossiers archéologique, historiques et Culturels du Nord-Pas-de-Calais*. 2003, Vol. 54, pp. 27-55.

Introduction
The Travel Editor, 'Old Picardie. Montreuil sur Mer. Part I Personal'. *The Queen. The Lady's Newspaper*, 26th September, 1896.
Morgan, Bryan, *The End of the Line. A Book about Railways and Places Mainly Continental*. London: Cleaver-Hulme Press, 1955.

Chapter One
Northern France and the Paris Region, Michelin Green Guide, 2006 (in English).
Nord Pas-de-Calais Picardie, Paris: Le Guide Vert Michelin, 2006 (in French, but more
    detailed than the English equivalent above).
Baedeker, Karl, *Northern France from the English Channel to the Loire excluding Paris and its
    Environs. Handbook for Travellers*. Karl Baedeker, Leipsic, 1894.
Banaudo, J., *Trains Oubliés. Volume 4: L'État - Le Nord - Les Ceintures*. Menton: Les Éditions
    du Cabri, 1982.
Les Chemins de Fer du Nord. Paris: Rimage, 1979.
Angelier, Maryse, *La France Ferroviaire en Cartes Postales. Nord-Pas-de-Calais*. Paris: Éditions
    La Vie du Rail, 2001.

Chapter Five
Taylor, A.J.P., *The First World War. An illustrated history*, New York: Perigee Books, The
    Berkley Publishing Group, 1963 (original publishers Hamish Hamilton).
Johnson, J.H., *1918, The Unexpected Victory*. London: Arms and Armour Press, Cassell Group, 1997.
Henniker, A.M., *Transportation on the Western Front 1914-1918*, London: Imperial War Museum, 1937.
Le Hénaff and Bornecque, H., *Les Chemins de Fer Français et la Guerre*, Paris: Librairie Chapelot, 1922.

Chapter Six
Gottwaldt, Alfred, *Heeresfeldbahnen*. Motor Buch Verlag, 1986 (in German).
Anvin-Calais Railcar, *The SNCF Society Journal* September 1997, No. 87, pp. 32-33.
Thomas, David, Coordination (parts 1 & 2). *The SNCF Society Journal* March 2006, No. 121,
    & June 2006, No. 122.

Chapter Seven
Delaforte, P., *Smashing the Atlantic Wall, The Destruction of Hitler's Coastal Fortresses*, Cassell
    and Co., 2001.
Bailleul, L., *Les Sites V1 en Flandres et en Artois*, Hazebrouck: S.A. Presse Flamande, 2000.
Despriet, Phillipe, (2004) *Onbekend Frans-Vlaanderen. De vliegende bom in Frans-Vlaanderen,
    Gids voor de V 1-installaties in Nord, Pas-de-Calais en Somme*, Kortrijk, 2004 (in Flemish).
Boulogne-sur-Mer, *La Vie du Rail* 27th September, 1953, pp. 2-17.
Ligne d'Autocars Fruges-Aire-Berguette, *L'Echo de la Lys* , 29th August, 1952, p. 3.
Fauquembergues, Le service d'autobus de la C.G.L., *Journal du Pas-de-Calais et de la Somme*,
    1st September, 1952, p. 5.
Après 3/4 de siècle de service public, la Gare d'Aire (Voyageurs) vient de fermer. *L'Echo
    de la Lys* , 8th October, 1954, p. 2.
Le petit train de Guînes est mort au champ d'honneur du modernisme. *Nord-Littoral*, 1st
    March, 1955, p. 5.
Fourrier, Albert and Chaussois, Robert. Deux vieux serviteurs sont congédiés, *La Voix du
    Nord* , 2nd March, 1955, p. 3.
Les horaires des autobus empêchent les gens de la vallée de la Course, *Journal du Pas-de-
    Calais et de la Somme*, 2nd March, 1955, p. 4.
Le "Tortillard" a veçu, *Journal du Pas-de-Calais et de la Somme*, 2nd March, 1955, p. 4.
Son dernier voyage. *Journal de Montreuil* , 6th March, 1955, p. 1.

Chapter Eight
Musée des Tramways à Vapeur et des chemins de fer Secondaires français (MTVS), *Guide
    de la Collection*, 2004 edition, Valmondois.
Haworth, Richard, *The Tourist railways of France*, Second edition, Rapid Transit
    Publications, London, 1996.
Jones, Mervyn, *The Essential Guide to French Heritage and Tourist Railways*: Oakwood Press,
    Usk, Mon., 2006.

Postscript
Comfort, Nicholas, *The Channel Tunnel and its High Speed Links*: Oakwood Press, Usk, Mon., 2006.